Springer Series in Statistics

Advisors:
P. Diggle, S. Fienberg, K. Krickeberg,
I. Olkin, N. Wermuth

Springer Series in Statistics

(continued after index)

Nicholas T. Longford

Models for Uncertainty in Educational Testing

With 31 Figures

Springer-Verlag
New York Berlin Heidelberg London Paris
Tokyo Hong Kong Barcelona Budapest

Nicholas T. Longford
Research Division
15-T Educational Testing Service
Rosedale Road
Princeton, NJ 08541 USA

Library of Congress Cataloging-in-Publication Data
Longford, Nicholas T., 1955–
    Models for uncertainty in educational testing / Nicholas T. Longford.
        p.   cm. — (Springer series in statistics)
    Includes bibliographical references and index.
    ISBN 0-387-94513-X (alk. paper)
    1. Educational tests and measurements.   2. Examinations — Validity.
3. Examinations — Interpretation.   4. Examinations — Design and
construction.   5. Examinations — Scoring.   6. Educational Testing
Service.   I. Title.   II. Series.
    LB3051.L625   1995
    371.2´6´013—dc20   95-8145

Printed on acid-free paper.

Production managed by Hal Henglein; manufacturing supervised by Jeffrey Taub.
Photocomposed pages prepared from the author's LaTeX file.
Printed and bound by Braun-Brumfield, Ann Arbor, MI.
Printed in the United States of America.

9 8 7 6 5 4 3 2 1

ISBN 0-387-94513-X Springer-Verlag New York Berlin Heidelberg

To Elyse and Kalman,
The children of the 'lesser' Dad

Preface

*Empirical Bayes and James-Stein estimation. This closely re-
lated pair of ideas is the biggest theoretical success on my list
and the biggest underachiever in number of practical applications. The irony here is that these methods potentially offer the
biggest practical gains over their predecessors.*

Bradley Efron, *The statistical century*[1]

The idea for this book came about with my growing realization that the
Educational Testing Service (ETS) and its databanks are a genuine treasure
trove of interesting statistical problems that are also encountered in many
other fields. That in itself is a rather unoriginal statement, which can be
found in one form or another in many other statistical texts motivated
by educational testing issues. However, recent changes in the educational
testing industry, especially the growing emphasis on constructed-response
items, have brought about new statistical challenges and novel areas of
application. This book is intended to be a tasting, rather than a complete
and integral enumeration of these challenges, which are likely to be in a
state of flux for a few years to come.

The title of the book, arrived at after umpteen revisions, is meant to
have no other than statistical connotation. The term 'uncertainty' may

---

[1]Bradley Efron's agreement and permission of the Royal Statistical Society to
reprint this passage from Efron (1995) are acknowledged.

sound somewhat negativist, but I hope that its appearance in the title will contribute to the emancipation of educational research from decades of futile attempts to find near-deterministic descriptions of educational phenomena with the aid of imperfect measurement instruments. I do not see the problem in the lack of perfection (when human subjects and observers are perfect and consistent, they are no longer human); it is rather in the reliance on statistical methods that assume perfect measurement and on cursory attention to problems of generalizability from one context (in which the study is conducted) to another (for which inference is desired). I find the term 'uncertainty' more appealing than 'variation' or *unexplained* variation to describe our inability to find a perfect explanation of an observed process.

The book is not intended as a celebration of ETS, but in part a piece of criticism, hopefully constructive, and principally a collection of case studies from educational testing. ETS has been generous in funding (in a piecemeal fashion but with good intentions) much of the research described in the book. I wish to express my gratitude to the research management for their patience and endurance with my criticism on a number of issues, and for giving me a go-ahead for this project. In brief, I acknowledge the flexible exercise of their authority. Where views are expressed, they are my own, unless stated otherwise, and ETS management has had little input in their formation. The book does not represent any aspects of official ETS policy, and I do not expect that it will do so at any time in the future.

One aspect in which my employer is beyond reproach is that I have always been granted leaves in response to invitations from academic institutions. I have done some of the work on this book while visiting the Zentrum für Umfragen, Methoden und Analysen in Mannheim, Germany (Michael Wiedenbeck), the Department of Statistics, University of Adelaide, Australia (Patty Solomon) and the Department of Economics, University of Pompeu Fabra in Barcelona, Spain (Albert Satorra). Their hospitality and stimulating environment are acknowledged. Research on the material presented in Chapter 7 was supported by a generous grant from the National Center for Educational Statistics.

The book would not have come about without the encouragement and exemplary cooperation of Martin Gilchrist of Springer-Verlag, who arranged for several detailed, informative, and insightful reviews of earlier drafts of the manuscript. I am grateful to several colleagues at ETS for their contribution to the book, in a variety of forms. Being mean by nature, I name only Eric Bradlow, Charlie Lewis, Gary Marco, Bob Mislevy, and Neal Thomas. I want to give credit to Bill Strawderman for several discussions and the resulting inspiration.

Those who provided the datasets analysed in the book are acknowledged in the text. Mike Wagner and Joe Bezek attended to the well-being of all the files on my Sun workstation. The production staff at Springer-Verlag helped to iron out the problems in wordprocessing and copy-editing.

My mother, Irena Lefkovičová, who introduced me many years ago to the charm and excitement of numbers, has been a staunch supporter throughout.

Princeton, NJ   Nicholas T. Longford
April 1995

Contents

1

Inference about variation

The advent and proliferation of computing technology is continually making us rethink the meaning of the adjectives 'large', 'extensive', and 'complex', as in large data, extensive computing, and complex computational algorithms. Our appetite for information has been enhanced to such a degree that our systems for digesting it are often under strain, and they crave for the substance of information to be presented in a more condensed manner.

Statistical software has taken over much of the business of digesting information. On the one hand, software packages are great labour-saving devices, sparing us from the anxieties of low-level programming; on the other hand, what the engaged software does to the input information is not necessarily under full control of the analyst. The full potential of the software is realized only when the analyst is a demanding and well-informed customer thoroughly acquainted with how the software functions, and when the analyst insists on good digestion without any loss of 'nutrients', rather than merely 'shopping' for the best that one particular or a narrow range of software products can offer.

Recent developments in statistical software have brought closer the prospect of doing statistical computing from basic principles, which substantially enhances the analyst's control of all the details of the analysis. Compact matrix languages implemented in Splus, matlab, or Gauss enable relatively effortless transcription of methods described by complex equations from print to the computer. This opens up the possibility of analysts having their own libraries of statistical procedures tailor-made to particular problems, with the analytical expertise being the only limiting factor.

The present book anticipates this trend and is aimed at a statistical analyst open to persuasion or sympathetic to such a development. All the computing and graphical presentations for the examples were done in Splus3.2 (Becker, Chamber, and Wilks, 1988; Chambers and Hastie, 1992), but other computing environments would probably have been just as suitable.

1.1   Imperfection and variation

The omnipresent problem in educational measurement is that the quantities of interest can be observed only indirectly. For example, when attempting to measure the ability in mathematics of a population of students, we require a definition of the population (say, all the 13-year-olds in a country), a definition of the 'mathematics ability', a representation of this ability by one or several tests (sets of questions and problems as well as their solutions), a procedure for administering the tests (including recruiting test-takers), a method for scoring these tests, a method of summarizing the scores, and, finally, an interpretation of the results that responds to the interest and needs that set off this process in the first place.

Each of these components of the (educational) measurement process involves elements of arbitrariness and uncertainty which should be reflected by reduced confidence about the final product of the measurement, be it an estimate of a student's ability or a summary for the population. For instance, if the test score were a perfect measure of the student's ability, our inference about a population summary (such as the mean of the scores) should have more confidence than if the test scores were an imperfect measure.

Imperfection of educational measurement instruments and of other procedures in education, and in social sciences in general, is an inescapable reality that no pursuit of quality control is likely to eradicate. Quality control does play an important role in educational measurement, as exemplified in the high standards of test assembly and review procedures, but it has obvious limitations. The main factor in these limitations is the human subject (test-taker) with the unpredictable temporal variation in his/her performance, judgement, response to intellectual stimuli, and behaviour in general.

A more pragmatic approach to imperfection in measurement of human ability is to limit the impact of the imperfection and gain a good understanding of the processes that give rise to it. This entails having standards for the 'amount of imperfection'. For example, consider a group of examinees who have the same ability in the domain of the test they are about to take. With an ideal test, these examinees would achieve identical scores, and these scores would differ from the scores attained by examinees with a different ability. In a more defensive posture, we would adopt some standard for the greatest (reasonably acceptable) magnitude of the differences among the scores for examinees who have the same ability. Assessment of imperfection is closely connected to inference about variation. Clearly, it is desirable that the scores of the examinees with the same ability have a small variance in relation to the variance of all the scores. (As a perverse example, suppose every examinee is awarded the same score.)

Whereas individual elements of imperfection, such as the impact of the actual test form used on an examinee's score or the impact of the scoring rule on the examinee's score, are a nuisance (using the statistical meaning of this term), their summaries may be much more useful. Often, the *mean* of these 'elements' is of little interest, because it is close to zero owing to the self-norming nature of their definition, and so inference about it is of little value.

The next candidate for a summary is the *variance*. One purpose of this monograph is to demonstrate that variances are rather underrated as compact and easy-to-interpret summaries in a variety of settings. Although educational testing is used as a background for the developments and examples, commonalities with other areas in social sciences are obvious.

Chapters 2–4 deal with problems of subjective assessment of examinees' responses by expert raters. Conceptually, we define the variance of the scores that an examinee would receive for an essay (or some other performance) from the engaged raters. However hard all the parties involved in the rating process try to fulfill their roles, the raters end up not agreeing in their assessments of the essays. The smaller the variance of the scores given to an examinee, relative to the variance of the scores across the examinees, the better.

Chapter 5 presents a general approach to summarizing a large number of quantities of the same kind, each estimated with little precision. A simple prescription is followed — the *distribution* of the quantities is estimated. In the examples discussed, related to differential item functioning (DIF), the variance of the elementary quantities is of principal interest. Although each of the quantities is estimated subject to a lot of uncertainty, the variance is estimated with much more precision.

Chapter 6 discusses methods for relating test forms that are supposed to be equivalent. For instance, the Scholastic Assessment Test (SAT) taken today should have characteristics identical to those of the SAT taken last year. Rest assured, it does not, and the more defensive position of making sure that they are not radically different is more realistic. A measure of the deviation from equivalence is defined in terms of the residual variance in the regression of the so-called 'true' scores.

Chapters 7 and 8 deal with making inferences from large-scale surveys. Although the stratified clustered design of a survey facilitates collection of data at a moderate cost, it exacts a price in the complexity of the statistical analysis due to clustering. Chapter 7 discusses methods for estimating the population mean and its standard error, with the emphasis on the latter, and Chapter 8 is devoted to small-area estimation, a generic term for methods of enhancing inferences about smaller sampling units by 'borrowing strength', that is, utilizing information contained in the data from the other sampling units as well as from other data sources.

Chapter 9 discusses the problem of eliciting and reconciling experts' judgements about setting cut points for passing (failing) in educational tests and presents an application of the logistic regression with random coefficients. The discrepancy of the expert's judgements is described by a variance of the logits of certain underlying conditional probabilities.

The subject of Chapter 10 is analysis of longitudinal surveys involving incomplete cooperation of the subjects. The focus of the chapter is on efficient use of data from incomplete records assuming an informative pattern of missingness. Since the test instruments administered at each time point are on more-or-less arbitrary scales, the correlation structure of the true scores underlying the examinees' responses is the most important summary of the data.

Borrowing strength and using variances as the agents for it are a theme common to all the chapters. In Chapter 3, essay scores for examinees are estimated using methods based on the variances that summarize disagreement among the raters and differences in ability of the examinees. In Chapter 4, we extend this approach to representing the essay topics as a sample from the domain of topics that cover the tested subject area. The summaries defined in Chapter 5 provide an effective feedback to estimation of the elementary quantities. In Chapter 6, the variance is used for the description of distance between two tests. Section 7.9 describes how estimation of subpopulation means can be improved when a large number of such means is estimated. Chapter 8 deals with a similar issue in a different context. Chapter 9 returns to the issue of imperfect judgement of experts in a context different from Chapters 2–4. Chapter 10 revisits the issue of estimating variances and variance matrices or indirectly observed quantities, addressed in Chapters 5 and 6, with the added complexity due to incompleteness of the data.

The chapters are motivated by problems encountered during my practice at the Educational Testing Service (ETS) in the period 1989–94. Most of the examples are drawn from standardized tests administered by ETS, and in some instances the operational procedures are contrasted with those developed here. In several examples, it was necessary to omit a number of details that would have diluted the focus of the chapter or deflected the reader's attention from it.

Although educational testing is central to the exposition, the book is intended as a *statistical* text. For that purpose, I attempted to minimize the use of educational measurement terminology as well as the reader's need for a background in educational testing. Section 1.2 introduces the most important terms and describes the context in which they are used in the book.

Section 1.3 gives a summary of the statistical notation, definitions, and other conventions, and outlines the background needed for the book.

1.2   Educational measurement and testing

The principal goal of educational measurement is the development and application of methods for assessing knowledge, performance, skills, and abilities of examinees (members of populations of students, professionals, or the like) in domains that are the subjects of instruction at the various levels of educational or professional development. Educational testing is one form of implementation of these methods.

A typical domain of knowledge, such as arithmetic, English composition, or European history, does not have an explicit definition. Often, there is merely an *understanding* or a vague agreement about the body of knowledge that constitutes the domain. An educational test for a given domain is a representation of the domain by an instrument for assessing examinees' abilities in that domain. The assessment usually has the form of a score, an ordinal quantity. Higher scores correspond to higher ability, lower scores to lower ability.

The atomic unit in educational testing is an *item*. A typical item consists of a reading passage introducing the context of the problem, followed by a question, instruction to carry out a task or perform a procedure, or the like. In some cases, the item is concluded by a list of response options. Rules for scoring the responses (number of points) and available time are an integral part of the item. Of course, a single item is not sufficient for assessment of ability in a typical domain because any single item is a poor representation of the domain and the response of an examinee contains too little information about his/her ability.

Usually, an examinee is administered a *test form*, that is, a collection of items. The test form is assembled so as to enable a faithful and precise assessment of each examinee's ability. Faithfulness, or *validity*, refers to a balanced coverage of the domain and the requirement that the abilities from other domains be as unimportant as possible. Balanced coverage is effective only if it is accompanied by an appropriate scoring rule.

The term *test performance* refers to the entirety of an examinee's responses. The scoring rule is a mapping of test performances to scores. The simplest scoring rule is to count the number of correct responses. The score is usually defined for each examinee but may sometimes be defined only for groups of examinees, such as a classroom, a school, or a university department. The scoring rule is an integral component of validity; as a perverse example, counting the number of instances that the examinee selected the first response option would render most test forms not valid.

Validity of a test form can be interpreted as the strength of the association of the score with the ability being assessed. In general, this association is rather tenuous and applicable only in the narrow context of a population. For instance, a test form consisting of items very difficult for third-graders has little validity for this population but may have much more validity for a population of older students.

In an extreme case, if the examinee is informed in advance of the location of the correct answers on the response sheet, the validity is breached. The examinee may receive an outstanding score even with a rudimentary ability in the tested domain. Examples of more subtle breaches of validity are good mental preparation, practice with test forms with similar format and/or content, using strategies vis-à-vis allocated time, and the like. In principle, any preparation other than study and practice within the tested domain is a threat to the association of ability with test performance. Unfortunately, when examinees have high stakes in the outcome of the test administration, most of the ways of breaching this association are regarded as fair. In fact, the association would be maintained if all examinees 'breached' the validity to the same extent, that is, if they were equally well prepared in the 'art' of test-taking.

An important contribution to the maintenance of validity are the standardized conditions for test administration. Suitable environment (comfortable temperature, quiet, suitable furniture), supervision, assistance in the elements of the test not related to the tested domain, and guarding against gross breaches of validity are some of the elements of standardized conditions. The same conditions, the same equipment (e.g., calculators), are clearly an imperative for a valid test.

There is a considerable burden on the examinee to maintain the validity of the test. If examinees misunderstand the instructions, fill in responses in wrong locations, or make similar mistakes as a result of lack of concentration, the validity is eroded. One function of the standardized conditions is to minimize the chances of such mistakes and thus promote validity.

Ability of an examinee is conceptualized as a variable that is not subject to radical variation within a short time span. Whereas a typical test assesses ability, it is more appropriate to refer to the subject of assessment as *performance*. Most of us have heard the complaint 'I was unlucky, just did not have a good day', or similar, implying a discrepancy between the realized performance and the underlying (*latent*) ability.

A typical test is comprised of many test forms. For instance, SAT is administered several times a year, and a test form can be used only on one administration date. This is necessary, for example, because prospective examinees may obtain the items from past examinees and engage assistance in finding the correct responses in advance of the test administration.

A test can be defined as a set, or a population, of test forms, including not only future, not as yet assembled test forms but also test forms that could have been assembled. The term 'test', or testing programme, is also used to designate the entire process associated with assembly, administration, and scoring of test forms.

Ability is popularly regarded as a unidimensional quantity. Any examinee is either more than, less than, or as able as another examinee. This allows for a representation of the ability by real numbers. Of course, ability is observed only indirectly, through performance on a test form, which itself is subject to temporal variation. When the test has a number of test forms, the scores are meaningful only if examinees would not have systematically different scores from one test form to another had they taken each test form. Since a typical examinee takes the test only once, systematic differences cannot be assessed in such a way. Instead, more elaborate methods have to be applied to check, or to arrange, that test form scores are *equivalent*. For example, assuming that the distribution of ability among the examinees is the same for each test form, equivalence of test form scores corresponds to identical distributions of scores across the test forms.

Test scores are not absolute quantities; if each score is, say, increased tenfold, the scores are effectively unaltered. Any linear transformation of the scores brings about no effective change, because the rank ordering and the relative differences of the scores are unchanged. More generally, we can regard any monotone transformation of the scores as leaving the scores effectively unaltered. In a test with many test forms, using a suitable transformation of the scores in each test form can lead to the test form scores being equivalent.

Test forms may consist of sections, or subforms. These subforms may be associated with subdomains (such as addition, multiplication, and fractions in arithmetic). Each form of a test may have the same composition of subforms, in which case it is meaningful to consider the *subtest* as a partition of the test.

Subtests may be associated with *subscores*. The issues of equivalence carry over from scores to subscores. In addition, an important issue is whether there are systematic differences among the subscores of a test or whether the subscores are merely less reliable versions of the test score. In the latter case, there is little point in reporting the subscores. However, if the subscores measure essentially different elements of ability, attention has to be paid to the relative contributions of the subscores to the test score. In order to maintain equivalence, even the subscores have to be equivalent across the test forms.

In summary, sets of items comprise test forms, and a test may have several test forms. A test is associated with a domain of knowledge and a tested population. Test forms involve representation of the tested domain and a scoring rule. Ideally, the representation should be balanced and complete and the scoring rule should be such that there would be no systematic differences in the scores across the test forms. Tests may consist of subtests reflecting the composition of the tested domain by subdomains. Subtests are represented in the test forms by sections; the sections are associated with subscores.

1.3   Statistical context

Most statistical textbook exercises are concerned with single datasets, in contrast to the statistical practice where datasets are rarely analysed in isolation and a lot of attention is paid to collating information across several datasets (survey samples, experiments, or the like). In standard Bayesian approaches, information contained in the analysed dataset is combined with a *prior* distribution of the parameters of interest. In practice, we have to face the problem of expressing prior information in terms of the prior distribution. This entails an element of uncertainty which we would like to sidestep.

Datasets are never 'large enough' because our appetite for statistical detail grows with the size of the data. Many industrial processes are not unique but are repeated many times, possibly in slightly different circumstances. For instance, a test such as SAT is administered several times a year, it has been around for decades, and it is likely to be around for a few more. Different examinees take the test on each occasion, but the cohorts of examinees have gone through similar processes of instruction and preparation for the test, as well as general maturing. Similarly, the test is somewhat different on each occasion but is constructed to the same or only slightly altered specifications, and the processes of pretesting and review of items are standardized. Past administrations can tell us a lot about what the next administration is going to be like, and the analysis of the current administration could be improved by incorporating information from the past administrations.

How informative are old data? If we knew that, in a particular aspect of interest, all the past administrations were identical, it would be reasonable to expect that the current administration is also the 'same', and so old data would be as informative as the current dataset. In a more realistic setting, the administrations (experiments, surveys) are not identical, but they differ only slightly, and so the 'old' data are relatively less informative than the current dataset. Of course, when there are a large number of 'old' datasets, their importance may match or even overwhelm the importance of the current dataset. This is not counterintuitive; if the current data are not very informative, then past data should be given much more weight.

1.3.1   Statistical objects

The processes we are interested in are observed by imperfect measurement instruments which, together with other (background) information, yield a data record. A typical data record contains only a modest amount of information about the studied process, and so a number of measurements have to be made. Design of the study (the collection of measurements) is concerned with the setting of the aspects of the measurement that are under our control. Examples of these aspects are the time of measurement, the background of the subjects (if they are recruited or selected for the study), and the choice of the measurement instrument.

The properties of the studied process are described by a set of *parameters* that are linked to the observed data through a *model*. The model may be a mechanical encoding of the process that gave rise to the data, or it may merely capture some of the transparent properties of the process. Apart from the parameters of interest, the model may contain so-called *nuisance* parameters which have an impact on the association of the parameters of interest and the data (outcomes) but are themselves of only secondary interest.

A typical model involves two kinds of uncertainty. First, we do not know the values of the parameters (otherwise we would not need to invest any effort to gain information about them), but we believe that these values are in some sense 'present' in every observation. Second, there are influences specific to each observation that are not replicable and are associated exclusively with this observation. These influences can often be regarded as nuisance because if they were absent our task of making inference about the parameters would be much easier. In a typical model, these influences are represented by systematic and random components, respectively. For instance, in the ordinary regression model

$$y_i = a + bx_i + \varepsilon_i, \qquad\qquad i = 1, \ldots, N,$$

the linear function $f(x) = a + bx$ relating the outcomes y to the background variable x is the systematic component, and the deviations $\varepsilon_i = y_i - (a + bx_i)$ are the random component. If we replicated the data collection exercise, possibly using different values of x_i (assuming that we could set their values by will), we would expect the same function $f(x)$ to relate the outcomes to the background, but different terms ε_i would be realized. However, these terms would have the same description in both exercises; ε_i would be random draws from the centred normal distribution with an unknown variance σ^2. This variance is also a parameter, and not necessarily a nuisance one.

The random terms are often referred to as random errors, implying either that they represent error of measurement or error in our construction of the model. In the case studies described in this book, the term 'error' is highly inappropriate because we do not have the ambition to define the 'correct' model (perfect description of the studied process), attach any blame for the size of the 'error', or devise corrective measures that would reduce or eradicate the 'error'. Random variation is an integral part of the models for human performance or behaviour. There is nothing erroneous about one individual being different from another, even if they are matched on several factors. In fact, in several cases the size of the variation is of substantive interest.

The distinction between the systematic and random components in the ordinary regression is straightforward. In other models, it is much less so. In several cases discussed in the book, we consider a large number of what could be regarded as nuisance parameters (for instance, one associated with each of a large number of essay raters in Chapter 2). We prefer models in which the raters are represented by random terms for several reasons. First, we wish to make inferences that refer to the 'average' rater, and to the differences among the raters, and so instead of each rater's severity, we estimate a summary of the severities. Second, if the rating exercise were repeated, different sets of raters would grade most essays, because the assignment of each particular essay to raters is not prescribed by design but is left to chance. Third, the quality of the rating would be described rather poorly by rater-specific quantities. Summaries of these quantities are easier to comprehend because they comprise a small number of parameters even when a large number of raters is engaged. Finally, these summaries are important for score adjustment schemes described in Chapter 3. Rating exercises are conducted after every administration of a test, and if the quality of the rating process is the same (or similar) in every administration, inference about the quality can be strengthened by collating information across the administrations.

Models are often rather modest and oversimplified descriptions of studied phenomena because reality has such a lot of facets and is understood only rudimentarily. Therefore, no amount of skepticism about the adopted model is unwarranted. Criticism of the model, comparison of the conclusions based on alternative models, and speculation of how the results would be altered if our data were supplemented by further information are all part-and-parcel of the effort to arrive at a well-informed conclusion.

1.3.2 Estimation

With rare and uninteresting exceptions, the exact values of the parameters cannot be recovered from the data. The parameters are *estimated*; that is, the values best supported by the data are adopted as estimates. We distinguish between *estimators*, random variables that are functions of the data, and *estimates*, which are the realizations of such random variables. Prior to the data collection, there is uncertainty about what values the anticipated data will attain, and so there is uncertainty about the value of the estimator, that is, the estimate that the data would yield.

Quality of an estimator is measured by its proximity to the value of the estimated parameter. Little can be said about how close the estimate (the realized value) is to the estimated parameter, because the latter is not known, and if there was any information about its value not already incorporated in the estimate, we could improve the estimator by incorporating this information. The actual data values are assumed to arise partly by a chance mechanism, and so the distance of the estimate from the estimated parameter is also subject to chance. Therefore, this distance, if it were known, would not characterize the quality of the estimator. As a measure of the quality of an estimator, we take the average of the distances of the estimates from the estimated parameter; the average is taken over all the samples (datasets) that could have been drawn, assuming that the adopted model is correct. Formally, let $\hat{\theta}$ be an estimator of the univariate parameter θ. The estimate of θ based on a given dataset is also denoted by $\hat{\theta}$. Usually, it is easy to distinguish from the context whether $\hat{\theta}$ is meant to be an estimator or an estimate. The deviation $\hat{\theta} - \theta$ is the estimation error of $\hat{\theta}$. The mean squared error is defined as

$$\text{MSE} = \mathbf{E}\left(\hat{\theta} - \theta\right)^2$$

($\mathbf{E}$ stands for expectation, that is, for averaging over all datasets that could have been collected). The mean squared error may depend on the unknown parameters, and so its exact value can only be estimated, for instance, by substituting the estimates of the parameters in place of their unknown values. In this book, and elsewhere in literature, when a mean squared error (MSE) is given as a (positive) number, it is usually an estimate, most often depending on the realized value of the estimator assessed by the MSE. A notable exception to this incestuous feature of the estimation of the MSE are simulations, in which datasets are generated multiply according to a model with preset parameter values. In simulations, the MSE can be determined with arbitrarily high precision, given sufficient computing facilities.

An estimator with the minimum MSE is often difficult to find, and such an estimator may attain the minimum MSE for certain values of the parameters but not for others. The *maximum likelihood* is a general prescription for constructing parameter estimates. For a given a matrix $\mathbf{X}$ we consider the joint density of the outcomes $\mathbf{y}$, $f(\mathbf{y}; \boldsymbol{\theta}, \mathbf{X})$, and seek the values of the parameter vector $\boldsymbol{\theta}$ for which the log-likelihood $l(\boldsymbol{\theta}; \mathbf{y}) = \log f(\mathbf{y}; \boldsymbol{\theta}, \mathbf{X})$ attains its maximum. Taking the logarithm does not affect the location of the maximum; it is mainly of practical importance, as we see later. Note that the log-likelihood depends on the model; different models result in different log-likelihood functions.

In general, the maximum may not exist, or there may be multiple maxima. However, in 'well-behaved' (regular) situations there is a unique maximum, and for large samples the maximum likelihood estimator has several desirable properties. We omit the details — in particular, the definition of the terms 'well-behaved' and 'large samples'. Edwards (1972) presents a very readable yet in-depth introduction to and a profound justification of the maximum likelihood method.

Apart from the estimator, the log-likelihood also yields an estimator of the MSE. In well-behaved cases and for large samples, the maximum likelihood estimator has small bias, $\mathbf{E}(\hat{\boldsymbol{\theta}}) \doteq \boldsymbol{\theta}$, and its sampling variance is approximately equal to the negative expectation of the matrix of second-order partial derivatives:

$$\text{var}(\hat{\boldsymbol{\theta}}) \doteq -\mathbf{E}\left(\frac{\partial^2 l}{\partial\boldsymbol{\theta}\partial\boldsymbol{\theta}^\top}\right). \tag{1.1}$$

In the absence of bias, $\text{var}(\hat{\boldsymbol{\theta}}) = \text{MSE}(\hat{\boldsymbol{\theta}})$. The standard error of the estimator is defined as $\sqrt{\text{var}(\hat{\boldsymbol{\theta}})}$. In most contexts, it is estimated, but this estimate is also referred to as 'standard error', without the qualifying adjective 'estimated'. We will adhere to this abuse of terminology so as to avoid lengthy expressions. The term 'standard error' will always stand for an estimate or estimator, not for the estimated quantity (the 'true' standard error, a function of model parameters).

Likelihood is dealt with in detail in most statistical textbooks. Mardia, Kent, and Bibby (1979, Ch. 4) provides sufficient background on likelihood for this book. Cox and Hinkley (1974) contains a comprehensive background to maximum likelihood estimation.

The maximum likelihood method cannot be applied without a complete specification of the model, that is, of the joint distribution of the outcomes $\mathbf{y}$. This is greatly simplified if the outcomes are independent, because then

$$l(\boldsymbol{\theta};\mathbf{y},\mathbf{X}) = \sum_{i=1}^{N} l(\boldsymbol{\theta};y_i,\mathbf{x}_i),$$

and the (univariate) distributions of y_i specify the log-likelihood.

The ordinary least squares is a simple example of maximum likelihood. Suppose the outcomes y_i are related to the vectors of covariates $\mathbf{x}_i$ by the linear regression

$$\mathbf{E}(y_i) = \mathbf{x}_i\boldsymbol{\beta}, \tag{1.2}$$

where $\boldsymbol{\beta}$ is a vector of (regression) parameters, $\mathbf{x}_i$ are given (say, set by the analyst), and the deviations $y_i - \mathbf{x}_i\boldsymbol{\beta}$ are independent and normally distributed with zero mean and variance σ^2. An alternative description of the model is

$$y_i \sim \mathcal{N}(\mathbf{x}_i\boldsymbol{\beta},\sigma^2), \qquad \text{independently},$$

or, in matrix notation:

$$\mathbf{y} \sim \mathcal{N}_N(\mathbf{X}\boldsymbol{\beta},\sigma^2\mathbf{I}_N),$$

where $\mathbf{I}_N$ denotes the $N \times N$ identity matrix and $\mathcal{N}_N$ denotes the N-dimensional normal distribution. Note that the model parameters are $\boldsymbol{\theta} = (\boldsymbol{\beta},\sigma^2)$, not merely $\boldsymbol{\beta}$. Depending on the specific case, σ^2 and/or a subset of the vector $\boldsymbol{\beta}$ are nuisance parameters.

Many other examples of statistical models have some of the features of the ordinary regression model, in particular, linearity of the systematic component and a simple description of the residual variance $\text{var}(\varepsilon_i)$. Most chapters of the book deal with models in which there are several variances, and they are by no means nuisance parameters.

1.3.3   Correlation structure and similarity

When the observations are independent, as in the ordinary regression, each observation's contribution to the log-likelihood is determined by the outcome y_i, the vector of covariates $\mathbf{x}$ and the parameters $\boldsymbol{\theta}$. In some way, each observation is autonomous; observations are interrelated only through their values of the covariates $\mathbf{x}$. A variety of important cases fall outside this framework, notably time series and clustered data. Our focus is on correlated data and on making inference about the correlation structure of the observations.

Clustered observational units, such as students within schools and multiple measurements of the same quantity over time, are frequently encountered examples of correlated observations. Suppose each elementary unit (student or a measurement) is associated with a 'true' value μ_{ij} (observation on subject i in cluster j), but imperfection of the measurement causes the observed value to be $\mu_{ij} + \varepsilon_{ij}$. Further, the cluster has an impact on the measurement (such as the effect of the instruction at a school), so that the actual observed value is

$$y_{ij} = \mu_{ij} + \delta_j + \varepsilon_{ij} . \tag{1.3}$$

For simplicity, assume that $\{\delta_j\}_j$ and $\{\varepsilon_{ij}\}_{ij}$ are mutually independent random samples (identically distributed sets of random variables), and μ_{ij} is a function of the covariates and of some parameters.

This example can be forced into the standard regression framework by subsuming δ_j in the regression part μ_{ij}, in essence, declaring δ_j as nuisance parameters. A disadvantage of such an approach becomes obvious when there are a large number of clusters — a large number of parameters have to be estimated. Alternatively, if δ_j are regarded as random they are represented in the model and the corresponding log-likelihood only by a small number of parameters that characterize their distribution, often a single variance.

In the example given by (1.3), $\mathbf{E}(\mathbf{y}) = \boldsymbol{\mu}$ and

$$\text{var}(\mathbf{y}) = \sigma_\delta^2 \mathbf{J} + \sigma_\varepsilon^2 \mathbf{I}_N ,$$

where the subscript of σ^2 refers to the random term, and $\mathbf{J}$ is the $N \times N$ matrix with its elements equal to unity if the row and column indices belong to the same cluster and equal to zero otherwise. The variance σ_δ^2 is the covariance of two observations in the same cluster, $\text{cov}(y_{i_1 j}, y_{i_2 j}) =$

σ_δ^2, and the corresponding correlation is $\sigma_\delta^2/(\sigma_\delta^2 + \sigma_\varepsilon^2)$. The importance of this covariance (or correlation) is as a measure of the relative similarity of the observations within clusters. In some problems, the covariance can be interpreted as a measure of risk associated with the allocation of an elementary unit to one cluster or another. The terms δ_j would convey such information only indirectly.

1.3.4   Notation

We have introduced some notation in the previous section. Here we give a summary and describe some of the conventions. Vectors will be denoted by bold lowercase characters, Latin or Greek, and matrices by bold capitals. Elements of the matrices are denoted by the same capital character, in italics lightface, with the row and column subscripts. Similarly, elements of the vectors are denoted by the same character, in italics lightface, with its order index. A row of a matrix is denoted by the same bold character in lowercase and subscripted by its row index.

An array (finite or infinite) of objects is denoted by the braces { } with the subscript(s) indexing the array. For instance, $\{\mathbf{A}_{ij}\}_i$ is the sequence of matrices $\mathbf{A}_{1j}, \mathbf{A}_{2j}, \ldots, \mathbf{A}_{n_j j}$. Matrices and vectors may have multiple subscripts. For instance, the elements of a vector of values associated with individuals that are clustered in groups (and groups further clustered in areas, and so on) would have an index for each level of clustering. Of course, such an object can be described by a multiway array in which some elements are not realized (not associated with any values).

The notation in Chapters 7 and 8 departs from these conventions considerably. There, dealing with survey samples, capitals are used for the population quantities and lowercase for sample quantities.

Some symbols are reserved for specific objects. Throughout, $\mathbf{I}$ will denote the identity matrix and, with the exception above, $\mathbf{J}$ will be the matrix of ones. The sizes of these matrices, when relevant, will be given in the subscript. Similarly, $\mathbf{1}$ and $\mathbf{0}$ will stand for the column vector of ones and zeros, respectively. The direct sum symbol $\oplus$ will be used only in conjunction with $\mathbf{I}, \mathbf{J}, \mathbf{1}$, and $\mathbf{0}$, explaining in every instance the effect of the operation. For instance, $\mathbf{I}_K \oplus \{\mathbf{A}_k\}$ is the block-diagonal matrix with the matrices $\mathbf{A}_1, \mathbf{A}_2, \ldots, \mathbf{A}_K$ in its diagonal blocks. Whenever possible, we use a capital to denote the number of units, and the corresponding lowercase as the index for these units (say, $i = 1, 2, \ldots, I$).

Further, capital script characters will denote some of the familiar distributions: $\mathcal{N}$ (normal), $\mathcal{B}$ (binomial), and $\mathcal{U}$ (continuous uniform). The expectation is denoted by $\mathbf{E}$ and probability (of an event) by P throughout.

Estimates and estimators are denoted by the same symbol as the estimated quantity, with a 'hat' ($\hat{}$). When several estimators for the same quantity are considered, they are distinguished by either a subscript or a superscript.

Real functions are denoted by lowercase Latin characters. A function f is said to be increasing if for any pair of points $x_1 < x_2$ implies $f(x_1) < f(x_2)$. A function is said to be non-decreasing if for any such points $f(x_1) \leq f(x_2)$. Decreasing and non-increasing functions are defined analogously.

2
Reliability of essay rating

2.1 Introduction

Standardized educational tests have until recently been associated almost exclusively with multiple-choice items. In such a test, the examinee is presented items comprising a reading passage stating the question or describing the problem to be solved, followed by a set of response options. One of the options is the correct answer; the others are incorrect. The examinee's task is to identify the correct response. With such an item format, examinees can be given a large number of items in a relatively short time, say, 40 items in a half-hour test. Scoring the test, that is, recording the correctness of each response, can be done reliably by machines at a moderate cost. A serious criticism of this item format is the limited variety of items that can be administered and that certain aspects of skills and abilities cannot be tested by such items. Many items can be solved more effectively by eliminating all the incorrect response options than by deriving the correct response directly. Certainly, problems that can be formulated as multiple-choice items are much rarer in real life; in many respects, it would be preferable to use items with realistic problems that require the examinees to construct their responses.

The principal problem with such *constructed-response* items is that they have to be graded by (human) experts. The response, that is, an essay, a mathematical proof, or the performance of a task, typically takes much longer time to produce than the response to a multiple-choice item, but much more information about the examinee is disclosed. For instance, an essay written on a given topic can inform about several aspects of the examinee's ability: correct grammar, spelling and punctuation, clarity of expression, content, adherence to the topic, suitable composition and style, and the like. An expert could assess a small number of essays on all these aspects and produce a verbal description of this assessment. The next step would be to define a formal ordinal scale for each aspect, such as integer scores 1–5, together with a correspondence of the verbal description to these scores, and then find the best match for the assessment on this scale.

In order for this process to function as desired, it is necessary to recruit raters who are experts in the tested subject area, to train them in the task of rating, and to instruct them about the details of the rating scale. Clearly, this and the rating itself are a costly enterprise that can be justified only if the experts' ratings accurately reflect each examinee's performance. A form of quality control for this process is provided by multiple rating of essays. Disagreement of the experts' ratings of an essay is a sure sign that the rating process is not perfect. Measures of imperfection, the subject of this chapter, can be constructed from the frequency and extent of disagreement.

In summary, multiple-choice items make life easier for the administration and scoring of the test, whereas constructed-response items are more realistic and may come closer to gauging examinees' abilities, especially when the rating process is (almost) perfect.

Imperfection of the rating process has traditionally been described in terms of various correlations, often referred to as *reliability*, and in terms of the probability of agreement. This chapter develops an alternative approach based on a description by variance components of the ways in which the raters disagree. First, one rater may be stricter or more lenient than another rater. This may become apparent when a pair of raters grades a large number of essays in common and one rater gives a higher score than the other for most essays. Next, raters may disagree on the merit of the essays: rater A gives a higher rating for essay P than for essay Q, while rater B gives a higher rating for essay Q. Finally, a rater might have given a different rating to an essay had he/she graded it on a different occasion. These three sources of imperfection can be referred to as

- difference in severity;

- disagreement in merit;

- temporal variation.

Insight into temporal variation could be gained only if a rater graded an essay more than once and 'forgot' everything about the essay between consecutive ratings. This is relatively easy to arrange when the raters grade a large number of essays. However, such an experiment can rarely be afforded on a meaningful scale, and so disagreement in merit usually cannot be distinguished from temporal variation. The ideal situation when there is no temporal variation and no disagreement in merit is referred to as *consistent rating*.

We consider first the case of I examinees writing an essay each on a given topic, and every essay being graded by each of J raters. Throughout, we assume that the raters do not discuss any of the essays, so that their ratings for each essay are mutually independent. The ratings can be represented by an $I \times J$ table, or array, with rows representing the examinees/essays and the columns the raters. Perfect rating (no disagreement) corresponds to constant rows. When the between-column differences are constant, the ratings are consistent; the differences can be attributed to the raters' severities.

Usually, estimating the ability of each examinee is of principal interest. In the narrow context of a single item (essay), this can be represented as the score that would be given by the 'ideal' or average rater. Since we want to define this score without a reference to the actual raters who happen to have graded the essay, it is useful to consider the *population* of raters from which the engaged raters have been drawn. Thus, we define the *true* score of an examinee as the mean of the ratings that would have been given by the raters in this population. This will enable us to establish a framework in which the true score is an unknown quantity estimable from the raters' grades.

When there are a large number of examinees, it may be impractical to have each essay graded by every rater. This is the case in standardized educational tests where there are thousands of examinees and the scores have to be provided in a relatively short time. Reading and handling the essays takes a lot of time and effort, and a rater can reasonably be expected to grade, at most, a few hundred essays a day.

Essay rating in large-scale test administrations is usually organized in *sessions*. Each essay is rated once in every session, and no essay is graded twice by the same rater. For instance, when two sessions are used, each essay is graded by two distinct raters; in the examinee-by-rater table, there are two ratings in each row, and the other cells of the table are empty. For illustration, Table 2.1 depicts an example with 12 examinees and 5 raters. The scores, in the cells corresponding to the examinee (row) and rater (column), are accompanied by the subscript indicating the session (1 or 2). For instance, examinee 9 was graded in session 2 by rater 4 and was awarded five points.

The focus of a typical rating exercise is on estimation of the true score and the standard error of this estimator for each examinee. The obvious choice for the estimator is the mean of all the grades assessed to the examinee's essay. When an essay is graded only by some of the raters, this estimator is problematic, especially when the raters have different severities. An examinee might be disadvantaged if his/her essay happens to be graded by more severe raters. When a rater grades a large number of essays,

TABLE 2.1. Example of an examinee-by-rater table.

Examinee	Rater 1	2	3	4	5
1	3_1				2_2
2		2_2	2_1		
3	5_2		5_1		
4	1_1	0_2			
5	3_2	3_1			
6		1_2		2_1	
7	3_1			4_2	
8		3_2		3_1	
9	3_1			5_2	
10		2_2		2_1	
11			4_1	4_2	
12		1_2	2_1		

Note: The cells contain the score subscripted by the session number.

his/her severity can be estimated by comparing the rater's mean grade with the other raters' means, and so the examinee's score could be adjusted.

The subject of this chapter is assessment of the quality of the rating process. The approach adopted is motivated by generalizability theory (Shavelson and Webb, 1991) and variance component analysis (Searle, Casella, and McCulloch, 1992). In brief, a variance component model is adopted, and the correlation of the grades given by a pair of raters for the same essay is expressed in terms of the model parameters (variances). As an alternative, the quality of the rating process can be assessed by the (average) squared deviation, or the mean squared error (MSE), of the estimator of the true score from the true score itself. The advantage of this approach becomes more obvious when the issue of score adjustment is discussed in Chapter 3.

Section 2.2 introduces the notation and defines the models for subjectively rated essay scores. Section 2.3 deals with estimation of the model parameters. Section 2.4 discusses extensions of the models for non-standard situations, such as the different behaviours of raters from session to session and unequal number of ratings of the essays. Diagnostic procedures are discussed in Section 2.5. The methods are illustrated by examples in Section 2.6. Approaches to determining the standard errors of the estimated variances and to assessing the impact of uncertainty about the variances on estimation of the true scores are outlined and demonstrated in Section 2.7. The chapter is concluded with a summary and a literature review.

2.2   Models

Suppose there are I examinees, each having written an essay on the same topic. Each essay is graded by K raters selected from a pool of J raters; in general, different essays have different sets of raters. The rating process is organized into K sessions; each essay is rated once in every session. Let y_{ij} be the grade given by rater $j = 1, 2, \ldots, J$ for essay $i = 1, 2, \ldots, I$. Since an essay is not graded by all the raters, only some of the scores y_{ij} are realized. To associate an examinee–rater pairing with a session, we denote by j_{ik} $(k = 1, \ldots, K)$ the rater who graded essay i in session k.

The essay written by examinee i has an unknown true score α_i. The severity of rater j is defined as the difference between the mean of the grades that the rater would give to all the examinees (I grades of which only some are realized) from the mean of the grades that would be given by all the raters to all the examinees (IJ grades, of which only IK are realized). To avoid the dependence of the rater severity on the examinees who happen to be taking the test containing the essay, we consider a *population* of examinees from which the actual examinees have been drawn. Similarly, instead of the finite 'sample' of J raters, we consider an infinite population of raters. Now, the severity of rater j, denoted by β_j, is defined as the difference of the rater's mean score (over the population of examinees) from the mean score of all the raters (mean over the populations of examinees and raters). Note that positive severity corresponds to being more lenient and negative severity to being stricter than the average rater. Admittedly, it would be more appropriate to refer to β_j as leniency, or to define severity as $-\beta_j$.

With the populations of examinees and raters, we have a symmetric setup: in the examinee-by-rater table of grades, the rows are a sample from the population of examinees and the columns are a sample from the population of raters. The rows are associated with true scores and the columns with rater severities. An important element of asymmetry is that although it is desirable to have raters with identical severities ($\beta_j \equiv 0$), no differences in true scores correspond to a degenerate case. If the examinees had identical true scores, there would be no point in administering the test.

For the realized scores y_{ij} we posit the additive model

$$y_{i,j_{ik}} = \alpha_i + \beta_{j_{ik}} + \varepsilon_{i,j_{ik}} . \tag{2.1}$$

The residual terms $\varepsilon_{i,j_{ik}}$ represent the amalgam of disagreement in merit (raters' idiosyncracies), temporal variation, and other departures from the simpler model

$$y_{i,j_{ik}} = \alpha_i + \beta_{j_{ik}} ,$$

which applies when the scores are consistent and are transformed to be on an additive scale. . The true scores α_i are assumed to be a random sample (a set of independent identically distributed random variables) from a distribution with unknown mean μ and variance σ_a^2. Similarly, the rater severities β_j are assumed to be a random sample from a distribution with zero mean and variance σ_b^2. The inconsistency terms ε_{ij}, sometimes referred to as rater-by-examinee interactions, are also assumed to be a random sample from a distribution with zero mean and variance σ_e^2. The three random samples are mutually independent. Note that the shape or type of the distribution is not specified. This is of importance particularly when the score scale consists of only a small number of integers (such as 1–5), because these distributions may be rather unusual and difficult to describe.

Note also that the variances σ_a^2, σ_b^2, and σ_e^2 depend on the score scale. If the scores y_{ij} are transformed linearly, say, they are replaced by $y_{ij}^* = C + Dy_{ij}$, then the mean of the transformed scores y_{ij}^* is $C + D\mu$ and the variances are $D^2\sigma_a^2$, $D^2\sigma_b^2$, and $D^2\sigma_e^2$. It is much more difficult to foresee what happens when a non-linear transformation is applied.

In conclusion, the mean μ and the variances σ_a^2, σ_b^2, and σ_e^2, as summaries of the examinee population and of the rating process, depend on the score scale, and so a judicious choice of the scale, together with the correspondence of essay quality to each score (referred to as the *rubric*) is essential.

Vanishing variance of the true scores, $\sigma_a^2 = 0$, corresponds to a degenerate case; if every examinee attained the same true score, there would be no point in rating the essay other than to study the severity and inconsistency of the raters. When $\sigma_b^2 = 0$, that is, the raters' severities are identical, there is, on average, no advantage or disadvantage for the examinees to be graded by one rater or another. When $\sigma_e^2 = 0$, ratings of a pair of raters differ by the same quantity, the difference of their severities, for each essay graded by both of them. This is rather unlikely when an integer scale with few distinct scores is used. When $\sigma_e^2 = 0$, the severities can be determined without error. Perfect rating corresponds to $\sigma_b^2 = \sigma_e^2 = 0$; then $y_{ij} = \alpha_i$ for each rating.

Agreement of the raters can be summarized by the correlation of grades given by two distinct raters for the same essay. According to the model in (2.1), this correlation is

$$r_1 = \operatorname{cor}(y_{i,j_{i1}}, y_{i,j_{i2}}) = \frac{\sigma_a^2}{\sigma_a^2 + \sigma_b^2 + \sigma_e^2}. \qquad (2.2)$$

If we could arrange two *independent* ratings of the same essay by the same rater, the correlation of the two grades would be

$$r_2 = \operatorname{cor}(y_{i,j_{i1}}, y_{i,j_{i1'}}) = \frac{\sigma_a^2 + \sigma_b^2}{\sigma_a^2 + \sigma_b^2 + \sigma_e^2}. \qquad (2.3)$$

When the focus is on estimating the true scores, of main interest is how close, on average, the estimate of the true score is to the true score itself. A trivial estimator of the true score is the mean of the grades given for the essay,

$$y_{i,\cdot} = \frac{1}{K} \sum_{k=1}^{K} y_{i,j_{ik}} .$$

Of course, there may be more efficient estimators of the true score, which are more highly correlated with it. Several such estimators are discussed in Chapter 3. The correlation of the mean score $y_{i,\cdot}$ with the true score is

$$r_a = \mathrm{cor}(\alpha_i, y_{i,\cdot}) = \frac{\sigma_a^2}{\sqrt{\sigma_a^2(\sigma_a^2 + \sigma_b^2/K + \sigma_e^2/K)}}$$

$$= \left(1 + \frac{\tau_b + \tau_e}{K}\right)^{-\frac{1}{2}}, \qquad (2.4)$$

where $\tau_b = \sigma_b^2/\sigma_a^2$ and $\tau_e = \sigma_e^2/\sigma_a^2$ are the *relative* variances of severity and inconsistency, respectively.

An alternative way of assessing the quality of the ratings is by computing the MSEs of the ratings around the true score. We have

$$\begin{aligned}
\mathbf{E}(y_{i,j} - \alpha_i)^2 &= \sigma_b^2 + \sigma_e^2 , \\
\mathbf{E}(y_{i,\cdot} - \alpha_i)^2 &= \frac{\sigma_b^2 + \sigma_e^2}{K} ,
\end{aligned} \qquad (2.5)$$

for one rating and for the mean of the K ratings of an essay, respectively. The obvious dependence of the MSEs on the score scale can be removed by defining the *relative* MSEs, relative to the unconditional variances of $y_{i,j}$ and $y_{i,\cdot}$, respectively, as

$$\frac{\sigma_b^2 + \sigma_e^2}{\sigma_a^2 + \sigma_b^2 + \sigma_e^2}$$

and, since $\mathrm{var}(y_{i,\cdot}) = \sigma_a^2 + (\sigma_b^2 + \sigma_e^2)/K$, as

$$\frac{\sigma_b^2 + \sigma_e^2}{K\sigma_a^2 + \sigma_b^2 + \sigma_e^2} ,$$

which correspond to (2.5). The (relative) MSEs can be easily related to the reliabilities.

The principal obstacle in computing a reliability or MSE is that neither the variances nor the relative variances involved in equations (2.4) and (2.5) are known, and they have to be estimated. When there are two sessions, the sample correlation of the ratings from the first session with those from the second session would appear to be a suitable estimator of the reliability r_a. This estimator is

$$\hat{r} = \frac{\sum_i (y_{i,j_{i1}} - \bar{y}_1)(y_{i,j_{i2}} - \bar{y}_2)}{\sqrt{\sum_i (y_{i,j_{i1}} - \bar{y}_1)^2 \sum_i (y_{i,j_{i2}} - \bar{y}_2)^2}} , \qquad (2.6)$$

where $\bar{y}_k$, $k = 1, 2$, is the mean rating in session k. When there are more than two sessions, the mean of the sample correlations for every pair of sessions could be used instead of $\hat{r}$ in (2.6).

The following example illustrates a serious deficiency of the correlation $\hat{r}$. For a given test item, consider a population of consistent raters, that is, $\sigma_e^2 = 0$. Suppose first that in each session only one rater is engaged, and he/she grades all the essays (in this case $J = K$). Then the between-session correlation is equal to unity because the ratings differ from one session (k_1) to another (k_2) by the constant $\beta_{k_1} - \beta_{k_2}$, which, incidentally, could be estimated without error. For a contrast, consider now the scheme in which each rater grades only one essay (in this case $J = IK$; there are more raters than examinees). In the presence of varying severities, $\sigma_b^2 > 0$, the correlation in (2.6) may be much smaller than unity. Thus, the correlation $\hat{r}$ depends on the assignment design, that is, how the essays are assigned to raters. This is a rather undesirable property.

However, when the severities are constant, $\sigma_b^2 = 0$, $\hat{r}$ is a good estimator of r_a. To see this, consider the between-session differences

$$y_{i,j_{i1}} - y_{i,j_{i2}} = \varepsilon_{i,j_{i1}} - \varepsilon_{i,j_{i2}} .$$

They are mutually independent and their variances are equal to $2\sigma_e^2$. Using the identity

$$\text{cov}(y_1, y_2) = \frac{\text{var}(y_1) + \text{var}(y_2) - \text{var}(y_1 - y_2)}{2}$$

for a pair of ratings of the same essay and noting that $\text{var}(y_1) = \text{var}(y_2) = \sigma_a^2 + \sigma_e^2$, we obtain

$$\text{cor}(y_1, y_2 \mid \sigma_b^2 = 0) = \frac{\sigma_a^2}{\sigma_a^2 + \sigma_e^2} ,$$

which coincides with r_1 and r_2. Hence, the sample correlation $\hat{r}$ is a good estimator of the reliabilities r_1 and r_2, when $\sigma_b^2 = 0$. What happens when σ_b^2 is positive is not easy to explore, though.

2.3   Estimation

The example in the last section highlights the importance of knowing the sizes, or at least the relative sizes, of the variances σ_a^2, σ_b^2, and σ_e^2. In this section, we describe a simple and elementary method for estimating these variances. In brief, we define three sums-of-squares statistics, compute their expectations, and then solve the equations that match these expectations with the sum-of-squares statistics. This method, used in a variety of contexts, is called the *method of moments*. It is very convenient that the method can be applied without any distributional assumptions.

We define the following statistics:

1. the *within-examinee* sum of squares,

$$S_E = \sum_{k=1}^{K}\sum_{i=1}^{I}(y_{i,j_{ik}} - y_{i,.})^2 \; ; \tag{2.7}$$

2. the *within-rater* sum of squares,

$$S_R = \sum_{k=1}^{K}\sum_{i=1}^{I}(y_{i,j_{ik}} - z_{j_{ik}})^2 \, , \tag{2.8}$$

where z_j is the mean grade given by rater j,

$$z_j = \frac{1}{n_j}\sum_{k=1}^{K}\sum_{(i;j_{ik}=j)} y_{i,j_{ik}}$$

(n_j is the workload of rater j, and the summations are over all the essays graded by rater j);

3. the *total* sum of squares,

$$S_T = \sum_{k=1}^{K}\sum_{i=1}^{I}(y_{i,j_{ik}} - \bar{y})^2 \, , \tag{2.9}$$

where $\bar{y}$ is the mean of all the ratings,

$$\bar{y} = \frac{1}{IK}\sum_{k=1}^{K}\sum_{i=1}^{I} y_{i,j_{ik}} \, .$$

The expectations of these statistics are

$$\begin{aligned}
\mathbf{E}(S_E) &= I(K-1)(\sigma_b^2 + \sigma_e^2) \, , \\
\mathbf{E}(S_R) &= (IK - J)(\sigma_a^2 + \sigma_e^2) \, , \\
\mathbf{E}(S_T) &= K(I-1)\sigma_a^2 + \left(IK - \frac{\sum_{j=1}^{J} n_j^2}{IK}\right)\sigma_b^2 + (IK-1)\sigma_e^2 \, .
\end{aligned} \tag{2.10}$$

Note that these expectations are linear functions of the variances. This makes the application of the method of moments very simple.

The identities in (2.10) are proved by elementary operations. For S_E, we have

$$\mathbf{E}(S_E) = \sum_{k=1}^{K}\sum_{i=1}^{I}\mathbf{E}\left(\beta_{j_{ik}} - \frac{1}{K}\sum_{k'=1}^{K}\beta_{j_{ik'}} + \varepsilon_{i,j_{ik}} - \frac{1}{K}\sum_{k'=1}^{K}\varepsilon_{i,j_{ik'}}\right)^2 .$$

The β's are independent of the ε's and have zero expectations. Therefore,

$$\mathbf{E}(S_E)$$

$$= \sum_{k=1}^{K} \sum_{i=1}^{I} \left\{ \mathrm{var}\left(\beta_{j_{ik}} - \frac{1}{K} \sum_{k'=1}^{K} \beta_{j_{ik'}} \right) + \mathrm{var}\left(\varepsilon_{i,j_{ik}} - \frac{1}{K} \sum_{k'=1}^{K} \varepsilon_{i,j_{ik'}} \right) \right\}.$$

Each variance above is evaluated using the identity

$$\mathrm{var}\left(\gamma_m^* - \frac{1}{M} \sum_{m=1}^{M} \gamma_m \right) = \mathrm{var}\left\{ \gamma_m^* \left(1 - \frac{1}{M} \right) \right\} + \sum_{m \neq m^*} \mathrm{var}\left(\frac{\gamma_m}{M} \right)$$

$$= \sigma_g^2 \left\{ \left(\frac{M-1}{M} \right)^2 + \frac{M-1}{M^2} \right\}$$

$$= \sigma_g^2 \frac{M-1}{M}, \tag{2.11}$$

where γ_m, $m = 1, 2, \ldots, M$, are independent and identically distributed random variables with variance σ_g^2. Using this identity with $M = K$ and suitable random variables for γ_m yields

$$\mathbf{E}(S_E) = \sum_{k=1}^{K} \sum_{i=1}^{I} \frac{K-1}{K} (\sigma_b^2 + \sigma_e^2)$$

$$= I(K-1)(\sigma_b^2 + \sigma_e^2). \tag{2.12}$$

For brevity, we omit the proof for $\mathbf{E}(S_R)$ but give details of the proof for $\mathbf{E}(S_T)$, which is slightly more complex. First,

$$\mathbf{E}(S_T)$$

$$= \sum_{k=1}^{K} \sum_{i=1}^{I} \mathbf{E}\left(\alpha_i - \sum_{i'=1}^{I} \frac{\alpha_{i'}}{I} + \beta_{j_{ik}} - \sum_{j=1}^{J} \frac{n_j \beta_j}{IK} + \varepsilon_{i,j_{ik}} - \sum_{k'=1}^{K} \sum_{i'=1}^{I} \frac{\varepsilon_{i',j_{i'k'}}}{IK} \right)^2$$

$$= K \sum_{i=1}^{I} \mathrm{var}\left(\alpha_i - \frac{1}{I} \sum_{i'=1}^{I} \alpha_{i'} \right) + \sum_{j^*=1}^{J} n_{j^*} \mathrm{var}\left(\beta_{j^*} - \frac{1}{IK} \sum_{j=1}^{J} n_j \beta_j \right)$$

$$+ \sum_{k=1}^{K} \sum_{i=1}^{I} \mathrm{var}\left(\varepsilon_{i,j_{ik}} - \frac{1}{IK} \sum_{k'=1}^{K} \sum_{i'=1}^{I} \varepsilon_{i',j_{i'k'}} \right).$$

The variances involving the severities β_j are equal to

$$\mathrm{var}\left(\beta_{j^*} - \frac{1}{IK} \sum_{j=1}^{J} n_j \beta_j \right) = \sigma_b^2 \left\{ \left(\frac{IK - n_{j^*}}{IK} \right)^2 + \sum_{j \neq j^*} \frac{n_j^2}{(IK)^2} \right\}$$

$$= \sigma_b^2 \left(1 - \frac{2n_{j*}}{IK} + \sum_{j=1}^{J} \frac{n_j^2}{I^2 K^2} \right) .$$

The variances involving the other terms (α's and ε's) can be evaluated using (2.11). Substitution yields

$$\mathbf{E}(S_T) = \sigma_a^2 N \frac{I-1}{I} + \sigma_b^2 \left(N - \sum_{j*=1}^{J} \frac{2n_{j*}^2}{N} + \sum_{j*=1}^{J} n_{j*} \sum_{j=1}^{J} \frac{n_j^2}{N^2} \right)$$

$$+ \sigma_e^2 N \frac{N-1}{N}$$

$$= \sigma_a^2 (N - K) + \sigma_b^2 \left(N - n^{(2)} \right) + \sigma_e^2 (N - 1) ,$$

where, for brevity, we set $N = IK$ (the total number of ratings) and $n^{(2)} = (n_1^2 + \ldots + n_J^2)/N$.

In the next step, the expectations in (2.10) are matched with the sum-of-squares statistics (2.7)–(2.9):

$$(N - I)(\hat{\sigma}_b^2 + \hat{\sigma}_e^2) = S_E ,$$

$$(N - J)(\hat{\sigma}_a^2 + \hat{\sigma}_e^2) = S_R , \qquad (2.13)$$

$$\hat{\sigma}_a^2 (N - K) + \hat{\sigma}_b^2 \left(N - n^{(2)} \right) + \hat{\sigma}_e^2 (N - 1) = S_T$$

(the hats ˆ are added to the variances to indicate estimates). This is a linear system of equations in the variances. It can be solved in a number of ways by linearly combining the equations. Existence and uniqueness of the solution can be discussed by evaluating the determinant of the matrix associated with the left-hand sides in (2.13). It is equal to

$$\det \begin{pmatrix} 0 & N-I & N-I \\ N-J & 0 & N-J \\ N-K & N-n^{(2)} & N-1 \end{pmatrix}$$

$$= (N - I)(N - J) \left(N - K + 1 - n^{(2)} \right) . \qquad (2.14)$$

This determinant vanishes only when there is a single session ($K = 1$ and $N = I$), when each rater grades only one essay ($N = J$), when there is only one rater ($J = 1$; then necessarily $K = 1$ and $n_1 = I = N$), or when $n^{(2)} = N - K + 1$. To rule out the latter identity, we search for the maximum possible value of $n^{(2)}$. Consider a particular decomposition of the total number of ratings N into the sum of raters' workloads, $N = n_1 + \ldots + n_J$. Suppose $n_1 > n_2$. It is easy to check that $(n_1 + 1)^2 + (n_2 - 1)^2 > n_1^2 + n_2^2$. Therefore, $n^{(2)}$ can be increased by reducing the workload of the raters who have small workloads and giving the essays to the busiest raters (so long as they do not grade an essay twice). Ultimately, it can be arranged that only K raters are engaged, each of them grading every essay. The corresponding (maximum possible) $n^{(2)}$ is equal to $KI^2/N = I$. Hence, $N - K + 1 - n^{(2)} > (I - 1)(K - 1) \geq 0$. Incidentally, the determinant in (2.14) has a lower bound $I(I - 1)(K - 1)^2(N - J)$.

The estimates of the variances are

$$\hat{\sigma}_e^2 = \frac{\frac{N - n^{(2)}}{N - I} S_E + \frac{N - K}{N - J} S_R - S_T}{N - n^{(2)} - K + 1},$$

$$\hat{\sigma}_b^2 = \frac{S_E}{N - I} - \hat{\sigma}_e^2, \tag{2.15}$$

$$\hat{\sigma}_a^2 = \frac{S_R}{N - J} - \hat{\sigma}_e^2.$$

Obtaining the sampling variances of these estimators in closed form is rather arduous and requires assumptions about the skewnesses and kurtoses of the random variables involved. An alternative approach based on simulations is discussed in Section 2.7.

The number of examinees is usually much greater than the number of raters. Then the standard error of the severity variance σ_b^2 cannot be smaller than the standard error in the hypothetical situation in which the severities of each rater are known exactly. Note that this standard error depends on σ_b^2 itself. In general, the true score variance σ_a^2 and the inconsistency variance σ_e^2 are estimated with greater precision, even though these variances are often much greater than the severity variance.

Positive true-score variance σ_a^2 is imperative for the rating process to be a meaningful exercise in rating examinees. In fact, the rating process in educational testing is regarded as highly unsatisfactory even when the variance σ_a^2 is of the same order as $\sigma_b^2 + \sigma_e^2$. Usually, $\sigma_b^2 < \sigma_e^2$, that is, imperfection of the rating is mainly due to inconsistency.

A rater who has given a low average grade is either a severe rater or one who has been assigned examinees with lower than average true scores. Since the true scores are not known in advance, severity variance can be estimated only if the essays are assigned to raters by a *non-informative* design. The means of the true scores may vary from region to region, or across other divisions of the examinees, and so there are only two foolproof ways of ensuring non-informative design: assigning essays to raters according to a systematic design or assigning them completely at random. The latter is difficult to implement when there are a lot of essays to be graded, but the approximate (agreed) workloads of the raters are easy to accommodate. The systematic design (such as spiralling over the raters) is easy to implement, but difficulties may arise when there are constraints on the workloads. A satisfactory compromise is achieved by packaging the essays into bundles of, say, 20, which are then treated as a single unit and are assigned to a rater in each session.

2.4   Extensions

Of course, situations may arise where the assumptions adopted in the previous section are too restrictive. First, essays may be graded by unequal numbers of raters. For instance, some essays may be graded twice and the rest only once. The method of moments can readily accommodate this generalization. The derivation of the expectations of the sum-of-squares statistics is somewhat more tedious, but no new tricks are required. Some notational difficulties may be encountered. It is practical to consider *incomplete sessions*, that is, sessions in which not all the essays are rated. The resulting equations are similar to those in (2.10); see Longford (1994b).

After completing a session, the raters may discuss their experiences or may receive additional instructions. The raters may also reflect on the completed work. The effect of these influences may be that each rater applies a different severity in the next session. The inconsistency variance may also be altered. For instance, inconsistency may be due to raters applying different emphasis on the various aspects of the essay (form, content, spelling, and the like). Discussion of these issues or merely reflection on new experiences or on some unexpected problems in rating may contribute to lowering the inconsistency variance in the next session. In an extreme case, the raters may be instructed to pay more attention to certain aspects of the essays, which would result, in effect, in a different test item.

These features of the rating process can be accommodated by extending the model in (2.1). Let β_j be the *average severity* of rater j, averaged over the sessions $k = 1, \ldots, K$, and let δ_{kj} be the deviation of his/her severity in session k from the average severity ($\beta_j + \delta_{kj}$ is the severity of rater j in session k). Then the grade given to examinee i in session k can be modelled as

$$y_{i,j_{ik}} = \alpha_i + \beta_{j_{ik}} + \delta_{kj_{ik}} + \varepsilon_{i,j_{ik}}, \qquad (2.16)$$

with the assumptions about α_i and β_j as in (2.1); δ_{kj} are assumed to be a random sample from a distribution with zero mean and variance σ_d^2, and $\{\varepsilon_{i,j_{ik}}\}_i$ are random samples from distributions with zero means and variances $\sigma_{e,k}^2$ ($k = 1, \ldots, K$). The model in (2.1) corresponds to $\sigma_d^2 = 0$ and $\sigma_{e,k}^2 \equiv \sigma_e^2$. The random samples in (2.16) are assumed to be mutually independent.

The model in (2.16) can be further generalized by allowing for session-specific means of the grades. Then it is necessary to separate these means from the mean of the true scores. This can be done by adding session-specific terms in (2.16), for instance, by replacing α_i with $g_k + \alpha_i$, where g_k, $k = 1, \ldots, K$, are unknown constants. To avoid confounding with the true-score mean μ, a linear constraint on the constants g_k has to be imposed. Practical choices are $g_1 = 0$ and $g_1 + g_2 + \ldots + g_K = 0$.

It would normally be expected that the inconsistency variances are reduced as a result of practice and experience. The raters may have consistent components of severity; that is, despite fluctuations in their severities from session to session, the raters also differ in their average severities. Then the average severity variance σ_b^2 is greater than the variance of the severity fluctuation, σ_d^2.

Differences in rating may be attributed to variables such as gender, age, and experience of the raters. These can be modelled in a similar fashion, although when there are only a moderate number of raters there may be scope for considering no more than one such variable.

Systematic differences, such as the average difference between male and female raters, can be estimated by their natural sample counterparts. Since these are linear functions of the data, their sampling variances can also be obtained. By way of illustration, let $\bar{y}_M$ be the mean grade given by the male raters and $\bar{y}_F$ the mean grade given by the female raters. Then $\bar{y}_M - \bar{y}_F$ is an estimate of the difference of severity between an average male and female rater. Suppose the raters are indexed so that the indices $j = 1, \ldots, J_1$ correspond to male and $j = J_1 + 1, \ldots, J$ to female raters. Let N_m and N_f be the workloads (the total numbers of rated essays) of the male and female raters, respectively, and let m_i and f_i $(i = 1, \ldots, I)$ be the respective numbers of male and female raters who rated essay i. Then, assuming the model in (2.1), the sampling variance of the difference $\bar{y}_M - \bar{y}_F$ is

$$
\sigma_a^2 \left(\frac{1}{N_m^2} \sum_{i=1}^I m_i^2 - \frac{2}{N_m N_f} \sum_{i=1}^I f_i m_i + \frac{1}{N_f^2} \sum_{i=1}^I f_i^2 \right)
$$

$$
+ \sigma_b^2 \left(\frac{1}{N_m^2} \sum_{j=1}^{J_1} n_j^2 + \frac{1}{N_f^2} \sum_{j=J_1+1}^J n_j^2 \right) + \sigma_e^2 \left(\frac{1}{N_m} + \frac{1}{N_f} \right).
$$

(2.17)

The sampling variances of other differences, such as between two sessions, are derived similarly.

2.5   Diagnostic procedures

Diagnostic procedures should accompany the application of every model-based statistical procedure. With the rater reliability models (2.1) and (2.16), a number of possible departures from the model assumptions may also be of substantive interest. First, the size of the severity variance may be to a large extent due to a single rater who has an outlying severity. This could be detected by estimating the severities of the raters. The mean grades z_j are estimates of the severities, but they are particularly unsatisfactory for raters with small workloads n_j. We return to diagnostics for severity in Chapter 3.

The inconsistency variance may also be excessively inflated by an aberrant rater. Clearly, inconsistency is an attribute of pairs of raters, and therefore it can be explored only when there are at least two sessions. Then the grades given to the essays read by a given pair of raters yield information about inconsistency. However, some disagreement between any two raters is to be expected; the conditional variance of the differences in grades given to the same essay is

$$\mathrm{var}(y_{i,j_1} - y_{i,j_2} \mid \beta_{j_1}, \beta_{j_2}) = 2\sigma_e^2.$$

This suggests the following procedure: for each pair of raters who rated more than a certain number of essays in common (say, ten), calculate the mean squared difference of the pairs of ratings

$$S_{j_1,j_2} = \frac{1}{m_{j_1,j_2}} \sum_{(i;j_1,j_2)} (y_{i,j_1} - y_{i,j_2})^2$$

(m_{j_1,j_2} is the number of essays rated by the raters j_1 and j_2 in common), and compare $S_{j_1,j_2}/2\sigma_e^2$ to unity. Large values of $S_{j_1,j_2}/2\sigma_e^2$ indicate more disagreement, and low values indicate more agreement than expected. Of course, grades given by a rater who is identified in several pairings should be subjected to scrutiny. When some ratings can be discarded (for instance, when the essays can be rerated), it may be worthwhile to consider rerating the essays that were graded by a rater who has been judged aberrant. If this rater is replaced, the inconsistency variance may be reduced substantially, and the reduction may be worth the additional ratings.

Another model assumption to be subjected to diagnosis is that of variance homogeneity (equal variance of ε's). Conceivably, a very strict (or lenient) rater would give the extreme grade (the lowest or the highest) to most of the essays, and so the variance of the inconsistency terms $\varepsilon_{.,j}$ would be smaller than for the rest of the raters. In this case, the extreme severity would be accompanied by excessive disagreement with the fellow raters.

The conditional variance of the grades given by a rater is

$$\mathrm{var}(y_{.,j} \mid \beta_j) = \sigma_a^2 + \sigma_e^2.$$

This suggests calculating the within-rater sample variances (within sessions and across sessions) and comparing them with $\sigma_a^2 + \sigma_e^2$. Small values of these sample variances indicate raters who gave almost the same grade to each examinee (narrow effective scale), and large values correspond to raters who gave the lowest and/or the highest scores more frequently than would be expected. Of course, non-informative assignment of examinees to raters is crucial for validity of such an interpretation.

It is difficult to set a formal criterion for a sample variance (for pairs of raters or within a rater) to be judged an outlier. Being committed to no distributional assumptions, we have no 'null' distribution for these sample variances either. Informal rules of thumb can be based on the χ^2 distribution which corresponds to the normality assumptions. For instance, the within-rater sample variance for rater j,

$$V_j = \frac{1}{n_j - 1} \sum_{k=1}^{K} \sum_{(i; j_{ik}=j)} (y_{ij} - z_j)^2,$$

is a corrected mean square of n_j independent identically distributed random variables. If these variables were normally distributed, $(n_j - 1)V_j/(\sigma_a^2 + \sigma_e^2)$ would have a χ^2 distribution with $n_j - 1$ degrees of freedom, and therefore $W_j = V_j/(\sigma_a^2 + \sigma_e^2)$ would have unit expectation and variance $\sqrt{2/(n_j - 1)}$. Of course, any diagnostic procedure is meaningful only for raters with large workloads n_j. Using the normal approximation to the χ^2 distribution, rater j could be considered an outlier when the value of W_j is outside the interval $1 \pm c\sqrt{2/(n_j - 1)}$, where c is a suitably chosen constant. A similar rule can be defined for the within-pair sample variances $S_{jj'}$. Note that W_j is a normalized subtotal of S_R. In addition, when $K = 2$, $S_{jj'}$ is related to subtotals of S_E.

2.6   Examples

The English Language and Literature (ELL) and Social Science (SSc) tests are two components of the Content Area Performance Assessment (CAPA) which is used in conjunction with a battery of multiple-choice tests for teacher certification in California. The Assessment was developed jointly by the Educational Testing Service (ETS) and the California Commission on Teacher Credentialing. The dataset analysed in this section is from the November 1992 operational administration in which 419 examinees took part. The data were kindly provided by David Anderson from ETS.

The ELL and SSc tests consist of two essays each; we denote them by ELL1, ELL2, SSc1, and SSc2. Each essay was graded by a pair of raters. The two tests use disjoint pools of raters, but the pools for the pair of essays in each test are identical. The scoring scale is 1–6 for both essays. The workloads of the raters are summarized in Table 2.2. Rater 570 graded only 2 ELL1 essays in the first session and rater 501 graded only 9 ELL1 essays and 22 ELL2 essays in the respective second sessions. The other raters took part in all four sessions, grading betweeen 19 and 82 essays on each topic.

The agreement of the raters can be straightforwardly summarized by cross-tabulating the ratings from the sessions. This is done in Table 2.3. No

TABLE 2.2. Workloads of the raters for the ELL essays.

			Essay ELL1			
Rater	501	510	511	512	513	514
Workload	0+9	19+17	14+22	33+19	23+32	31+47
Rater	515	516	517	521	522	523
Workload	17+19	25+39	23+28	31+ 9	34+24	21+44
Rater	524	525	526	527	528	570
Workload	29+35	21+25	34+29	36+ 9	28+10	2+ 0
			Essay ELL2			
Rater	501	510	511	512	513	514
Workload	0+22	9+10	19+10	33+13	9+32	23+49
Rater	515	516	517	521	522	523
Workload	24+20	40+17	14+34	28+23	34+24	41+17
Rater	524	525	526	527	528	
Workload	41+41	30+ 4	28+36	28+28	18+29	

Notes: Each rater's workload is given by essay and session. For instance, rater 511 graded 14 ELL1 essays in the first session and 22 in the second session.

disagreement corresponds to all the off-diagonal entries in the tables being equal to zero (the diagonal entries are printed in boldface). Of particular concern are the pairs of scores given for the same essay, which differ by more than one point. Such differences may arise when an essay is graded by a pair of raters with very different severities, although these differences may also be attributed to disagreement in merit. The disagreements can be further summarized as follows: the pairs of raters agree on their grades for 192 ELL1 essays (46 percent), differ by a point for 195 essays (46.5 percent), by 2 points for 24 essays (6 percent), and by 3 or 4 points for 8 essays (2 percent). There appears to be somewhat less disagreement for the ELL2 essays. There is agreement for 233 essays (55.5 percent), difference of 1 point for 167 essays (40 percent), and difference of 2 or more points for 19 essays (4.5 percent).

Estimation of the variances is based on the sum of squares defined in (2.7)–(2.9). For the two ELL essays, we have

$$\textbf{ELL1}: \quad S_E = 181.50, \quad S_R = 902.82, \quad S_T = 969.36,$$
$$\textbf{ELL2}: \quad S_E = 124.00, \quad S_R = 822.37, \quad S_T = 881.80, \qquad (2.18)$$

TABLE 2.3. Tables of agreement.

	Essay ELL1						Essay ELL2					
Rating	1	2	3	4	5	6	1	2	3	4	5	6
1	**4**	2	0	1	0	0	**1**	3	0	0	0	0
2	0	**17**	24	5	2	0	1	**9**	17	1	0	0
3	1	14	**51**	38	7	0	1	7	**56**	38	4	0
4	2	5	35	**76**	31	0	0	0	22	**95**	33	3
5	0	2	3	33	**37**	3	0	1	3	25	**60**	8
6	0	0	1	3	15	**7**	0	0	0	6	13	**12**
Session 1	7	48	111	149	78	26	4	28	106	153	97	31
Session 2	7	40	114	156	92	10	3	20	98	165	110	23

Notes: The rows refer to the ratings in the first session and the columns to the second session. For instance, two ELL1 essays were rated 5 in the first session and 2 in the second session. The diagonal entries are printed in boldface. The lower panel contains the distribution of the scores within sessions.

and the resulting estimates of the variances are

$$\textbf{ELL1:} \quad \hat{\sigma}_a^2 = 0.730, \quad \hat{\sigma}_b^2 = 0.062, \quad \hat{\sigma}_e^2 = 0.371\,;$$
$$\textbf{ELL2:} \quad \hat{\sigma}_a^2 = 0.762, \quad \hat{\sigma}_b^2 = 0.056, \quad \hat{\sigma}_e^2 = 0.240\,. \tag{2.19}$$

The estimated total variances of the grades, $\hat{\sigma}_a^2 + \hat{\sigma}_b^2 + \hat{\sigma}_e^2$, are 1.16 and 1.06 for ELL1 and ELL2, respectively. This is rather low for a score scale with the range of 5 points (1–6). Inspection of the score distributions, as well as of the tables of agreement, provides an explanation. The lowest grade, 1, is apparently given only in exceptional circumstances, and the grades 2 and 6 are also given to very few examinees. Thus, the effective score scale is only 3–5. Of the total variance, $100 \times 0.73/1.16 = 63$ percent (ELL1) and 72 percent (ELL2) are due to true scores. Variation in severity is only a modest component of the total variation due to rater disagreement; $100 \times 0.062/(0.062 + 0.371) = 14$ percent for ELL1 and 19 percent for ELL2 essay. The MSE of the mean grade around the true score, $\mathbf{E}(y_{i,\cdot} - \alpha_i)^2$, is $(0.062 + 0.371)/2 = 0.22$ for essay ELL1 and 0.15 for ELL2.

Although the true scores are on a continuous scale, the observed scores and their means are on a very coarse scale. In a sense, the best that can be achieved with the observed scores is to match the true scores after rounding. If the true scores had the uniform distribution on $(0.5, 6.5)$, rounding would contribute to the inconsistency variance by 0.083, the variance of a uniform distribution on $[0, 1]$. This is about 20–25 percent of the rating error variance $\sigma_b^2 + \sigma_e^2$ for the ELL essays. Thus, rounding is a sizeable but not a dominant component of the rating error.

TABLE 2.4. Pairwise sample variances for essay ELL2.

Raters	501 524	510 524	512 521	512 525	513 525
$\frac{1}{2}S_{jj'}/\hat{\sigma}_e^2$	0.17	0.66	1.16	2.73	0.76
Counts	12	15	14	13	11
Raters	513 526	514 521	514 526	515 528	516 523
$\frac{1}{2}S_{jj'}/\hat{\sigma}_e^2$	0.26	1.04	0.56	1.75	0.56
Counts	15	18	13	15	13
Raters	516 524	516 527	517 522	517 526	523 527
$\frac{1}{2}S_{jj'}/\hat{\sigma}_e^2$	0.64	1.44	2.38	1.10	1.01
Counts	17	19	13	18	17

Notes: Only pairs of raters with more than 10 essays graded in common are listed. The statistics are normalized by dividing by $2\hat{\sigma}_e^2$.

For comparison, we give the corresponding results for the SSc essays. The estimates of the variances are

$$\textbf{SSc1:}\quad \hat{\sigma}_a^2 = 0.707,\quad \hat{\sigma}_b^2 = 0.077,\quad \hat{\sigma}_e^2 = 0.321\,;$$
$$\textbf{SSc2:}\quad \hat{\sigma}_a^2 = 1.358,\quad \hat{\sigma}_b^2 = 0.064,\quad \hat{\sigma}_e^2 = 0.264\,. \tag{2.20}$$

The true-score variance for essay SSc2 is almost twice as large as that of the other three items. High true-score variance is a very desirable feature, because, given fixed variances associated with the raters, it is a greater component of the total variance $\sigma_a^2 + \sigma_b^2 + \sigma_e^2$, and the relative variances τ_b and τ_e are smaller.

We return to the analysis of ELL essays to explore the within-rater and pairwise sample variances for diagnostic purposes. To avoid a lot of duplication in illustrating the diagnostic procedures, we consider only essay topic ELL2. Since the workloads of the raters are only moderate, there are very few pairs of raters that have rated enough essays in common for the pairwise sample variances to be useful for diagnostics. Table 2.4 lists all the normalized sample variances $\frac{1}{2}S_{jj'}/\hat{\sigma}_e^2$ for the pairs of raters who rated more than 10 essays in common.

There is a remarkable agreement between raters 501 and 524 (they disagree in 2 essays out of 12, by 1 point each), whereas the pairs (512, 525) and (517, 522) disagree more than what would be expected. For orientation, the nominal standard errors associated with these statistics are $\sqrt{2/m_{jj'}}$, where $m_{jj'}$ is the number of essays rated in common (row 'Counts' in Table 2.4). Thus, the standard errors associated with the sampled variances quoted above are about 0.4. The importance of the deviations of these statistics from unity can be more appropriately assessed by a reference to the critical values of the χ^2 distribution.

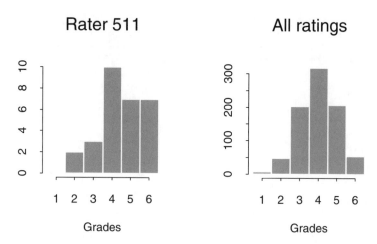

FIGURE 2.1. Histograms of rater 511 and of all the ratings.

A finer insight could be gained by distinguishing the order of rating, that is, computing separate sample variances for essays graded by rater j in the first session and rater j' in the second session. This is not useful in these examples, however, because the counts of essays in common are very small.

The normalized within-rater sample variances W_j are listed in Table 2.5. The three pairs of columns give these statistics for the first session, the second session, and for the aggregate of the sessions, respectively. Raters who graded fewer than 10 essays are omitted. Raters 515 and 522 have the smallest normalized sample variances W_j; they appear to have been more reluctant to give the highest and lowest grades than the other raters. On the other hand, raters 511 and 525 have the largest normalized sample variances; they have given the extreme grades more frequently than the other raters. Further, the raters' frequencies of the grades can be compared to the frequencies of all the grades. For illustration, Figure 2.1 displays the histograms of the grades given by rater 511 and all the raters. Rater 511 was more lenient than the average rater, and yet he/she gave grades on the entire scale. No strong conclusions about the rater are warranted because, as can be observed in the histogram, small counts are involved. Grades given by other raters can be explored similarly.

The estimates in (2.19) and (2.20) can be put in an appropriate perspective only when they are associated with standard errors or some other measure of sampling variation and when they can be compared with the corresponding variances for tests in similar and different subject areas as well as with tests for different populations of examinees. Estimation of standard errors is dealt with in Section 2.7. In the next section, we discuss variance estimation for several test administrations that involve subjective scoring by raters.

TABLE 2.5. Within-rater statistics for essay ELL2.

Rater	Session 1		Session 2		Both sessions	
	$W_{j,1}$	Count	$W_{j,2}$	Count	W_j	Count
501			1.11	22	1.11	22
510					0.88	19
511	1.37	19			1.40	29
512	0.75	33	1.16	13	0.84	46
513			0.74	32	0.77	41
514	0.91	23	0.77	49	0.82	72
515	0.86	24	0.43	20	0.66	44
516	1.33	40	0.57	27	1.25	67
517	1.17	14	0.94	34	1.12	48
521	0.85	28	0.86	23	0.90	51
522	0.59	34	0.58	24	0.58	58
523	1.10	41	1.37	17	1.32	58
524	1.09	41	1.32	41	1.20	82
525	1.45	30			1.58	34
526	0.88	28	0.83	36	0.84	64
527	1.51	28	1.22	28	1.35	56
528	0.82	18	1.17	29	1.02	47

Notes: The statistics based on fewer than ten ratings are omitted. Raters referred to in the text are indicated by boldface print.

2.6.1 Advanced Placement tests

Advanced Placement (AP) is a collection of tests for a number of academic subject areas, administered by ETS. The test is taken by high school juniors and seniors and provides a means for colleges to grant credit to students who have achieved a certain level of mastery in a particular subject area, as indicated by a good results in an AP test.

The AP tests use both multiple-choice and constructed-response items. The score for the multiple-choice part of the test is derived as the number of correct responses, with an appropriate adjustment for non-response. The constructed-response items (essays) are scored by raters; each essay is rated only once, but so-called 'reliability studies' are carried out on a regular schedule. These studies involve rescoring a small fraction of the essays from an administration so as to assess the quality of the rating process.

In the operational scoring, the multiple-choice scores are combined with the raters' scores (one for each item) with relative weights that reflect the perceived importance of the sections of the test and the ranges of the effective scales of the sections. The resulting scores are then coded on a discrete scale 1–5 (the so-called AP grade) according to a set of cut points. A college may award a freshman credit for a course if the student's AP grade is 3 or higher (4 or higher in some colleges).

Some details of the analyses are postponed to Chapter 3. Here we give the estimates of the variances for the administrations of the AP tests in Psychology, Computer Science, and English Composition, so as to bring the corresponding estimates from the CAPA administrations into a better perspective. All the administrations took place in autumn 1993. All the items (essay topics) referred to were rated on the scale 0–9.

In a reliability study, for each topic a small number of essays (in the range 250–400) are selected at random and are rescored by a pool of raters selected from the raters who graded the essays in the operation. In fact, the essays are usually added to the workload, so that the raters do not know that they are grading an essay for the second time. No essay is graded twice by the same rater.

Information about the inconsistency variance is contained only in multiple ratings. Therefore, we proceed as follows. First, the pairs of ratings are analysed. Of the estimated variances based on these data, the inconsistency variance is retained as the estimate for the entire (operational) scoring, and the other two variances are reestimated using the operational scores for all the examinees.

The Psychology AP test was taken by 6259 examinees. The test contained two essays, denoted by PSY1 and PSY2. In the reliability study, the essays submitted by 299 examinees were rescored for both topics. The estimates of the variances based on these ratings are

$$
\begin{aligned}
\textbf{PSY1:} \quad & \hat{\sigma}_a^2 = 5.165, \quad \hat{\sigma}_b^2 = 0.023, \quad \hat{\sigma}_e^2 = 1.089\,; \\
\textbf{PSY2:} \quad & \hat{\sigma}_a^2 = 4.547, \quad \hat{\sigma}_b^2 = 0.339, \quad \hat{\sigma}_e^2 = 1.315\,.
\end{aligned}
\tag{2.21}
$$

Then, using the statistics S_R and S_T for the operational scores (one score from each of the 6259 examinees) and the estimate $\hat{\sigma}_e^2$ based on the reliability study data (299 students), the variances due to true scores and rater severity are reestimated. We obtained the following estimates:

$$
\begin{aligned}
\textbf{PSY1:} \quad & \hat{\sigma}_a^2 = 6.067, \quad \hat{\sigma}_b^2 = 0.041, \quad \hat{\sigma}_e^2 = 1.089\,; \\
\textbf{PSY2:} \quad & \hat{\sigma}_a^2 = 5.277, \quad \hat{\sigma}_b^2 = 0.113, \quad \hat{\sigma}_e^2 = 1.315
\end{aligned}
\tag{2.22}
$$

(the inconsistency variance estimates are added for completeness). A striking feature of these estimates is the large variance of the true scores, not only in relation to the other variance components but also relative to the estimates in the CAPA test. The score scale for the AP topics has a range of nine points, while for the CAPA topics it is five points. Roughly twice as wide a range should correspond to about four times greater variance. However, with the exception of the topic SSc2, the increase in the variance of the true scores is about 7–8-fold. The inconsistency variances for the AP

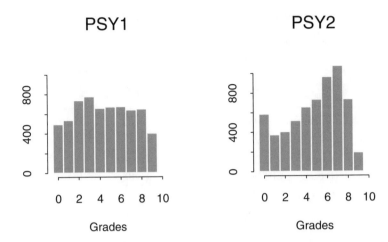

FIGURE 2.2. Histograms of score distributions for the topics PSY1 and PSY2 in AP Psychology.

Psychology topics are only 3–5 times greater than for the CAPA topics. Remarkably, even the severity variance for PSY1 is smaller than for either of the CAPA topics. Also, the severity variance for PSY2 is only 1.5–2 times greater than its CAPA counterparts. The rating of the Psychology essays is much more precise than the rating of the CAPA essays.

When deciding on the essay topics for a particular AP test, a number of criteria are considered. An important objective is to ensure that the level of difficulty of the essay topic is such that not too many examinees obtain the highest or the lowest scores. Setting the rubric, that is, describing what kind of performance corresponds to each grade, may help to avoid this problem. In terms of the variances, this corresponds to having large true-score variance, σ_a^2, or large total variance, $\sigma_a^2 + \sigma_b^2 + \sigma_e^2$, of which the true-score variance is the dominant component.

Usually, the distribution of the scores is unimodal, with the mode closer to the maximum score than to the minimum score. Figure 2.2 displays the histograms for the scores in the two Psychology AP topics. The distribution of the scores for the topic PSY1 is close to uniform, whereas the scores for PSY2 have a mode at 7 points.

The estimated variances can be compared with benchmarks, such as the variance of the discrete uniform distribution or of a distribution that has been anticipated based on past experience. The uniform distribution on the integers $0, 1, \ldots, m$ has the mean $m/2$ and variance

$$\frac{1}{m+1} \sum_{i=0}^{m} i^2 - \frac{m^2}{4} = \frac{m(m+1)(2m+1)}{6(m+1)} - \frac{m^2}{4} = \frac{m(m+2)}{12},$$

TABLE 2.6. Variance estimates for the Computer Science AP test forms.

Item No.	Form A			Form B		
	$\hat{\sigma}_a^2$	$\hat{\sigma}_b^2$	$\hat{\sigma}_e^2$	$\hat{\sigma}_a^2$	$\hat{\sigma}_b^2$	$\hat{\sigma}_e^2$
1	9.06 (7.46)	0.053 (0.027)	0.333	5.62 (5.15)	0.301 (0.010)	0.522
2	10.04 (8.89)	0.096 (0.000)	0.702	6.39 (6.38)	0.284 (0.186)	0.411
3	8.03 (7.80)	0.064 (0.000)	0.488	6.04 (5.89)	0.204 (0.000)	0.464
4	5.63 (7.50)	0.027 (0.000)	0.248	5.39 (4.75)	0.114 (0.000)	0.429

Notes: Estimates based on the data from the reliability studies are given in parentheses. The estimates of the inconsistency variances are taken from the reliability studies and are used for the analysis of the operational scores.

which, for $m = 9$, is equal to 8.25. The estimated total variance for the topic PSY1 comes close to this figure; it is equal to $6.067 + 0.041 + 1.089 \doteq 7.2$. The estimated total variance for PSY2 is about 6.7.

In summary, the rating in AP Psychology appears to be more reliable than the rating in CAPA. However, the more homogeneous population of examinees in CAPA may be a factor contributing to this difference. In the extreme, if all the examinees were equally able/prepared, the description of the rating process in terms of the reliabilities would indicate very low quality. This demonstrates the advantage of the description in terms of the variances; they are likely to be much less related to the examinee population.

Reliability studies with a similar design were carried out for two administrations of the Computer Science AP test which involved 6100 and 4400 examinees each. Each test contained four essays. The reliability studies involved about 248 examinees for test form A and 250 examinees for test form B; for these examinees, each essay was rerated. Table 2.6 summarizes the results of these studies. The estimates based on the combination of the operational and the second ratings, which correspond to (2.22), are given at the top of each cell, and the estimates based on the pairs of ratings, which correspond to (2.21), are given underneath in parentheses. Recall that the estimates of the inconsistency variances are derived from the paired ratings and are used in the analysis of the operational scores.

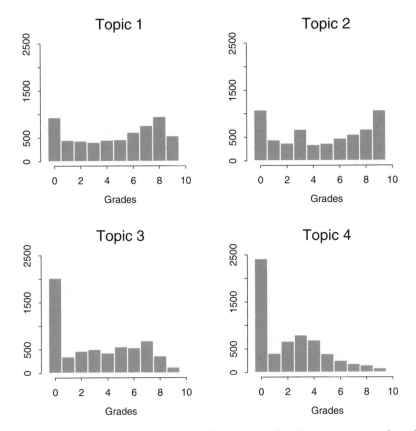

FIGURE 2.3. Histograms of the score distributions for the topics in test form B of AP Computer Science.

The rating process for the essays in these tests appears to have a higher quality than the essays in the Psychology test. The true-score variance estimates for several topics exceed the variance of the corresponding uniform distribution (for the topics in Psychology AP they are all smaller). In addition, the estimates of the inconsistency variances are all smaller than unity. The topics in test form B are associated with much greater severity variance than those in form A. More detailed exploration of the scores shows that they are essentially bimodal with one mode at zero. For each essay, a large proportion of the examinees gained no score. Figure 2.3 displays the histograms for the four topics in form A. The results for the topics in form B are similar.

In the AP test of English Composition, there are three essay topics. The analysed administration involved about 36 000 examinees. Reliability studies were carried out for two of the three essay topics by rerating the essays of a random sample of 250 examinees. The estimates based on these essays are

$$\textbf{Topic 1:} \quad \hat{\sigma}_a^2 = 1.08, \quad \hat{\sigma}_b^2 = 0.31, \quad \hat{\sigma}_e^2 = 1.13;$$
$$\textbf{Topic 2:} \quad \hat{\sigma}_a^2 = 1.80, \quad \hat{\sigma}_b^2 = 0.13, \quad \hat{\sigma}_e^2 = 0.62. \tag{2.23}$$

The inconsistency variances $\hat{\sigma}_e^2$ are imputed in the analysis of the operational scores. In the absence of an estimate for the third topic, we use the mean of the estimates for the other two topics, equal to 0.87. The resulting estimates are

$$\textbf{Topic 1:} \quad \hat{\sigma}_a^2 = 1.23, \quad \hat{\sigma}_b^2 = 0.12, \quad \hat{\sigma}_e^2 = 1.13;$$
$$\textbf{Topic 2:} \quad \hat{\sigma}_a^2 = 2.03, \quad \hat{\sigma}_b^2 = 0.15, \quad \hat{\sigma}_e^2 = 0.62; \tag{2.24}$$
$$\textbf{Topic 3:} \quad \hat{\sigma}_a^2 = 1.87, \quad \hat{\sigma}_b^2 = 0.14, \quad \hat{\sigma}_e^2 = 0.87.$$

The rating process is rather unsatisfactory in this case because the inconsistency variances are almost of the same order of magnitude as the variances of the true scores. The true-score variances are small because the scores 0, 1, 8, and 9 are given to very few essays; the effective scale is very narrow.

2.7   Standard errors

It is customary, and often very informative, to assess the uncertainty associated with estimating a parameter of interest. In a principled approach, we consider the sampling distribution of the estimator, that is, the distribution of the values of the estimator in a long sequence of hypothetical replications of the rating process, or, more generally, the process that generates the data. The most important summaries of this distribution are its mean and variance. The bias of an estimator is defined as the difference of its mean (expectation) and the parameter value. Clearly, the absence of bias is a desirable property of an estimator. The variance of an estimator is a summary of the spread of the would-be values of the estimator around its mean in a large number of replications. In general, small variance (less uncertainty) is preferred, although there is a tradeoff between bias and variance. Small variance of an estimator is a dubious property when the estimator has a substantial bias. Small bias is of little value when the sampling variance is large. To balance the requirements of small variance and small bias, we define the MSE of an estimator $\hat{\theta}$ of the parameter θ as

$$\mathrm{MSE}(\hat{\theta}) = \mathbf{E}\left(\hat{\theta} - \theta\right)^2.$$

It can be shown that

$$\mathrm{MSE}(\hat{\theta}) = \mathrm{var}(\hat{\theta}) + \left\{\mathbf{E}(\hat{\theta}) - \theta\right\}^2.$$

The difference $\mathbf{E}(\hat{\theta}) - \theta$ is the bias of $\hat{\theta}$.

The standard error of an estimator is the square root of MSE; it has the advantage that it is defined on the same scale as the outcome variable. Usually, bias and standard error depend on the unknown parameters, and so they themselves are estimated.

In principle, the sampling variance matrix of the variance estimators $\hat{\sigma}_a^2$, $\hat{\sigma}_b^2$, and $\hat{\sigma}_e^2$ can be obtained by evaluating the variances and covariances of the summands of the statistics S_E, S_R, and S_T. However, this may very quickly become unmanageable because a large number of cases have to be distinguished when computing the covariances of the squares contributing to these statistics . In addition, the variances of the squares depend on the skewnesses and kurtoses of the random terms α_i, β_j, and ε_{ij}. These cannot be estimated from the realized scores y_{ij} in any straightforward way. As an approximation, the skewness and kurtosis of the normal distribution may be used.

As a rough-and-ready method, we consider the hypothetical situation in which the random terms in (2.1) are known exactly. Then, assuming normality, the sampling variance of the estimated variance σ_b^2 is $2\sigma_b^4/J$, so that the standard error is approximated as $\sigma_b^2\sqrt{2/J}$. Thus, J is in the role of 'degrees of freedom', as frequently encountered in the analysis of variance. For illustration, the approximate lower bound for the standard error of the severity variance estimate for ELL1 [see (2.19)] is $0.062 \times \sqrt{2/18} = 0.021$, and so if this bound were attained there would be little support for the hypothesis that $\sigma_b^2 = 0$.

When most of the raters have very large workloads n_j, so that β_j are effectively known, this is a reasonable approximation; otherwise it is an approximate lower bound. The other variance parameter estimates can be considered by a similar approach. On the one hand, usually there are many more examinees than raters, $I \gg J$; on the other hand, there is much less information about the true score of an essay because it is rated only a small number of times. Similarly, the number of inconsistency terms ε_{ij}, equal to the number of ratings, N, is large, but it is more meaningful to associate them with $N - I$ degrees of freedom. Similarly, $I - J$ is a more appropriate number of degrees of freedom for the true scores. Because these numbers are usually large, the sampling variances of the variance parameters σ_a^2 and σ_e^2 are small, and, as such, are of little interest. Estimating the sampling variance of σ_b^2 is often much more important, because it delimits the scope for adjustment of the scores.

2.7.1 Simulations

A more formal approach, requiring substantially more computing, is based on simulations. In each simulation, the realized scores of the examinees are replaced by computer-generated scores. The simulated severities β_j are

TABLE 2.7. Summary of the simulations for essay ELL1.

	Normal scores			Rounded scores		
	σ_a^2	σ_b^2	σ_e^2	σ_a^2	σ_b^2	σ_e^2
True value	0.730	0.062	0.371	0.730	0.062	0.371
Mean	0.749	0.077	0.350	0.722	0.074	0.421
Std. deviation	(0.067)	(0.038)	(0.040)	(0.065)	(0.038)	(0.041)

Notes: Two hundred simulations were used. The left-hand part refers to simulated data using normally distributed random terms; the right-hand part refers to their rounded and truncated values.

drawn at random from a distribution with mean zero and variance equal to the estimated severity variance (estimated from the real data), and the true scores are generated similarly, using the estimated mean and variance of the true scores. The simulated scores are then generated according to the model in (2.1), with randomly generated inconsistency terms ε_{ij}. Each random variable $(\alpha, \beta, \varepsilon)$ is assumed to be normally distributed. The simulated data are used to compute the estimates of the variances. A large number of simulations (say, 100) is carried out, each resulting in a set of estimates of the variances. Regarding them as draws from the sampling distribution of the corresponding estimators, their standard deviations are obtained in a straightforward fashion.

The realistic nature of the simulations can be enhanced by rounding the simulated scores y_{ij} to integers. Of course, that is likely to inject a bias in the estimates of the variances. This bias can be compensated by an ad hoc adjustment of the variances used for generating the random terms.

Two hundred simulations were carried out for the essay topic ELL1. The variance estimates given in (2.19) were used for generating the artificial scores. Table 2.7 gives a summary of the simulations. The left-hand part gives the details for the scores generated according to the model in (2.1), without rounding the scores. The right-hand part gives details for the scores that have been rounded and truncated, so that they are on the integer scale 1–6. For each estimator, its parameter value (used for simulation), the mean of the simulated estimates, and the standard deviation of these estimates are given.

The bias of the estimator for the 'normal' scores is of little consequence. The bias for the truncated scores is somewhat greater but remains unimportant. Considering the magnitude of the variances, the standard errors (that is, the standard deviations of the estimators) are relatively the largest for the severity variance. The standard errors are only marginally affected by rounding. For comparison, using the method based on the degrees of freedom, we obtained a lower bound of 0.021 for the standard error for $\hat{\sigma}_b^2$. The simulations yield the estimated standard error equal to 0.038.

The results cannot be generalized to other assignment designs, score scales, or relative sizes of the variance components. However, such simulations are easy to carry out for any specific case. The normal distributions used in the simulations can be replaced by any other easy-to-generate distributions with given variances.

2.8 Summary

This chapter described a variance component method for summarizing the quality of the rating process for a test item with free-response format. The variance parameters refer to underlying populations of examinees and raters, and so they are not applicable to different examinee and rater populations. In particular, different methods of training and instruction of the raters may change the characteristics of the process. Of course, the variance components are affected by the topic of the essay. The examples suggest that the underlying parameters for topics within a test do not differ a great deal, although they do differ much more across subject areas.

The computational algorithm for estimating the variance components is non-iterative and is easy to implement. Its extensions for unequal number of ratings, session-specific behaviour of raters, and the like are conceptually straightforward. Diagnostic procedures for various kinds of deviations from the model assumptions are an integral part of the method. Standard errors for the estimated variances can be estimated by simulations.

2.9 Literature review

Issues of rater reliability and agreement of experts' judgements are by no means restricted to educational testing. The topic has received a lot of attention, especially in medical applications. In a typical problem in medical research, there are surgeons (experts) who rate the severity of a set of medical cases (patients) or the appropriateness of the treatment applied. Such situations are analysed by Landis and Koch (1977), Agresti (1988), and Uebersax (1990 and 1993). Two important features common to these approaches that distinguish them from the approach adopted in this chapter are the application of the logistic models for ordinal categorical responses and estimation of the rater severities.

The logistic models of analysis of variance, or other models for binary and ordinal categorical data, reflect the discrete nature of the data. Their application leads to the description of a rater's severity in terms of probabilities corresponding to each category (scale score). This may be useful when there are a small number of raters, but for situations with large numbers of raters, further summaries of these quantities would be required. The models do not provide an overall assessment of the rating process. This deficiency could be resolved by imposing a distribution on the raters' severities. This is rather difficult to implement for the discrete data models for several reasons. First, extensions of the random-effects models to ordinal categorical data are not straightforward. Next, fitting logistic regression models with random coefficients requires complex iterative algorithms. Further, estimating a larger number of parameters (for instance, nine sets for the score scale 0–9) inevitably results in greater standard errors of the estimates. These methods have been adapted for the educational testing context by Lunz, Wright, and Linacre (1990), although they are not suitable for test administrations with large numbers of raters.

The term *generalizability theory* is attributed to Cronbach *et al.* (1972); see Shavelson and Webb (1991) for a more recent exposition. The focus of this approach is on the global description of the rating process rather than on individual raters. In this respect, the method described here is motivated by generalizability theory; see Braun (1988) for another application. Chapter 4 discusses an extension of our approach, within the framework of generalizability theory, to a sample of essay topics.

An important hypothesis that has received relatively little attention is that the raters' severities may depend on the true score. For example, a rater may be relatively stricter on essays with high true scores, and more lenient on essays with low true scores. This corresponds to having a narrower effective score scale, which can be detected by the diagnostic procedures described in Section 2.5. However, the diagnostic procedures cannot quantify the association of the true scores and severity.

An approach to improved estimation of severity variance, as yet unexplored, is to pool information across several essay topics from the same subject area, not necessarily used in the same test form, but for which raters are drawn from the same population. In brief, if it can be established that the severity variances for all the topics are similar, the average of the estimates based on each topic may be a more efficient even if slightly biased estimator of the severity variance for each topic. As a compromise between the unbiased but inefficient estimator based exclusively on one essay topic and the estimator common to all essay topics, a variety of so-called *shrinkage* estimators can be considered, which, in essence, combine these two 'extreme' estimators. Shrinkage estimators will be discussed in a different context in Chapter 3.

3

Adjusting subjectively rated scores

3.1 Introduction

In the context of educational testing, estimation of the variance components and of the reliability coefficients is at best of secondary importance to the pivotal task — assigning scores to the essays (performances, problem solutions, or the like) in a way that reflects their quality as faithfully as possible. In ideal circumstances, this would correspond to reconstructing the true score α_i for each essay. A more realistic target is to get as close to α_i as possible. This chapter discusses improvements on the trivial estimator of the true score, the mean score over the K sessions, $y_{i,\cdot} = (y_{i,j_{i1}} + \ldots + y_{i,j_{iK}})/K$, by means of several adjustment schemes. The variance components σ_a^2, σ_b^2, and σ_e^2 play an important role in these schemes. To motivate them, consider the following extreme cases: when everybody has the same true score, $\sigma_a^2 = 0$, each examinee should be given the same score, irrespective of the grades given by the raters. Similarly, when the raters vary a great deal in their severities (large σ_b^2), or the rating is very inconsistent (large σ_e^2), an extreme score (say, 0 or 9 on the scale 0–9) is not a strong evidence of very poor or very high quality of the essay. On average, it may be prudent to 'pull' the extreme scores closer to the mean, so as to hedge our bets against the largest possible errors.

We are cautious with using the term *estimate* because, according to the model in (2.1), α_i is not a parameter but a random variable. Nevertheless, it is legitimate to consider estimation of α_i as the *i*th *realization* of the random variable α. See Robinson (1991) for a thoughtful discussion of this issue.

This chapter explores improvements of $y_{i,.}$ as an estimator of α_i. We refer to $y_{i,.}$ as the *unadjusted* mean score, to distinguish it from a score derived by its adjustment. Assuming known variance components σ_a^2, σ_b^2, and σ_e^2, the mean squared error (MSE) of this estimator is

$$\mathbf{E}(y_{i,.} - \alpha_i)^2 = \frac{\sigma_b^2 + \sigma_e^2}{K}. \tag{3.1}$$

Estimation of α_i can be trivially improved by having the essay graded by many raters. However, this may not be feasible for the thousands of examinees involved in the administration of a test.

Our general strategy can be described as follows: we define a class of statistics linear in the unadjusted mean score $y_{i,.}$, the raters' mean scores $z_j = \sum_{i \in [j]} y_{i,j}/n_j$ (the sum is over all the scores given by rater j), and the overall mean score $\bar{y} = \sum_{k=1}^{K} \sum_{i=1}^{I} y_{i,j_{ik}}/N$. Then we search for the coefficients in these statistics that minimize the MSE $\mathbf{E}(\hat{\alpha}_i - \alpha_i)^2$.

We depart slightly from this general strategy to discuss an estimator of α_i that conforms closely with the traditional approach in educational testing. First, we estimate the severities β_j, and then adjust the mean scores $y_{i,.}$ for the mean severity of the raters, $y_{i,.} - (\hat{\beta}_{j_{i1}} + \ldots + \hat{\beta}_{j_{iK}})/K$. Details of this approach are given in Section 3.2.

Section 3.3 describes two other adjustment schemes. Their main transparent advantage is that they do not require intermediation of the severity estimates. Section 3.4 describes a scheme based on a general class of linear combinations. This scheme is computationally more complex, but it yields more efficient estimators of true scores than the simpler schemes. Section 3.5 expands on the diagnostic methods presented in Section 2.5. Section 3.6 discusses several examples. Section 3.7 deals with combining observed scores. The chapter is concluded with a summary.

3.2   Estimating severity

The severity of each rater j with workload $n_j > 1$ is estimable because the random term β_j is realized in each rating performed by this rater. The naive estimator of β_j is the difference of the rater's and the overall means,

$$b_j = z_j - \bar{y}.$$

This estimator, although unbiased, is particularly unsatisfactory when the workload n_j is small because the mean z_j of a small number of ratings has a large sampling variance; $\text{var}(z_j \mid \beta_j) = (\sigma_a^2 + \sigma_e^2)/n_j$. Also, if the severity variance σ_b^2 were small, zero might be a more efficient estimator of β_j. When the severity variance is large, or the workload n_j is large, the estimator b_j is satisfactory. For intermediate values of σ_b^2 and small or moderate n_j, we consider a compromise, $\hat{\beta} = s_j b_j$, where s_j is the rater-specific coefficient which minimizes the MSE $\mathbf{E}(\hat{\beta}_j - \beta_j)^2$. The coefficient s_j can be interpreted as a *shrinkage* coefficient, shrinking the estimator b_j toward zero.

Let $[j, k]$ denote the set of essays graded by rater j in session k, and let $[j]$ denote the set of all essays graded by rater j; we will use this notation for summing over all the essays graded by rater j. According to the model in (2.1),

$$
\begin{aligned}
y_{i,.} &= \alpha_i + \frac{1}{K}\sum_{k=1}^{K}\beta_{jik} + \frac{1}{K}\sum_{k=1}^{K}\varepsilon_{i,jik}, \\
z_j &= \frac{1}{n_j}\sum_{i\in[j]}\alpha_i + \beta_j + \frac{1}{n_j}\sum_{i\in[j]}\varepsilon_{i,j}, \\
\bar{y} &= \frac{1}{I}\sum_{i=1}^{I}\alpha_i + \frac{1}{N}\left(\sum_{j=1}^{J}n_j\beta_j + \sum_{k=1}^{K}\sum_{i=1}^{I}\varepsilon_{i,jik}\right).
\end{aligned}
\tag{3.2}
$$

Using these identities, we obtain

$$
\begin{aligned}
\hat{\beta}_j &= s_j\left(\frac{1}{n_j} - \frac{1}{I}\right)\sum_{i\in[j]}\alpha_i - \frac{s_j}{I}\sum_{i\notin[j]}\alpha_i \\
&\quad + s_j\left(1 - \frac{n_j}{N}\right)\beta_j - \frac{s_j}{N}\sum_{j'\neq j}n_{j'}\beta_{j'} \\
&\quad + s_j\left(\frac{1}{n_j} - \frac{1}{N}\right)\sum_{k=1}^{K}\sum_{i\in[j,k]}\varepsilon_{i,jik} - \frac{s_j}{N}\sum_{k=1}^{K}\sum_{i\notin[j,k]}\varepsilon_{i,jik}.
\end{aligned}
$$

By taking advantage of independence of the random samples $\{\alpha_i\}$, $\{\beta_j\}$, and $\{\varepsilon_{i,j}\}$, the MSE can be expressed as the total of three variances:

$$
\begin{aligned}
\mathbf{E}(\hat{\beta}_j - \beta_j)^2 &= s_j^2\,\mathrm{var}\left\{\left(\frac{1}{n_j} - \frac{1}{I}\right)\sum_{i\in[j]}\alpha_i - \sum_{i\notin[j]}\frac{\alpha_i}{I}\right\} \\
&\quad + \mathrm{var}\left\{\left(s_j - 1 - \frac{s_j n_j}{N}\right)\beta_j - \frac{s_j}{N}\sum_{j'\neq j}n_{j'}\beta_{j'}\right\} \\
&\quad + s_j^2\,\mathrm{var}\left\{\left(\frac{1}{n_j} - \frac{1}{N}\right)\sum_{k=1}^{K}\sum_{i\in[j,k]}\varepsilon_{i,jik} - \sum_{k=1}^{K}\sum_{i\notin[j,k]}\frac{\varepsilon_{i,jik}}{N}\right\}.
\end{aligned}
$$

Owing to independence of the random terms, the variances can be further decomposed:

$$
\begin{aligned}
\mathbf{E}(\hat{\beta}_j - \beta_j)^2 &= s_j^2 \sigma_a^2 \left\{ n_j \left(\frac{1}{n_j} - \frac{1}{I} \right)^2 + \frac{I - n_j}{I^2} \right\} \\
&\quad + \sigma_b^2 \left\{ \left(s_j - 1 - \frac{s_j n_j}{N} \right)^2 + \frac{s_j^2}{N^2} \sum_{j' \neq j} n_{j'}^2 \right\} \\
&\quad + s_j^2 \sigma_e^2 \left\{ n_j \left(\frac{1}{n_j} - \frac{1}{N} \right)^2 + \frac{N - n_j}{N^2} \right\} \\
&= s_j^2 \sigma_a^2 \left(\frac{1}{n_j} - \frac{1}{I} \right) + s_j^2 \sigma_e^2 \left(\frac{1}{n_j} - \frac{1}{N} \right) \\
&\quad + \sigma_b^2 \left\{ (1 - s_j)^2 + 2 s_j (1 - s_j) \frac{n_j}{N} + \frac{s_j^2}{N^2} \sum_{j'=1}^{J} n_{j'}^2 \right\}.
\end{aligned}
$$

This is a quadratic function of s_j:

$$
\mathbf{E}(\hat{\beta}_j - \beta_j)^2 = C_{j,0} - 2 C_{j,1} s_j + C_{j,2} s_j^2, \tag{3.3}
$$

where

$$
\begin{aligned}
C_{j,0} &= \sigma_b^2, \\
C_{j,1} &= \sigma_b^2 \left(1 - \frac{n_j}{N} \right), \\
C_{j,2} &= \sigma_a^2 \left(\frac{1}{n_j} - \frac{1}{I} \right) + \sigma_b^2 \left(1 - \frac{2 n_j}{N} + \frac{n^{(2)}}{N} \right) + \sigma_e^2 \left(\frac{1}{n_j} - \frac{1}{N} \right),
\end{aligned}
$$

and $n^{(2)} = (n_1^2 + \ldots + n_J^2)/N$. The coefficient -2 is included in (3.3) only for notational convenience. Since

$$
1 - \frac{2 n_j}{N} + \frac{n^{(2)}}{N} \geq \left(1 - \frac{n_j}{N} \right)^2, \tag{3.4}
$$

the quadratic coefficient $C_{j,2}$ is non-negative. It is equal to zero only when $\sigma_a^2 = \sigma_e^2 = 0$ and either $\sigma_b^2 = 0$ or a single rater is engaged ($J = K = 1$ and $n_1 = n^{(2)} = I = N$). However, $\sigma_a^2 = 0$ and $J = 1$ correspond to unrealistic scenarios in which the issue of score adjustment does not arise.

The quadratic function in (3.3) attains its minimum for $s_j^* = C_{j,1}/C_{j,2}$, and the corresponding minimum value is $C_{j,0} - C_{j,1}^2/C_{j,2}$. Since $C_{j,2} > 0$, the optimal coefficient s_j^* is non-negative and is equal to zero only when $\sigma_b^2 = 0$. However, s_j^* may be greater than unity. To show this we first prove the inequality $n^{(2)} < \max_j n_j$. For $n^* = \max_j n_j$, $n_j^2 \le n_j n^*$ for each j, and so

$$n^{(2)} \le \frac{n^*}{N} \sum_{j=1}^{J} n_j = n^*.$$

Thus, s_j^* could be greater than unity for raters with the largest workloads when σ_b^2 is much greater than σ_a^2 and σ_e^2. In practice, this is very unlikely.

The MSE of the adjusted score $y_{i,.} - \sum_k s_{jik}^* b_{jik}$ around α_i is obtained using (3.2). We refer to the adjustment scheme which assigns this score as **sAdj**. Let $r_{ii',k}$ be the indicator for the event that essays i and i' are graded by the same rater in session k; $r_{ii',k} = 1$ if $j_{ik} = j_{i'k}$, and $r_{ii',k} = 0$ otherwise. Note that $\sum_{k=1}^{K} \sum_{i'=1}^{I} r_{ii',k} = n_{j_{ik}}$. For arbitrary coefficients s_j, we have

$$\mathbf{E}\left(y_{i,.} - \frac{1}{K} \sum_{k=1}^{K} s_{jik} b_{jik} - \alpha_i \right)^2$$

$$= \mathrm{var}\left\{ \left(-\frac{1}{K} \sum_{k=1}^{K} \frac{s_{jik}}{n_{jik}} \sum_{i'=1}^{I} r_{ii',k} - \frac{s_i^+}{I} \right) \alpha_i \right\}$$

$$+ \mathrm{var}\left\{ \frac{1}{K} \sum_{k=1}^{K} (1 - s_j)\beta_{jik} + \frac{s_i^+}{N} \sum_{j=1}^{J} n_j \beta_j \right\}$$

$$+ \mathrm{var}\left(\frac{1}{K} \sum_{k=1}^{K} \varepsilon_{i,jik} - \frac{1}{K} \sum_{k=1}^{K} \frac{s_{jik}}{n_{jik}} \sum_{i'=1}^{I} r_{ii',k} \varepsilon_{i',j_{i'k}} + \frac{s_i^+}{N} \sum_{k=1}^{K} \sum_{i'=1}^{I} \varepsilon_{i',j_{i'k}} \right),$$

where $s_i^+ = (s_{j_{i1}} + \ldots + s_{j_{iK}})/K$ is the mean of the coefficients of the raters who graded essay i. Each variance above can be expressed as the total of variances involving the individual random terms; the MSE is

$$\sigma_a^2 \left\{ \frac{1}{K^2} \sum_{i'=1}^{I} \left(\sum_{k=1}^{K} \frac{r_{ii',k} s_{jik}}{n_{jik}} \right)^2 - \frac{s_i^{+2}}{I} \right\}$$

$$+ \sigma_b^2 \left\{ \frac{1}{K^2} \sum_{k=1}^{K} (1 - s_{jik})^2 + \frac{2 s_i^+}{KN} \sum_{k=1}^{K} n_{jik}(1 - s_{jik}) + \frac{n^{(2)}}{N} s_i^{+2} \right\}$$

$$+ \sigma_e^2 \left\{ \frac{1}{K} - \frac{1}{K^2} \sum_{k=1}^{K} \frac{s_{jik}(2 - s_{jik})}{n_{jik}} + \frac{s_i^+(2 - s_i^+)}{N} \right\}. \tag{3.5}$$

This is a rather unwieldy equation and is of little use for analytical discussion; recall that s_j^* itself has a complex form. For instance, for $s_j \equiv 0$ we obtain the MSE of the unadjusted mean score, in agreement with (3.1).

Full adjustment corresponds to $s_j \equiv 1$. Then

$$\mathbf{E}\left(y_{i,.} - b_j - \alpha_i\right)^2 = \sigma_a^2 \left(\frac{R_i}{K} - \frac{1}{I}\right) + \sigma_b^2 \frac{n^{(2)}}{N} + \frac{\sigma_e^2}{K}\left(1 - n_i^- + \frac{1}{I}\right),$$

(3.6)

where $n_i^- = (n_{j_{i1}}^{-1} + \ldots + n_{j_{iK}}^{-1})/K$ and

$$R_i = \frac{1}{K} \sum_{i'=1}^{I} \left(\sum_{k=1}^{K} \frac{r_{ii',k}}{n_{j_{ik}}}\right)^2.$$

Traditionally, only two options for score adjustment have been considered: no adjustment ($s_j = 0$) and full adjustment ($s_j = 1$). Considering the entire continuum, $s_j \in [0,1]$, is clearly preferable. Nevertheless, if restricted to the two extreme options, a simple way of arbitrating between them is to compare the MSEs. We have

$$\mathbf{E}(y_{i,.} - b_j - \alpha_i)^2 - \mathbf{E}(y_{i,.} - \alpha_i)^2$$

$$= \sigma_a^2 \left(\frac{R_i}{K} - \frac{1}{I}\right) + \sigma_b^2 \left(\frac{n^{(2)}}{N} - \frac{1}{K}\right) + \frac{\sigma_e^2}{K}\left(\frac{1}{I} - n_i^-\right).$$

(3.7)

This quantity is relatively easy to calculate. Since the MSE in (3.6) is positive even when $\sigma_b^2 = \sigma_e^2 = 0$, $R_i/K > 1/I$. The fraction $n^{(2)}/N$ attains its highest value when there are K raters, each with workload equal to I; then $n^{(2)}/N = 1/K$. Since $n_j \leq I$, $n_i^- \geq 1/I$. Therefore, the coefficients of σ_b^2 and σ_e^2 in (3.7) are non-positive.

Suppose the assignment design is fixed. As we increase the true-score variance σ_a^2, keeping the other variances fixed, the difference in (3.7) becomes positive, that is, full adjustment becomes detrimental. As we increase the severity variance σ_b^2, keeping the other two variances fixed, the difference in (3.7) is bound to become negative, so that for large σ_b^2 adjustment is useful. However, the difference may be positive even for $\sigma_b^2 = 0$, particularly when σ_e^2 is large relative to σ_a^2. Adjustment for 'severity' is useful even when there is no variation in severity. This seeming contradiction is due to a different role of the adjustment $z_j - \bar{y}$. When the unadjusted scores $y_{i,.}$ have very large sampling variances, their adjustment by much less noisy quantities, $z_j - \bar{y}$, reduces the MSEs.

Similarly, as we increase the inconsistency variance σ_e^2, keeping the other two variances fixed, the full adjustment becomes useful. In brief, for unadjusted scores with a lot of uncertainty, almost any adjustment by a quantity with small variance is useful. When is no adjustment, $s_j = 0$, optimal? Let i be an examinee graded by rater j, so that $j = j_{ik}$ for some k. The first-order partial derivative of the MSE given by (3.5), evaluated at $s_j = 0$, is

$$\left.\frac{\partial \mathbf{E}\left(y_{i,.} - s_{j_{ik}} b_j - \alpha_i\right)^2}{\partial s_{j_{ik}}}\right|_{s_{j_{ik}}=0} = \frac{2\sigma_b^2}{K}\left(\frac{n_i^+}{N} - 1\right) + \frac{2\sigma_e^2}{K}\left(\frac{1}{N} - \frac{1}{Kn_{j_{ik}}}\right),$$

which is negative, unless $\sigma_b^2 = \sigma_e^2 = 0$ or a single rater is engaged in each session. Therefore, barring these trivial cases, the unadjusted score can always be improved.

We return to the discussion of the optimal coefficient s_j^*. When $\sigma_b^2 = 0$, $s_j^* = 0$ for all raters j. Thus, as expected, in the absence of differences in severity, $\hat{\beta}_j \equiv 0$. When σ_b^2 is much greater than $\sigma_a^2 + \sigma_e^2$ and n_j much smaller than N, the optimal coefficient s_j^* is approximately equal to

$$\frac{1 - \frac{n_j}{N}}{1 - \frac{2n_j}{N} + \frac{n^{(2)}}{N}} \doteq 1 + \frac{n_j - n^{(2)}}{N - n_j} = \frac{N - n^{(2)}}{N - n_j}. \tag{3.8}$$

For balanced (equal) workloads, $n_j = N/J$, $n^{(2)} = n_j$, and so the ratio in (3.8) is equal to unity. When the workload n_j is large, the terms in (3.3) involving σ_b^2 dominate. When many raters are engaged and the workloads n_j are much smaller than N, the approximation in (3.8) also applies.

The reduction of the MSE of $\hat{\beta}_j$ is

$$\frac{C_{j,1}^2}{C_{j,2}} = \frac{\sigma_b^4 (1 - n_j/N)^2}{C_{j,2}}. \tag{3.9}$$

Holding the variances σ_a^2, σ_b^2, and σ_e^2 as well as I, N, and $n^{(2)}$ constant, the reduction is an increasing function of n_j. This can be proved by differentiation; lengthy algebra is avoided if the logarithm is differentiated instead of the expression in (3.9):

$$\frac{\partial \log(C_{j,1}^2/C_{j,2})}{\partial n_j} = \frac{-2}{N - n_j} + \frac{\sigma_a^2/n_j^2 + 2\sigma_b^2/N + \sigma_e^2/n_j^2}{C_{j,2}},$$

which is positive unless n_j is a substantial fraction of N, or all three variances are small. Estimation of severity is more precise for raters with higher workloads. However, as we discussed earlier, improved estimation of severity cannot be equated with improved estimation of true scores. In general, it is advantageous to spread the total workload N evenly among the raters, avoid having to use raters who do very little work, and in multiple ratings make sure that no essay is graded by more than one rater with a small workload. The shrinkage coefficient s_j^* is small when σ_b^2 is small or when the rater's workload n_j is small; the coefficient is large (close to unity) when σ_b^2 is large or the workload n_j is large.

The adjustment for severity is problematic when a rater's workload n_j is a large fraction of the total number of ratings N. In such a case, z_j and $\bar{y}$ are highly correlated and s_j^* is a ratio of two relatively small numbers. Intuitively, this is close to the case of a single rater, $J = 1$; then there is no information about the rater's severity. Of course, estimation of the severities of the other raters is also problematic because their workloads are small.

The adjustment is far from perfect in some extreme scenarios. For instance, when $\sigma_a^2 = 0$, $\bar{y}$ is a suitable estimate of the true score for each essay. However, the adjusted score $y_{i,\cdot} - s_j b_j$ cannot be constant unless also $\sigma_e^2 = 0$. When $\sigma_e^2 = 0$ and there is more than one session, $K > 1$, the severity β_j can be estimated without error, irrespective of the value of σ_a^2. However, the MSE of $\hat{\beta}_j$, $C_{j,0} - C_{j,1}^2/C_{j,2}$, is a decreasing function of σ_a^2, and so it cannot vanish for all values of σ_a^2. In more typical situations, when σ_a^2 is greater than σ_e^2, and σ_e^2 is greater than σ_b^2, the adjustment performs satisfactorily.

3.3   Examinee-specific shrinkage

Although we started with the idea of adjusting for raters' severities, we discovered that another kind of adjustment is taking place, namely, adjustment for rater inconsistency. Good estimation of raters' severities does not imply good estimation of true scores, especially when the inconsistency variance σ_e^2 is large. Although it may be advantageous to have to compute only the J pairs of quantities (s_j^* and $b_j = z_j - \bar{y}$) on which the adjustments are based, a more flexible adjustment scheme may result in more efficient estimation of α_i.

In this section, we explore an alternative scheme which differs from **sAdj** in only one essential feature. We consider shrinkage coefficients specific to each examinee, based on the adjustment

$$\hat{\alpha}_{i,u} = y_{i,\cdot} - \frac{u_i}{K} \sum_{k=1}^{K} (z_{j_{ik}} - \bar{y}) \quad \left(= y_{i,\cdot} - \frac{u_i}{K} \sum_{k} b_{j_{ik}} \right), \qquad (3.10)$$

where u_i is chosen so as to minimize the MSE $\mathbf{E}(\hat{\alpha}_{i,u} - \alpha_i)^2$. The subscript u is used to distinguish $\hat{\alpha}_{i,u}$ from other estimators of α_i. The estimator in (3.10) differs from the adjustment for severity,

$$\hat{\alpha}_{i,s} = y_{i,\cdot} - s_j \frac{b_{j_{i1}} + \ldots + b_{j_{iK}}}{K},$$

only in that the rater-specific coefficient s_j is replaced by an essay-specific coefficient u_i.

To find the optimal shrinkage coefficient u_i, we follow the outline from the previous section. The deviation $y_{i,\cdot} - u_i(b_{j_{i1}} + \ldots + b_{j_{iK}})/K - \alpha_i$ is expressed in terms of the random variables α_i, β_j, and ε_{ij} as

$$-\frac{u_i}{K} \sum_{k=1}^{K} \frac{1}{n_{j_k}} \sum_{i'=1}^{I} r_{ii',k} \alpha_{i'} + \frac{u_i}{I} \sum_{i'} \alpha_{i'}$$

$$+ \frac{1 - u_i}{K} \sum_{k=1}^{K} \beta_{j_{ik}} + \frac{u_i}{N} \sum_{j=1}^{J} n_j \beta_j$$

$$+\frac{1}{K}\sum_{k=1}^{K}\varepsilon_{i,j_{ik}}+u_i\sum_{k=1}^{K}\frac{1}{n_{j_k}}\sum_{i'=1}^{I}r_{ii',k}\varepsilon_{i',j_{ik}}$$

$$+\frac{u_i}{N}\sum_{k=1}^{K}\sum_{i'=1}^{I}\varepsilon_{i',j_{i'k}}.$$

The MSE is obtained using the same steps as in Section 3.2:

$$\mathbf{E}(y_{i,.}-u_ib_j-\alpha_i)^2 = u_i^2\sigma_a^2\left(\frac{R_i}{K}-\frac{1}{I}\right)$$

$$+\sigma_b^2\left\{\frac{(1-u_i)^2}{K}+2u_i(1-u_i)\frac{n_i^+}{N}+u_i^2\frac{n^{(2)}}{N}\right\}$$

$$+\sigma_e^2\left\{\frac{1}{K}+u_i(2-u_i)\left(\frac{1}{N}-\frac{n_i^-}{K}\right)\right\},$$

where $n_i^+=(n_{j_{i1}}+\ldots+n_{j_{iK}})/K$ and $n_i^-=(n_{j_{i1}}^{-1}+\ldots+n_{j_{iK}}^{-1})/K$. This is a quadratic function of the coefficient u_i;

$$\mathbf{E}(y_{i,.}-u_ib_j-\alpha_i)^2 = D_{i,0}-2D_{i,1}u_i+D_{i,2}u_i^2, \qquad (3.11)$$

where

$$D_{i,0} = \frac{\sigma_b^2+\sigma_e^2}{K},$$

$$D_{i,1} = \sigma_b^2\left(\frac{1}{K}-\frac{n_i^+}{N}\right)+\frac{\sigma_e^2}{K}\left(\frac{n_i^-}{K}-\frac{1}{N}\right),$$

$$D_{i,2} = \sigma_a^2\left(\frac{R_i}{K}-\frac{1}{I}\right)+\sigma_b^2\left(\frac{1}{K}-\frac{2n_i^+}{N}+\frac{n^{(2)}}{N}\right)$$

$$+\sigma_e^2\left(\frac{n_i^-}{K}-\frac{1}{N}\right).$$

It is easy to show that $D_{i,2}\geq 0$ and that the identity occurs only when $\sigma_a^2=\sigma_e^2=0$ and either $\sigma_b^2=0$ or only one rater is engaged in each session ($K=J$ and $n_j\equiv I$). Unless $D_{i,2}=0$, the minimum MSE is attained for $u_i^*=D_{i,1}/D_{i,2}$, and the minimum value attained is $D_{i,0}-D_{i,1}^2/D_{i,2}$. In fact, in the expression for $D_{i,2}$, the coefficient with each variance is positive unless $J=1$. For instance,

$$1/K-2n_i^+/N+n^{(2)}/N \geq (1-n_j/I)^2/K > 0;$$

see (3.4) for a similar argument.

This adjustment scheme, denoted by **uAdj**, has weak points similar to the adjustment for severity, **sAdj**. When σ_a^2 is small relative to σ_b^2 and σ_e^2, the adjustment will not result in a near-constant score for all the essays. When $\sigma_e^2 = 0$ and the severities β_j, and therefore also the true scores, can be determined without error, the adjustment scheme produces estimated true scores with positive MSEs.

3.3.1   Rating in a single session

The scores can be adjusted even when only one session of rating is conducted, so long as the variances σ_a^2, σ_b^2, and σ_e^2 are known (or, as in practice, estimated). The adjustment equations simplify considerably. When $K = 1$, there are n_{j_i} non-zero terms in the expression for R_i, each corresponding to an essay graded by the same rater as essay i. Each of these terms is equal to $1/n_{j_i}$, and so $R_i = 1/n_{j_i}$. Further, $n_i^+ = n_{j_i}$ and $n_i^- = 1/n_{j_i}$. The coefficients in (3.11) are reduced to

$$D_{i,0} = \sigma_b^2 + \sigma_e^2,$$

$$D_{i,1} = \sigma_b^2 \left(1 - \frac{n_{j_i}}{I}\right) + \sigma_e^2 \left(\frac{1}{n_{j_i}} - \frac{1}{I}\right),$$

$$D_{i,2} = \sigma_a^2 \left(\frac{1}{n_{j_i}} - \frac{1}{I}\right) + \sigma_b^2 \left(1 - \frac{2n_{j_i}}{I} + \frac{n^{(2)}}{I}\right) + \sigma_e^2 \left(\frac{1}{n_{j_i}} - \frac{1}{I}\right).$$

The adjustment scheme based on these equations depends on the assignment design only through the workload of the rater, n_{j_i}, and so, just like the adjustment for severity, it is constant within raters. Yet, the respective quadratic equations, (3.3) and (3.11), differ in their linear terms; we have

$$C_{j,1} = \sigma_b^2 \left(1 - \frac{n_j}{I}\right).$$

Whereas the adjustment for severity, **sAdj**, does not change the score when $\sigma_b^2 = 0$, in the adjustment scheme **uAdj** the scores are changed unless also $\sigma_e^2 = 0$. The scheme **uAdj** yields a greater coefficient, $u_i > s_{j_i}$, but the difference is small when σ_b^2/n_i^+ is small relative to σ_b^2. Adjustment for severity is more conservative than the adjustment given by (3.11).

When σ_a^2 is at least of the same order of magnitude as the other variance components, $D_{i,1} < D_{i,2}$, and so u_i^* can be interpreted as a shrinkage coefficient. In general, higher workloads are associated with less shrinkage (greater u^*), greater severity variance σ_b^2 with less shrinkage, and higher true-score variance σ_a^2 with more shrinkage.

In the case of multiple sessions, it is difficult to compare the two adjustment schemes analytically. Intuitively, the adjustment based on (3.11) is more flexible because it allows for differential adjustment, which depends on the raters who graded the essay, but through R_i it is also affected by the assignment design. The term $\sigma_e^2(1/n_{j_i} - 1/I)$ in $D_{i,1}$ appears to adjust for inconsistency. Further flexibility could be achieved by allowing unequal coefficients for the terms b_j in (3.10). For small n_j, the coefficient $u_{i,j}$ in

$$\hat{\alpha}_{i,u^*} = y_{i,\cdot} - \sum_{k=1}^{K} u_{i,j} (z_{j_i k} - \bar{y})$$

should also be smaller. The optimal coefficients $u_{i,j}$ can be found by the method used for the scheme **uAdj**. The additional complexity is rewarded by non-trivial gains only for essays graded by raters with vastly different workloads.

3.3.2 Shrinking to the rater's mean

Another way of using the information about the raters for score adjustment is to combine the mean score for an essay and the mean of the raters' scores:

$$\hat{\alpha}_{i,t} = (1 - t_i)y_{i,\cdot} + \frac{t_i}{K} \sum_{k=1}^{K} z_{j_{ik}} \, .$$

This scheme, denoted by **tAdj**, does not have a natural interpretation; the main purpose of introducing it here is to help understand the deficiencies of the other two schemes. This will be illustrated on the examples analysed in Section 3.6. The MSE of $\hat{\alpha}_{i,t}$ is

$$\mathbf{E} \left(\hat{\alpha}_{i,t} - \alpha_i \right)^2$$

$$= \operatorname{var} \left\{ -t_i \alpha_i + \frac{t_i}{K} \sum_{k=1}^{K} \sum_{i'=1}^{I} r_{ii',k} \alpha_{i'} \right\} + \operatorname{var} \left(\frac{1}{K} \sum_{k=1}^{K} \beta_{j,ik} \right)$$

$$+ \operatorname{var} \left\{ \frac{1 - t_i}{K} \sum_{k=1}^{K} \varepsilon_{i,j_{ik}} + \frac{t_i}{K} \sum_{k=1}^{K} \frac{1}{n_{j_{ik}}} \sum_{(i';j,k)} \varepsilon_{i',j_{i'k}} \right\}$$

$$= \frac{\sigma_b^2 + \sigma_e^2}{K} - 2t_i \frac{\sigma_e^2}{K} (1 - n_i^-)$$

$$+ t_i^2 \left\{ \sigma_a^2 \left(1 - 2n_i^- + \frac{R_i}{K} \right) + \frac{\sigma_e^2}{K} (1 - n_i^-) \right\} . \tag{3.12}$$

As in the adjustment schemes **sAdj** and **uAdj**, this MSE is a quadratic function in t_i,

$$\mathbf{E} \left(\hat{\alpha}_{i,t} - \alpha_i \right)^2 = E_{i,0} - 2E_{i,1} t_i + E_{i,2} t_i^2 , \tag{3.13}$$

where

$$E_{i,0} = \frac{\sigma_b^2 + \sigma_e^2}{K} ,$$

$$E_{i,1} = \frac{\sigma_e^2}{K} (1 - n_i^-) ,$$

$$E_{i,2} = \sigma_a^2 \left(1 - 2n_i^- + R_i/K \right) + E_{i,1} .$$

The MSE in (3.13) attains its minimum for $t_i = E_{i,1}/E_{i,2}$, and the attained minimum value is $E_{i,0} - E_{i,1}^2/E_{i,2}$. It is easy to see that $0 \le t_i \le 1$ and that the boundary values are attained only in degenerate cases. Interestingly, this adjustment scheme involves the severity variance σ_b^2 only in the constant term $E_{i,0}$. This suggests that the scheme may be deficient, for instance, when σ_b^2 is large. However, when inconsistency variance dominates variation in severity, shrinking to the rater mean is useful because it is a much more stable quantity than $y_{i,.}$, and the conditional bias of $\hat{\alpha}_{i,t}$, given the severities of the raters involved, is more than compensated by reduced variance of the estimated true score. Examples analysed in Section 3.6 suggest that the scheme performs satisfactorily when σ_e^2 is large relative to σ_b^2.

3.4   General scheme

The schemes introduced in the previous section can be effectively combined into an adjustment scheme in which the MSE is minimized over the class of all linear combinations of $y_{i,.}$, z_i, and $\bar{y}$:

$$\hat{\alpha}_{i,v} = v_{1i}y_{i,.} - \frac{v_{2i}}{K}\sum_{k=1}^{K} z_{jik} + v_{3i}\bar{y}. \tag{3.14}$$

For the examinee-specific coefficients, we impose the condition

$$v_{1i} - v_{2i} + v_{3i} = 1, \tag{3.15}$$

so that $\hat{\alpha}_{i,v}$ is conditionally unbiased given α_i;

$$\mathbf{E}(\hat{\alpha}_i - \alpha_i \mid \alpha_i) = 0.$$

Assuming known variances σ_a^2, σ_b^2, and σ_e^2, this scheme, denoted by **AAdj**, yields an estimator of the true score that has MSE not greater than either of the two schemes introduced in Section 3.3 because the class of statistics in (3.14) contains the classes on which the other schemes are based.

Calculating the MSE of $\hat{\alpha}_{i,v}$ is rather tedious, but only the tools used in Section 3.3 are required. The derivation is outlined in the Appendix; here we give only the final expression:

$$\mathbf{E}(\hat{\alpha}_{i,v} - \alpha_i)^2$$
$$= \left\{(1 - v_{1i})^2 + 2(1 - v_{1i})(v_{2i}n_i^- - v_{3i}/I)\right\}\sigma_a^2$$
$$+ \left\{v_{2i}^2 R_i/K - 2v_{2i}v_{3i}/I + v_{3i}^2/I\right\}\sigma_a^2$$
$$+ \left\{(v_{1i} - v_{2i})^2/K + 2(v_{1i} - v_{2i})v_{3i}n_i^+/N + v_{3i}^2 n^{(2)}/N\right\}\sigma_b^2$$
$$+ \left\{v_{1i}^2/K + 2(v_{1i} - v_{2i})v_{3i}/N - (2v_{1i} - v_{2i})v_{2i}n_i^-/K + v_{3i}^2/N\right\}\sigma_e^2. \tag{3.16}$$

The minimum of this quadratic function in v_{hi}, $h = 1, 2, 3$, can be found as the roots of the first-order partial derivatives. This leads to a system of three linear equations,

$$\begin{aligned}
A_{11}v_{1i} - A_{12}v_{2i} + A_{13}v_{3i}/I &= K\sigma_a^2, \\
A_{12}v_{1i} - A_{22}v_{2i} + A_{13}v_{3i}/I &= Kn_i^-\sigma_a^2, \\
A_{13}v_{1i} - A_{13}v_{2i} + A_{33}v_{3i} &= K\sigma_a^2,
\end{aligned} \tag{3.17}$$

where

$$\begin{aligned}
A_{11} &= K\sigma_a^2 + \sigma_b^2 + \sigma_e^2, \\
A_{12} &= Kn_i^-\sigma_a^2 + \sigma_b^2 + n_i^-\sigma_e^2, \\
A_{13} &= K\sigma_a^2 + n_i^+\sigma_b^2 + \sigma_e^2, \\
A_{22} &= R_i\sigma_a^2 + \sigma_b^2 + n_i^-\sigma_e^2, \\
A_{33} &= K\sigma_a^2 + n^{(2)}\sigma_b^2 + \sigma_e^2.
\end{aligned}$$

The constraint in (3.15) can be enforced by applying the method of Lagrange multipliers. When the variance of $\bar{y}$ is negligible in comparison to that of z_j and $y_{i,.}$, it suffices to solve the system of linear equations in (3.17) and then alter the solution v_{3i} so as to conform with the linear constraint in (3.15).

3.4.1 Sensitivity and robustness

In practice, the variances σ_a^2, σ_b^2, and σ_e^2 are not known, and their estimates are used instead. It is of interest then whether substitution of slightly different variances would result in small changes of the score adjustments. This is relatively easy to explore for the simpler adjustment schemes **sAdj**, **uAdj**, and **tAdj** because the shrinkage coefficients are simple functions of the variances. Analytic exploration of the adjustment scheme based on (3.17) is much more difficult, and so the advantage gained by the apparently more efficient estimation of the true scores may be eroded by substituting estimates of the variance components in place of the true values.

Properties of the general scheme given by (3.17) can be explored for the case of single rating, $K = 1$. Then $A_{22} = A_{12}$ and $A_{13} = n_{j_i}A_{12}$, and the determinant of the system of linear equations in (3.17) is

$$\det\begin{pmatrix}
A_{11} & -A_{12} & n_{j_i}A_{12}/I \\
A_{12} & -A_{12} & n_{j_i}A_{12}/I \\
n_{j_i}A_{12} & -n_{j_i}A_{12} & A_{33}
\end{pmatrix}$$

$$= A_{12}(A_{11} - A_{12})\left(\frac{n_{j_i}^2}{I}A_{12} - A_{33}\right)$$

$$= - \left(\frac{\sigma_a^2 + \sigma_e^2}{n_{j_i}} + \sigma_b^2 \right) \left(1 - \frac{1}{n_{j_i}} \right) (\sigma_a^2 + \sigma_e^2)$$

$$\times \left\{ \left(1 - \frac{n_{j_i}}{I} \right) (\sigma_a^2 + \sigma_e^2) + \left(n^{(2)} - \frac{n_{j_i}^2}{I} \right) \sigma_b^2 \right\}. \qquad (3.18)$$

Since n_j^2/I is a summand of $n^{(2)}$, each factor of the determinant is positive, so long as $\sigma_a^2 + \sigma_e^2 > 0$ and $J > 1$. Thus, barring these degenerate cases, the equations in (3.17) have a unique solution. Note that the determinant in (3.18) depends on the variances σ_a^2 and σ_e^2 only through their total, $\sigma_a^2 + \sigma_e^2$. When there is no rater who grades most of the essays, and the workloads are large, that is, $n_j \gg 1$ and $n^{(2)} \gg n_j^2/I$ for most j, the severity variance σ_b^2 is accompanied in (3.18) by relatively large coefficients (1 vs. $1/n_{j_i}$ and $n^{(2)}$ vs. n_j^2/I). Therefore, estimation of σ_b^2 is the key to the efficiency of the adjustment scheme. Yet σ_b^2 is estimated with least precision because the number of raters is relatively small.

In principle, the coefficients v_{hi} can be expressed in a closed form because the inverse of the matrix associated with the linear equations can be derived using the determinant in (3.18). This is of limited interest, however, and so we do not pursue it here.

3.5   More diagnostics

The estimates of the raters' severities are an important diagnostic tool. Although the raters' severities β_j are not associated with any distributional assumptions, the raters with outlying severities are of considerable interest because of their impact on the severity variance. An interesting, and in many contexts, a controversial issue may arise when making the decision to discard the ratings of an apparently outlying or aberrant rater. Apart from the practical concerns, such as having to rescore essays, exclusion of such a rater should be followed by reestimation of the variance components, unless their estimation is based on a previous administration. The updated estimates of the variances yield different estimates of severities as well as different score adjustments.

Recall that the variance component model in (2.1) does not assume any particular shape of the distribution of raters' severities. Therefore, outliers in the conventional sense (vis-à-vis the normal distribution) do not represent a departure from the model assumptions. None the less, without a 'flagged' rater, the rating process would be of much higher quality and the true scores would be estimated more efficiently both for examinees who were graded by the outlying rater(s) and those who were not. Exclusion of a rater should be based on evidence that the rater does not belong to the population of raters, so that the resulting estimated variances would refer to the appropriate population.

3.6   Examples

We return to the analysis of the English Language and Literature (ELL) and Social Sciences (SSc) tests in the Content Area Performance Assessment (CAPA) to explore the impact of the adjustment schemes. The estimates of the variance components for the pairs of essays in each test are given in (2.19) and (2.20). These values are used in place of the true variances in the equations for each score adjustment scheme. Since there are a large number of examinees, it is not practical to list the adjustments nor is it very informative to discuss the adjusted scores for a selected subset of examinees. Therefore, it is essential to have effective and informative summaries of the adjustments.

One important aspect of the adjustment is the MSE of the adjusted score. When each essay is rated the same number of times, each unadjusted score has the same MSE for every examinee, equal to $(\sigma_b^2 + \sigma_e^2)/K$. However, the MSEs for the adjustment schemes are not constant because they depend on the raters' workloads n_j and, through R_i, on their overlap. The estimated MSEs (using the estimated variances in place of their parameter values) can be summarized by their ranges, as done in Table 3.1 for no adjustment, **NAdj**, and four adjustment schemes: adjustment by the mean of the estimated severities, **sAdj**, discussed in Section 3.2; adjustment by shrinking to the rater mean, **tAdj**, Section 3.3.2; essay-specific adjustment for severity, **uAdj**, Section 3.3; and the general adjustment scheme, **AAdj**, Section 3.4.

The benefit of the adjustment schemes is obvious. By substituting the estimates instead of the true values of the variance components, the MSEs are themselves estimated. This is unlikely to substantially alter the differences between the (estimated) MSEs for no adjustment (**NAdj**) and the adjustment schemes **sAdj**, **tAdj**, and **uAdj**. The MSEs for **sAdj** and **uAdj** are almost identical. In itself this would not imply that the two adjustment schemes themselves are almost identical, but the corresponding quadratic equations in (3.3) and (3.11) are also similar. The scheme **tAdj** performs better than **sAdj** and **uAdj** for essay ELL1 but not for the other three essays. The differences are modest in comparison with the gains over no adjustment. The scheme **AAdj** stands out as the most efficient, and its gains over the simpler adjustment schemes are of the same order of magnitude as the gains of these schemes over no adjustment. However, the full gain in efficiency would be realized only if the variance components were known exactly. That is clearly an unrealistic proposition. It is unlikely, though, that the scheme **AAdj** is outperformed by any other scheme.

Table 3.2 gives the workloads and the estimated severities of the raters engaged to grade essays ELL1 and ELL2. The workloads are given by session (for instance, rater 510 graded 19 essays in session 1 and 17 essays in session 2). The estimates of the severities (rows labeled 'Severity') for essay ELL1 are in the range –0.34 to 0.26; there appear to be no pronounced

TABLE 3.1. Ranges of MSEs for the adjustment schemes in CAPA tests.

Essay	Adjustment scheme				
	NAdj	**sAdj**	**tAdj**	**uAdj**	**AAdj**
ELL1	0.217	0.191–0.197	0.182–0.188	0.190–0.195	0.152–0.161
ELL2	0.148	0.125–0.128	0.132–0.133	0.124–0.127	0.108–0.112
SSc1	0.199	0.167–0.175	0.170–0.171	0.166–0.173	0.136–0.143
SSc2	0.164	0.141–0.146	0.152–0.153	0.142–0.144	0.130–0.132

Note: The adjustment schemes are: **NAdj** — no adjustment; **sAdj** — adjustment for severity; **tAdj** — shrinkage to the rater mean; **uAdj** — essay-specific shrinkage; and **AAdj** — the general adjustment scheme.

outliers. For completeness, the shrinkage coefficients and the square roots of the MSEs of the severity estimates are given in the rows labeled 'Shrinkage' and '$\sqrt{\text{MSE}}$', respectively. For rater 570, who graded only two essays, a tenfold shrinkage takes place (shrinkage coefficient 0.10); this reflects the large sampling variation of his/her mean z_j. The shrinkage coefficients for the majority of raters, with workloads in the range 36–78, are between 0.63 and 0.75. The square roots of the MSE errors for these raters are in the range 0.15–0.17; of course, they are much higher for the raters with small workloads. Similar observations can be made on the results for essay ELL2.

For administrations of moderate size, such as the analysed CAPA tests, the scatterplots of the adjustments are informative. The matrix of pairwise plots of the adjustments for essay ELL1 is presented in Figure 3.1. The distinct pattern of points on approximately parallel lines is due to the coarse nature of scoring. The plots confirm that the schemes **sAdj** and **uAdj** are very similar; the adjustments are highly correlated. On the other hand, the adjustments in either of these schemes are almost uncorrelated with those using the scheme **tAdj**. Note that plotting the adjustments against the unadjusted score would be less informative because the unadjusted scores are on a very coarse scale.

In general, the adjustments appear to be small in comparison with the coarseness of the rating scale. Most of the adjustments would be negated if the adjusted scores were rounded. This is an indication of the conservative nature of the adjustment, rather than of proximity of the unadjusted scores to the true scores. The magnitude of the MSEs indicates that a large proportion of the unadjusted (or, for that matter, adjusted) scores departs from the true score by more than 0.5. As we observed in Chapter 2, rounding is a small component of the deviation of the adjusted scores from the true scores.

TABLE 3.2. Raters' workloads and estimates of their severities in grading essays ELL1 and ELL2.

	Raters' workloads and severity estimates								
	Essay ELL1								
Rater Id.	501	510	511	512	513	514	515	516	517
Workload	0+9	19+17	14+22	33+19	23+32	31+47	17+19	25+39	23+28
Severity	−0.25	0.17	0.26	0.02	−0.34	0.04	0.20	−0.14	0.06
Shrinkage	0.33	0.63	0.63	0.69	0.70	0.75	0.63	0.69	0.65
$\sqrt{\text{MSE}}$	0.21	0.16	0.16	0.16	0.16	0.16	0.16	0.15	0.16
Rater Id.	521	522	523	524	525	526	527	528	570
Workload	31+9	34+24	21+44	29+35	21+25	34+29	36+9	28+10	0+2
Severity	−0.15	0.20	0.19	0.02	0.02	−0.10	−0.12	−0.08	−0.13
Shrinkage	0.65	0.71	0.73	0.73	0.67	0.72	0.67	0.64	0.10
$\sqrt{\text{MSE}}$	0.16	0.15	0.15	0.15	0.16	0.15	0.16	0.16	0.24
	Essay ELL2								
Rater Id.	501	510	511	512	513	514	515	516	517
Workload	0+22	9+10	19+10	33+13	9+32	23+49	24+20	40+27	14+34
Severity	0.10	0.06	0.29	0.00	0.02	0.13	−0.12	−0.05	−0.04
Shrinkage	0.53	0.49	0.59	0.67	0.65	0.74	0.67	0.73	0.68
$\sqrt{\text{MSE}}$	0.17	0.17	0.16	0.15	0.15	0.15	0.15	0.15	0.15
Rater Id.	521	522	523	524	525	526	527	528	
Workload	28+23	34+24	41+17	41+41	30+4	28+36	28+28	18+29	
Severity	−0.16	0.19	0.19	−0.18	−0.14	0.04	−0.23	0.05	
Shrinkage	0.69	0.71	0.71	0.76	0.62	0.72	0.71	0.68	
$\sqrt{\text{MSE}}$	0.15	0.15	0.15	0.15	0.16	0.15	0.15	0.15	

3.6.1 Advanced Placement tests

In this section, we apply the adjustment schemes to the administrations of the Advanced Placement (AP) tests analysed in Section 2.6. For motivation, we adhere to a practical concern:

> What proportion of examinees would receive an altered grade
> if the scores for the essay part of the test used in the operation
> were adjusted?

We focus on the Psychology test and then discuss results for the other AP tests. We do not consider the most complex scheme, **AAdj**, because of the large number of examinees and because the scheme is not robust with respect to imperfect variance estimation.

We start with estimating the severities of the raters. The results are summarized in Table 3.3. Although there are no apparent outliers in rating

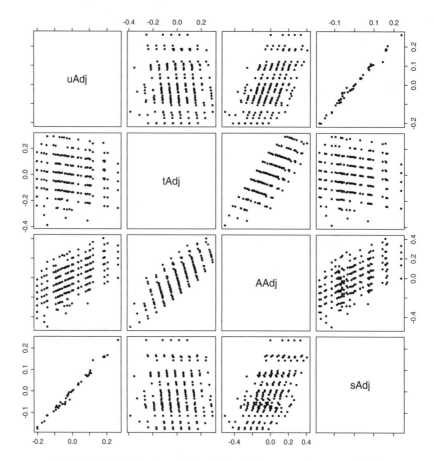

FIGURE 3.1. Pairwise plots of the adjustments for essay ELL1.

essay A, raters 100, 123, and 181 have very large estimates of severities in essay B (–0.51, 0.37, and –0.45, respectively). Also, rater 190 has a large estimate of severity, –0.40; however, it is based on only 21 essays, and so it has a large MSE, 0.29^2.

Since each essay is rated only once, the adjustments in the schemes **sAdj** and **uAdj** depend only on the rater's workload. Thus, for comparing these schemes it suffices to consider the adjustment for an arbitrary essay graded by each rater. Figure 3.2 displays the plots of the adjustments for essays A and B. Each rater is represented by a single point; raters with workloads greater than 100 are marked by black squares and those with smaller workloads by white squares. The identity is marked by a dashed line. The plots indicate that the adjustment schemes **sAdj** and **uAdj** are essentially identical for raters with large workloads. For raters with small workloads, **sAdj** is more conservative than **uAdj**.

TABLE 3.3. Raters' workloads and estimates of their severities in grading the essays of the Psychology AP test.

	Raters' workloads and severity estimates							
	Essay A							
Rater Id.	103	104	106	107	108	111	112	113
Workload	368	350	25	439	442	399	574	551
Severity	−0.08	0.13	0.03	−0.07	−0.03	0.06	−0.21	−0.25
Shrinkage	0.67	0.66	0.12	0.71	0.71	0.69	0.77	0.76
$\sqrt{\text{MSE}}$	0.12	0.12	0.19	0.12	0.12	0.12	0.11	0.11
Rater Id.	114	115	120	122	124	182	183	190
Workload	538	580	657	552	582	72	59	37
Severity	0.19	0.09	−0.03	0.20	0.17	−0.13	−0.11	−0.03
Shrinkage	0.76	0.78	0.81	0.76	0.78	0.29	0.25	0.17
$\sqrt{\text{MSE}}$	0.11	0.11	0.11	0.11	0.11	0.17	0.18	0.18
	Essay B							
Rater Id.	**100**	101	102	106	109	110	116	117
Workload	451	405	563	726	535	495	295	413
Severity	**−0.51**	0.03	−0.02	0.11	−0.19	0.10	−0.06	0.17
Shrinkage	0.88	0.87	0.92	0.97	0.91	0.90	0.82	0.87
$\sqrt{\text{MSE}}$	0.14	0.15	0.14	0.13	0.14	0.14	0.16	0.15
Rater Id.	118	119	121	**123**	125	180	**181**	**190**
Workload	321	353	498	484	433	125	115	21
Severity	0.24	−0.06	−0.01	**0.37**	0.12	0.16	**−0.45**	**−0.40**
Shrinkage	0.83	0.84	0.90	0.90	0.88	0.66	0.64	0.26
$\sqrt{\text{MSE}}$	0.16	0.15	0.14	0.14	0.14	0.20	0.21	0.29

Notes: Estimates for raters who graded fewer than 20 essays are omitted. Figures referred to in the text are printed in boldface.

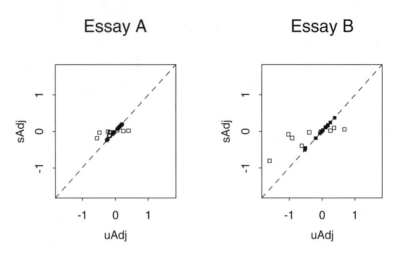

FIGURE 3.2. Adjustments of essay scores in Psychology AP.

Of course, an examinee may feel the impact of the adjustment only through the 'final' score of the test, the so-called AP grade. When free-response items are only one component of the test and their scores are given a relatively small weight in calculating the composite score, this score may be affected by the raters only to a small extent. In the analysed administration of the Psychology test, the composite score is calculated as the total of the score from the multiple-choice section of the test and the 2.778-multiple of the total of the essay scores. The multiple-choice section of the test consists of 100 items, each scored as correct or incorrect. An adjustment is applied for omitted responses by taking into account the chance of selecting the correct response at random. The multiple-choice scores are in the range 0–97.75, with mean and median around 60 and standard deviation equal to 16. In comparison, the total of the two unadjusted essay scores has mean 9.24 and standard deviation 4.40. Thus, the standard deviations of the multiple-choice and (2.778-multiples of) the essay components of the total score have comparable standard deviations (16.2 vs. 12.2).

In the Advanced Placement tests, the examinees are awarded AP grades on the integer scale 1–5. The AP grade is determined by applying *a priori* set cut points to the composite score. These cut points are 50.5, 73.5, 93.5, and 111.5. The resulting distribution of the AP grades, using the unadjusted essay scores, is

1	2	3	4	5
712	1270	1729	1562	986

Naturally, it is of interest how the AP grades would be changed if the unadjusted scores were replaced with the scores adjusted by each scheme. The total scores using the unadjusted and adjusted essay scores are plotted

TABLE 3.4. Cross-tabulation of the operational and adjusted AP grades in Psychology AP test.

NAdj grades	Adjustment sAdj					Adjustment uAdj				
	1	2	3	4	5	1	2	3	4	5
1	703	9	0	0	0	704	9	0	0	0
2	10	1240	20	0	0	9	1241	20	0	0
3	0	28	1678	23	0	0	27	1681	21	0
4	0	0	42	1504	16	0	0	40	1507	15
5	0	0	0	24	962	0	0	0	24	962

in Figure 3.3. Since there are a large number of examinees, the size of the adjustments can be best assessed by the thickness of the cloud of points in the plot. Thus, the schemes **uAdj** and **sAdj** are very similar, and they differ from **tAdj** even more than from **NAdj**. The differences in the AP grades using these scoring schemes are summarized by cross-tabulations of each set of the adjusted and operational grades; see Table 3.4. For the vast majority of examinees, the adjustment results in no change of the AP grade. In fact, the grades are altered by the scheme **uAdj** for only 2.75 percent of the examinees and by 2.62 percent using the scheme **sAdj**. Further examination reveals that the schemes **sAdj** and **uAdj** yield identical AP grades for all but eight examinees (0.13 percent). Each of these examinees was graded by a rater with a small workload on one of the essays. For each of them, the operational AP grade coincides with the u-adjusted grade but differs from the s-adjusted grade.

The AP grades adjusted using the scheme **tAdj** are substantially different from **uAdj** and **sAdj**. The radical shrinkage of the essay scores to the rater means, which are close to the overall mean, reduces the variation in the essay component of the score. This reduction could be compensated by changing the cut points and increasing the weight of the essay scores to reflect their improved reliability. Therefore, comparison of the t-adjusted AP grades may exaggerate the real differences in the AP scores and grades.

For comparison, we discuss the results of score adjustment for the other analysed AP test administrations. The multiple-choice sections of the Computer Science test were comprised of 40 items, with examinees' scores in the range 0–40. The multiple-choice and the essay scores were combined as $0.972M + 0.875F$ and $1.389M + 1.250F$ for the respective tests A and B, where M is the score from the multiple-choice section and F is the score from the essay component comprising four essays in each test. The cross-tabulations of the operational and adjusted grades for the two tests are given in Table 3.5.

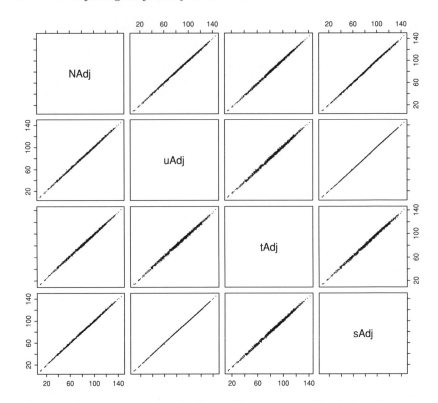

FIGURE 3.3. Operational and adjusted final scores for Psychology AP test.

The two scoring schemes differ only for five examinees, each of them having been graded by at least one rater with a small workload. The adjusted scores differ from the operational scores for only 2 percent of the examinees in test A and 3 percent in test B. The percentages of disagreement are somewhat higher for the adjustment scheme **tAdj** (2.5 and 3.3 percent, respectively).

For the English Composition test, the adjustments of the essay scores result in an altered AP grade for more than 6 percent of the examinees. This can largely be attributed to considerable inconsistency variation in the essay rating; see (2.24). The scheme **tAdj** alters the AP grade for an incredible 43 percent of the examinees because owing to the poor quality of rating it is impossible to have extreme estimates of the true scores for the essays. The essay scores are so radically shrunk toward the average score that extreme AP grades, 1 and 5, cannot be attained with the scheme **tAdj**.

Yet another means of improving estimation of the AP grades is provided in the next section. We have not applied it earlier so as to focus on the uncertainty due to subjective scoring.

TABLE 3.5. Cross-tabulation of the operational and adjusted AP grades in the Computer Science test forms.

| | Form A | | | | | | | | | |
| | Adjustment sAdj | | | | | Adjustment uAdj | | | | |
NAdj grades	1	2	3	4	5	1	2	3	4	5
1	2012	15	0	0	0	2013	14	0	0	0
2	14	1160	19	0	0	14	1160	19	0	0
3	0	23	1407	11	0	0	24	1406	11	0
4	0	0	15	809	5	0	0	15	809	5
5	0	0	0	16	560	0	0	0	16	560

| | Form B | | | | | | | | | |
| | Adjustment sAdj | | | | | Adjustment uAdj | | | | |
NAdj grades	1	2	3	4	5	1	2	3	4	5
1	696	15	0	0	0	696	15	0	0	0
2	14	887	7	0	0	14	886	8	0	0
3	0	21	1134	9	0	0	22	1132	10	0
4	0	0	26	502	4	0	0	27	500	5
5	0	0	0	33	1066	0	0	0	33	1066

3.7 Estimating linear combinations of true scores

In Section 3.6.1, we analysed test scores from the Advanced Placement tests. Many other educational tests are also comprised of separately scored sections. A typical such test has a multiple-choice and a free-response section. The multiple-choice section is machine-scored (say, as the number of correct responses), and the free-response section is scored by expert readers. Prior to the administration, a panel of experts decides how the scores from the two sections should be combined. The experts are usually not informed about measurement error problems, and so the consensus they arrive at is meant to apply to the underlying true scores. Often the 'measurement' error variance of the free-response section is much greater than that of the multiple-choice section. The analysis in Section 3.6.1 provided several examples.

Intuitively, when combining a pair of scores, both subject to measurement error, it would be prudent to reduce the weight assigned to the score with the greater measurement error variance, so as to reduce its contribution to the error variance in the combination of the scores. We show that neither this approach nor using the coefficients meant for the true scores is fully efficient, because the optimal combination of the observed scores depends also on the covariance structure of the true scores.

In the remainder of this section, we state the problem formally, and in Section 3.7.1, we derive solutions based on three optimality criteria. The solutions coincide and have a natural interpretation as a multivariate shrinkage estimator.

Let $\mathbf{a}$ be the vector of unknown *true scores* of an examinee. Say, $\mathbf{a} = (a_1, a_2)$, where a_1 and a_2 are the scores for the multiple-choice and the free-response sections of a test. It is of interest to estimate the total score $a = a_1 + a_2$ or, more generally, $a = \mathbf{a1}$ (**1** is the vector of ones of the same length as $\mathbf{a}$), based on the vector of observed scores $\hat{\mathbf{a}}$. Suppose $\hat{\mathbf{a}}$ is unbiased, that is, $\mathbf{E}(\hat{\mathbf{a}} \mid \mathbf{a}) = \mathbf{a}$.

Let $\mathbf{S}$ be the measurement error variance matrix for $\hat{\mathbf{a}}$, that is, $\mathbf{S} = \mathrm{var}(\hat{\mathbf{a}} - \mathbf{a})$. Typically, the measurement errors (components of $\hat{\mathbf{a}} - \mathbf{a}$) are mutually independent, and so $\mathbf{S}$ is a diagonal matrix. Let $\boldsymbol{\mu}$ be the vector of (population) means of the true scores, $\boldsymbol{\mu} = \mathbf{E}(\mathbf{a})$, and $\boldsymbol{\Sigma}$ be the variance matrix of the true scores, $\boldsymbol{\Sigma} = \mathrm{var}(\mathbf{a})$. Usually, the true scores are highly correlated, and so $\boldsymbol{\Sigma}$ may be singular or close to singularity. The measurement errors are assumed to be independent of the true scores, so that the unconditional variance matrix of the observed scores is $\mathrm{var}(\hat{\mathbf{a}}) = \boldsymbol{\Sigma} + \mathbf{S}$.

No generality is lost by restricting our attention to the total of the section scores, $\mathbf{a1}$, instead of a linear combination $\mathbf{aw}$ for a given vector of constants $\mathbf{w}$. These constants can be absorbed in $\mathbf{a}$ with the appropriate adjustments of the observed scores $\hat{\mathbf{a}}$ and the variance matrices $\boldsymbol{\Sigma}$ and $\mathbf{S}$.

Instead of the trivial estimator $\hat{a} = \hat{\mathbf{a}}\mathbf{1}$, we consider the class of linear combinations $\hat{a}_v = c + \hat{\mathbf{a}}\mathbf{v}$ and select the constant c and the vector of weights $\mathbf{v}$ so as to satisfy one of the following criteria:

- minimize the MSE, $\mathbf{E}(\hat{a}_v - a)^2$;

- minimize the conditional MSE given the observed scores, $\mathbf{E}\left\{(\hat{a}_v - a)^2 \mid \hat{\mathbf{a}}\right\}$;

- maximize the correlation with the true score, $\mathrm{cor}(\hat{a}_v, a)$.

Note that in the latter case the solution is not unique because the correlation is invariant with respect to linear transformations.

3.7.1 Optimal linear combinations

Denote
$$S(c, \mathbf{v}) = \mathbf{E}\left\{(\hat{a}_v - a)^2\right\}.$$
Elementary operations yield the identity
$$S(c, \mathbf{v}) = \left\{c + \boldsymbol{\mu}(\mathbf{v} - \mathbf{1})\right\}^2 + (\mathbf{v} - \mathbf{1})^\top \boldsymbol{\Sigma}(\mathbf{v} - \mathbf{1}) + \mathbf{v}^\top \mathbf{S}\mathbf{v}.$$

This is a quadratic function of the unknown coefficient c and the vector $\mathbf{v}$, with positive quadratic terms, and so its unique minimum is found by setting its partial derivatives to zero:

$$\frac{1}{2}\frac{\partial S}{\partial c} = c + \mu(\mathbf{v} - \mathbf{1}),$$

$$\frac{1}{2}\frac{\partial S}{\partial \mathbf{v}} = \{c + \mu(\mathbf{v} - \mathbf{1})\}\,\mu + (\mathbf{v} - \mathbf{1})^\top\Sigma + \mathbf{v}^\top\mathbf{S}.$$

Substituting $c^* = -\mu(\mathbf{v} - \mathbf{1})$ in the equation for $\mathbf{v}$ yields the solution

$$\mathbf{v}^* = (\Sigma + \mathbf{S})^{-1}\Sigma\mathbf{1}.$$

Noting that

$$\mathbf{v}^* - \mathbf{1} = \{(\Sigma + \mathbf{S})^{-1}\Sigma - \mathbf{I}\}\,\mathbf{1}$$
$$= -(\Sigma + \mathbf{S})^{-1}\mathbf{S}\mathbf{1},$$

the optimal estimator of the true-score combination is

$$\hat{a}_v = \mu(\Sigma + \mathbf{S})^{-1}\mathbf{S}\mathbf{1} + \hat{a}(\Sigma + \mathbf{S})^{-1}\Sigma\mathbf{1}$$
$$= \hat{a}\mathbf{1} - (\hat{a} - \mu)(\Sigma + \mathbf{S})^{-1}\mathbf{S}\mathbf{1}. \tag{3.19}$$

Since $\mathbf{S}(\Sigma + \mathbf{S})^{-1}\Sigma$ is a symmetric matrix, the minimum MSE is

$$\mathrm{E}(\hat{a}_v - a)^2 = \mathbf{1}^\top\Sigma(\Sigma + \mathbf{S})^{-1}\mathbf{S}(\Sigma + \mathbf{S})^{-1}\Sigma\mathbf{1}$$
$$+ \mathbf{1}^\top\mathbf{S}(\Sigma + \mathbf{S})^{-1}\Sigma(\Sigma + \mathbf{S})^{-1}\mathbf{S}\mathbf{1}$$
$$= \mathbf{1}^\top\mathbf{S}(\Sigma + \mathbf{S})^{-1}\Sigma\mathbf{1}$$
$$= \mathbf{1}^\top\left(\Sigma^{-1} + \mathbf{S}^{-1}\right)^{-1}\mathbf{1};$$

the last identity is appropriate only when both Σ and $\mathbf{S}$ are non-singular.

For comparison, the MSE for the trivial estimator $\hat{a} = \hat{a}\mathbf{1}$ is equal to $S(0, \mathbf{1}) = \mathbf{v}^\top\mathbf{S}\mathbf{v}$. The difference of the MSEs of $\hat{a}$ and $\hat{a}_v$ is

$$(\Delta =)\quad S(0,\mathbf{1}) - S(c^*,\mathbf{v}^*) = \mathbf{1}^\top\mathbf{S}\mathbf{1} - \mathbf{1}^\top\Sigma(\Sigma + \mathbf{S})^{-1}\mathbf{S}\mathbf{1}$$
$$= \mathbf{1}^\top\mathbf{S}(\Sigma + \mathbf{S})^{-1}\mathbf{S}\mathbf{1}.$$

Since $\mathbf{S}(\Sigma + \mathbf{S})^{-1}\mathbf{S}$ is a non-negative definite matrix, Δ is non-negative. Moreover, when $\mathbf{S}$ is positive definite Δ is positive.

Positive definiteness is commonly used for partial ordering of matrices. A matrix $\mathbf{A}$ is said to be 'smaller' than matrix $\mathbf{B}$ if $\mathbf{A}$ and $\mathbf{B}$ have the same dimensions and $\mathbf{B} - \mathbf{A}$ is positive definite. Note that $(\Sigma + \mathbf{S})^{-1}\mathbf{S}$ is 'smaller' than the unit matrix $\mathbf{I}$ because $\mathbf{I} - (\Sigma + \mathbf{S})^{-1}\mathbf{S} = (\Sigma + \mathbf{S})^{-1}\Sigma$.

For the case of combining two section scores, let $\boldsymbol{\Sigma} = \begin{pmatrix} \sigma_1^2 & \sigma_{12} \\ \sigma_{12} & \sigma_2^2 \end{pmatrix}$ and $\mathbf{S} = \mathrm{diag}(s_1^2,\, s_2^2)$. Then

$$\hat{a}_v = \hat{a} - (\hat{a}_1 - \mu_1)\frac{s_1^2(\sigma_2^2 + s_2^2) - s_2^2\sigma_{12}}{z} - (\hat{a}_2 - \mu_2)\frac{s_2^2(\sigma_1^2 + s_1^2) - s_1^2\sigma_{12}}{z},$$

where $z = \det(\boldsymbol{\Sigma} + \mathbf{S}) = (\sigma_1^2 + s_1^2)(\sigma_2^2 + s_2^2) - \sigma_{12}^2$. Note that the coefficient with $\hat{a}_1 - \mu_1$ (or $\hat{a}_2 - \mu_2$) may be negative, for instance, when s_2^2 is much greater than s_1^2 and σ_{12} is large and positive. Even though the estimator in (3.19) has the form of multivariate shrinkage, it does not correspond to componentwise shrinkage.

It would appear that a further improvement in estimation of a would be gained by conditioning on the observed scores $\hat{a}$, that is, minimizing the conditional MSE

$$T(c, \mathbf{v}) = \mathbf{E}\left\{(\hat{a}_v - a)^2 \mid \hat{a}\right\}.$$

Assuming normality of $\hat{a}$ and $\mathbf{a}$, the conditional distribution of $\mathbf{a}$ given $\hat{a}$ is normal,

$$(\mathbf{a} \mid \hat{a}) \sim \mathcal{N}\left\{\boldsymbol{\mu} + (\hat{a} - \boldsymbol{\mu})(\boldsymbol{\Sigma} + \mathbf{S})^{-1}\boldsymbol{\Sigma},\, \boldsymbol{\Sigma} - \boldsymbol{\Sigma}(\boldsymbol{\Sigma} + \mathbf{S})^{-1}\boldsymbol{\Sigma}\right\}.$$

Since the conditional variance does not depend on $\hat{a}$, the maximum of $T(c, \mathbf{v})$ is found by matching $\hat{a}_v$ to the conditional expectation of a. This yields

$$\hat{a}_v = \mathbf{E}(a \mid \hat{a}) = \boldsymbol{\mu}\mathbf{1} + (\hat{a} - \boldsymbol{\mu})(\boldsymbol{\Sigma} + \mathbf{S})^{-1}\boldsymbol{\Sigma}\mathbf{1},$$

which coincides with (3.19). Thus, conditioning on the observed scores does not improve the estimator of a when the observed and true scores are normally distributed. In practice, the observed scores are often distinctly non-normally distributed, although the distribution of the 'measurement' errors is difficult to describe because it contains elements of rounding and misclassification. Conditioning can be interpreted as ordinary regression, and so the assumptions of normality can be relaxed to that of linearity (adopted a priori) and homoscedasticity (equal conditional variance), which are often more palatable.

Another meaningful criterion is to maximize the correlation of the combination of the observed scores with the true-score total. For an arbitrary constant c and vector $\mathbf{v}$, we have

$$\{R(\mathbf{v}) = \} \quad \mathrm{cor}(\hat{a}_v,\, a) = \frac{\mathbf{v}^\top\boldsymbol{\Sigma}\mathbf{1}}{\sqrt{\mathbf{1}^\top\boldsymbol{\Sigma}\mathbf{1}\,\mathbf{v}^\top(\boldsymbol{\Sigma} + \mathbf{S})\mathbf{v}}}.$$

To find the maximum of this function of $\mathbf{v}$, it is easier to differentiate its logarithm:

$$\frac{1}{2}\frac{\partial\log(R)}{\partial\mathbf{v}} = \frac{\boldsymbol{\Sigma}\mathbf{1}}{\mathbf{v}^\top\boldsymbol{\Sigma}\mathbf{1}} - \frac{(\boldsymbol{\Sigma} + \mathbf{S})\mathbf{v}}{\mathbf{v}^\top(\boldsymbol{\Sigma} + \mathbf{S})\mathbf{v}}.$$

An optimal vector $\mathbf{v}$ is found by setting this expression to zero. By absorbing the denominators in a constant, we obtain the solution

$$\mathbf{v}^* = d(\mathbf{\Sigma} + \mathbf{S})^{-1}\mathbf{\Sigma}\mathbf{1},$$

where d is a positive constant. Its value is irrelevant, just as that of c, because it has no impact on the correlation. This solution, chosen with the appropriate constants c and d, coincides with (3.19). The maximum correlation is

$$R(\mathbf{v}^*) = \frac{\mathbf{1}^\top \mathbf{S}(\mathbf{\Sigma} + \mathbf{S})^{-1}\mathbf{1}}{\sqrt{\mathbf{1}^\top \mathbf{\Sigma}\mathbf{1} \cdot \mathbf{1}^\top \mathbf{S}(\mathbf{\Sigma} + \mathbf{S})^{-1}\mathbf{S}\mathbf{1}}}.$$

Note that, in general, $R(\mathbf{v}^*) > R(\mathbf{1})$ even when the measurement error variances are identical, $\mathbf{S} = s^2\mathbf{I}$.

In practice, the vector $\boldsymbol{\mu}$ and the matrices $\mathbf{\Sigma}$ and $\mathbf{S}$ are not known and have to be estimated. However, in large-scale test administrations involving thousands of examinees, these objects are estimated with high precision. Using optimal combinations of the observed or adjusted scores in the Advanced Placement tests would result in the change of the AP grade for a few percent of the examinees in addition to those whose grades would have been altered by the adjustment schemes described earlier in this chapter.

3.8   Summary

Three schemes for adjustment of subjectively rated scores were studied in this chapter. The schemes pool information about the true scores by utilizing the variance components and by applying shrinkage estimators. The schemes **sAdj** and **uAdj** are almost identical when each essay is rated only once and the raters have moderate to large workloads. The scheme **tAdj** is efficient when inconsistency variation dominates variation in severity. The scheme **AAdj** combines the advantages of these schemes but is computationally the most complex and the least robust when the variance components are not known precisely.

A typical adjustment scheme is defined as follows. First, a class of linear combinations of the essay scores is defined. The coefficients of such a combination are defined so as to minimize its MSE around the true score or around the rater's severity. The adjustment depends on the variance components; in practice, these variances are replaced by their estimates. Simulation methods can be applied to explore robustness of the schemes when such a substitution takes place.

Information about the variance components could be supplemented from administrations using similar items and the same populations of examinees and raters (for instance, older versions of the same test). Also, information about each rater could be supplemented by the raters' estimated severities from other administrations of the same test. Because of a sizeable inconsistency in rating, the score adjustment usually amounts to only a modest reduction of the MSE of the score. Another potential source of improvement is in pooling information about examinees' true scores from other tests. This may be controversial in tests with high stakes because an examinee's past test-taking record would have an impact on his/her future test scores.

When a test comprises both multiple-choice and free-response sections, the weight assigned to the sections is usually set so as to reflect the importance of the true scores for the sections. It may be more appropriate to take into account the differential measurement error variances associated with the sections as well as the correlation structure of the true scores. This leads to a multivariate shrinkage estimator of the composite score.

The score adjustment derived from the traditional ANOVA model ('full' adjustment) corresponds to $u_i = 1$ in the scheme **uAdj**. In the studied examples, such a scheme can be improved considerably. By analogy, methods based on logistic models for ordinal categorical response (Agresti, 1988; Uebersax, 1993), which represent each rater by a parameter, are likely to be deficient. Versions of these models in which raters are represented by random variables are computationally very intensive, but they do not present an insurmountable hurdle. See Longford (1993a) and Hedeker and Gibbons (1994) for applications in different areas.

Appendix
Derivation of MSE for the general adjustment scheme

To prove (3.16), we express the deviation $\hat{\alpha}_{i,v} - \alpha_i$ in terms of the random variables α, β, and ε:

$$
\begin{aligned}
\hat{\alpha}_{i,v} - \alpha_i ={} & (v_{i1} - 1)\alpha_i - \frac{v_{2i}}{K} \sum_{k=1}^{K} \frac{1}{n_{j_{ik}}} \sum_{i'=1}^{I} r_{ii',k}\, \alpha_{i'} + \frac{v_{3i}}{I} \sum_{i'=1}^{I} \alpha_{i'} \\
& + \frac{v_{1i} - v_{2i}}{K} \sum_{k=1}^{K} \beta_{j_{ik}} + \frac{v_{3i}}{N} \sum_{j'=1}^{J} n_{j'} \beta_{j'} \\
& + \frac{v_{1i}}{K} \sum_{k=1}^{K} \varepsilon_{i,j_{ik}} - v_{2i} \sum_{k=1}^{K} \sum_{i';j_{i'k}} \frac{\varepsilon_{i',j_{i'k}}}{n_{j_{i'k}}} + \frac{v_{3i}}{N} \sum_{i'=1}^{I} \sum_{k=1}^{K} \varepsilon_{i',j_{i'k}}.
\end{aligned}
$$

The variance of this deviation can be decomposed into variances involving the random variables from only one random sample, and these can be further decomposed to variances involving the individual random variables.

For instance, using the identities $r_{ii,k} = 1$, and $r_{i1,k} + \ldots + r_{iI,k} = n_{jik}$, the contribution due to the true scores α_i becomes

$$
\text{var} \left\{ \left(v_{i1} - 1 - \frac{v_{2i}}{K} \sum_k \frac{1}{n_{jik}} + \frac{v_{3i}}{I} \right) \alpha_i - \sum_{i' \neq i} \left(\frac{r_{ii',k} v_{2i}}{K} - \frac{v_{3i}}{N} \right) \alpha_{i'} \right\}
$$

$$
= \sigma_a^2 \left\{ (1 - v_{i1})^2 + 2(1 - v_{i1}) \left(v_{2i} n_i^- - \frac{v_{3i}}{I} \right) + v_{2i}^2 \frac{R_i}{K} - \frac{2 v_{2i} v_{3i}}{I} + \frac{v_{3i}^2}{I} \right\},
$$

as in the second line of (3.16). The contributions due to β_j and ε_{ij} are derived by the same method.

4

Rating several essays

4.1 Introduction

Chapters 2 and 3 were concerned with the measurement of examinees' performances on a single item. Even though an essay written by an examinee may be much more informative about his/her ability than a multiple-choice item, a single essay is unlikely to provide sufficient information, especially in the presence of imperfect grading by the raters. Also, the examinee's performance may be unduly affected by the essay topic, and no single topic can represent the tested domain in a balanced way.

In this chapter, we explore extensions of the methods for measurement of ability based on a set of constructed-response items. Ideally, the tested domain would be represented by a large number of items, ensuring complete and balanced coverage of the domain. Administering a large number of constructed-response items is often impractical because each examinee can cope with only a few items (write two or three essays at most). Completeness and balanced coverage of the domain are always problematic when the domain is defined only vaguely, and there is no precise description of the skills tapped by an item (essay topic). This problem is often compounded by the context associated with the small number of administered items that is irrelevant to the domain of the test.

In high-stakes tests, identical essay topics for each examinee are often preferred so as to avoid the problem of differential difficulty of the essay topics. Of course, the essay topic may introduce other measurement problems. For instance, a typical examinee may have certain strengths and weaknesses in the tested domain, and they may be disproportionately represented among the assigned topics. An innovative but as yet insufficiently understood method of administration that addresses this issue is to allow each examinee to choose a given number of topics from a presented list. For instance, the examinees may be presented with six topics and be asked to write essays on any three of them. The examinees can therefore choose topics on which they would perform best.

When the objective is to describe the distribution of ability in a population, examinees may be given different tasks. A particularly appealing design combines the use of many items interspersed among the examinees. The examinees are assigned subsets of the items by a non-informative design. The subsets may be overlapping, so as to enable various within-examinee comparisons of the item properties. The large pool of topics promotes good representation of the domain.

Just as in the classical rectangular design (each item assigned to every examinee), each item in this incomplete design is presented to a sample of examinees representing the examinee population, and so the methods developed in Chapters 2 and 3 can be applied to one item at a time. The drawback of such an approach is that information is not combined across the items, across examinees' performances, or across the raters. Combining information is of particular importance when most raters grade essays on several topics.

In order to divorce the analysis from the particular items to the domain represented by the items, we consider a sample of rating exercises, one for each item, and posit a model in which we consider the rating exercise for an 'average' item and item-level variation in all aspects of rating: item difficulty, rater severity, and inconsistency. We prefer to associate the items with variation so as to emphasize the random and unreplicable nature of assembly of the pool of items. Also, our focus is on measurement of ability (performance) on a domain of knowledge for which the particular items used are incidental; other items that might have been selected by the same test construction process would have served the purpose equally well.

Our approach is motivated by the generalizability theory model of Cronbach et al. (1972). Examinees, items, raters, and sessions are considered as factors or *facets*, each of them being a source of variation, that is, an element contributing to the uncertainty of the outcomes. Variation associated with the examinees is to be expected, and its size is of substantive interest. In a well-informed process of test assembly and instruction of the raters, the variation associated with the items is under partial control of the test developers. Very difficult or very easy items (vis-à-vis the tested population) are screened out in the review process, and it is ensured that not all the items have the same difficulty. In other words, there is an (informal) standard for the variation in item difficulty.

In the previous chapters, we presented strong evidence that raters are associated with substantial variation, both in terms of severity and inconsistency. A rater may exercise the same severity for every item in a test, but a less restrictive assumption is that each rater has an 'average' strictness, referring to an 'average' item, and that his/her strictness for each item differs from the average by a random quantity. Similarly, sessions may be associated with a variety of possible changes in the conduct of the raters; the raters may become uniformly more lenient, or stricter, in a session, may become so only for some of the items, may become less inconsistent, and similar.

The next section describes the models for subjective rating of several essay topics. Section 4.3 deals with estimation of the variances that characterize items, examinees, and raters. An application to a large-scale survey of U.S. secondary education is presented in Section 4.4. In Section 4.5, we address some of the issues that arise when examinees can choose among the presented topics. The chapter is concluded with a summary.

4.2   Models

If every examinee $i = 1, \ldots, I$ wrote an essay on each topic $h = 1, \ldots, H$, and each essay, indexed by hi, were graded by every rater $j = 1, \ldots, J$, the data could be organized in a three-way $H \times I \times J$ array of scores. Of course, in practice only a small fraction of these scores may be realized.

As a starting point, we assume for each item the basic model from Chapters 2 and 3:

$$y_{hijk} = \alpha_{hi} + \beta_{hj} + \varepsilon_{hijk} , \qquad (4.1)$$

where the index k denotes the session, $k = 1, \ldots, K$, α_{hi} is the true score of examinee i on topic h, β_{hj} is the severity of rater j when grading topic h, and ε_{hijk} is the residual term attributed to inconsistency. The true scores α_{hi} are assumed to have topic-specific means (difficulties) μ_h; the β's and ε's in (4.1) have zero expectations.

The scores for each topic could be analysed separately. Such an analysis is fairly efficient when each examinee takes every item and each rater specializes in grading a single topic. If we believed that the topics share their values of the severity and inconsistency variances, these variances could be estimated more efficiently by pooling information across the analyses. Examinees' true scores, defined as $(\alpha_{1i} + \ldots + \alpha_{Hi})/H$, or as their infinite-item (population) versions, can be estimated as the weighted sums of the estimated true scores for the topics, $\hat{\alpha}_{hi}$, with weights reciprocally proportional to the estimated mean squared errors (MSE). Section 3.7 presented a more efficient alternative.

When many raters grade several topics, raters are bound to grade some essays on most of the topics. As a consequence, the topic-specific severity and inconsistency variances are poorly estimated, and the estimation errors will permeate into estimation of the true scores. If a rater exercises the same or similar severity in every essay he/she grades, then some information about the rater ends up not being exploited. If there is a large number of essays, a lot of information is discarded. Recall that the raters' workloads play an important role in the score adjustment schemes discussed in Chapter 3.

This deficiency motivates the extension of the model in (4.1) which would accommodate between-item differences or the raters' characteristics and examinees' abilities. If the true scores on the topics were identical for each examinee, each rater had the same severity for each topic, and each topic were associated with the same inconsistency variance, the topics could be regarded as perfect replicates and all the ratings of an examinee's essays could be regarded as multiple ratings of the same essay. Most likely, the true scores are highly, though not perfectly, correlated, and the raters' severities are similar but not identical across the items.

We assume that the items $h = 1, \ldots, H$ are randomly drawn from an appropriately defined population of items. This population is characterized by an unknown mean μ and variance σ_μ^2. For each examinee, we assume an average ability, α_i, defined as the mean of the true scores over the population of items in the tested domain. The examinee's ability specific to item h is α_{hi}; the deviations $\gamma_{hi} = \alpha_{hi} - \alpha_i$ are assumed to be a random sample from a centred distribution with variance σ_γ^2. By symmetry, rater j has the average severity β_j, defined as the mean of the item-specific severities $\beta_j + \delta_{hj}$ over the population of topics. Assuming additivity of these terms leads to the model

$$ y_{hijk} = \mu_h + \alpha_i + \gamma_{hi} + \beta_j + \delta_{hj} + \varepsilon_{hijk} , \qquad (4.2) $$

where ε_{hijk} represents the deviation from the case that corresponds to consistent rating. The terms α_i, γ_{hi}, β_j, δ_{hj}, and ε_{hijk} are random samples from centred distributions with respective variances σ_α^2, σ_β^2, σ_γ^2, σ_δ^2, and σ_ε^2. All the random variables in (4.2) are mutually independent. Table 4.1 summarizes the interpretation of these variables and the notation for their variances. Note that the residual terms ε_{hijk} in (4.2) do not coincide with those in (4.1), although both of them represent inconsistency.

The true score of examinee i on item h is $\mu_h + \alpha_i + \gamma_{hi}$, and its variance, averaged over the items and examinees, is $\sigma_\mu^2 + \sigma_\alpha^2 + \sigma_\gamma^2$. Given the item difficulty μ_h, the conditional variance is $\sigma_\alpha^2 + \sigma_\gamma^2$. The variance σ_γ^2 describes the uncertainty about an examinee's score, associated with the choice of the items. The average of the item-specific true scores $\alpha_i + \gamma_{hi}$ over the items is $\alpha_i + (\gamma_{1i} + \ldots + \gamma_{Hi})/H$, which has MSE σ_γ^2/H. Thus, the true scores α_i cannot be estimated with precision when either σ_γ^2 is large or H is small.

To estimate a rater's item-specific severity $\beta_j + \delta_{hj}$, the rater has to grade many essays on topic j. To estimate the 'general' severity β_j, the rater has to grade many essays on several topics, unless σ_δ^2 is very small, in

TABLE 4.1. Random variables and variance components in equation (4.2).

Interpretation	Notation		Mean	Variance
Item difficulty	μ_h	$h = 1, \ldots, H$	μ	σ_μ^2
Average item ability	α_i	$i = 1, \ldots, I$	0	σ_α^2
Item-specific ability	γ_{hi}		0	σ_γ^2
Rater average severity	β_j	$j = 1, \ldots, J$	0	σ_β^2
Item-specific severity	δ_{hj}		0	σ_δ^2
Rater inconsistency	ε_{hijk}	$k = 1, \ldots, K$	0	σ_ε^2

which case grading essays on one topic is very informative about how the rater would have graded essays on a different topic. However, in the spirit of borrowing strength across items, ratings on other topics can contribute to inference about the topic-specific severity of a rater even when σ_δ^2 is positive. The smaller the variance σ_δ^2, the more informative are the ratings on items $h' \neq h$ about the item-specific severity $\beta_j + \delta_{hj}$.

In a general setup considered in Section 4.4, each examinee is assigned a small number of topics, but each of a large number of topics is assigned to a non-informative sample of examinees. We assume that the raters grade essays only on some of the topics and that the raters' workloads may vary both within and between essay topics. Also, although a large number of raters is engaged, each essay is graded by a small number of raters.

Because of the dispersed nature of the information about the examinees, items, and raters, it is advantageous to carry out a simultaneous analysis of the data for all items rather than to analyse the subsets of data corresponding to the items separately. The model in (4.2), suitable for a simultaneous analysis, implies variance homogeneity for a variety of subsets of the data. Analyses of such subsets are an integral component of model diagnostics.

The numbers of items, examinees, raters, and sessions are denoted by the respective capitals H, I, J, and K. For counts of grades within various combinations of the facets, we introduce the '+' notation. Thus, n_{h+++} denotes the number of ratings of essays written on topic h, n_{+ij+} is the number of times rater j graded an essay written by examinee i, and so on. In particular, when the first session is complete, n_{+++1} is the number of essays written in the entire administration. For brevity, we denote by $N = n_{++++}$ the total number of ratings. An essay is graded by a rater at most once, and so $n_{hij+} \leq 1$.

For convenience, we use the abbreviated notation $\sum_{hijk}$ to denote the summation over all the *realized* combinations of the subscripts $hijk$, that is, over all the N ratings. Summation over subsets of these indices is defined similarly. We use the 'dot' notation for arithmetic means of grades. For instance, $y_{hi\cdot\cdot}$ denotes the mean grade given to examinee i for essay h, and

$y_{....}$ is the overall mean, $y_{....} = N^{-1} \sum_{hijk} y_{hijk}$. To avoid confusion, we will refer to the response of an examinee as an *essay* and to an item as an (essay) *topic*.

4.3   Estimation

The variance components σ^2 are estimated by the method of moments. For each variance, we define a sum-of-squares (SSQ) statistic and match it with its expectation. The expectation of each statistic turns out to be a linear function of the variance components, and so the estimates of the variances are the solutions of a linear system of equations.

We define the following statistics:

1. itemwise SSQ:
$$S_1 = \sum_{hijk} (y_{hijk} - y_{h...})^2 \, ;$$

2. examinee SSQ:
$$S_2 = \sum_{hijk} (y_{hijk} - y_{\cdot i \cdot \cdot})^2 \, ;$$

3. rater SSQ:
$$S_3 = \sum_{hijk} (y_{hijk} - y_{\cdot\cdot j \cdot})^2 \, ;$$

4. item-by-examinee SSQ:
$$S_4 = \sum_{hijk} (y_{hijk} - y_{hi..})^2 \, ;$$

5. item-by-rater SSQ:
$$S_5 = \sum_{hijk} (y_{hijk} - y_{h \cdot j \cdot})^2 \, ;$$

6. total SSQ:
$$S_6 = \sum_{hijk} (y_{hijk} - y_{....})^2 \, .$$

For large numbers of examinees, these statistics are more economically calculated from the totals of squares and mean scores over certain combinations of the facets. For instance, we have

$$S_4 = \sum_{hijk} y_{hijk}^2 - \sum_{hi} n_{hi++} \, y_{hi..}^2 \, .$$

Moreover, these two summations can be restricted to the multiply graded essays (that is, hi such that $n_{hi++} > 1$).

Using elementary properties of the expectation, we obtain

$$\mathbf{E}(S_1) = \sum_{hijk} \text{var}(y_{hijk} - y_{h\cdots}), \qquad (4.3)$$

and similarly for other SSQ statistics. For evaluation of these variances, the following identity is useful. Let η_l, $l = 1, \ldots, L$, be a random sample from a distribution with arbitrary mean μ_η and variance σ_η^2, and let s_l, $l = 1, \ldots, L$, be a sequence of real numbers. Denote their total by $S = (s_1 + \ldots + s_L)$. Then

$$\text{var}\left(\eta_{l*} - \frac{1}{S}\sum_{l=1}^{L} s_l \eta_l\right) = \sigma_\eta^2 \left(1 - \frac{2s_{l*}}{S} + \frac{1}{S^2}\sum_{l=1}^{L} s_l^2\right). \qquad (4.4)$$

The identity is proved using elementary operations:

$$\text{var}\left(\eta_{l*} - \frac{1}{S}\sum_{l=1}^{L} s_l \eta_l\right) = \text{var}\left(\frac{S - s_{l*}}{S}\eta_{l*} + \frac{1}{S}\sum_{l \neq l*} s_l \eta_l\right)$$

$$= \sigma_\eta^2 \left\{\frac{(S - s_{l*})^2}{S^2} + \frac{1}{S^2}\sum_{l \neq l*} s_l^2\right\},$$

from which equation (4.4) follows directly. Note that

$$\sum_{l*=1}^{L} s_{l*} \text{var}\left(\eta_{l*} - \frac{1}{S}\sum_{l=1}^{L} s_l \eta_l\right) = \sigma_\eta^2 \left(S - \frac{1}{S}\sum_{l=1}^{L} s_l^2\right).$$

When $s_l = 1$ for each l,

$$\text{var}\left(\eta_{l*} - \frac{1}{S}\sum_{l=1}^{L} s_l \eta_l\right) = \sigma_\eta^2 \left(1 - \frac{1}{L}\right). \qquad (4.5)$$

Derivation of the expectations of the SSQ statistics is elementary but lengthy. To avoid a lot of repetitious equations, we give details only for S_1. First,

$$y_{h\cdots} = \mu_h + \frac{1}{n_{h+++}}\sum_{i=1}^{I} \alpha_i n_{hi++} + \frac{1}{n_{h+++}}\sum_{i=1}^{I} \gamma_{hi} n_{hi++}$$

$$+ \frac{1}{n_{h+++}}\sum_{j=1}^{J} \beta_j n_{h+j+} + \frac{1}{n_{h+++}}\sum_{j=1}^{J} \delta_{hj} n_{h+j+} + \frac{1}{n_{h+++}}\sum_{ijk} \varepsilon_{hijk}.$$

Using the mutual independence of the random terms, a summand in (4.3) is decomposed as

$$\mathrm{var}(y_{hijk} - y_{h\cdots}) = \mathrm{var}\left(\alpha_i - \frac{1}{n_{h+++}}\sum_{i=1}^{I}\alpha_i n_{hi++}\right)$$

$$+ \mathrm{var}\left(\gamma_{hi} - \frac{1}{n_{h+++}}\sum_{i=1}^{I}\gamma_{hi} n_{hi++}\right)$$

$$+ \mathrm{var}\left(\beta_j - \frac{1}{n_{h+++}}\sum_{j=1}^{J}\beta_j n_{h+j+}\right)$$

$$+ \mathrm{var}\left(\delta_{hj} - \frac{1}{n_{h+++}}\sum_{j=1}^{J}\delta_{hj} n_{h+j+}\right)$$

$$+ \mathrm{var}\left(\varepsilon_{hijk} - \frac{1}{n_{h+++}}\sum_{ijk}\varepsilon_{hijk}\right),$$

where the last summation is over all the grades given for essays on topic h. Equation (4.4) or, when appropriate, (4.5) applied to each term yields

$$\mathbf{E}(S_1) = \sigma_\alpha^2 \sum_{h=1}^{H}\sum_{i^*=1}^{I} n_{hi^*++}\left(1 - \frac{2n_{hi^*++}}{n_{h+++}} + \frac{1}{n_{h+++}^2}\sum_{i=1}^{I} n_{hi++}^2\right)$$

$$+ \sigma_\gamma^2 \sum_{h=1}^{H}\sum_{i^*=1}^{I} n_{hi^*++}\left(1 - \frac{2n_{hi^*++}}{n_{h+++}} + \frac{1}{n_{h+++}^2}\sum_{i=1}^{I} n_{hi++}^2\right)$$

$$+ \sigma_\beta^2 \sum_{h=1}^{H}\sum_{j^*=1}^{J} n_{h+j^*+}\left(1 - \frac{2n_{h+j^*+}}{n_{h+++}} + \frac{1}{n_{h+++}^2}\sum_{j=1}^{J} n_{h+j+}^2\right)$$

$$+ \sigma_\delta^2 \sum_{h=1}^{H}\sum_{j^*=1}^{J} n_{h+j^*+}\left(1 - \frac{2n_{h+j^*+}}{n_{h+++}} + \frac{1}{n_{h+++}^2}\sum_{j=1}^{J} n_{h+j+}^2\right)$$

$$+ \sigma_\varepsilon^2 \sum_{h=1}^{H} n_{h+++}\left(1 - \frac{1}{n_{h+++}}\right),$$

which simplifies to

$$\mathbf{E}(S_1) = (\sigma_\alpha^2 + \sigma_\gamma^2)\left(N - \sum_{h=1}^{H}\frac{1}{n_{h+++}}\sum_{i=1}^{I} n_{hi++}^2\right) + \sigma_\varepsilon^2(N - H)$$

$$+ (\sigma_\beta^2 + \sigma_\delta^2)\left(N - \sum_{h=1}^{H}\frac{1}{n_{h+++}}\sum_{j=1}^{J} n_{h+j+}^2\right). \tag{4.6}$$

Expressions for the other SSQ statistics are derived by the same method. We give them below without proof.

$$\mathbf{E}(S_2) = (\sigma_\mu^2 + \sigma_\gamma^2)\left(N - \sum_{i=1}^{I} \frac{1}{n_{+i++}} \sum_{h=1}^{H} n_{hi++}^2\right)$$

$$+ \sigma_\beta^2\left(N - \sum_{i=1}^{I} \frac{1}{n_{+i++}} \sum_{j=1}^{J} n_{+ij+}^2\right)$$

$$+ (\sigma_\delta^2 + \sigma_\varepsilon^2)(N - I), \tag{4.7}$$

$$\mathbf{E}(S_3) = (\sigma_\mu^2 + \sigma_\delta^2)\left(N - \sum_{j=1}^{J} \frac{1}{n_{++j+}} \sum_{h=1}^{H} n_{h+j+}^2\right)$$

$$+ \sigma_\alpha^2\left(N - \sum_{j=1}^{J} \frac{1}{n_{++j+}} \sum_{i=1}^{I} n_{+ij+}^2\right)$$

$$+ (\sigma_\gamma^2 + \sigma_\varepsilon^2)(N - J), \tag{4.8}$$

$$\mathbf{E}(S_4) = (\sigma_\beta^2 + \sigma_\delta^2 + \sigma_\varepsilon^2)(N - n_{+++1}), \tag{4.9}$$

$$\mathbf{E}(S_5) = (\sigma_\alpha^2 + \sigma_\gamma^2 + \sigma_\varepsilon^2)\left(N - \sum_{h=1}^{H} J_h\right), \tag{4.10}$$

where J_h is the number of raters who graded at least one essay on topic h and

$$\mathbf{E}(S_6) = \sigma_\mu^2\left(N - \frac{1}{N} \sum_{h=1}^{H} n_{h+++}^2\right)$$

$$+ \sigma_\alpha^2\left(N - \frac{1}{N} \sum_{i=1}^{I} n_{+i++}^2\right)$$

$$+ \sigma_\gamma^2\left(N - \frac{1}{N} \sum_{h=1}^{H} \sum_{i=1}^{I} n_{hi++}^2\right)$$

$$+ \sigma_\beta^2\left(N - \frac{1}{N} \sum_{j=1}^{J} n_{++j+}^2\right)$$

$$+ \sigma_\delta^2\left(N - \frac{1}{N} \sum_{h=1}^{H} \sum_{j=1}^{J} n_{h+j+}^2\right) + \sigma_\varepsilon^2(N - 1). \tag{4.11}$$

The population mean μ can be estimated as the sample mean of all the ratings, $y_{....}$, or as the mean of the topic-wise means, $(y_{1...} + \ldots + y_{H...})/H$. Alternative estimators may be based on the mean grades for each essay, $n_{hi.1}^{-1} \sum_{hi} y_{hi..}$, or similar. Efficiency of estimation of μ is rarely an issue because usually a large number of essays are written. The variance of the sample mean $y_{....}$ is

$$\operatorname{var}(y_{....}) = \frac{\sigma_\varepsilon^2}{N} + \frac{1}{N^2} \left(\sigma_\mu^2 \sum_h^H n_{h...}^2 + \sigma_\alpha^2 \sum_i^I n_{.i..}^2 \right)$$

$$+ \frac{1}{N^2} \left(\sigma_\gamma^2 \sum_h^H \sum_i^I n_{hi..}^2 + \sigma_\beta^2 \sum_j^J n_{..j.}^2 + \sigma_\delta^2 \sum_h \sum_j n_{h.j.}^2 \right).$$

When the test consists of a single item, the six moment matching equations collapse to just three because the variance due to item differences, σ_μ^2, cannot be distinguished from the overall mean μ, and the general and item-specific true scores and severities cannot be separated. The model in (4.2) then simplifies to the model in (2.1).

4.4 Application

The National Assessment of Educational Progress (NAEP) is an extensive programme of educational surveys designed to monitor primary and secondary education in the United States. In the Writing Assessment of NAEP for grade 8 students in 1992, examinees were assigned 2 essay topics out of a pool of 11 topics by a systematic non-informative design (spiralling). The survey sample comprised 11 112 students. The students' essays were assessed by 27 raters of whom 2 graded a total of 3 essays, and the other 25 graded 350–1700 essays each. The essay topics were classified into three categories according to the nature of the writing task (persuasive writing, informative writing, and story-telling). Each rater graded essays from one category of topics. The integer scoring scale 1–6 was used, with other grades for non-response, writing off topic, and the like. The essays were first graded once each by non-informatively assigned raters. Then the essays written by a random sample of students were regraded, with the 'second' raters assigned at random with the proviso that no essay be graded twice by the same rater. However, a rater may have graded both essays written by a student. The data were provided by John Mazzeo and Steve Wang of ETS.

In the analysis, non-response, writing off topic, and the like were disregarded. As a consequence, 225 students (2 percent) were excluded from the analysis. If an essay received a score in the range 1–6 and another score outside this range (for instance, judged to be off topic by one rater), the former score was retained and the latter discarded. In total, 10 887 students

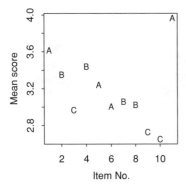 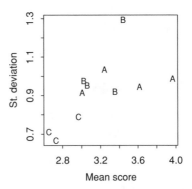

FIGURE 4.1. Mean scores for the item topics in NAEP Writing Assessment. The symbols 'A', 'B', and 'C' indicate the classification of the topic.

submitted 18 035 essays that were awarded a score in the range 1–6 by at least one rater; 3739 students submitted only one essay each (they failed to score on the other essay). Altogether, 4767 essays had second ratings in the range 1–6; 2730 students received one grade in the range 1–6 (one essay, rated once), 6268 students received two grades (one essay rated twice or two essays each rated once), 20 students three grades, and 1869 four grades.

The numbers of essays written on each topic were in the range 1597–1671, of which 414–462 were graded twice. The 11 essay topics were classified into the three categories as follows: persuasive writing — topics 1, 5, 6, and 11; informative writing — topics 2, 4, 7, and 8, and story-telling — topics 3, 9, and 10. Figure 4.1 summarizes the difficulties of topics. In the left-hand-side panel, the mean score for each item is plotted against the index (Item No.); the symbols 'A', 'B', and 'C' denote the three categories of topics. In calculating the means, each rating is given the same weight, and so an essay that has been rated twice is effectively given double weight. We checked that other weighting schemes do not alter the means appreciably. The means are based on more than 2000 ratings each, and so they are associated with very small sampling variation. The diagram shows a strong association of difficulty with item order (with the exception of item 11), although it also seems that topics 'C' are more difficult than 'A' or 'B'.

The right-hand-side panel of the diagram contains the plot of the (raw) standard deviations of the ratings against the mean scores. There is a strong association of difficulty with dispersion; more difficult items (lower mean scores) are associated with a smaller variance. The variance is calculated as the sample variance of all the ratings, so that an essay that has been rated twice is given more weight. Other weighing schemes do not alter the impression of the strong association. Figure 4.2 displays the histograms of the first ratings for each essay. The score distributions differ a great deal from essay to essay.

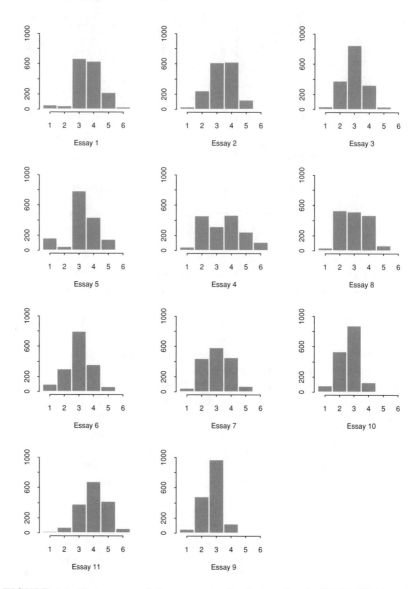

FIGURE 4.2. Histograms of the scores in the first rating in NAEP Writing Assessment. Each histogram represents an essay topic.

TABLE 4.2. Raters' workloads in NAEP Writing Assessment.

Essay topic	Topics A									
	400	402	403	404	405	406	407	408	427	607
1	177	184	297	270	163	255	313	437	1	0
5	171	172	274	287	167	253	289	404	0	1
6	161	176	262	268	171	267	330	420	0	0
11	196	180	281	265	165	266	315	437	0	0
Total	705	712	1114	1090	666	1041	1246	1697	1	1

	Topics B									
	400	410	411	412	413	414	415	416	417	418
2	0	115	181	204	222	362	216	311	229	255
4	0	107	179	201	228	359	214	314	236	254
7	0	123	158	197	209	365	198	296	244	253
8	1	133	179	198	220	361	214	309	241	243
Total	1	478	697	800	879	1447	842	1230	950	1005

	Topics C										
	400	415	420	421	422	423	424	425	426	427	428
3	0	1	183	342	391	316	211	358	1	147	106
9	0	1	181	359	382	311	221	360	0	138	122
10	1	0	185	350	400	311	198	363	1	139	120
Total	1	2	549	1051	1173	938	630	1081	2	426	348

Note: The panels in the first column correspond to the topics in category A (persuasive writing), those in the second column to the topics in category B (informative writing), and those in the third column to the topics in category C (story-telling).

Disregarding five ratings, the raters were divided into three non-overlapping categories that were engaged solely for grading one category of essays. Table 4.2 summarizes the rater's workloads. Apart from a few ratings, each essay topic was graded by eight to nine raters with workloads in the range 106–437.

4.4.1 Itemwise analyses

We consider first each essay topic separately and estimate the sources of variation due to (essay-topic specific) true scores, rater severity, and inconsistency. The estimates of the variance components are given in Table 4.3.

The estimates of the variances indicate that the rating process is of very high quality, even though the true-score variance is small relative to the scoring scale. The correlations of the grades with the true scores, $\sqrt{\hat{\sigma}_a^2/(\hat{\sigma}_a^2 + \hat{\sigma}_b^2 + \hat{\sigma}_e^2)}$, are in the range 0.908–0.957. Since the rater severity variance is much greater than inconsistency variance and most raters have large workloads, the scheme adjusting for rater severity (**sAdj**, see Chapter 3) is likely to be very effective, although the MSEs of the scores are very low. In fact, the severities of most raters are estimated with high precision. For instance, the mean score for item 1 is 3.625, and the trivial estimate of severity of rater 400 is $3.790 - 3.625 = 0.175$. Ignoring the sampling variance of the overall mean of the grades for item 1, the standard deviation of the severity estimate is $\sqrt{(0.854 + 0.027)/177} = 0.066$. Using the scheme **sAdj**, the estimate of severity is adjusted to 0.147 with MSE equal to 0.058^2.

Since most raters have large workloads and have graded several topics, we can explore how raters' severities change from topic to topic. For instance, rater 400 graded 177, 171, 161, and 196 essays on the respective topics 1, 5, 6, and 11. The estimates of the corresponding severities are 0.147, 0.070, –0.022, and –0.035. Figure 4.3 displays the pairwise scatterplots of the estimated severities for the eight raters who graded more than 100 essays on each of these topics. The small number of raters does not permit reliable estimation of the association of the severities across the topics. However, a strong association of the severities is rather unlikely. In the next section, variation of raters' severities across topics is assessed more formally.

Small true-score variances, for topics C in particular, suggest that the scoring scale is not used effectively. In fact, these topics are more difficult than the rest; the scores 5 and 6 are awarded very rarely.

4.4.2 Simultaneous analysis

The simultaneous analysis of the 11 essay topics yields the following estimates:

TABLE 4.3. Variance component estimates for the essay topics in NAEP Writing Assessment.

Essay topic	Counts		Variances		
	Students	Graded twice	True scores $\hat{\sigma}_a^2$	Severity $\hat{\sigma}_b^2$	Inconsistency $\hat{\sigma}_e^2$
		Topics A			
1	1656	439	0.854	0.097	0.027
5	1597	422	1.043	0.088	0.019
6	1641	414	0.812	0.133	0.021
11	1643	462	0.935	0.112	0.028
		Topics B			
2	1671	424	0.823	0.128	0.019
4	1661	431	1.652	0.133	0.019
7	1621	422	0.851	0.144	0.037
8	1648	451	0.908	0.158	0.032
		Topics C			
3	1640	416	0.606	0.058	0.013
9	1638	437	0.436	0.035	0.006
10	1639	429	0.494	0.056	0.010

$$\hat{\sigma}_\mu^2 = 0.152, \qquad \hat{\sigma}_\alpha^2 = 0.329, \qquad \hat{\sigma}_\gamma^2 = 0.432,$$
$$\hat{\sigma}_\beta^2 = 0.059, \qquad \hat{\sigma}_\delta^2 = -0.050, \qquad \hat{\sigma}_\varepsilon = 0.116.$$

The occurrence of a negative estimated variance is somewhat disconcerting. The fitted model suggests that variation in severity across the topics (σ_δ^2) is small. This is clearly not borne out by the scatterplots in Figure 4.3. Also, the estimated inconsistency variance, σ_ε^2, is much greater than either of its topic-specific counterparts. The results are in conflict with our expectations because the model assumptions are grossly violated. According to the model in (4.2), the variance of each score is constant:

$$\text{var}(y_{hijk} \mid h) = \sigma_\alpha^2 + \sigma_\gamma^2 + \sigma_\beta^2 + \sigma_\delta^2 + \sigma_\varepsilon^2.$$

However, the analysis in the previous section showed that these variances are vastly different. The results in Table 4.3 imply that it may be appropriate to analyse separately each category of topics. This is meaningful because the categories represent different writing skills. The fact that each category is represented by too few topics affects mainly the estimation of the difficulty variance σ_μ^2, which happens to be of least interest.

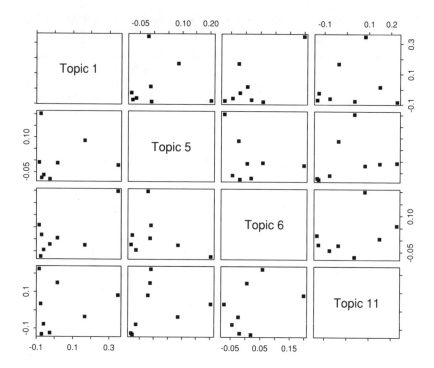

FIGURE 4.3. Scatterplots of the topic-specific severities for Topics A in NAEP Writing Assessment.

For illustration, we analyse the essays writen on topics A (items 1, 5, 6, and 10). The estimates of the variances are

$$\hat{\sigma}^2_\mu = 0.139, \qquad \hat{\sigma}^2_\alpha = 0.616, \qquad \hat{\sigma}^2_\gamma = 0.361,$$
$$\hat{\sigma}^2_\beta = 0.037, \qquad \hat{\sigma}^2_\delta = 0.022, \qquad \hat{\sigma}_\varepsilon = 0.040.$$

These estimates are much closer to what we would expect from the item-wise analyses (Table 4.3), and so the results are easier to interpret. The within-examinee variance σ^2_γ is quite large. A possible explanation is that examinees concentrated on their first essays, and then performed with less enthusiasm on their second essays. Indeed, the mean score for the first essays is 3.42, and the mean for the second essays 3.03. This comparison is compounded by the possibly informative missingness; it is feasible that the examinees who did not score on their second essays would have scored lower than if they had made an effort. Certainly, many more examinees (2664) failed to score on their second essays than on their first essays (149).

However, this observation defeats the purpose of the survey as well as of the analysis, because our most important findings relate to the following artefacts: quality of rating, stability of raters' severities, informative missingness, motivation of the examinees, and the like. Nevertheless, it is

TABLE 4.4. Variance component estimates for the essay topics in NAEP Reading Assessment.

Essay topic	Counts		Variances		
	Students	Graded twice	True scores $\hat{\sigma}_a^2$	Severity $\hat{\sigma}_b^2$	Inconsistency $\hat{\sigma}_e^2$
1	1443	367	0.714	0.054	0.0077
2	1187	299	0.752	0.079	0.0150
3	1375	371	0.954	0.056	0.0064
4	1524	419	0.816	0.072	0.0134
5	1252	306	0.842	0.031	0.0033
6	1543	421	0.653	0.049	0.0058

intriguing that the rating in NAEP assessment is so much more consistent than in any of the AP tests analysed in Chapter 3. We can only speculate that the target population is so diverse in ability that their classification into a small number of categories is straightforward. However, borderline cases are bound to arise, and disagreement in the rating of such essays is likely. The results suggest that there are very few such cases or that the adopted scoring rubric was well understood and almost identically interpreted by the engaged raters.

High quality of rating in NAEP is not confined to the Writing Assessment. Table 4.4 summarizes the itemwise analyses for six items in the NAEP Reading Assessment of the eighth-graders. Here the rating is just as consistent as in the Writing Assessment.

4.5   Choice of essay topics

Compared to responding to a multiple-choice item, writing an essay takes much longer and it is usually a much more complex and strenuous mental exercise. As a consequence, an examinee cannot be subjected to a test comprising a large number of essay topics. Essay topics are unavoidably associated with a lot of context unrelated to the assessed trait. When ability to compose text in English is to be measured, the actual topic is an undesirable element of the context. An examinee's performance may be severely hampered by a lack of interest in the topic, no experience or relevance of the topic, or some other objection to the topic. Similarly, when factual knowledge of a domain (say, history) is measured, ability to compose text is an undesirable, yet unavoidable, element of the context.

The representation of the domain is also under threat because of the small number of topics that can be administered. An attractive alternative to the standard test format is to offer the examinees a choice of essay topics. For instance, the examinees may be asked to write essays on any two out of a set of six topics. In this way, given an intelligent choice by the examinee, the undesirable elements of the context may be minimized.

Choice of essay topics raises a host of issues associated with 'fair' or valid (performance) assessment. Some topics may be more difficult than others, or relatively more difficult for examinees of high (low) ability. Inference about such properties of the topics is hard to come by because the (self-)assignment of the topics to examinees is, by design, informative; examinees write on the topics on which they believe they can do best. Unlike multiple-choice items, topics cannot be pretested because, owing to their small numbers, they can be easily memorized by the examinees. Just as for multiple-choice items, prediction of the item properties without a trial administration is subject to too much uncertainty.

Suppose each essay is rated on the same scale. For the moment, assume that the rating is perfect, so that the true scores are available for each essay. In designing a scoring rule (combining the essay scores), we may want to compensate for the differential difficulty of the essay topics, about which the examinees would have no information. What strategy should an examinee adopt? Write an essay on the most difficult, but otherwise favoured, topic, or write on the easiest topic, even though the essay will not attest fully to the examinee's ability? It is important that the uneven ability to make such a decision does not erode the validity of the test. Yet, without information about the item properties of the topics, the administrators cannot give any intelligent advice on how to choose among the topics with a view toward their difficulty. Even if such information were available and appropriately phrased for the examinees, it may not be fully understood or perfectly implemented by them.

In some domains, choice of topics is in concordance with the generally accepted notion of validity. For instance, in a history test, it may be appropriate to assess an examinee's ability by his/her specialty; good knowledge of a narrow but important period in the history of a country, which demonstrates the grasp of general principles of the academic field, would be sufficient and rated higher than superficial acquaintance with historical events spanning several eras. On the other hand, the lack of proficiency in a subdomain, say, of mathematics, is generally regarded as a cause for a lower grade; comprehensive mastery of the domain is desired. Even here, choice may be justified, for instance, to avoid unfamiliar context in the verbal passages of some of the problems.

Choice is certainly a very convenient feature for the examinees and may contribute to the validity of the test. Choice may enhance the motivation of the examinees by enabling them to focus on their strengths. The difficulties associated with the choice of topics are the dependence of performance on the choice made by the examinee, the administrator's inability to assist in this choice, and the definition of a scoring rule that would take account of the differential difficulties of the items, which are themselves difficult to estimate. Of course, all these issues are further compounded by imperfect (subjective) rating of the essays.

In the next section, we consider a model for examinee behaviour in choosing essay topics. In Section 4.5.2, we set up a simulation framework to study the impact of choice on the scores. We illustrate how simulated data can be used to explore when the assumptions of non-informative selection, which would lead to a simple analysis of the topics and a simple scoring rule, are inappropriate.

4.5.1 Modelling choice

Suppose each examinee $i = 1, \ldots I$ has a true score θ_i for a given domain represented by essay topics $h = 1, \ldots, H$. For each essay, we define the topic-specific true score, θ_{hi}. We assume that if a topic were somehow separated from the context irrelevant to the domain, the topic-specific true scores would be linearly related to the domain-true score; that is, there are constants a_h and b_h such that

$$\theta_{hi}^* = a_h + b_h \theta_i \,,$$

where θ_{hi}^* is the context-free topic-specific true score. The constants a_h and b_h can be interpreted as the *difficulty* and *discrimination* of topic h. To avoid problems with identification, assume that the true scores θ_i are centred around zero and have unit variance. Then a_h is the context-free true score for topic h for an examinee with domain-true score $\theta = 0$, and b_h is the difference of context-free true scores corresponding to a unit difference (one standard deviation) of the domain-true scores. The difference $\delta_{hi} = \theta_{hi}^* - \theta_{hi}$ is the impact of the context of topic h on examinee i. Note that δ_{hi} does not involve any measurement (score assignment) error.

The relative importance of the context is described by the variance of context deviations δ_{hi}, denoted by σ_δ^2. The greater the variance σ_δ^2, the more important the context, that is, the greater the uncertainty associated with selection of the topic using a non-informative strategy (disregarding the knowledge of $\{\theta_{hi}\}_h$).

Of the true scores defined, θ_i, θ_{hi}^*, and θ_{hi}, θ_i is of principal interest, but only some scores θ_{hi} are realized through the observed scores s_{hi}. Suppose the deviations $\varepsilon_{hi} = s_{hi} - \theta_{hi}$ have (measurement error) variance σ_ε^2. The deviations ε_{hi} and δ_{hi} and the true scores θ_i are mutually independent.

A general class of non-informative selection strategies are given by probability distributions on the sets of all possible topic selections; each examinee selects a set of topics by a random draw from this distribution. Such a strategy is clearly unrealistic. In a more realistic strategy, each examinee selects the subset of topics that yields the highest true-score total $\theta_{h_1,i} + \ldots + \theta_{h_L,i}$, where L is the number of topics to be selected and $h_1, \ldots, h_L$ are the topics selected by examinee i. We refer to this strategy as *score maximization*.

In the scoring rule implied by this strategy (adding up the essay scores), examinees who select more difficult topics are disadvantaged because, on average, a performance of the same quality is converted to lower scores. If the difficulty and discrimination parameters a_h and b_h were known (or estimated), adding up the normalized observed scores,

$$\sum_{l=1}^{L} \frac{s_{h_l,i} - a_{h_l}}{b_{h_l}},$$

would be more appropriate. Therefore, the optimal strategy of an examinee would be to maximize the true-score version of this score. We refer to this strategy as *normalized score maximization.*

These strategies, although reasonable, are also unrealistic because an examinee is unlikely to assess his/her strengths accurately and pick the 'optimal' topics. A more realistic scenario is that an examinee selects the optimal strategy with a certain probability, selects all but one of the 'optimal' topics and the remaining one at random with a smaller probability, and so on. Such strategies are akin (though not identical) to mixtures of the optimal and the non-informative strategies. The examinees' responses contain no information about the strategy adopted. Even if interviewed after the test, an examinee may neither precisely formulate the strategy adopted nor assess with desired accuracy how he/she would have performed on the other topics.

The examinees may select the topics and, after writing the essays, may be asked to write essays on the topics they did not select. Such a scheme may provide some information about the selection strategies, although by its nature the scheme fails to be realistic; the examinees' performances are affected by the circumstances.

4.5.2 Simulations

To gain insight into the impact of choice on the scores and their validity, we consider a number of setups and generate data artificially according to the model described in the previous section. For simplicity, we assume that all the random variables are normally distributed. We intend to give no definite answers but merely to indicate how the impact of choice can be explored.

Suppose, for illustration, that there are 1000 examinees and they have to select $L = 2$ out of $H = 6$ topics. The domain-true scores of the examinees are generated as random draws from $\mathcal{N}(0, 1)$. The difficulty parameters are randomly drawn from $\mathcal{U}(5, 7)$ and the discrimination parameters are drawn from $\mathcal{U}(1, 3)$. All the random draws are mutually independent. These quantities define the context-free true scores θ_{hi}^{*}.

Next, we generate the true scores θ_{hi} and then the observed scores s_{hi} by adding randomly drawn deviations δ_{hi} and ε_{hi}, drawn from $\mathcal{N}(0, 2)$

and $\mathcal{N}(0, 1)$, respectively. For the non-informative selection strategy, we generate the probabilities of the pairs of selected items as follows: we define an order for the set of all possible choices and draw a random sample of the same length, $6 \times 5/2 = 15$, from $\mathcal{U}(0, 1)$. The normalized cumulative totals of these draws (normalized, so as to add up to unity) are formed. An examinee is simulated to have selected the pair corresponding to the interval of the cumulative totals into which a new draw from $\mathcal{U}(0, 1)$ falls. To enhance the realistic nature of the simulation, all the observed scores can be rounded.

Note that the variance components σ_δ^2 and σ_ε^2 cannot be identified from the totals $\delta_{hi} + \varepsilon_{hi}$. Nevertheless, we generate the topic-specific true scores θ_{hi} because they play a role in the informative strategies.

Apart from the three true scores defined earlier, we have the total of the true scores for the selected items. Each examinee has the following 'observed' scores:

- the total for all the topics, $s_{1i} + s_{2i} + \ldots + s_{Hi}$;

- the total for the selected topics $s_{h_1,i} + \ldots + s_{h_L,i}$ (for each strategy);

- the normalized versions;

- the rounded versions.

The normalization of the scores, $(s_{hi} - a_h)/b_h$, can be carried out using the true values of a_h and b_h, their estimates based on all the HI observed scores s_{hi}, the estimates based on the realized observed scores (assuming non-informative selection of topics), or by assuming a specific informative selection process. Of interest is for how many examinees the strategy applied makes a difference, and to what extent. A secondary issue is the bias incurred in estimating the topic parameters.

In the simulation, the following difficulty and discrimination parameters were generated:

Difficulty:	6.15	5.08	5.61	6.08	6.47	6.46
Discrimination:	1.31	1.28	1.23	1.40	1.99	1.24

The realized abilities θ_i, $i = 1, \ldots, 1000$, were in the range -2.88 to 3.41. The context-free true scores θ_{hi}, $h = 1, \ldots, 6$, were in the range 0.75–12.25. Since only 17 scores were greater than 10.5, this is a reasonable simulation of the scores on the scale 1–10. The mean and median score was 5.93, and the topic-specific means and medians were in the range 5.03–6.46, very close to the difficulty parameters. The context-specific true scores add a further source of variation to the scores. These scores are in the range -3.5 to 16.4. Observed scores contain yet another source of variation; these are in the range -4.1 to 16.6, with about 100 negative scores and 400 scores (out of 6000) greater than 10.0. The test-form scores are computed as the

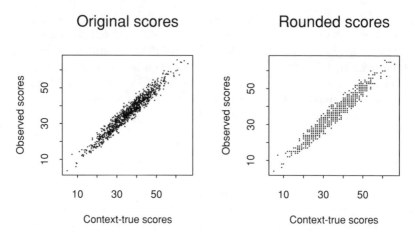

FIGURE 4.4. Simulated observed and context-specific true scores; totals over the six topics.

totals of the scores over the six essays. Their observed and context-specific true-score versions are plotted in Figure 4.4. In the right-hand plot, the rounded versions of these scores are used.

Of course, in a realistic setting, these scores would not be realized because each examinee would select only two topics. First, we consider non-informative selection of the pairs of items. Using the random mechanism described above, the pairs of items were assigned probabilities in the range 0.0015–0.101, and random drawing using these probabilities resulted in the assignment of the following numbers of essays for the topics 1–6: 304, 373, 402, 322, 190, and 409. Topics 5 and 6 happen to be the easiest, and so the 'unpopularity' of topic 5 may be an unrealistic feature of the simulation.

For the selected pair of topics, we calculate the corresponding true and observed scores. They are only modestly correlated with the true scores because of the sources of uncertainty as well as being based on fewer topics. For orientation, Figure 4.5 contains plots of the true and observed scores for the selected items (top panels). The bottom panels of the diagram plot the scores for the selected pair against the total scores for the six (hypothetical) essays. Note that the association of the scores for the selected pair of items and the total scores would be easy to evaluate only if the items had identical parameters.

Next, we apply the three informative strategies and two scoring rules. For each examinee, we select the pair of topics on which he/she would attain the highest

- true-score total $\theta_{h_1,i} + \theta_{h_2,i}$;

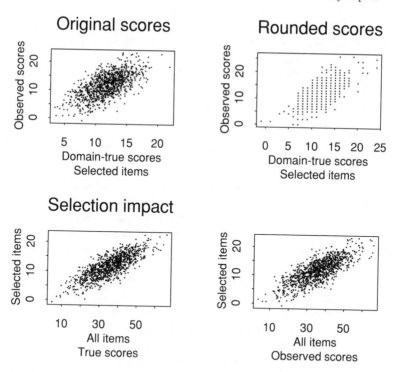

FIGURE 4.5. The impact of selection on the true and observed scores.

- normalized true-score total

$$\frac{\theta_{h_1,i} - a_{h_1}}{b_{h_1}} + \frac{\theta_{h_2,i} - a_{h_2}}{b_{h_2}} ;$$

- estimated normalized true-score total

$$\frac{\theta_{h_1,i} - \hat{a}_{h_1}}{\hat{b}_{h_1}} + \frac{\theta_{h_2,i} - \hat{a}_{h_2}}{\hat{b}_{h_2}} ,$$

where $\hat{a}_h$ and $\hat{b}_h$ are estimates of the difficulty and discrimination parameters. For simplicity, we estimate them from the observed scores realized by the non-informative strategy. The estimates are obtained by matching the means and variances of the observed scores.

For each strategy, we consider two scoring rules: the total score and the normalized total score. Thus, each examinee has six different scores, and of interest is the association of these scores with the domain-true score θ_i.

For 627 examinees, all three selection strategies yield the same pair of topics. Whether the exact or estimated normalization is applied makes little difference in comparison to the maximum score strategy. The two strategies based on the normalized scores agree for 857 examinees and have one item in common for another 61 examinees. The maximum score and maximum normalized score strategies coincide for 653 examinees and another 95 examinees have one item in common.

Figure 4.6 contains pairwise plots of the six different scores and the true score. The first three rows and columns correspond to total scores, the next three to the totals of the normalized scores, and the last one to the domain-true score. In the plots, a large number of points are on the identity line $y = x$ because the different strategies lead to the selection of the same topics. We see that the scores are about equally strongly associated with the domain-true score. However, the choice of the strategy matters for a large number of examinees and to an appreciable extent, and so does the scoring method. We emphasize that this conclusion is contingent on the several sets of parameters (item difficulty and discrimination parameters in particular), as well as on the realized samples of small size. A more thorough insight, which nevertheless confirms our observations, can be gained by replicating the simulation.

Is choice a good idea? If the same pair of topics were assigned to each examinee, these topics would be a poor representation of the tested domain. If each examinee were assigned a pair of topics at random, would the resulting scores be more closely associated than if a choice of topics were permitted? The plots of the domain-true score against the total scores derived by the three strategies considered and the content true-score total over all six essays in Figure 4.7 indicate that the perfect selection strategies yield scores that are more strongly associated with the domain-true score than if non-informative selection were applied. In the figure, the total scores, without normalization, are used. Normalization has a negligible impact on these associations. The correlations of the selection strategy scores with the domain-true score are 0.71 and 0.72, whereas the correlation for the non-informative selection is 0.65. For comparison, the correlation of the total context-specific true scores (totals for six items) with the domain-true score is 0.86 and the correlation of the total of the observed scores is 0.83.

Most likely, examinees do not adhere to the simulated strategies because the examinees are not perfectly informed about their own abilities or the abilities of their peers, and they have to make judgements in a short time and in stressful circumstances. Note that a guess of the item difficulty and discrimination involves information about the population of examinees. The perfectly informed and non-informative strategies represent the extremes that delineate the dependence of the examinee scores on their choice behaviour. More realistic selection strategies can be devised by mixing the informed and non-informative strategies. For instance, we set the probability of an examinee making a perfect selection, the probability of selecting the best item informatively and the second one at random, and so on, and mix the strategies with these proportions. The realistic nature of the simulation can be further enhanced by setting these probabilities as functions of ability, although difficulties are likely to be encountered in setting these

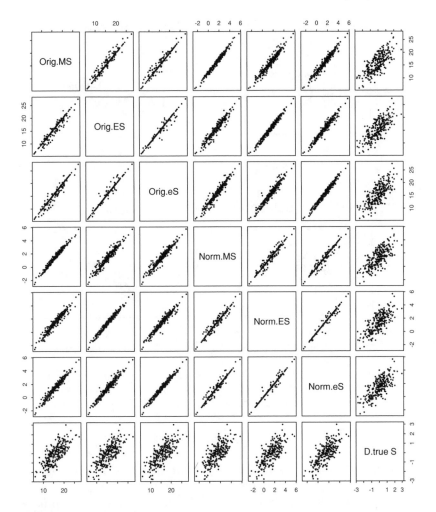

FIGURE 4.6. Pairwise plots of the scores for topics selected by perfectly informed selection strategies. The first three rows and columns correspond to total scores, the next three to normalized scores, and the last row and column correspond to the domain-true scores. The selection strategies are score maximization (rows 1 and 4), normalized score maximization using the 'true' difficulty and discrimination parameters (rows 2 and 5), and normalized maximization using estimated difficulty and discrimination (3 and 6).

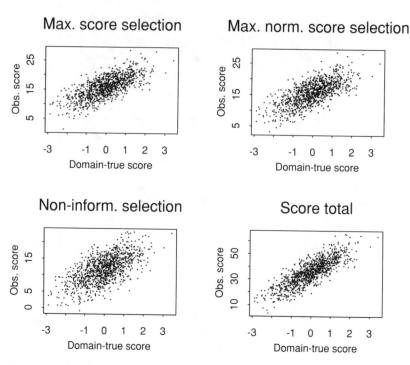

FIGURE 4.7. Association of the observed scores using the three selection strategies with ability. The strategies are: maximum score selection, maximum normalized score selection, and non-informative selection. The lower right-hand panel contains the plot of the total observed score (total for the six essays) against the domain-true score.

functions. But the principal difficulty is in making educated guesses about the parameters used in the simulation, based on the knowledge of the tested domain, population of examinees, and of the characteristics of the processes associated with test-taking and essay scoring.

4.6 Summary

The first part of the chapter developed models for simultaneous analysis of a pool of constructed-response items graded by raters. Pairs of variances are associated with examinees, items, and raters; within each pair, one component refers to the pool as a unit, and the other component describes variation across the items. The variances are estimated by the method of moments, which leads to a system of linear equations. In a realistic setting, the models are of limited applicability because they involve stringent variance homogeneity assumptions. However, when these assumptions are palatable, the models combine information across the items, thus enabling a compact description of a complex essay-rating exercise. The presented approach is motivated by generalizability theory; see Cronbach *et al.* (1972) and Brennan (1983) for more detailed background.

As yet unexplored extensions of these models allow for some of the variances themselves to vary across the items. This would accommodate variance heterogeneity observed in the analysed examples. However, a number of difficulties arise both with model specification and estimation.

In the second part, models for behaviour of examinees confronted with a choice of essay topics were discussed and a simulation-based approach to assessing the impact of the choice strategies on the examinees' scores was demonstrated. Although choice is a very desirable element of many educational tests, the validity of the scores awarded by trivial schemes is doubtful because of the number of unexplored factors associated with the choice. An examinee may write a better essay had he/she selected the topic than if he/she were assigned the same topic. This hypothesis is untestable, and so even if the estimates were in some way adjusted for non-informative assignment they would apply only to the same test format.

Experiments embedded in high-stakes administrations, such as asking the examinees to respond to the items they have not chosen [see Wang, Wainer, and Thissen (1993) for an example], are not satisfactory because the realistic nature of the experiment is undermined. For another perspective, see Wainer and Thissen (1994).

5

Summarizing item-level properties

5.1 Introduction

A typical educational test consists of a large number of multiple-choice items. In the construction and pretesting of a test form, particular attention is paid to every item of the form. Each item is screened for a number of possible faults, such as non-existence or non-uniqueness of the correct answer among the response options, use of words or expressions that may have a different connotation or may be more (or less) familiar to an ethnic category of examinees, may require non-elementary knowledge from a different subject area, and the like.

Without empirical data, a number of characteristics, such as difficulty and differential performance of the subpopulations of examinees, can at best only be conjectured from the reading passage of the item. They can be estimated much more reliably, although not without sampling error, from a trial administration of the test form. When such estimates are available, accompanied by their standard errors, it may not be a trivial task to sift through their values and assess whether the test form would be improved by excluding a particular item, by replacing it with a different item, or by altering it after a review.

From a different perspective, even a careful screening of the items may be insufficient to ensure that the test form has the desired characteristics. A situation may arise in which every item is 'good' (it satisfies a well-defined criterion), yet the test form as a unit has some undesirable properties. For some characteristics, the goal is an optimal *distribution* of the characteristic in the test form.

The traditional approach to refining of test forms is based on screening the items one by one. This avoids the impasse in which no item can be improved, yet the test form remains unsatisfactory. However, to an anxious examinee, all that matters is the *test score*; to other users of the test score, its validity is paramount. In a word, the test is perceived as an indivisible unit. One bad item among many good ones is not likely to erode the validity of the test as much as if a large proportion of the items were on the borderline between being 'good' and 'bad' items.

Construction of an item is a complex process comprising several rounds of reviews and fitting the item into the context of the test form. For testing programmes that administer high-stakes tests, such as SAT or GRE, several new forms are constructed for each administration date and annually there may be several administration dates. Each item is used only once and then it is discarded. Thus, over several years, thousands of discarded items are accumulated. When each item is associated with the estimate of an underlying quantity, these estimates can be comprehended in a meaningful way only through their formwise summaries.

This chapter discusses a method of summarizing itemwise characteristics at the test-form level. In brief, we consider the distribution of the 'true' values of the itemwise variables and put forward their mean and variance as compact test-level summaries of the characteristic. These summaries can then be used for comparisons across test forms, over time, and indeed, across tests.

We present the perspective that each item is too small a fraction of the test form to have a non-trivial impact on the test score. Therefore, item characteristics of interest are too 'fractured' elements of information about the properties of the test form. In this respect, it is more appropriate to regard them as a nuisance and focus on their test-level summaries, which are much more informative about the impact of the test form on the examinees' scores. But foremost, a test-level summary presents the information about the items in a much more digestible form, suitable for comparisons with other test forms and for setting standards for item characteristics and their distribution in a test form.

A parallel can be drawn with the rater reliability and score adjustment issues discussed in Chapters 2–4 where the raters represented a nuisance, yet the summaries of their impact on the essay scores, the severity and inconsistency variances, were instrumental in assessing the quality of the rating process. These summaries were also important for adjusting the scores so as to reduce the impact of the raters.

Trial administrations, also called pretests, are frequently used to verify that newly assembled test forms have the desired properties. Data from a pretest can be used to 'fine-tune' the test form, for instance, by reviewing some of the items. An item characteristic is likely to depend on the examinee population, and so the examinees for the pretest have to be recruited from the same population as the examinees in a future administration. It is important to arrange that the trial administration (pretest) is conducted under conditions as close as possible to those in the operational administration. Motivating the examinees to perform to the best of their abilities, to use the same strategies as in a 'real' test, is often a considerable challenge. Comparisons of item characteristics across administrations of the same test form are useful for assessing the dependence of the characteristic on the context: the examinee population, time, motivation, or a combination of these. Item-by-item comparisons are problematic because they involve a large number of quantities, each subject to sizeable sampling error. Variance summaries defined in this chapter resolve these problems by collating information about the item characteristic of interest over the test form.

We illustrate these summaries in examples concerned with screening of items for differential item functioning (DIF). Section 5.2 gives the substantive background to DIF and defines the Mantel-Haenszel statistic (Mantel and Haenszel, 1959). In Section 5.3, a test-level summary of DIF, called the DIF variance, is introduced. Section 5.4 discusses estimation of the DIF variance. In Section 5.5, several examples are analysed. Section 5.6 illustrates how estimation of the DIF coefficients can be improved by incorporating information about the DIF variance or, equivalently, by borrowing strength from the other items. Model criticism and diagnostic procedures are discussed in Section 5.7.

Extensions of the approach, discussed in Section 5.8, provide effective summaries for differences in DIF from one population of examinees to another and for exploration of the association of DIF with other item-level attributes. The chapter is concluded with a summary outlining a fuller potential of the approach.

5.2   Differential item functioning

In a test for high school students, a mathematics problem requiring understanding of baseball rules can be justifiably criticized that it puts female students and those not acquainted with the game at a disadvantage. Had another problem requiring the same *mathematical* skills, insight, and manipulation been posed, female students would have performed, on average, much better. Of course, an item may have a similar deficiency that is much more difficult to identify by a mere inspection. It is desirable to have an alternative (empirical) method that would complement the subjective judgement of expert reviewers.

Consider the hypothetical situation in which each examinee's ability is known. The examinees take a test form and their responses to each item are classified as correct or incorrect. Suppose the examinees belong to two well-identified categories, such as men and women, called the *reference* and the *focal* groups. An item is said to be unbiased if within every level of ability, the chance of a correct response to the item does not depend on the examinee's group.

In practice, the ability of an examinee is not known and is estimated as the test score from his/her responses to the items. Suppose there are K possible test scores, t_k, $k = 1, \ldots, K$. For each item i and a pair of categories of examinees, we consider the set of K 2×2 tables:

	Correct	Incorrect
Reference	A_{ik}	B_{ik}
Focal	C_{ik}	D_{ik}

where 'Reference' and 'Focal' are the designations of the two subpopulations (groups), and A_{ik}, B_{ik}, C_{ik}, and D_{ik} are the counts of examinees in the respective cells, whose test scores are equal to t_k. Let $n_{ik} = A_{ik} + B_{ik} + C_{ik} + D_{ik}$ be the total number of examinees with total score t_k who attended item i (when each examinee responds to every item, n_{ik} does not depend on i). Underlying the counts $A_{ik}, \ldots, D_{ik}$ are the population proportions $p_{A,ik}, \ldots, p_{D,ik}$. No association of the group (reference/focal) with the response to item i (correct/incorrect) corresponds to the odds ratio

$$\psi_{ik} = \frac{p_{A,ik}\, p_{D,ik}}{p_{B,ik}\, p_{C,ik}}$$

being equal to unity for every score category k. This odds ratio can be estimated as $\hat{\phi}_{ik} = A_{ik}D_{ik}/B_{ik}C_{ik}$. In practice, there are usually many score categories, and so there may be many small counts n_{ik} even in very large administrations. For such pairs ik, the odds ratio ψ_{ik} would be poorly estimated. Instead, the odds ratio is assumed to be common to all score categories, $\psi_{ik} \equiv \psi_i$, and this common odds ratio is estimated by pooling information across the K tables:

$$\hat{\psi}_i = \frac{\sum_{k=1}^{K} A_{ik}\, D_{ik}}{\sum_{k=1}^{K} B_{ik}\, C_{ik}} \tag{5.1}$$

(Mantel and Haenszel, 1959). The total score is in the role of a conditioning variable (ψ_i is a conditional odd-ratio, given the total score). When a large number of total scores is realized, it may be necessary to group these scores (for instance, by rounding). In principle, any other variable interpretable as a stratifying variable closely related to the ability can be used instead. This variable is called the *matching variable*. A matching variable defined as a function of the responses to the analysed test form is called *internal*. If the matching variable is based on a different test(s), it is called *external*.

It is more convenient to work with the log-odds ratios, $\log(\psi_i)$, estimated by $\log(\hat{\psi}_i)$, so that the ideal corresponds to $\log(\psi_i) = 0$. Robins, Breslow, and Greenland (1986) derived an approximation to the sampling variance of $\log(\hat{\psi}_i)$:

$$
\begin{aligned}
S_i^2 &= \widehat{\mathrm{var}}\{\log(\hat{\psi}_i)\} \\
&= \frac{\sum_{k=1}^{K} n_{ik}^2 (A_{ik}D_{ik} + \hat{\psi}_i B_{ik}C_{ik})\{A_{ik} + D_{ik} + \hat{\psi}_i(B_{ik} + C_{ik})\}}{2\left(\sum_{k=1}^{K} A_{ik}D_{ik}/n_{ik}\right)^2}.
\end{aligned}
\tag{5.2}
$$

Also, in order to conform with certain conventions, instead of the log-odds ratio $\log(\psi_i)$ and its estimator $\log(\hat{\psi}_i)$, their –2.35 multiples are used,

$$
\alpha_i = -2.35\log(\psi_i), \qquad \hat{\alpha}_i = -2.35\log(\hat{\psi}_i).
$$

The sampling variance of $\hat{\alpha}_i$ is approximated by $s_i^2 = 2.35^2 S_i^2$. We refer to α_i as the DIF *coefficient* for item i, and to $\hat{\alpha}_i$, its estimate, as the DIF *statistic*. It is essential to distinguish between the DIF coefficient and the DIF statistic. The former is an unknown real number, interpretable as the 'true' DIF for the given test and administration, the latter, a function of the data, is a random variable. The DIF statistic is a consistent estimator of the DIF coefficient; that is, for very large sample sizes of the reference and focal groups within each test-score category, the DIF statistic is very close to the DIF coefficient.

An easy way of gaining a perspective of the value of a DIF coefficient is by making a connection to the probability scale. Suppose the DIF coefficient of an item is equal to unity. This corresponds to the log-odds ratio of $-1/2.35 = -0.43$, that is, odds ratio $\exp(-0.43) = 0.65$. If, given a value of the matching variable, the probability of a correct response is 0.5 in one group, the corresponding probability in the other group is $0.65/1.65 \doteq 0.4$; the conditional probability 0.3 for one group corresponds to 0.22 for the other group. Roughly, one point on the DIF scale corresponds to the difference of 0.10 on the probability scale for probabilities close to 0.5 and to somewhat smaller differences for probabilities closer to zero and unity. We see that differential item functioning is attempting to identify relatively small differences in probabilities, and so estimation of DIF coefficients is meaningful only when the sample sizes for both groups are large.

For a typical test-form administration, several pairs of reference and focal groups are defined (such as Male/Female, White/Black, White/Hispanic, White/Asian), and for each pair, the estimates $\hat{\alpha}_i$, $i = 1, \ldots, I$, and their approximate standard errors s_i are calculated. When the matching variable is the number of correct responses on the studied test form, the DIF statistics are self-norming in the sense that their total is $\hat{\alpha}_1 + \ldots + \hat{\alpha}_I \doteq 0$. In an ideal test form, the DIF coefficient is equal to zero for every item.

Of course, owing to the sampling errors, the DIF statistics would not be identically equal to zero even for such an ideal form.

Trivial summaries of DIF for a test form include counting the number of items with outlying DIF statistics (such as $|\hat{\alpha}_i| > 1$), the number of items with DIF statistics nominally significantly different from zero (say, $|\hat{\alpha}_i|/s_i > 1.96$), or a combination of such criteria. These summaries have very poor resampling properties because they involve small counts and they capitalize on chance. A simple simulation experiment can be conducted to show that the number of items i with $|\hat{\alpha}_i| > 1$ is a biased estimator of the number of items with $|\alpha_i| > 1$, unless the standard errors s_i are negligible.

See Holland and Thayer (1988) and Holland and Wainer (1993) for further background to DIF. There are two notable alternatives to the method based on the Mantel-Haenszel DIF statistic: the standardization method (Dorans and Kulick, 1986) and an item-response model based method (Shealy and Stout, 1993). Our approach is applicable for either method because its focus is on secondary processing (summarizing) of the item-level estimates. We accept the definition of the DIF coefficient and its interpretation as an indicator of bias without any criticism.

5.3   DIF variance

Consider two test forms with 10 items each, having the following sets of DIF coefficients for a given pair of reference and focal groups:

Item No.	1	2	3	4	5	6	7	8	9	10
Form A DIFs:	−1.6	0	0	0	0	0	0	0	0	1.6
Form B DIFs:	−0.9	0.9	0.9	−0.9	0.9	−0.9	0.9	−0.9	0.9	−0.9

Suppose an item is regarded as acceptable if the corresponding DIF coefficient is smaller than unity in absolute value. Test form A has eight 'perfect' items and two items with high DIF, whereas all items in the test form B are acceptable. If these DIF coefficients were estimated subject to no sampling error, a typical screening procedure would lead to the review of items 1 and 10 of test form A, whereas form B would be approved intact. However, arguably, DIF in form B is a greater problem than in form A, because of the substantial *dispersion* of the DIF coefficients.

This example provides the motivation for defining the variance of the DIF coefficients across the test form as a test-level summary of DIF. The ideal of no DIF corresponds to

$$\text{var}_f(\alpha.) = 0;$$

we use the subscript f to signify that the variance (or expectation) is taken over the items of a test form. Whenever confusion may arise, we will refer to the variance over the items of a form as the *form-variance*. For instance, the form-variance of the DIF statistics, $\mathrm{var}_f(\hat{\alpha}_i)$, is itself a random variable dependent on the responses of the examinees. The form-variance of the DIF statistics is likely to be greater than the form-variance of the DIF coefficients because the former is inflated by the sampling errors of $\hat{\alpha}_i$.

The items of a test form can be regarded as outcomes of a complex process of test assembly. In principle, if such a process were to be replicated, the resulting test form would be composed of different items. This justifies the association of the DIF coefficients with variation.

We consider the model

$$\hat{\alpha}_i = \alpha_i + \varepsilon_i, \tag{5.3}$$

where ε_i are the errors due to estimation of α_i by $\hat{\alpha}_i$; we assume that ε_i, $i = 1, \ldots, I$, are mutually independent with variances s_i^2 given by (5.2), with the appropriate multiplicative adjustment. The DIF coefficients α_i are regarded as a random sample from a distribution with mean μ and variance σ_f^2. Combined with the model in (5.3), we have

$$\hat{\alpha}_i = \mu + \delta_i + \varepsilon_i, \tag{5.4}$$

where δ_i is the deviation of the DIF coefficient of item i from the mean DIF ($\delta_i = \alpha_i - \mu$). The random variables δ_i and ε_i are assumed to be mutually independent. At first, the model in (5.4) appears not to be fully identified because each outcome $\hat{\alpha}_i$ is associated with two random terms. However, the sampling variance of one of them, ε_i, is assumed to be known. Hence, the DIF variance $\mathrm{var}_f(\delta.)$ is the form-variance of the DIF coefficients in excess of what can be attributed to the estimation errors.

Several assumptions of the model in (5.4) are not satisfied in a realistic setting and are adopted purely for simplicity. First, the variances s_i^2 are assumed to be known, even though they are estimated; in fact, their *approximations* are estimated. Next, the estimation errors ε_i may not be independent because they are based on the same set of data. Further, the estimation errors ε_i may be correlated with the DIF coefficients. These issues are discussed in Section 5.7. For the time being, we accept these assumptions without criticism. In addition, we assume that the random variables δ_i and ε_i are normally distributed.

The model in (5.4) can be expanded to accommodate linear regression. Suppose each item is associated with a $1 \times p$ (row) vector of explanatory variables $\mathbf{x}_i$. The association of these variables with DIF can be modelled by the equation

$$\hat{\alpha}_i = \mathbf{x}_i \boldsymbol{\beta} + \delta_i + \varepsilon_i, \tag{5.5}$$

where $\boldsymbol{\beta}$ is a $p \times 1$ (column) vector of regression parameters. The components of $\boldsymbol{\beta}$ may be known or unknown. We adopt the convention that the first element of $\mathbf{x}_i$ represents the intercept, that is, it is equal to unity for each item i. Since any component of $\boldsymbol{\beta}$ may be assumed to vanish, this convention is not restrictive. The model in (5.4) corresponds to $p = 1$, $\boldsymbol{\beta} = \mu$, and $x_i = 1$ for each item i.

5.4 Estimation

Assuming normality, the log-likelihood associated with the model in (5.5) is

$$l = -\frac{1}{2}\left\{I \log(2\pi) + \sum_{i=1}^{I} \log(\sigma_f^2 + s_i^2) + \sum_{i=1}^{I} \frac{(\hat{\alpha}_i - \mathbf{x}_i\boldsymbol{\beta})^2}{\sigma_f^2 + s_i^2}\right\}. \tag{5.6}$$

Let $\mathbf{X}$ be the $I{\times}p$ matrix composed of rows $\mathbf{x}_i$, that is, $\mathbf{X} = \mathbf{1}_I{\oplus}\{\mathbf{x}_i\}$, where $\mathbf{1}_I$ is the column vector of ones of length I. We assume that $\mathbf{X}$ is of full rank p, so that no problems with confounding of regression parameters would arise. Let $\hat{\boldsymbol{\alpha}}$ be the $I \times 1$ vector of the DIF statistics $\hat{\alpha}_i$, $\hat{\boldsymbol{\alpha}} = \mathbf{1}_I \oplus \{\hat{\alpha}_i\}$, and let $\boldsymbol{\Sigma}$ be the $I \times I$ diagonal matrix with elements $\sigma_f^2 + s_i^2$, that is, $\boldsymbol{\Sigma} = \mathbf{I}_I \oplus \{\sigma_f^2 + s_i^2\}$. Using this notation, the log-likelihood in (5.6) can be expressed in a compact form as

$$l = -\frac{1}{2}\left\{I \log(2\pi) + \log(\det \boldsymbol{\Sigma}) + \mathbf{e}^\top \boldsymbol{\Sigma}^{-1}\mathbf{e}\right\}, \tag{5.7}$$

where $\mathbf{e} = \hat{\boldsymbol{\alpha}} - \mathbf{X}\boldsymbol{\beta}$ is the vector of residuals.

For estimating the parameters $\boldsymbol{\beta}$ and σ_f^2, we apply the Fisher scoring algorithm. It requires expressions for the first- and second-order partial derivatives of the log-likelihood. Formal matrix differentiation with respect to the vector $\boldsymbol{\beta}$ yields

$$\begin{aligned}
\frac{\partial l}{\partial \boldsymbol{\beta}} &= \mathbf{X}^\top \boldsymbol{\Sigma}^{-1}\mathbf{e}, \\
-\frac{\partial^2 l}{\partial \boldsymbol{\beta}\partial \boldsymbol{\beta}} &= \mathbf{X}^\top \boldsymbol{\Sigma}^{-1}\mathbf{X}.
\end{aligned} \tag{5.8}$$

Note that these identities hold for a general non-singular matrix $\boldsymbol{\Sigma}$, so long as $\boldsymbol{\Sigma}$ is functionally independent of $\boldsymbol{\beta}$. For the DIF variance σ_f^2, we have

$$\frac{\partial l}{\partial \sigma_f^2} = \frac{1}{2}\left\{-\mathrm{tr}\left(\boldsymbol{\Sigma}^{-1}\right) + \mathbf{e}^\top \boldsymbol{\Sigma}^{-2}\mathbf{e}\right\} \tag{5.9}$$

($\mathrm{tr}\boldsymbol{\Sigma}$ stands for the trace of the matrix $\boldsymbol{\Sigma}$) and

$$-\frac{\partial^2 l}{\left(\partial \sigma_f^2\right)^2} = \frac{1}{2}\left\{-\mathrm{tr}\left(\boldsymbol{\Sigma}^{-2}\right) + 2\mathbf{e}^\top \boldsymbol{\Sigma}^{-3}\mathbf{e}\right\}.$$

Using the identity $\mathbf{E}(\mathbf{e}\mathbf{e}^\top) = \mathbf{\Sigma}$ and the commutative property of the trace operator, we obtain

$$\mathbf{E}\left(\mathbf{e}^\top\mathbf{\Sigma}^{-3}\mathbf{e}\right) = \mathbf{E}\left\{\mathrm{tr}\left(\mathbf{\Sigma}^{-3}\mathbf{e}\mathbf{e}^\top\right)\right\} = \mathrm{tr}\left(\mathbf{\Sigma}^{-2}\right),$$

and so

$$-\mathbf{E}\left\{\frac{\partial^2 l}{\left(\partial\sigma_f^2\right)^2}\right\} = \frac{1}{2}\mathrm{tr}\left(\mathbf{\Sigma}^{-2}\right). \qquad (5.10)$$

Since $\mathbf{E}(\mathbf{e}) = \mathbf{0}_I$ and $\mathbf{e}$ does not depend on σ_f^2,

$$-\mathbf{E}\left(\frac{\partial^2 l}{\partial\beta\partial\sigma_f^2}\right) = \mathbf{X}^\top\frac{\partial\mathbf{\Sigma}^{-1}}{\partial\sigma_f^2}\mathbf{E}(\mathbf{e}) = \mathbf{0}_p.$$

This enables the iterations of the Fisher scoring algorithm to be split into two parts, updating of the regression parameter estimates $\hat{\boldsymbol{\beta}}$ and updating of the DIF variance estimate $\hat{\sigma}_f^2$.

The updating equation for the regression parameter estimates is

$$\hat{\boldsymbol{\beta}}_{new} = \hat{\boldsymbol{\beta}}_{old} + \left(\mathbf{X}^\top\hat{\mathbf{\Sigma}}_{old}^{-1}\mathbf{X}\right)^{-1}\mathbf{X}^\top\hat{\mathbf{\Sigma}}_{old}^{-1}\mathbf{e}_{old},$$

where the subscripts old and new refer to the current and updated estimates of $\boldsymbol{\beta}$ or $\mathbf{\Sigma}$, and $\mathbf{e}_{old} = \hat{\boldsymbol{\alpha}} - \mathbf{X}\hat{\boldsymbol{\beta}}_{old}$. Substituting for $\mathbf{e}_{old}$ yields

$$\hat{\boldsymbol{\beta}}_{new} = \left(\mathbf{X}^\top\hat{\mathbf{\Sigma}}_{old}^{-1}\mathbf{X}\right)^{-1}\mathbf{X}^\top\hat{\mathbf{\Sigma}}_{old}^{-1}\hat{\boldsymbol{\alpha}}, \qquad (5.11)$$

which is the generalized least squares (GLS) estimator.

The updating equation for the DIF variance estimate is

$$\hat{\sigma}_{f,new}^2 = \hat{\sigma}_{f,old}^2 - \frac{\mathrm{tr}\left(\hat{\mathbf{\Sigma}}_{old}^{-1}\right) - \mathbf{e}_{old}^\top\hat{\mathbf{\Sigma}}_{old}^{-2}\mathbf{e}_{old}}{\mathrm{tr}\left(\hat{\mathbf{\Sigma}}_{old}^{-2}\right)}. \qquad (5.12)$$

The Fisher scoring algorithm proceeds by iterations of equations (5.11) and (5.12). The estimates from the ordinary regression,

$$\left(\mathbf{X}^\top\mathbf{X}\right)^{-1}\mathbf{X}^\top\hat{\boldsymbol{\alpha}},$$

are a suitable starting solution for $\boldsymbol{\beta}$. When no explanatory variables are used, $\mathbf{X} = \mathbf{1}_I$, this is the arithmetic mean $(\hat{\alpha}_1 + \ldots + \hat{\alpha}_I)/I$. Zero is a suitable starting solution for the DIF variance σ_f^2. The iterations are terminated when a convergence criterion is satisfied. This criterion can be based on the changes $\hat{\boldsymbol{\beta}}_{new} - \hat{\boldsymbol{\beta}}_{old}$ and $\hat{\sigma}^2_{f,old} - \hat{\sigma}^2_{f,new}$, the change in the fitted log-likelihood, $l_{new} - l_{old}$, or their combination. In the examples discussed in Section 5.5, we use the criterion

$$\frac{\left(\hat{\boldsymbol{\beta}}_{new} - \hat{\boldsymbol{\beta}}_{old}\right)^\top \left(\hat{\boldsymbol{\beta}}_{new} - \hat{\boldsymbol{\beta}}_{old}\right) + \left(\hat{\sigma}^2_{f,new} - \hat{\sigma}^2_{f,old}\right)^2}{p+1} < 10^{-6}.$$

The estimate of the variance σ^2_f resulting from the Fisher scoring iterations may be negative, in which case it is meaningful to reset it to zero. When no explanatory variables are used, the GLS estimator in (5.11) is

$$\hat{\mu} = \frac{\sum_i \hat{\alpha}_i \left(\hat{\sigma}^2_f + s^2_i\right)^{-1}}{\sum_i \left(\hat{\sigma}^2_f + s^2_i\right)^{-1}}, \tag{5.13}$$

which has the form of a weighted mean. Since the variance estimate $\hat{\sigma}^2_f$ is altered at each iteration, $\hat{\mu}$ is an *iteratively reweighted* mean. Thus, the maximum likelihood estimator is well motivated even when the outcomes $\hat{\alpha}_i$ are not normally distributed.

Owing to the diagonal form of $\boldsymbol{\Sigma}$, we have

$$\log(\det \boldsymbol{\Sigma}) = \sum_{i=1}^{I} \log(\sigma^2_f + s^2_i),$$

$$\mathrm{tr}\left(\boldsymbol{\Sigma}^{-k}\right) = \sum_{i=1}^{I} \frac{1}{\left(\sigma^2_f + s^2_i\right)^k},$$

$$\mathbf{e}^\top \boldsymbol{\Sigma}^{-k} \mathbf{e} = \sum_{i=1}^{I} \frac{e^2_i}{\left(\sigma^2_f + s^2_i\right)^k}$$

($k = 1, 2$), and so equation (5.12) and the log-likelihood in (5.7) can be evaluated by summing certain functions of the outcomes and the current parameter estimates over the items i.

The sampling variance of the maximum likelihood estimator $\hat{\boldsymbol{\beta}}$ is approximated as

$$\widehat{\mathrm{var}}(\hat{\boldsymbol{\beta}}) \approx \left(\mathbf{X}^\top \hat{\boldsymbol{\Sigma}}^{-1} \mathbf{X}\right)^{-1}.$$

This equation is obtained as the inverse of the expected information matrix [see (5.8)] with the unknown matrix $\boldsymbol{\Sigma}$ replaced by its estimate. Also, if $\boldsymbol{\Sigma}$ were known, the sampling variance matrix of $\hat{\boldsymbol{\beta}}$ would be

$$\mathrm{var}(\hat{\boldsymbol{\beta}}) = \left(\mathbf{X}^\top \boldsymbol{\Sigma}^{-1} \mathbf{X}\right)^{-1} \mathbf{X}^\top \boldsymbol{\Sigma}^{-1} \mathbf{E}\left(\mathbf{e}\mathbf{e}^\top\right) \boldsymbol{\Sigma}^{-1} \mathbf{X} \left(\mathbf{X}^\top \boldsymbol{\Sigma}^{-1} \mathbf{X}\right)^{-1}$$

$$= \left(\mathbf{X}^\top \boldsymbol{\Sigma}^{-1} \mathbf{X}\right)^{-1},$$

since $\mathbf{E}(\mathbf{ee}^\top) = \boldsymbol{\Sigma}$. Note that this derivation does not rely on any asymptotics. The sampling variance is estimated by replacing $\boldsymbol{\Sigma}$ with its estimate.

The asymptotic sampling variance of the estimator $\hat{\sigma}_f^2$ is $2/\mathrm{tr}\left(\boldsymbol{\Sigma}^{-2}\right)$. The sampling distribution of $\hat{\sigma}_f^2$ tends to deviate substantially from normality, and so using multiples of the standard deviation $\sqrt{2/\mathrm{tr}\left(\boldsymbol{\Sigma}^{-2}\right)}$ for the bounds of confidence intervals may be misleading. The Fisher scoring algorithm can be easily adapted to estimate a transformation of the variance, such as $\log(\sigma_f^2)$ or the standard deviation σ_f. However, the estimators of these parameters are usually also distinctly non-normally distributed.

Uncertainty about $\boldsymbol{\Sigma}$, that is, about σ_f^2, should inflate the sampling variance matrix of $\hat{\boldsymbol{\beta}}$, and, of course, the uncertainty about $\boldsymbol{\beta}$ should inflate the sampling variance of $\hat{\sigma}_f^2$. However, the equations derived for the maximum likelihood estimation do not reflect this reasonable expectation. This problem can be interpreted in terms of the familiar degrees of freedom. Using the standard notation in ordinary regression, which corresponds to $s_i^2 = 0$ for all i, the maximum likelihood estimator of the residual variance σ^2 is

$$\hat{\sigma}^2 = \frac{\mathbf{e}^\top \mathbf{e}}{I},$$

whereas, in general, we prefer the unbiased estimator

$$\hat{\sigma}^2 = \frac{\mathbf{e}^\top \mathbf{e}}{I - p},$$

which takes account of the p degrees of freedom associated with estimation of the regression parameters. When the interest is in summaries for large numbers of items, $I \gg p$, this issue of correcting for degrees of freedom is of little importance.

In most contexts, the focus of inference is on testing the hypothesis that all the DIF coefficients are equal to zero. Since this corresponds to $\sigma_f^2 = 0$, the likelihood ratio test can be applied. Under this null hypothesis, the maximum likelihood estimator of $\boldsymbol{\beta}$ is obtained by the weighted least squares (WLS), and the corresponding value of the log-likelihood is

$$l_0 = -\frac{1}{2} \left\{ I \log(2\pi) + \sum_{i=1}^{I} \log(s_i^2) + \sum_{i=1}^{I} \frac{e_i^2}{s_i^2} \right\}.$$

Denote the log-likelihood evaluated at the maximum likelihood solution by $l(\hat{\boldsymbol{\beta}}, \hat{\sigma}_f^2)$. The likelihood ratio statistic is

$$-2\left\{ l_0 - l(\hat{\boldsymbol{\beta}}, \hat{\sigma}_f^2) \right\},$$

and under certain regularity conditions it has asymptotically χ^2 distribution with one degree of freedom. The degree of freedom is due to estimation of the variance σ_f^2 under the alternative.

5.5   Examples

In this section, we discuss two sets of examples from large-scale educational tests. In these examples, the outcome variables are the DIF statistics for the following reference–focal group pairs: Men–Women (M–F), White–Black (W–B), White–Hispanic (W–H), and White–American Asian examinees (W–A). The DIF statistics were computed using an ETS operational computer programme.

5.5.1   National Teachers' Examination

We explore DIF in three administrations of non-overlapping test forms (denoted A, B, and C) of the core battery of the National Teacher's Examination test (NTE). The data were kindly provided by David Anderson from ETS. The forms were administered in 1990 and have since been disclosed. In the DIF analyses, the number of correct responses on the studied test form is used as the matching variable. The administered forms had 112–115 dichotomously scored items. The administration sizes for forms A, B, and C were about 22 000, 15 000, and 13 000, respectively. The tests were taken by many more women than men, and by only hundreds of examinees in each ethnic minority group. In the administration of form C, there were fewer than 100 American Asian examinees, and so, in accordance with operational rules at ETS, no DIF analysis was carried out because the standard errors associated with these DIF statistics would be very large.

For orientation, Figure 5.1 displays the scatterplots of the DIF statistics $\hat{\alpha}_i$ and their standard errors s_i for the four pairs of reference and focal groups for form A. The standard errors are, on average, the smallest for Men–Women DIF, and the largest for White–American Asian DIF; they are negatively associated with the smaller of the sample sizes for the two groups. Note also that the dispersion of the DIF statistics is the smallest for Men–Women DIF, and largest for White–American Asian DIF; the sampling variance of the DIF statistics contributes to the dispersion, and so it is essential to disentangle it from the observed form-variance of the DIF statistics.

Association among the DIF statistics across the reference–focal group pairs can be informally assessed in the pairwise scatterplots of the DIF statistics drawn in Figure 5.2. Any hypothesis about such an association is tentative at best, maybe with the exception of a positive association of the White–Hispanic and White–American Asian DIF statistics. We make no attempt here to find an explanation for this finding. It is not replicated for the forms B or C; for brevity, we omit the details.

Estimation of the DIF variances is summarized in Table 5.1. The left-hand side of the table gives the numbers of examinees in the reference and focal groups. The estimates of the variances are in the range 0.24–0.32, with the exception of the two DIF variances for White–American

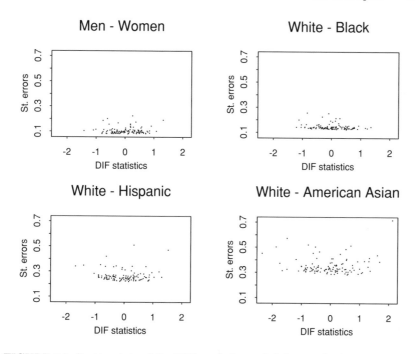

FIGURE 5.1. Scatterplots of the DIF statistics and their standard errors for form A of the NTE test.

Asian DIF. Both the standard errors and the likelihood ratio test statistics suggest that zero DIF variance is extremely unlikely for either set of DIF statistics. By the same token, values of the DIF variance greater than, say, unity, are also not supported by the model fit. The estimates of the means $\hat{\mu}$ are of no interest, and so they are omitted from the table. The estimates differ from zero by less than 0.02.

The standard errors of the DIF variances are negatively associated with the number of examinees in the focal group. The size of the standard errors for $\hat{\sigma}_f^2$ suggests that even when each DIF statistic is associated with a large standard error, the DIF variance as a summary of the DIF coefficients is estimated with reasonable precision. If the White–American Asian DIF statistics were available for form C, the standard error of the corresponding DIF variance would not be greater than, say, 0.15.

Just how much DIF is there in a test form with DIF variance of 0.25? For simplicity, consider a normally distributed set of DIF coefficients in such a form. Then, approximately 70 percent of the items have DIF coefficients in the range $(-0.5, 0.5)$ and about 5 percent have DIF coefficients outside the range $(-1, 1)$. These percentages may be somewhat different when the coefficients are distinctly non-normally distributed, but a small variance excludes the possibility of many items with large DIF coefficients. Large

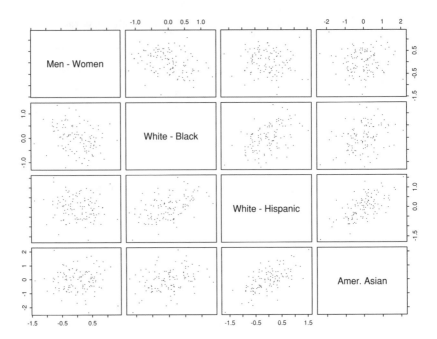

FIGURE 5.2. Pairwise scatterplots of the DIF statistics for the pairs of reference and focal groups, form A of the NTE test.

variance implies the presence of several such items. Note that the DIF variance does not identify any items with large or outlying DIF coefficients.

5.5.2 GRE Verbal test

We analyse a set of four test forms of the Graduate Record Examination (GRE) Verbal test, administered in October 1990. The data were kindly provided by Sue Vitella and Robin Durso of ETS. For each test form, the DIF analyses for the same four focal–reference group pairs were carried out as in the previous section. The number of correct responses was used as the matching variable. The test forms comprised 75 items each. As in the previous example, the DIF statistics for Men–Women comparisons have a smaller dispersion than the DIF statistics involving ethnic minorities. The standard errors for the former are, on average, also smaller. The estimates of the DIF variances, summarized in Table 5.2 in the same format as Table 5.1, display a lot of consistency. The DIF variance in each form is greatest for the White–American Asian groups and smallest for the White–Black groups. The examples from NTE and those presented here do not warrant the generalization that the DIF variance in all educational tests tends to be greater for White–American Asian comparisons than for the other pairs of reference and focal groups. However, the estimated DIF variances from

TABLE 5.1. DIF variance estimates in the NTE test forms.

R – F	Examinees R – F		DIF variance	(Std. error)	Likelihood ratio
	Form A		115 items,	22,248 examinees	
M – F	4 747	17 501	0.238	0.033	49.5
W – B	18 929	1 938	0.263	0.038	57.1
W – H		525	0.243	0.041	25.6
W – A		304	0.417	0.071	58.8
	Form B		112 items,	15,017 examinees	
M – F	3 328	11 689	0.241	0.035	45.2
W – B	12 985	1 116	0.318	0.048	69.8
W – H		353	0.268	0.050	25.4
W – A		220	0.469	0.086	59.3
	Form C		114 items,	13,025 examinees	
M – F	2 753	10 272	0.308	0.044	80.8
W – B	11 410	892	0.240	0.038	32.6
W – H		274	0.258	0.052	17.9

a wide range of tests and several test forms from each test could be much more informative about such hypotheses.

The standard errors of the DIF variances as well as the likelihood ratio test statistics suggest that zero DIF variance is an unrealistic assumption. At the same time, a DIF coefficient outside the interval $(-1, 1)$ is very rare because a typical DIF variance for a focal–reference group pair other than W–A is unlikely to be greater than, say, 0.6.

5.6 Shrinkage estimation of DIF coefficients

If the DIF variance were equal to zero, all the DIF coefficients in the test form would be equal, and so their mean would be a more efficient estimator of each coefficient than the DIF statistic. Although the DIF variance is not likely to vanish, it is moderate, and a large value of the DIF statistic is not a clear indication of a large DIF coefficient because the statistic may be inflated by the sampling error. For instance, form kgr1 contains 25 items with DIF statistics for White–Asian American comparisons outside the range $(-1, 1)$. However, the estimated variance of 0.66 implies that it is extremely unlikely that 25 items would have DIF *coefficients* outside this range. The DIF variance can be effectively used to improve the estimator

TABLE 5.2. DIF variance estimates in GRE Verbal test forms.

R − F group	Examinees (R − F)		DIF variance	Std. error	Likelihood ratio
Form kgr1			75 items,	10 447 examinees	
M − F	4 151	6 296	0.323	0.056	63.3
W − B	8 363	748	0.285	0.057	28.9
W − H	8 363	296	0.449	0.093	48.5
W − A	8 363	201	0.660	0.137	67.9
Form kgr2			75 items,	10 385 examinees	
M − F	4 227	6 158	0.259	0.045	38.2
W − B	8 268	767	0.269	0.054	25.4
W − H	8 268	311	0.325	0.072	23.7
W − A	8 268	202	0.428	0.100	26.2
Form kgr3			75 items,	14 667 examinees	
M − F	5 917	8 748	0.298	0.051	51.3
W − B	12 182	617	0.233	0.048	16.4
W − H	12 182	453	0.419	0.082	49.9
W − A	12 182	459	0.464	0.091	58.6
Form kgr4			75 items,	14 751 examinees	
M − F	5 891	8 860	0.384	0.065	91.7
W − B	12 234	615	0.199	0.043	9.6
W − H	12 234	474	0.328	0.067	30.9
W − A	12 234	438	0.449	0.088	54.1

of the DIF coefficient by incorporating information about the rest of the items. This leads to shrinkage estimation of the DIF coefficients.

We consider the conditional expectation of the DIF coefficient given the data and the parameters:

$$\tilde{\alpha}_i = \mathbf{E}\left(\alpha_i \mid \hat{\alpha}_i ; \mu, \sigma_f^2, s_i^2\right).$$

Relying on the assumptions of normality, we obtain

$$\tilde{\alpha}_i = \mu + \frac{\sigma_f^2}{\sigma_f^2 + s_i^2}\left(\hat{\alpha}_i - \mu\right) = \frac{\mu s_i^2 + \hat{\alpha}_i \sigma_f^2}{\sigma_f^2 + s_i^2}. \tag{5.14}$$

When both σ_f^2 and s_i^2 are positive, the conditional variance of α_i is

$$\sigma_f^2 - \frac{\sigma_f^4}{\sigma_f^2 + s_i^2} = \frac{1}{1/\sigma_f^2 + 1/s_i^2},$$

Form A

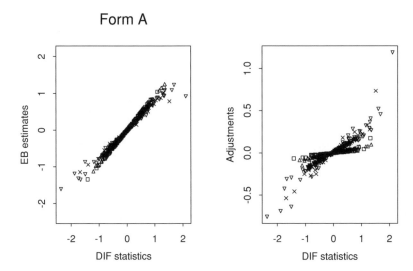

FIGURE 5.3. Scatterplots of the DIF statistics and the EB estimates of the DIF coefficients (left-hand side) and of the DIF statistics and the differences (DIF statistics – EB estimates) for the four pairs of reference and focal groups; form A of the NTE test. The symbols ⊔, △, ×, and ▽ distinguish the comparisons Men–Women, White–Black, White–Hispanic, and White–American Asian, respectively.

which is smaller than either σ_f^2 or s_i^2. The estimator in (5.14) can also be obtained as the linear combination of the DIF statistic and the overall mean, $a\hat{\alpha}_i + b\mu$, which has the smallest mean squared error. No distributional assumptions are involved in this derivation.

If the DIF variance were known, it could be regarded, in a Bayesian approach, as the *prior* variance for the DIF coefficients. In the approach described below, we use the 'prior' variance estimated from the same data (therefore, empirical) for which we are going to use it. We define the *empirical Bayes* (EB) estimator of α_i by (5.14) with the unknown parameters μ and σ_f^2 replaced by their estimates. This replacement may erode the advantage of the EB estimator when the number of items is small and σ_f^2 is poorly estimated, or when the standard errors s_i are large and themselves estimated with little precision. The EB estimator can be interpreted as a shrinkage estimator, because the original estimator $\hat{\alpha}_i$ is pulled toward the (estimated) overall mean $\hat{\mu}$; the extent of the shrinkage is determined by the relative sizes of the variances σ_f^2 and s_i^2.

We illustrate the effect of such shrinkage for form A of the National Teacher's Examination, analysed in Section 5.5.1. The left-hand-side plot in Figure 5.3 contains the scatterplot of the DIF statistics and the EB estimates of the DIF coefficients. The estimates for all four pairs of reference and focal groups are included in the plot, attempting to demonstrate

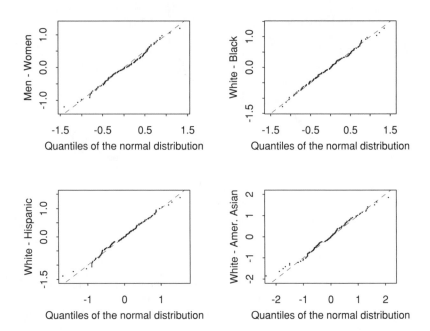

FIGURE 5.4. Normal quantile plots of the DIF statistics for the four reference–focal groups; form A of the NTE test. The dashed line represents the identity, $y = x$.

the differential amounts of shrinkage for the pairs (the symbols □, △, ×, and ▽ distinguish the respective pairs Men–Women, White–Black, White–Hispanic, and White–American Asian).

Because of the superior resolution, this is much more clearly demonstrated in the right-hand-side plot, where the DIF statistics are plotted against the *differences* $\hat{\alpha}_i - \tilde{\alpha}_i$, that is, the adjustments of the DIF statistics. The adjustments for the Men–Women DIF statistics are the smallest in absolute value and the adjustments for the White–American Asian DIF the greatest, reflecting the substantial uncertainty of the DIF statistics for the latter, which overrides the impact of the greater estimated DIF variance.

5.7 Model criticism and diagnostics

Several assumptions of the models in (5.5) were made so as to lead to a relatively simple estimation procedure for σ_f^2. Although realistic, these assumptions should always be subjected to scrutiny. In this section, we discuss model diagnostic procedures and outline methods for assessing the importance of some of the untestable assumptions.

We address first the assumption of normality of the DIF coefficients. Figure 5.4 presents the normal quantile plots for the DIF statistics for form A of the NTE test. In each panel, the normal quantiles of the fitted normal distribution are plotted against the DIF statistics sorted in ascending order. Normality corresponds to the proximity of the plotted points to the line $y = x$, drawn by a dashed line, and this assumption would apparently present no problems had the DIF statistics been equal to the DIF coefficients. However, since the standard deviations s_i do not vary a great deal for the DIF statistics within a reference–focal group pair, a similar picture would have arisen even if the DIF coefficients were known exactly. Certainly, the plots of the EB estimates display a similar pattern because they are simple transformations of the DIF statistics.

Outlying DIF statistics are likely to correspond to outlying DIF coefficients. They represent a departure from normality that also happens to be of substantive importance because an item with an outlying DIF statistic would be a prime candidate for a review or replacement. Exclusion of such an item may result in a reduced estimate of the DIF variance σ_f^2. However, if the excluded item is replaced by another one, we run the risk that the new item would have an even more outlying DIF coefficient than the old one.

The sampling errors ε_i, and therefore the DIF statistics $\hat{\alpha}_i$, are assumed to be independent, even though the statistics are self-norming, $\sum_i \hat{\alpha}_i \doteq 0$. In any case, the DIF statistics are interdependent because they are based on the data from the same or overlapping sets of examinees. If the covariance structure of the deviations $\delta_i + \varepsilon_i$ were known, the algorithm described in Section 5.4 could be adapted. The variance matrix Σ would no longer be diagonal, but its pattern could be exploited to obtain a computationally tractable form for its inverse and determinant.

Suppose the deviations $\delta_i + \varepsilon_i$ have a common covariance τ, so that

$$\Sigma = D + \tau J_I, \tag{5.15}$$

where $D = I_I \oplus \{\sigma_f^2 - \tau + s_i^2\}$, and J_I is the $I \times I$ matrix of ones, $J_I = 1_I 1_I^\top$. Then

$$\Sigma^{-1} = D^{-1} - \frac{\tau}{1 + \tau 1_I^\top D^{-1} 1_I} D^{-1} J_I D^{-1},$$

$$\det(\Sigma) = \det(D) \left(1 + \tau 1_I D^{-1} 1_I\right). \tag{5.16}$$

The first equation is verified directly by multiplication ($\Sigma \Sigma^{-1} = I$). The second equation can be proved by applying linear operations on the blocks of the matrix

$$\begin{pmatrix} D + \tau 1_I 1_I^\top & 0_I \\ \tau 1_I^\top & 1 \end{pmatrix}.$$

First, subtract the $\mathbf{1}_I$-multiple of the lower submatrices from the upper submatrices. Then add the $\mathbf{D}^{-1}\mathbf{1}_I$-multiple of the left-hand submatrices from the right-hand submatrices. These operations lead to the matrix

$$\begin{pmatrix} \mathbf{D} & \mathbf{0}_I \\ \tau\mathbf{1}_I^\top & 1 + \tau\mathbf{1}_I^\top\mathbf{D}^{-1}\mathbf{1}_I \end{pmatrix},$$

and since they do not change the determinant, the second identity in (5.16) follows.

The identities in (5.16) facilitate an adaptation of the Fisher scoring algorithm discussed in Section 5.4. We omit the details because the next section deals with a further extension of this algorithm. The algorithm can be applied using imputed (guessed) values of the covariance τ. In general, greater covariance is associated with greater DIF variance, but a substantial increase is obtained only for unrealistically large values of the covariance.

Another diagnostic concern is that the sampling variances s_i^2 are estimated subject to error, whereas the adopted model assumes that these values are precise. The impact of violating this assumption can be assessed by conducting simulations using randomly perturbed values of s_i^2. The sampling variances s_i^2 are replaced by altered (perturbed) values, such as $s_i^2\exp(\eta_i)$, where η_i, $i = 1,\ldots,I$, are a random sample from the normal distribution with mean zero and a set variance. This corresponds to adding a normally distributed error term to $\log(s_i^2)$ to simulate the imprecision of s_i^2. Variation of the estimates across the simulations provides a measure of robustness of the estimator with respect to the imprecision of s_i^2.

The estimates of the DIF variance are quite robust against this form of perturbation. In general, an increase in the sampling variances s_i^2 is compensated by a reduction of the estimated DIF variance. Thus, estimation of the DIF variance relies on approximate unbiasedness of the estimators of the sampling variances s_i^2.

5.8   Multiple administrations

Although the DIF coefficients, as well as other item attributes, are perceived to be measures of item properties, they depend on the population of examinees, and there is evidence that they may be affected by very innocuous changes in the test form, such as a change in the order of the items, alteration of some of the preceding items, and the like. Since test forms are often used on several occasions (for instance, in a trial and an operational administration), stability of the DIF coefficients across the occasions is a serious concern, especially when inference about DIF in an earlier (trial) administration is to be applied to a future (operational) administration. Also, it is of interest to assess the chances that an item with a small or moderate DIF has an outlying DIF in a slightly altered context. Skaggs and Lissitz (1992) address this issue by correlating the pairs of estimates from the two administrations, using several measures of DIF. Of course, one source of imperfect correlation is due to the sampling errors in estimation.

This section develops models for assessing changes of the DIF coefficients from one administration to another. Section 5.8.1 describes an estimation procedure, Section 5.8.2 discusses examples, and Section 5.8.3 outlines diagnostic procedures and some applications.

Suppose two administrations of a test form yield pairs of DIF statistics, $\hat{\alpha}_{1i}$ and $\hat{\alpha}_{2i}$, $i = 1, \ldots, I$, using the same matching variable (say, the number of correct responses). A naive way of comparing DIF in these two administrations is to inspect the itemwise differences of the DIF statistics, $\hat{\alpha}_{1i} - \hat{\alpha}_{2i}$. Since the differences add up approximately to zero, no trend among them can be observed. Each difference $\hat{\alpha}_{1i} - \hat{\alpha}_{2i}$ is a rather poor estimator of $\alpha_{1i} - \alpha_{2i}$, and the large number, I, of such differences makes any substantive inference about them very difficult. Some of the large differences $\alpha_{1i} - \alpha_{2i}$ may arise purely by chance owing to the magnitude of the sampling variances $\mathrm{var}(\hat{\alpha}_{1i} - \hat{\alpha}_{2i})$.

A formal approach to summarizing between-administration differences of the DIF coefficients can be based on the form-variance $\mathrm{var}_f(\alpha_{1i} - \alpha_{2i})$. More generally, we consider the DIF coefficient for item i in a hypothetical *average* administration, denoted by γ_i, and assume that the DIF coefficient in a realized administration, one of a population of hypothetical administrations that could have taken place, is drawn from a distribution with mean γ_i and variance σ_A^2. Thus, the estimator $\hat{\alpha}_{hi}$ for item i in administration $h = 1, \ldots, H$ involves two sources of uncertainty: the administration that happens to have been realized and the sampling error of the DIF statistic as an estimator of the DIF coefficient. These sources of uncertainty are captured in the model

$$\hat{\alpha}_{hi} = \mu + \delta_i + \xi_{hi} + \varepsilon_{hi}, \qquad (5.17)$$

where $\gamma_i = \mu + \delta_i$ is the DIF coefficient in the average administration, ξ_{hi} is the deviation of the DIF coefficient in administration h from the DIF coefficient in the average administration, and ε_{hi} is the estimation error of the DIF statistic for item i in administration h. The terms δ_i and ξ_{hi} are assumed to be mutually independent random variables with zero means and respective variances σ_f^2 (DIF variance) and σ_A^2 (between-administration DIF variance). The estimation error terms ε_{hi} are assumed to have known variances s_{hi}^2, which in reality are estimated by the method described in Section 5.2. This is a direct extension of the model in (5.5). When only a single administration takes place, $H = 1$, δ_i and ξ_{hi} are indistinguishable, and the model in (5.17) collapses to that in (5.4).

The expectation μ is an unknown constant. The model in (5.17) can be extended to allow for administration-specific means μ_h, applicable when different or external matching variables are used, and, more generally, for linear regression:

$$\hat{\alpha}_{hi} = \mathbf{x}_i \boldsymbol{\beta} + \delta_i + \xi_{hi} + \varepsilon_{hi}, \tag{5.18}$$

where the regressor variables in $\mathbf{x}$ may be defined for items (an item attribute), for forms (such as a categorical variable that allows for different means of the DIF coefficients), for sections of forms, and for interactions of such variables.

The variance σ_f^2 has the same interpretation as the DIF variance defined in Section 5.3, but now its estimation is improved because information is pooled over the H administrations. The variance σ_A^2 is a summary of the differences of the within-item DIF coefficients across the administrations; $\sigma_A^2 = \mathrm{var}_f(\alpha_{hi} - \gamma_i)$, where $\gamma_i = \mathbf{x}_i \boldsymbol{\beta} + \delta_i$ or $\gamma_i = \mu + \delta_i$ is the DIF coefficient in the hypothetical average administration, and $\alpha_i = \gamma_i + \xi_{hi}$ is the DIF coefficient in the administration h.

Owing to the independence of $\{\xi_{hi}\}$,

$$\mathrm{var}_f(\alpha_{1i} - \alpha_{2i}) = 2\sigma_A^2.$$

As pointed out earlier, it is important to distinguish between DIF coefficients and DIF statistics. The differences of the DIF statistics are more variable;

$$\mathrm{var}(\hat{\alpha}_{1i} - \hat{\alpha}_{2i}) = 2\sigma_A^2 + s_{i1}^2 + s_{i2}^2.$$

According to the models in (5.17) and (5.18), a pair of DIF statistics for the same item is correlated:

$$\mathrm{cov}(\hat{\alpha}_{1i}, \hat{\alpha}_{2i}) = \mathrm{var}(\delta_i) = \sigma_A^2, \tag{5.19}$$

and the model variance of a DIF statistic is $\sigma_f^2 + \sigma_A^2 + s_{hi}^2$. Thus, the variances σ_f^2 and σ_A^2 can be interpreted as *variance components*. In a single administration, only the sum $\sigma_f^2 + \sigma_A^2$ can be estimated, and so one can only speculate whether DIF is an attribute of the item (no variation across administrations, $\sigma_A^2 = 0$) or of the occasion and context (no DIF variance in the average administration, $\sigma_f^2 = 0$), or it arises as a mix of the two influences.

Suppose one administration has taken place and the DIF statistics $\hat{\alpha}_i$ and their standard errors s_i are available. What can we say about the DIF coefficients in a future administration of the same (or slightly altered) test form? Traditional approaches assume that the DIF coefficients in a future administration are the same as in the realized one, so that *prediction* of the DIF in a future administration is equivalent to estimation of the DIF coefficient in the realized administration. If $\sigma_A^2 > 0$, this assumption leads to a too optimistic assessment of uncertainty as well as to biased prediction.

5.8.1 Estimation

The principal difficulty in implementing maximum likelihood estimation for the models in (5.17) and (5.18) is that the outcomes are correlated; see

(5.19). However, the dependent outcomes (DIF statistics) are gathered in the sets of H statistics for each item. This pattern, as well as the equicovariance structure, can be effectively exploited to construct a relatively simple estimation algorithm.

Let $\mathbf{X}_i = \mathbf{1}_H \oplus \{\mathbf{x}_{hi}\}_h$ be the matrix of regressors for item i (stacked row-vectors $\mathbf{x}_{hi}$, $h = 1, \ldots, H$), and let $\mathbf{X} = \mathbf{1}_I \oplus \mathbf{X}_i$ be the matrix of regressors for all the DIF statistics. We denote the corresponding vectors of DIF statistics by $\hat{\boldsymbol{\alpha}}_i = \mathbf{1}_H \oplus \{\hat{\alpha}_{hi}\}_h$ and $\hat{\boldsymbol{\alpha}} = \mathbf{1}_I \oplus \{\hat{\boldsymbol{\alpha}}_i\}$. Assuming normality, the log-likelihood for the model in (5.18) is

$$l = -\frac{1}{2}\left\{HI\log(2\pi) + \log\left(\det \boldsymbol{\Sigma}\right) + \mathbf{e}^{\top}\boldsymbol{\Sigma}^{-1}\mathbf{e}\right\}, \qquad (5.20)$$

where $\mathbf{e} = \hat{\boldsymbol{\alpha}} - \mathbf{X}\boldsymbol{\beta}$ is the vector of residuals and $\boldsymbol{\Sigma}$ is the variance matrix $\mathrm{var}(\hat{\boldsymbol{\alpha}})$. The matrix $\boldsymbol{\Sigma}$ is block-diagonal, with blocks $\boldsymbol{\Sigma}_i$ corresponding to the items:

$$\boldsymbol{\Sigma} = \mathbf{I}_I \oplus \{\boldsymbol{\Sigma}_i\},$$

where

$$\boldsymbol{\Sigma}_i = \sigma_f^2 \mathbf{I}_H + \mathrm{diag}_h(s_{hi}^2) + \sigma_A^2 \mathbf{J}_H. \qquad (5.21)$$

In Section 5.7, we considered a similar covariance structure for the outcomes; see (5.15).

The log-likelihood involves the inverses and determinants of these matrices. Since H is usually small, the inversion can be carried out numerically, although an adaptation of equation (5.16) provides an elegant alternative.

The derivation of the iteratively reweighted least squares (IRLS) estimator in Section 5.4 [see (5.11)] is applicable for an arbitrary form of the variance matrix $\boldsymbol{\Sigma}$, so long as $\boldsymbol{\Sigma}$ does not involve the regression parameter vector $\boldsymbol{\beta}$. Also, since the first-order partial derivative $\partial l/\partial \boldsymbol{\beta}$ is a linear function of $\mathbf{e}$, the identity

$$-\mathbf{E}\left(\frac{\partial^2 l}{\partial\boldsymbol{\beta}\partial\sigma^2}\right) = \mathbf{0}_p$$

holds for either variance σ_f^2 or σ_A^2. Thus, iterations of the Fisher scoring algorithm comprise two independent updating procedures: IRLS for $\boldsymbol{\beta}$ and updating of the variance estimates $\hat{\sigma}_f^2$ and $\hat{\sigma}_A^2$. The first-order partial derivative with respect to a variance σ^2 is

$$\frac{\partial l}{\partial\sigma^2} = \frac{1}{2}\sum_{i=1}^{I}\left\{-\mathrm{tr}\left(\boldsymbol{\Sigma}_i^{-1}\frac{\partial\boldsymbol{\Sigma}_i}{\partial\sigma^2}\right) + \mathbf{e}_i^{\top}\boldsymbol{\Sigma}_i^{-1}\frac{\partial\boldsymbol{\Sigma}_i}{\partial\sigma^2}\boldsymbol{\Sigma}_i^{-1}\mathbf{e}_i\right\}, \qquad (5.22)$$

where the matrix derivatives are

$$\frac{\partial\boldsymbol{\Sigma}_i}{\partial\sigma_f^2} = \mathbf{I}_H,$$

$$\frac{\partial\boldsymbol{\Sigma}_i}{\partial\sigma_A^2} = \mathbf{J}_H.$$

The expectation of the second-order partial derivative with respect to a pair of variance parameters is

$$-\mathbf{E}\left(\frac{\partial^2 l}{\partial \sigma_1^2 \partial \sigma_2^2}\right) = \frac{1}{2}\sum_{i=1}^{I} \text{tr}\left(\mathbf{\Sigma}_i^{-1} \frac{\partial \mathbf{\Sigma}_i}{\partial \sigma_1^2} \mathbf{\Sigma}_i^{-1} \frac{\partial \mathbf{\Sigma}_i}{\partial \sigma_2^2}\right). \tag{5.23}$$

This is a generalization of (5.10) and is obtained analogously. By substituting the specific partial derivatives and using properties of the trace operator, we obtain

$$-\mathbf{E}\left\{\frac{\partial^2 l}{(\partial \sigma_f^2)^2}\right\} = \frac{1}{2}\sum_{i=1}^{I} \text{tr}\left(\mathbf{\Sigma}_i^{-2}\right),$$

$$-\mathbf{E}\left\{\frac{\partial^2 l}{(\partial \sigma_A^2)^2}\right\} = \frac{1}{2}\sum_{i=1}^{I} \left(\mathbf{1}_H^\top \mathbf{\Sigma}_i^{-1} \mathbf{1}_H\right)^2, \tag{5.24}$$

$$-\mathbf{E}\left\{\frac{\partial^2 l}{\partial \sigma_f^2 \partial \sigma_A^2}\right\} = \frac{1}{2}\sum_{i=1}^{I} \mathbf{1}_H^\top \mathbf{\Sigma}_i^{-2} \mathbf{1}_H.$$

Similarly, for the first-order partial derivatives, we have

$$\frac{\partial l}{\partial \sigma_f^2} = \frac{1}{2}\sum_{i=1}^{I} \left\{-\text{tr}\left(\mathbf{\Sigma}_i^{-1}\right) + \mathbf{e}_i^\top \mathbf{\Sigma}_i^{-2} \mathbf{e}_i\right\},$$

$$\frac{\partial l}{\partial \sigma_A^2} = \frac{1}{2}\sum_{i=1}^{I} \left\{-\mathbf{1}_H^\top \mathbf{\Sigma}_i^{-1} \mathbf{1}_H + \left(\mathbf{e}_i^\top \mathbf{\Sigma}_i^{-1} \mathbf{1}_H\right)^2\right\}. \tag{5.25}$$

Let $\mathcal{H}$ be the 2×2 information matrix for σ_f^2 and σ_A^2, containing the elements given by (5.24), and let $\mathcal{D}$ be the vector of first-order partial derivatives given by (5.25). The updating for the variance estimates is given by the formula

$$\begin{pmatrix} \sigma_{f,new}^2 \\ \sigma_{A,new}^2 \end{pmatrix} = \begin{pmatrix} \sigma_{f,old}^2 \\ \sigma_{A,old}^2 \end{pmatrix} + \mathcal{H}^{-1}\mathcal{D}. \tag{5.26}$$

Iterations of IRLS for $\boldsymbol{\beta}$ and the updating equation in (5.26) are terminated when the corrections for the estimated parameters are small, the change in the log-likelihood l is small, or the norm of the score vector $\mathcal{D}$ is small. The convergence criterion referred to in Section 5.4 can be adapted in a straightforward manner. The convergence properties of the algorithm are so good that choosing a 'good' starting solution is not essential. The WLS with weights reciprocal to s_i^2 (assuming $\sigma_f^2 = \sigma_A^2 = 0$) provides a natural starting solution for $\boldsymbol{\beta}$. As an alternative, the submodel assuming $\sigma_A^2 = 0$ can be fitted first; it is useful for testing the hypothesis of no differences among the administrations, $\sigma_A^2 = 0$.

Negative estimated variances can arise, especially for σ_A^2. It is meaningful to set such an estimated variance to zero and reestimate the other variance. The DIF variance σ_f^2 is unlikely to vanish. Examples in the next section indicate that $\sigma_A^2 = 0$ is a realistic hypothesis in many cases. An alternative approach to dealing with negative estimated variances is to estimate the corresponding standard deviations σ_f and σ_A. Using this parametrization, negative estimates of the variances cannot arise. However, since zero standard deviation is a stationary point of the Fisher scoring algorithm, the starting solution for the standard deviation has to be distant from zero.

The average DIF coefficient for item i can be estimated as the estimated conditional expectation of $\mu + \delta_i$ given the data and the parameter estimates:

$$\hat{\alpha}_i = \hat{\mu} + \hat{\sigma}_f^2 \mathbf{1}_H^\top \hat{\mathbf{\Sigma}}_i^{-1} \mathbf{e}_i,$$

with the estimated conditional variance $\hat{\sigma}_f^2 - \hat{\sigma}_f^4 \mathbf{1}_H^\top \hat{\mathbf{\Sigma}}_i^{-1} \mathbf{1}_H$. The conditional expectation can be interpreted as a shrinkage estimator.

5.8.2 Examples

A form of the College Board Biology Achievement Test was administered on three occasions between December 1983 and June 1986. On the first two occasions, identical forms were used, but prior to the third administration, 2 of the 95 items were reviewed. All the examinees in the first two administrations were high school juniors or seniors, whereas sophomores comprised almost 75 per cent of the examinees in the third administration. The administration sizes were 7400, 3000, and 17 000, respectively. Women were represented in the administrations by 53–58 percent, Black examinees by 2–4 percent, and Asian American examinees by 5–13 percent of the total. The data were provided by Anne Harvey of ETS.

We analysed the DIF statistics for Men–Women (M–F), White–Black (W–B), and White–Asian American groups (W–A) for the 93 items common to the three administrations. The number of correct responses was used as the matching variable. To explore the dependence of DIF on the populations of examinees, we analysed the administrations separately for juniors and seniors, and for all the examinees (including the sophomores in the third administration). The estimates of the DIF variances for the two sets of analyses are given in Table 5.3. The estimates of the between-administration variances σ_A^2 are 9–33 times smaller than the corresponding estimates of the DIF form-variances σ_f^2. The DIF coefficients exhibit considerable stability across the administrations, even when there are apparent differences in the populations from which the examinees are drawn.

The estimates of σ_A^2 are nominally significant (say, at a 5 percent level) for Men–Women DIF but not for White–Black DIF. There is no clear indication that the composition of the third administration (with or without

TABLE 5.3. DIF variance estimates in Biology Achievement test.

Groups	Without sophomores		With sophomores	
	$\hat{\sigma}_f^2$	$\hat{\sigma}_A^2$	$\hat{\sigma}_f^2$	$\hat{\sigma}_A^2$
M − F	0.405	0.0121	0.355	0.0194
	(0.062)	(0.0042)	(0.054)	(0.0040)
W − B	0.272	0.0206	0.270	0.0085
	(0.027)	(0.0254)	(0.048)	(0.0162)
W − A	0.358	0.0113	0.295	0.0334
	(0.056)	(0.0075)	(0.047)	(0.0085)

Note: Standard errors are given in parentheses.

sophomores) has a uniform impact on the between-administration DIF variance. Note that the addition of more than 10 000 sophomore students in the analysis is not accompanied by a marked reduction in the standard errors. In fact, for White–Asian American DIF, the standard error for $\hat{\sigma}_A^2$ is greater for the analysis with the larger dataset. The cause of this is that, in general, greater estimated variances are associated with greater standard errors.

The pairs of variance estimates $\hat{\sigma}_f^2$ and $\hat{\sigma}_A^2$ suggest that although the DIF coefficients change from administration to administration, the changes tend to be so small that it is unlikely that several items would have small DIF coefficients in one administration and outlying ones in another.

5.8.3   Other applications

With the emergence of new modes of administration, such as presenting the items on a computer screen as an alternative to the paper-and-pencil mode, concerns have been raised that some minority groups may be adversely impacted by the change. Studying how DIF changes as a test form is transcribed from the traditional mode to the computer can shed some light on this issue. Suppose one administration of a given test form is given in the traditional mode and another administration is given in the alternative mode. Considering these two administrations as using the same test form, the between-administration variance σ_A^2 is a summary measure of the changes in DIF from one mode to another.

This approach is not without deficiency, though. If the DIF coefficients were to change uniformly by the same quantity, this change would be negated by the self-norming property of the DIF coefficients. However, comparison of the test scores may indicate that a mode of administration is relatively more difficult for one group than for another. Equivalence of the populations of examinees could be ensured by some form of random or non-informative (representative) assignment of the examinees to the modes of administration. This is rarely feasible, though, because examinees' motivation and interest are an imperative, and inflexible assignment to a mode may be detrimental to motivation. On the other hand, if students select the mode of administration, the resulting assignment may be informative. Examinees might be asked to take the same test form in both modes, with a period of time between the two administrations that would ensure loss of the practice effect. Such experiments are very difficult to organize because the interest and motivation of the examinees is difficult to maintain on both occasions. Also, examinees' abilities may change considerably over the period between the administrations.

Because of the nature of the matching variable, which is usually an imperfect measure of ability, DIF coefficients are at best an imperfect measure of item bias. On the one hand, identified mistakes or biases in test items are likely to be associated with large DIF; on the other hand, large DIF may arise even when we are unable to identify a feature of the item that may have caused it.

The size of the change in DIF as a result of a deliberate 'mistake' can be assessed by constructing and administering alternate forms. For instance, to study the Men–Women DIF, test items may be constructed that use boy's or girl's names, or avoid any reference to gender. Alternate forms are then constructed, so that some items appear in 'male', 'female' or 'neutral' versions in the different test forms. The DIF statistics from (multiple) administrations of such forms can then be analysed using the explanatory variable indicating the version (male, female, or neutral). Longford, Holland, and Thayer (1993) give details of the analysis of such an experiment.

The utility of such experiments is limited by the uncertainty about the extent to which the results can be generalized. The findings may be dependent on the population of examinees, on the subject area tested, on the types of items used, and the like. The experiments require large numbers of well-motivated examinees, and the test results cannot be used in the same way as operational standardized tests (say, for admission to higher education) because of the experimental nature of the test.

5.9 Conclusion

A method for summarizing the properties of items in a test form was presented. The summaries are based on the *estimated* quantities for each item, but they refer to the *underlying* quantities. When there are a large number of items, each item-level estimate may be subject to substantial sampling error, yet the summary is quite precise. As a form of feedback, the summary can be used for improved estimation of the item-level quantities. Further improvement in estimation is achieved by pooling information across several administrations (replicates). All the methods can be expanded for linear regression to relate the quantities of interest to item attributes.

Variance of the itemwise differences across the administrations is a compact summary of the between-administration differences of the item properties. Such a summary is useful for evaluating the quality of inference for future administrations based on a realized (e.g., trial) administration. The EB approach enables improved estimation of the item characteristics by borrowing strength across the items.

Although the methods are illustrated by examples concerned with DIF, they are applicable to other item-level characteristics and are particularly relevant in situations where each of a large number of atomic quantities is estimated with little precision. A similar theme is pursued in Chapter 8, where estimation for a small geographical area is strengthened by incorporating information from the other areas; this improvement is mediated by the between-area variance.

6

Equating and equivalence of tests

6.1 Introduction

A test form serves its purpose of assessing an individual's skill, ability, or knowledge of a well-defined domain only if the test scores satisfy a number of conditions. First, the test scores have to be strongly associated (highly correlated) with the measured trait. This trait is an inherently unobservable quantity. How closely it is approximated by a test score (on average, in a population of examinees) is in most cases a matter of conjecture. At best, some faith in a test score can be generated by pursuing and documenting the usual elements of quality control: review of the composition of the test and scrutiny of every step in the test assembly.

Some evidence, although of a speculative nature, is provided by a comparison with other tests purported to measure the same or different traits. Such an approach does not address the dismissive hypothesis that all the tests may measure a common trait that is nevertheless distant from the trait of interest. When the measured trait is a future (potential) ability, some insight can be gained several years after the test administration by relating the past examinees' scores to their current status (employment, academic, and the like). Of course, this is difficult to accomplish in practice on a large scale, as the examinees disperse throughout the country and worldwide over the years. The numerous career, social, and health influences, in addition to imperfect measurement, blur the hypothetical 'clean' association between the test score and the trait of interest.

Reliability of the scores, or the 'measurement error' associated with scoring, has to be small enough so that most of the variation of the scores would be due to differences in ability of the examinees. Reliability is defined as the correlation of the scores of an examinee in a hypothetical replication of the test administration. The measurement error variance is the variance of the scores of an examinee over the replications. Different kinds of replication lead to different definitions of reliability and of measurement error variance.

Measurement error can be assessed by various methods that bypass the need for replication. For instance, test forms are often split into two halves deemed to be equivalent; each half is scored, and the variation of the between-half differences is used to estimate the measurement error variance. Details of this approach are given in Section 6.2.2.

The third condition applies to large-scale testing programmes that employ several forms and administer the test on many occasions. For instance, in a high-stakes test, a test form is used only on one occasion (in one administration), and on each occasion several forms may be used. To ensure continuity in the interepretation of the scores, it is essential that the association of the scores with the underlying trait does not depend on the form taken. The score of, say, 540 on SAT Verbal has to have, in some ways, the same meaning irrespective of the form taken and of the date on which the test was taken. We say that the scores are *equivalent* across the test forms and in time.

Since the scores are usually defined on an arbitrarily set scale, a transformation of one score may make it equivalent to another score. Methods for estimating such transformations are referred to as *equating*. In a typical context, an equating method is applied even when the scores may not be equatable, that is, when no transformation would make one score equivalent to the other. It is more appropriate to think of equating in this context as *projecting* of one score on the other. Then the distribution of the differences of one score from the projection of the other score characterizes the difference of the two test forms.

The expectation of these differences (over the population of the examinees) can be arranged to vanish, and so their variance is the principal descriptor of the distance between the two test forms (scores). To avoid some ambiguities, we may assume that each score, as well as the projection, has a zero mean and unit variance. Assuming normality, the differences are completely described by their variance.

This chapter discusses methods for assessing whether a pair of test forms can be equated, finding the appropriate transformation, and for evaluating how different are the traits measured by different tests or test forms. The centrepiece of our approach is in describing the difference of the traits underlying the tests by a variance. Zero variance corresponds to complete agreement; large variance corresponds to substantial differences between the traits for a large fraction of the population. The focus on inference about variation is a common link with the preceding chapters.

Although the motivation and focus of the chapter are exclusively from educational testing, similar problems arise in the development of diagnostic procedures in biomedical research; for instance, in studies attempting to establish equivalence of measurement methods or instruments for illnesses that could otherwise be diagnosed only by invasive and expensive surgery.

The next section discusses issues of score equivalence and score equating. Section 6.3 addresses estimation and related computational issues. An application is presented in Section 6.4. The chapter concludes with a summary.

6.2   Equivalent scores

For simplicity of the discourse, we consider the term 'test form' for the collection of items and a formula for assigning a score for each sequence of responses to the items. We consider the *observed* (manifest) or assigned score, and the *true* (latent) score for each examinee. The true score is defined as the expectation of the observed scores, for a given examinee, in a hypothetical (independent) replication of the test. There are several kinds of true scores, each associated with a type of replication. The true score for the domain may be different from the true score for the test form because, for instance, certain aspects of the domain may not be represented in the test form.

We use the term 'score' to denote two distinct entities. First, it refers to the quantitative assessment (number of points) of the responses of an examinee. The observed score is calculated directly from the pattern of responses to the multiple-choice items (such as the number of correct responses) or by combining the grades given for the constructed-response items. Conceptually, the true score is defined as the mean of a large number of replicated observed scores. Of course, this definition cannot be exploited directly because an examinee is rarely available to take the test more than once under the conditions that would warrant replication.

Another meaning of the term 'score' is to denote the *random variable* defined on the population of examinees. It is convenient to consider an infinite population (*super*population) of examinees, which is represented by the examinees who actually take the test. Thus, the term 'score' denotes both a random variable and its realization. Whenever we use this term, its meaning will be either stated explicitly or will be clear from the context.

The scores for a test have a multitude of equivalent representations. For instance, the scores on the SAT Verbal test are defined so as to be on the scale 200–800. If each score were divided by 10, so that the scores would be on the scale 20–80, no information would be discarded because the original scores could be recovered straightforwardly. The scale of 200–800 was set by a convention to begin with. A given score, say, 500 on the SAT Verbal test, does not correspond in any psychometrically meaningful way to the score of 500 on the SAT Mathematics test, nor to 500 on the GRE Verbal test and can in no way be interpreted as the score of an examinee who has mastered half of the tested domain.

The score as a random variable is defined on the population of examinees. To alleviate the dependence of the score on the essentially arbitrary scale, we declare two scores, say, x and y, to be *equivalent* if there is a (strictly) increasing transformation f of one score to the other, that is, $y = f(x)$. We exclude the decreasing functions from this definition because they reverse the order of the examinees' scores.

The relation of being 'equivalent' has the following properties:

- x is equivalent to itself;

- x is equivalent to y if and only if y is equivalent to x;

- if x is equivalent to y and y is equivalent to z, then x is equivalent to z.

In algebra, such a relation is called equivalence. An important property of equivalence is that it defines *classes of equivalence*. A pair of scores in the same class is equivalent and any pair of scores in different classes is not.

For examinee $i = 1, 2, \ldots, I$, we consider the *domain*-true score, x_i^d, the *test-form* true score x_i^t, and the observed score x_i^o. The domain- and the test-form true scores are not observed. Assuming a population of test forms that represent the domain, the domain-true score can be defined as the mean of the scores across the population of test forms. We assume that the deviations

$$\eta_i = x_i^t - x_i^d$$

have a distribution with mean zero (this is not a restrictive assumption if a normalization of the scores is adopted) and variance σ_d^2. The measurement error, that is, the deviation of the observed score from the test-form true score,

$$\varepsilon_i = x_i^o - x_i^t,$$

has zero expectation and variance σ_e^2. It is assumed that the deviations η_i and ε_i are mutually independent.

The variance σ_d^2 is usually not estimable because it requires replication of the domain trait on several test forms administered to the same set of examinees. Information about the variance σ_e^2 could, in principle, be gained by replication of the administration of the test form. This is rarely feasible; however, the test form may be regarded as two replicates (halves) from which an estimate of σ_e^2 can be obtained.

Large-scale educational testing programmes use many test forms and it is highly desirable that these test forms be equivalent. Ensuring equivalence of test forms is not a trivial matter. At the test assembly stage, attention is paid to the representation in the test form of the various subdomains, item types, and other item classifications. In principle, uneven representation of the subdomains can be compensated by attaching weights to the responses, although determining such weights may be difficult and subject to considerable uncertainty.

There are two parallel definitions of equivalence: one for the true scores and another for the observed scores. For test forms with extremely many items, the two definitions coincide. In the standard setting, when the measurement errors are mutually independent and not associated with the true scores, equivalence of the observed scores from two distinct forms is impossible unless the measurement errors vanish. The problematic nature of observed-score equating becomes transparent when realizing that it coincides with true-score equating, assuming that the observed scores are subject to no measurement error.

Psychometricians have for a long time been interested in the factor structure underlying human abilities. A practical consequence of these efforts is the almost universal belief of unidimensional traits for narrowly defined domains, such as an academic subject or a physical attribute. Unidimensionality is the raison d'être of the scores on a unidimensional scale, because if the values of the true scores were available, the examinees's abilities could be meaningfully ordered.

As a consequence of uncritical acceptance of unidimensionality, deviation of a test from unidimensionality is nowadays often interpreted as a form of its imperfection. Equivalence of tests is closely connected to unidimensionality. Suppose we define a new test consisting of the two original tests as its sections. Equivalence of these two sections corresponds to unidimensionality of the newly composed test. Within the traditional factor analysis, we can test the hypothesis of unidimensionality, and thereby assess the evidence against unidimensionality. However, the only available alternative to unidimensionality is the presence of two dimensions, represented by the section scores; see Bennett, Rock, and Wang (1991) for an example. A finer insight is gained by quantifying the departure from unidimensionality in terms of the variance of the difference of the equated (projected) scores.

6.2.1   Equating test forms

Equivalence of test forms is an ideal very unlikely to be achieved in practice. Most frequently, a defensive posture is adopted by showing that there is insufficient evidence that the test forms are not equivalent. The principal function of test-form equating is to estimate or, ideally, determine what each examinee's (true or observed) score would be had he/she been assigned the other form. Another motivation is to have a conversion formula that would estimate the score y that an examinee who scores x on test A would attain on test B. Equating is intimately connected with the populations of examinees. A pair of test forms may be equivalent, or close to being equivalent, for one population and distinctly not equivalent for another population.

There are a number of methods for equating of test forms, and there is a rich taxonomy for their classification. Most methods can formally be applied even when the equated test forms are not equivalent. In such a case, it is more appropriate to think of equating as a projection, that is, finding the transformation that minimizes the distance between the two scores. Since the scores are random variables, a suitable definition of the term 'distance' is required. The mean squared difference, $\mathbf{E}\{f(x) - y\}^2$, is an obvious criterion; the function f is chosen from a class of functions (say all the linear functions), so as to minimize the mean squared difference.

True-score equating methods attempt to find a transformation of the true score of one test form to match it to the true score of the other form. Most observed-score equating methods are direct applications of the true-score equating methods to observed scores.

Equating is routinely performed in several kinds of settings. In a simple setting, examinees are administered both test forms, so that scores on both forms are available for a sample from the population of examinees. In another setting, examinees are either randomly or non-informatively assigned to one of the two test forms. More complex designs can be conceptualized as combinations of these two settings. For instance, the two test forms to be equated are supplemented by a common section, and then equating of the two original test forms is mediated through this common section.

6.2.2 Half-forms

When the true scores of a pair of test forms coincide, the measurement errors of the observed scores and the transformation are the only sources of differences among the scores. The measurement error variances therefore represent the limit of how close the observed scores for two equated tests can be to one another. Departure from equivalence can be assessed as the distance between the scores of the compared test forms in excess of the measurement error variances.

Most methods of true-score equating rely on estimates of the measurement error variances. Since replication of the administration of a test form is difficult to arrange, other approaches have to be adopted to estimate this variance. A commonly used method relies on partitioning of the test form into two nearly equivalent sections. Assuming that the test form score is the total of the scores from the two sections, the true subscores underlying these two observed subscores are equivalent and equated. In other words, the true scores for the two sections are identical. An estimate of the variance of the true scores for the entire test form can then be obtained as the sample variance of the between-section differences.

Let the observed test score for a given form be x, and suppose the items of the test are partitioned into two subtests with corresponding observed scores $x^{(1)}$ and $x^{(2)}$. We assume that these scores are defined in such a manner that $x = x^{(1)} + x^{(2)}$. For instance, the score defined as the number of correct responses has this property. The variances of these observed scores have decompositions

$$\operatorname{var}(x) = \sigma_d^2 + \sigma_e^2,$$

$$\operatorname{var}\left(x^{(h)}\right) = \sigma_{d,h}^2 + \sigma_{e,h}^2$$

$(h = 1, 2)$ into the respective true-score variances (σ_d^2) and measurement error variances (σ_e^2). Suppose the two sections are equivalent and the corresponding true scores are identical (equated), so that $\sigma_{d,1}^2 = \sigma_{d,2}^2$ and $\sigma_{e,1}^2 = \sigma_{e,2}^2$. These are very strong assumptions warranted only by a judicious partitioning of the test form into its sections. The items in the sections do not have to be a contiguous sequence of the items in the test form. They may be selected by a random process or with the intention of obtaining a match of score distributions. They may correspond to two equally long timed sessions used in the test administration. The variance of the score difference $x^{(1)} - x^{(2)}$ is $\sigma_{e,1}^2 + \sigma_{e,2}^2$ which, owing to the additive nature of the scores from the sections, is equal to σ_e^2. Hence, the measurement error variance σ_e^2 can be estimated as the sampling variance of the realized differences of $x^{(1)} - x^{(2)}$,

$$\hat{\sigma}_e^2 = \frac{1}{I} \sum_{i=1}^{I} \left(x_i^{(1)} - x_i^{(2)}\right)^2. \tag{6.1}$$

In practice, the two sections are unlikely to be exactly equivalent, but correction for some deviations from equivalence can be made. For instance, if the sections differ in their mean scores, the estimator in (6.1) can be adjusted as

$$\hat{\sigma}_e^2 = \frac{1}{I-1} \sum_{i=1}^{I} \left(x_i^{(1)} - x_i^{(2)} - \Delta\right)^2, \tag{6.2}$$

where $\Delta = \bar{x}^{(1)} - \bar{x}^{(2)}$ is the difference of the mean scores for the two sections.

6.2.3 Linear true-score equating

Equating true scores for a pair of test forms consists of two tasks. First, we have to establish that the scores are equivalent (or not too distant) and then identify the appropriate transformation. The principal complicating factor in this process is that the true scores are not available. Yet, equivalence can be assessed even without recovering the true scores. For illustration, we consider the 'reverse' process. Suppose the true scores for a pair of test forms, x^* and y^*, are equivalent. Then the ranks of the scores x^* and y^* are identical for any random sample from the population of examinees and a transformation of x^*, $f(x^*)$, coincides with y^*. The function f could be identified directly from the scatterplot of x^* and y^*.

When only the observed scores x and y are available, the measurement errors $x - x^*$ and $y - y^*$ blur the strong association of the true scores. An appropriate model for the association of the observed scores is

$$y = f\left(x - \varepsilon^{(x)}\right) + \varepsilon^{(y)}, \tag{6.3}$$

where ε denotes the measurement error for the test indicated by the superscript. The objective is to recover the function (transformation) f. A standard approach would involve defining a parametric family of functions, such as monotone polynomials of a certain degree, and then searching for the coefficients of the polynomial f that minimizes the mean squared difference. For most functions f, the random term $\varepsilon^{(x)}$ is intractably entangled with the true score. We adopt the simplifying assumption that the function f is linear, $f(x) = a + bx$. This imposes a rather strong although not entirely unrealistic assumption on the association of the test form scores x and y.

In the linear regression model

$$y = a + bx^* + \varepsilon^{(y)}, \tag{6.4}$$

the (latent) variable x^* is observed subject to error through the (manifest) variable x,

$$x = x^* + \varepsilon^{(x)}. \tag{6.5}$$

It is easy to demonstrate that ordinary least squares (OLS) applied to x instead of x^* yields a biased estimator of the regression parameters (a, b). Figure 6.1 demonstrates this phenomenon. We generated x^* as a random sample of 50 observations from the standard normal distribution, $\mathcal{N}(0, 1)$, and set $y = x^* + \delta$, where δ has the distribution $\mathcal{N}(0, 0.16^2)$. Then we defined x by (6.5), with $\varepsilon^{(x)}$ as a random sample from $\mathcal{N}(0, 0.25^2)$. The OLS fit of y on x is drawn in the diagram by the dashed line, and it is much shallower than the identity, $y = x$, drawn by the solid line, which corresponds to true-score equating. For completeness, the ordinary regression of y on x^* is drawn by a dotted line.

The estimator of the regression slope on x^* is

$$\hat{b}^* = \frac{\sum_{i=1}^{I} y_i (x_i^* - \bar{x}^*)}{\sum_{i=1}^{I} (x_i^* - \bar{x}^*)^2}. \tag{6.6}$$

Since both scores x and y are random variables, the numerator and denominator in (6.6) can be approximated by their respective population

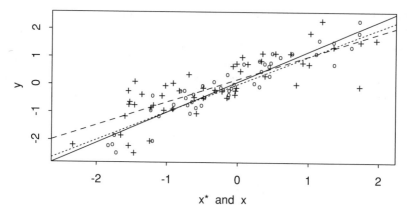

FIGURE 6.1. Scatterplot of the observed scores; a simulated example. The true-score points (x^*, y^*) are marked by the symbol 'o' and the observed-score points (x, y) by '+'. The regression of the observed scores is drawn by the dashed line, and the regression of the true scores by the dotted line. The solid line represents the identity, that is, the regression underlying the true scores.

versions,

$$I \operatorname{cov}(y, x^*) = I \operatorname{cov}(y, x) ,$$
$$I \operatorname{var}(x^*) = I \operatorname{var}(x) - I \sigma_e^2 .$$

Hence, for a large number of examinees, the regression slope in (6.6) is close to

$$\hat{b}^* = \frac{\operatorname{cov}(x, y)}{\operatorname{var}(x) - \sigma_e^2} ,$$

whereas the regression of the observed scores would yield

$$\hat{b} = \frac{\operatorname{cov}(x, y)}{\operatorname{var}(x)} .$$

Owing to the difference in the denominators, the regression of the observed scores is shallower than the regression for the true scores.

An alternative approach is based on the properties of the bivariate normal distribution. Let $\boldsymbol{\Sigma} = \operatorname{diag}(\sigma_{e,x}^2, \sigma_{e,y}^2)$ be the variance matrix of the measurement errors for x and y, and let $\boldsymbol{\Omega}$ be the variance matrix of the true scores. Owing to independence of the measurement errors and the true scores, the variance matrix of the observed scores is

$$[\operatorname{var}(x, y) =] \quad \boldsymbol{\Gamma} = \boldsymbol{\Omega} + \boldsymbol{\Sigma} .$$

Hence, $\boldsymbol{\Omega}$ can be estimated as

$$\hat{\boldsymbol{\Omega}} = \hat{\boldsymbol{\Gamma}} - \hat{\boldsymbol{\Sigma}} ,$$

where $\hat{\Gamma}$ is the sample variance matrix of (x, y), and $\hat{\Sigma} = \mathrm{diag}(\hat{\sigma}^2_{e,x}, \hat{\sigma}^2_{e,y})$ is the estimated measurement error variance matrix. Equivalence of the scores corresponds to their perfect correlation. Therefore, departure from equivalence can be inferred from $\hat{\Omega}$ by assessing how distant it is from being singular. This can be done by computing the eigenvalues of $\hat{\Omega}$, the estimated correlation,

$$\widehat{\mathrm{cor}}(x^*, y^*) = \hat{\Omega}_{xy}/\sqrt{\hat{\Omega}_{xx}\hat{\Omega}_{yy}},$$

or the estimated conditional variance,

$$\widehat{\mathrm{var}}(y^* \mid x^*) = \hat{\Omega}_{yy} - \hat{\Omega}^2_{xy}/\hat{\Omega}_{xx}$$

(assuming that $\hat{\Omega}_{xx} > 0$). This is an estimator of the residual variance of the linear regression of y^* on x^*. Furthermore, the estimated conditional expectation,

$$\hat{\mathbf{E}}(y^* \mid x^*) = \hat{\mu}_y + \hat{\Omega}_{xy}/\hat{\Omega}_{xx}(x^* - \hat{\mu}_x),$$

is the linear regression fit for the true scores. Thus, the two approaches, linear regression and decomposition of the variance matrix, coincide. The latter has the advantage that it requires minimal computing; the former is important as a link to the powerful tools of linear regression and maximum likelihood. The decomposition does not provide the sampling variances of the estimated parameters.

The sampling variances can be estimated by simulation. Having estimated all the model parameters, we generate a large number of sets of simulated true scores as random samples from the normal distribution with mean $\boldsymbol{\mu} = (\hat{\mu}_x, \hat{\mu}_y)^{\top}$ and variance matrix $\hat{\Omega}$. Each set has the same sample size as the realized sample. The simulated observed scores are computed from the true scores by adding the simulated measurement error, generated as a random sample from $\mathcal{N}(0, \hat{\Sigma})$. The variance matrix decomposition is then carried out for each dataset, and the sampling variance matrix of a set of parameters is estimated as the sample variance matrix of the simulated vectors of estimates. Such a simulation requires extensive computing, but it is relatively easy to implement. Note that in the simulations the true scores are computed, and so the simulated estimates can be compared with the estimates based on the realized values of the true scores. A more efficient alternative, but involving more computer programming, is to calculate the asymptotic standard errors from the inverse of the information matrix.

6.3   Estimation

This section discusses estimation of the linear transformation f, of the minimum variance σ^2_R, and of other quantities associated with equating.

In its entire generality (non-linear f), the problem is not tractable, and so we make several simplifying assumptions. We assume that all the random variables considered are normally distributed, that the transforming function f is linear, and that the measurement error variances are known.

The model specification for the true scores is

$$y^* = a + bx^* + \delta, \tag{6.7}$$

where the residual term δ is normally distributed with mean zero and variance σ_R^2. The true scores are represented by their observed counterparts, $x = x^* + \varepsilon^{(x)}$ and $y = y^* + \varepsilon^{(y)}$. The true scores x^* and y^* are normally distributed random samples with respective means μ_x and $\mu_y = a + b\mu_x$ and variances σ_x^2 and $\sigma_y^2 = b^2\sigma_x^2 + \sigma_R^2$. The model in (6.7) implies that $\text{cov}(x, y) = b\sigma_x^2$, and so

$$\begin{pmatrix} x \\ y \end{pmatrix} \sim N_2 \left\{ \begin{pmatrix} \mu_x \\ a + b\mu_x \end{pmatrix}, \begin{pmatrix} \sigma_x^2 + \sigma_{e,x}^2 & b\sigma_x^2 \\ b\sigma_x^2 & b^2\sigma_x^2 + \sigma_R^2 + \sigma_{e,y}^2 \end{pmatrix} \right\}. \tag{6.8}$$

Denote the mean vector and the variance matrix in (6.8) by $\boldsymbol{\mu}$ and $\boldsymbol{\Sigma}$, respectively, so that $(x, y)^\top \sim N(\boldsymbol{\mu}, \boldsymbol{\Sigma})$. The log-likelihood for the observed scores $\{x_i, y_i\}_i$ is

$$l = -\frac{1}{2}\left\{ I\log(2\pi) + I\det\boldsymbol{\Sigma} + \sum_{i=1}^{I} \mathbf{e}_i^\top \boldsymbol{\Sigma}^{-1}\mathbf{e}_i \right\}, \tag{6.9}$$

where $\mathbf{e}_i = \{(x_i, y_i)^\top - \boldsymbol{\mu}\}$. The maximum of this log-likelihood is found by the Fisher scoring method. Let $\mathbf{h}$ be the vector of the first-order partial derivatives of l with respect to the estimated parameters, $\mathbf{h} = \partial l/\partial\boldsymbol{\theta}$, and let $\mathbf{H}$ be the information matrix, $\mathbf{H} = -\partial^2 l/\left(\partial\boldsymbol{\theta}\partial\boldsymbol{\theta}^\top\right)$. The Fisher scoring algorithm for maximizing l can be described as iterations consisting of updating the vector $\hat{\boldsymbol{\theta}}$ of estimated parameters:

$$\hat{\boldsymbol{\theta}}_{new} = \hat{\boldsymbol{\theta}}_{old} + \mathbf{H}_{old}^{-1}\mathbf{h}_{old},$$

where the subscripts old and new refer to the current and the updated solutions. The iterations are terminated when the vector of corrections $\mathbf{H}_{old}^{-1}\mathbf{h}_{old}$, evaluated at the current solution, becomes small or the value of the log-likelihood l changes by a value smaller than a specified threshold.

For a general parameter θ, be it a regression parameter or a variance, we have

$$\frac{\partial l}{\partial\theta} = -\frac{I}{2}\text{tr}\left(\boldsymbol{\Sigma}^{-1}\frac{\partial\boldsymbol{\Sigma}}{\partial\theta}\right) + \frac{1}{2}\text{tr}\left(\boldsymbol{\Sigma}^{-1}\mathbf{S}\boldsymbol{\Sigma}^{-1}\frac{\partial\boldsymbol{\Sigma}}{\partial\theta}\right) + \sum_{i=1}^{I}\mathbf{e}_i\boldsymbol{\Sigma}^{-1}\frac{\partial\mathbf{e}_i}{\partial\theta}, \tag{6.10}$$

where $\mathbf{S} = \mathbf{e}_1\mathbf{e}_1^\top + \ldots + \mathbf{e}_I\mathbf{e}_I^\top$ is the matrix of totals of squares and cross-products of the (bivariate) residuals. The formal derivative $\partial\boldsymbol{\Sigma}/\partial\theta$ is the matrix of partial derivatives of the elements of $\boldsymbol{\Sigma}$ with respect to θ. Thus,

$$\frac{\partial \boldsymbol{\Sigma}}{\partial a} = \mathbf{0},$$

$$\frac{\partial \boldsymbol{\Sigma}}{\partial \mu_x} = \mathbf{0},$$

$$\frac{\partial \boldsymbol{\Sigma}}{\partial b} = \sigma_x^2 \begin{pmatrix} 0 & 1 \\ 1 & 2b \end{pmatrix},$$

$$\frac{\partial \boldsymbol{\Sigma}}{\partial \sigma_x^2} = \begin{pmatrix} 1 & b \\ b & b^2 \end{pmatrix} = \begin{pmatrix} 1 \\ b \end{pmatrix}\begin{pmatrix} 1 \\ b \end{pmatrix}^{\mathsf{T}},$$

$$\frac{\partial \boldsymbol{\Sigma}}{\partial \sigma_R^2} = \begin{pmatrix} 0 \\ 1 \end{pmatrix}\begin{pmatrix} 0 \\ 1 \end{pmatrix}^{\mathsf{T}}.$$

Further differentiation yields a rather formidable expression:

$$\frac{\partial l^2}{\partial \theta_1 \partial \theta_2} = \frac{I}{2} \mathrm{tr}\left(\boldsymbol{\Sigma}^{-1}\frac{\partial \boldsymbol{\Sigma}}{\partial \theta_1}\boldsymbol{\Sigma}^{-1}\frac{\partial \boldsymbol{\Sigma}}{\partial \theta_2}\right) - \mathrm{tr}\left(\boldsymbol{\Sigma}^{-1}\frac{\partial \boldsymbol{\Sigma}}{\partial \theta_1}\boldsymbol{\Sigma}^{-1}\mathbf{S}\boldsymbol{\Sigma}^{-1}\frac{\partial \boldsymbol{\Sigma}}{\partial \theta_2}\right)$$
$$- \sum_{i=1}^{I}\left(\frac{\partial \mathbf{e}_i}{\partial \theta_1}\right)^{\mathsf{T}}\boldsymbol{\Sigma}^{-1}\frac{\partial \mathbf{e}_i}{\partial \theta_2} - \sum_{i=1}^{I}\mathbf{e}_i^{\mathsf{T}}\boldsymbol{\Sigma}^{-1}\frac{\partial^2 \mathbf{e}_i}{\partial \theta_1 \theta_2}. \tag{6.11}$$

Since we use linear regression and none of the variance parameters are involved in the residuals $\mathbf{e}_i$, $\partial^2 \mathbf{e}_i/\partial \theta_1 \theta_2 \equiv \mathbf{0}$ for any pair of parameters θ_1 and θ_2. Also, $\partial \mathbf{e}_i/\partial \theta = -\partial \boldsymbol{\mu}/\partial \theta$. The matrix of totals of squares and cross-products $\mathbf{S}$ has expectation $I\boldsymbol{\Sigma}$, and so a general element of the information matrix is

$$-\mathbf{E}\left(\frac{\partial^2 l}{\partial \theta_1 \partial \theta_2}\right) = \frac{I}{2}\mathrm{tr}\left(\boldsymbol{\Sigma}^{-1}\frac{\partial \boldsymbol{\Sigma}}{\partial \theta_1}\boldsymbol{\Sigma}^{-1}\frac{\partial \boldsymbol{\Sigma}}{\partial \theta_2}\right) + I\frac{\partial \boldsymbol{\mu}^{\mathsf{T}}}{\partial \theta_1}\boldsymbol{\Sigma}^{-1}\frac{\partial \boldsymbol{\mu}}{\partial \theta_2}. \tag{6.12}$$

The Fisher scoring algorithm, using (6.12), is somewhat simpler than the Newton-Raphson algorithm based on (6.11). Further simplification in (6.12) takes place for specific pairs of parameters. When either θ_1 or θ_2 is a variance, $\partial \boldsymbol{\mu}/\partial \theta_h = \mathbf{0}$, and so only the first term in (6.12) has to be evaluated. Also, when θ_1 or θ_2 is not involved in $\boldsymbol{\Sigma}$, $\partial \boldsymbol{\Sigma}/\partial \theta_h = \mathbf{0}$, and only the second term has to be evaluated. The only parameter involved in both terms is the regression slope b. For completeness, we give the partial derivatives of the linear predictor $\boldsymbol{\mu}$:

$$\frac{\partial \boldsymbol{\mu}}{\partial a} = \begin{pmatrix} 0 \\ 1 \end{pmatrix},$$

$$\frac{\partial \boldsymbol{\mu}}{\partial b} = \begin{pmatrix} 0 \\ \mu_x \end{pmatrix},$$

$$\frac{\partial \boldsymbol{\mu}}{\partial \mu_x} = \begin{pmatrix} 1 \\ b \end{pmatrix}.$$

The unusual feature of the Fisher scoring algorithm based on (6.10) and (6.12) is the complex functional dependence of the information matrix and the score vector on the parameters. Although some of the elements of the information matrix vanish, the matrix is not block-diagonal. In many other settings, including the ordinary regression, the information matrix is block-diagonal with the blocks corresponding to the sets of the regression and variance parameters. In our model, all the parameters have to be estimated simultaneously. Some simplification would take place if the regression slope b were known.

Note that $(x_1 + \ldots + x_I)/I$ is not a fully efficient estimator of μ_x because the log-likelihood depends also on $\{y_i\}$. In most cases, the contribution of $\{y_i\}$ is only marginal, and the convergence of the Fisher scoring iterations is much slower than when $\hat{\mu}_x$ is set to the mean of $\{x_i\}$, which, in any case, is very close to the maximum likelihood estimate.

6.4 Application

When introducing a new format of an existing test, it is essential to demonstrate that the test forms in both formats measure the same domain of knowledge or ability; that is, the corresponding true scores are (almost) perfectly correlated. In other words, it is desirable that the format of the test have no impact on the scores. If we 'stripped' the test scores of the sources of uncertainty due to the selection of items and unpredictability of the examinees' responses, the score from a test with one format would be equivalent to the score from a test with the other format.

In recent years, this issue has received a lot of attention in educational testing as more emphasis is placed on the so-called authentic assessment. The thrust of this change of emphasis is on introducing test items that resemble much more closely the tasks that the examinees are expected to have mastered. Also, more accessible computer technology is contributing to the transformation of educational testing; in the future, examinees may be administered items and respond to them at a computer terminal. A truly vexing problem would arise if we found that the test administered by the traditional method (paper-and-pencil) was not equivalent to the test constructed to the same specifications (or even consisting of the same items) but administered on the computer.

The College Board SAT Programme conducted a study of different item types in 1992. The study applied the same design (but different tests) to two subpopulations of high school students defined by their achievement level (level I and level II). The recruited students, from high schools throughout the United States, selected their own level based on the description of the tests and in some cases with the advice of their teachers. For both achievement levels, students were administered tests on two days. On each day, a multiple-choice test and a separately timed test consisting of constructed-response items were administered. The domain of all the tests was high school mathematics. Anne Harvey from ETS provided the data generated by the study and the relevant background.

At each achievement level, four forms of the multiple-choice test were used, consisting of 35 items each. These forms were randomly assigned to classrooms. Each form was split into two sections consisting of 18 and 17 items which were administered on the separate days. These half-forms were constructed with a view toward equal score distribution on the two sections. The forms were randomly assigned to classrooms.

Test forms of three constructed-response item types were used: grid-in (GR), open-ended (OP), and extended open-ended (EX). Grid-in items require the examinees to enter their responses in a specified grid on the answer sheet. Such items provide a compromise between the need for computerized scoring and (essentially) unlimited number of response options. Open-ended items require the examinees to give an explanation or an example, to draw a diagram, or the like. Extended open-ended items present tasks such as explaining why a statement is true or false, giving an informal proof, or providing an alternative solution to a problem.

The half-forms of constructed-response items comprised 20 grid-in items, 10 open-ended items, or 3 extended open-ended items. The item types were assigned within classrooms by a spiralled design (GR, OP, EX, GR, OP, ...). Four half-forms, say, A, B, C, and D, were assembled for each item type. These half-forms were administered as four forms: sections A (on day 1) and B (on day 2); sections B (on day 1) and A (on day 2); sections C (on day 1) and D (on day 2); and sections D (on day 1) and C (on day 2). Thus, each examinee was administered two half-forms of a multiple-choice form (one on each day) and two half-forms of a constructed-response form (one on each day) containing items of one of the three non-standard item types.

Of interest to the programme direction is the proximity of the traits underlying the multiple-choice and non-standard forms. A hypothesis of interest is that the forms of grid-in items are closer to the multiple-choice forms than the open-ended and extended open-ended items. A factor analytic approach would not be suitable because the only alternative to unidimensionality is that of two factors underlying the scores from the multiple-choice and a non-standard form.

If the true scores were available, identity of the underlying traits would correspond to a deterministic relationship of the two scores, such as one score being a linear function of the other. Even if this were the case, the measurement 'error' (the deviation of the observed score from the true score) would cause the relationship among the observed scores to be

TABLE 6.1. Numbers of students in the study.

Item types	Achievement level I	Achievement level II
MC & GR	931	419
	245+241 + 213+232	102+ 98 + 103+116
MC & OP	571	354
	142+141 + 144+144	92+ 99 + 88+ 75
MC & EX	580	331
	140+140 + 151+149	93+108 + 70+ 60
Total	2082	1104

Notes: The quadruplets of numbers correspond to the forms. The numbers of students who took mutually reverse forms are separated by space. For example, 245 students took the form L1A (grid-in items), and 241 students took the form L1B, which differs from L1A only in the order of its half-forms.

blurred. The amount of blurring can be summarized by the variance of the measurement error; higher variance corresponds to more blurring.

6.4.1 Data and analysis

For simplicity, but also because we focus on comparison of item types, we do not distinguish among the four forms of each item type at each level of achievement, and we pool all estimates across these forms. Table 6.1 gives the sample sizes by the forms of the constructed-response items. The pairs of mutually reverse forms are separated by spaces. For instance, 245 examinees took form L1A of grid-in items for achievement level I, and 241 examinees took the form comprised of the same half-forms but administered in the reverse order (on different days). There were almost twice as many examinees at achievement level I than at level II.

Table 6.2 gives the sample means for each constructed-response form. The identification of the multiple-choice form taken was not available, and so only the mean across its four forms is given. The scores are integers, in the range –3 to 35 (number of correct responses with an adjustment for guessing). The means of the multiple-choice scores within the subsamples of students who were assigned a particular constructed-response item form are in the range 16.45–18.37 and 14.29–17.10 for the respective achievement levels I and II.

Figure 6.2 displays the scatterplots of the multiple-choice and grid-in scores for each form. An independent normal perturbation, $\mathcal{N}(0, 0.01)$, is added to each score in the diagram so as to distinguish between identical pairs of scores. The correlations for achievement level I are in the range

TABLE 6.2. Observed-score means for the four item types.

Item types	Achievement level I	Achievement level II
MC	17.27	15.61
GR	9.09	9.99
	8.52, 8.12, 9.84, 10.03	7.75, 7.94, 12.01, 11.91
OP	12.42	13.64
	13.73, 12.58, 12.17, 11.21	13.36, 12.26, 14.42, 14.87
EX	7.42	8.62
	7.34, 6.89, 7.99, 7.44	9.22, 8.51, 8.10, 8.52

Note: The test-form means for the constructed-response forms are given in the same order as the counts in Table 6.1.

0.73–0.79, and they are 0.71, 0.70, 0.81, and 0.75 for the forms at achievement level II. The correlations for the other item types are in the range 0.67–0.86. They exhibit no obvious pattern.

For each item type and achievement level, we consider the model relating the constructed-response test score to the multiple-choice test score by linear regression, assuming that both variables are measured subject to error with variances estimated from half-forms.

The results of the six analyses (two achievement levels and three item types) are summarized in Table 6.3. The estimates were obtained from variance decompositions and their standard errors from the inverses of the information matrices. The estimates of the measurement error variances of the multiple-choice test were not pooled across the three subsamples of examinees defined by the non-standard item type because, conceivably, the measurement error could be affected by the constructed-response items. However, the triplets of estimates of the measurement error variance are so close to one another, for both achievement levels, that pooling the estimates would lead to only slight changes. Note that all the scores are integers within a narrow range of values, which calls into question the ubiquitous assumption of normality.

The grid-in true scores at achievement level I are related to the multiple-choice form true scores by the estimated linear regression

$$y = -0.56 + 0.494x + \delta,$$

with estimated residual variance $\hat{\sigma}_R^2 = 1.58$. For contrast, the regression of the corresponding observed scores is $2.30 + 0.393x$, with estimated residual variance 6.97.

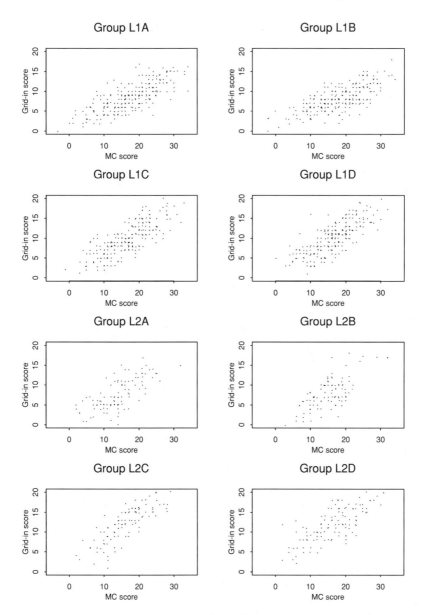

FIGURE 6.2. Scatterplots of the multiple-choice and grid-in form scores. 'L1' and 'L2' stand for achievement level. The pairs of plots in each row refer to forms that consist of the same half-forms in mutually reversed order. Each score is perturbed by a random draw from $\mathcal{N}(0, 0.01)$.

TABLE 6.3. Measurement error regression fits for the grid-in, open-ended, and extended open-ended test scores on the multiple-choice test scores.

Forms	Regression	Residual variance	Measurement error variance	True score variance	R^2
Achievement level I					
GR	−0.56 + 0.494x (0.005)	1.58 (0.33)	3.57 9.39	10.52 33.62	0.850
OP	−1.00 + 0.768x (0.009)	3.23 (0.99)	8.74 9.29	25.96 38.55	0.875
EX	−1.53 + 0.525x (0.007)	1.51 (0.57)	6.14 9.38	11.74 37.06	0.871
Achievement level II					
GR	−0.93 + 0.698x (0.010)	2.90 (0.71)	4.10 8.93	16.89 28.74	0.829
OP	−4.85 + 1.213x (0.015)	0.40 (1.61)	10.57 8.84	47.66 32.12	0.992
EX	−4.09 + 0.797x (0.011)	−2.05 (0.85)	8.88 8.74	14.59 26.21	1.141

Notes: Standard errors are given in parentheses underneath the estimates. In each cell in the columns 'Score variance' and 'True-score variance', the variance of the non-standard test form is given at the top and that of the multiple-choice form at the bottom. The column 'R^2' contains the estimated proportion of variation of the non-standard form true score explained by the multiple-choice true score.

If this equation were regarded as an equating formula, the examinees' equated scores would differ from the grid-in true scores on average by $\sqrt{1.58} \doteq 1.25$ in absolute value. In comparison, the variance of the grid-in true scores is 10.52 (standard deviation 3.24). Thus, the multiple-choice test true scores 'explain', in terms of the traditional R^2, $100 \times (1 - 1.58/10.52) =$ 85 percent of the variation in the grid-in true scores. The estimated measurement error variances are 3.57 (grid-in) and 9.39 (multiple choice). They were estimated from the half-form scores.

The proximity of the grid-in to the multiple-choice test is best assessed by comparing their association with the two competitors — the open-ended and extended open-ended tests. For achievement level I, the R^2 coefficients are almost identical and are much smaller than unity. The tests comprised of constructed-response items therefore do not represent the same trait as the multiple-choice tests, and their true scores deviate from the multiple-choice true scores by comparable amounts. The uncertainty about R^2 can

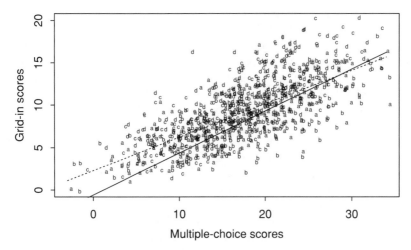

FIGURE 6.3. Fitted regressions for the multiple-choice and grid-in form scores, achievement level I. The OLS fit is drawn by the dashed line and the measurement error regression by the solid line. The plotting symbols differentiate among the four forms of grid-in items. The scores are perturbed by random draws from $\mathcal{U}(-0.25, 0.25)$ so as to avoid multiple points being drawn in the same location.

be highlighted as follows. The standard error of the residual variance for the grid-in test (equal to 0.33) is such that the values $\sigma_R^2 = 1.0$ and $\sigma_R^2 = 2.0$ are both feasible. The corresponding values of R^2 are $1 - 1/10.52 = 0.905$ and $1 - 2/10.52 = 0.810$. These would be, respectively, greater than and smaller than the R^2 coefficients for the other two item types. The fitted regression is drawn in the scatterplot of the multiple-choice and grid-in scores in Figure 6.3. So as to distinguish among points with the same coordinates, each score is perturbed by a randomly drawn variable from the uniform distribution on $(-0.25, 0.25)$.

In contrast, the R^2 coefficients for achievement level II differ substantially, although they are aligned in an unexpected order. A strange anomaly occurs for the extended open-ended test, for which the estimated true-score variance matrix $\hat{\Omega}$ has a negative eigenvalue. As a consequence, the estimated residual variance is negative, and R^2 is greater than unity. It would be reasonable to redefine the estimated residual variance to zero, so that $R^2 = 1$. In conclusion, we have found no evidence against the hypothesis that the open-ended and extended open-ended tests have the same underlying trait as the multiple-choice test. The grid-in test deviates from the multiple-choice test to about the same degree as do the tests for achievement level I.

The sample sizes would be sufficient for a reliable estimate of the measurement error variance if the half-forms were almost equivalent. When the half-forms contain a larger number of items, near-equivalence is likely to be attained by chance. However, the extended open-ended half-forms contain only three items, and so the pairs of half-forms may deviate from equivalence substantially. Since the scoring of these half-forms is rather coarse, the observed scores contain little information about departure from equivalence. Therefore, the measurement error variance may be overestimated, bringing about biased estimation of the true-score variance matrix $\boldsymbol{\Omega}$.

More detailed exploration can be conducted by separate analyses for each form. For instance, the substantial residual variance for the forms with grid-in items at achievement level II may be due to a single 'aberrant' form. However, this is not the case. For instance, the estimated residual variance for the grid-in forms L2A and L2B (mutually reverse forms) is 0.74 (standard error 0.97), and for the other two grid-in forms, L2C and L2D, it is 0.60 (standard error 0.94). Both estimated variances are smaller than the estimated variance from the pooled analysis (equal to 2.90). This suggests that the pairs of forms may be related to the multiple-choice test in different ways (for instance, they may represent different traits). Also, equating of the test forms may yield closer correspondence. However, the analyses of the smaller datasets are associated with greater uncertainty and they pertain to the issues of equivalence of test forms rather than tests (item types), and so the pooled analysis is preferred.

6.4.2 Comparing validity

It remains to address the issue of which item type is a better representation of the domain (high school mathematics). Since this trait is not observable, there is no unequivocal solution. Here we offer some insight by considering a narrow range of hypotheses about the tested domain.

Suppose the domain is perfectly represented by one of the true scores, x^* or y^*; denote this *trait score* by t. To fix the scale, let the trait scores have the same mean and variance as the true scores x^*. For each item type and achievement level, we consider the mean squared error (MSE) of the observed score, suitably rescaled, around the trait score. The true score y^* is brought onto the same scale as x^* and t by the linear transformation $y' = (y^* - a)/b$.

Assuming that $y' \equiv t$, the MSE for the observed score y, rescaled to $y^\dagger = (y - a)/b$, is $\mathbf{E}(y^\dagger - t)^2 = \sigma_{e,y}^2/b^2$, and for x, it is $\mathbf{E}(x - t)^2 = \sigma_{e,x}^2 + \sigma_R^2/b^2$. On the other hand, if $x \equiv t$, the MSEs for the observed scores are $\mathbf{E}(x - t)^2 = \sigma_{e,x}^2$ and $\mathbf{E}(y^\dagger - t)^2 = (\sigma_{e,y}^2 + \sigma_R^2)/b^2$. These MSEs are estimated by substituting the estimated slope and variances for the parameters. The estimates are given in Table 6.4. The columns contain the sets of four estimated MSEs for each level and item type. Thus, when the grid-in forms represent the trait perfectly for achievement level I, the grid-in and multiple-choice tests have similar MSEs (14.45 vs. 15.62), but the multiple-choice forms are clearly superior when they represent the trait

TABLE 6.4. Mean squared errors under the assumption that one of the true scores is the trait score.

MSE for	Achievement level I			Achievement level II		
	GR	**OP**	**EX**	**GR**	**OP**	**EX**
	Score trait y'					
$y^\dagger$	14.45	14.82	22.28	8.42	7.18	13.98
x^*	15.62	14.77	14.86	14.88	9.11	8.47
	Score trait x					
x^*	9.39	9.29	9.38	8.93	8.84	8.47
$y^\dagger$	20.69	20.29	27.76	14.37	7.46	13.98

Note: The negative estimate of the residual variance for the extended open-ended item type at achievement level II is reset to zero.

perfectly (9.39 vs. 20.69). At first, this appears to be a counterintuitive finding; however, it has a straightforward explanation. The measurement error variances of the constructed-response test are so much greater than that of the multiple-choice test that even perfect validity of their true scores would be a minor advantage over the multiple-choice tests because the true scores of the tests with different item types are so similar.

This finding is not replicated for achievement level II, and so its generalization, especially in view of the problems with estimating the measurement error variance for tests with few items, is not warranted. In any case, no generalization is warranted to other domains, populations, or other elements of the context. Note that the MSEs are also subject to sampling variation, more so for achievement level II, where the sample sizes are somewhat smaller.

The multiple-choice and constructed-response tests can be compared for a wider range of alternatives about the trait score, such as when the trait score is a linear combination of the true scores. Suppose the trait score is $t = cx^* + (1-c)y^\dagger$ for some $c \in [0, 1]$. Then the MSE for $y^\dagger$ is $(\sigma_{e,y}^2 + c^2\sigma_R^2)/b^2$ and the MSE for x is $\sigma_{e,x}^2 + (1 - c)^2\sigma_R^2/b^2$. Assuming that $\sigma_R^2 > 0$, these two MSEs coincide for

$$c^\dagger = \frac{b^2\sigma_{e,x}^2 + \sigma_R^2 - \sigma_{e,y}^2}{2\sigma_R^2}.$$

When $c^\dagger < 0$, x has a greater MSE for all $c \in (0, 1)$, and when $c^\dagger > 1$, x has a smaller MSE for all $c \in (0, 1)$; in these cases, one test is uniformly superior to the other. When $0 < c^\dagger < 1$, external information is required to establish which test has a smaller MSE around the trait score. In most practical settings, we can only speculate about the value of c or if indeed the domain of interest is equal or close to a linear combination of the true scores of the competing tests.

Many researchers and practitioners in the educational testing community believe that for the open-ended and extended open-ended item type, c is close to unity. This belief is based on the authentic nature of the items but otherwise has little empirical support. Nevertheless, there is considerable empirical evidence that the measurement error variance of a typical constructed-response test or section is much greater than a comparable test (section) of multiple-choice items. Therefore, uncritical preference for constructed-response items is poorly supported on the grounds of higher quality of examinee scores.

6.4.3   Model criticism

The assumptions of normality of all the random terms are adopted strictly for computational simplicity. The scores, being integers in a narrow range, are very coarse, and therefore distinctly non-normally distributed. It would be meaningful to assume that they are rounded versions of normally distributed random variables. In general, maximum likelihood estimators of the regression and variance parameters in measurement error models are fairly robust with respect to departures from normality, although the estimators of the *sampling variances* and standard errors are much less so. Normality is often promoted by the definition of the scores, because, for historic reasons, the bell-shaped distribution of test scores is preferred.

Another target for model criticism is linearity of the assumed association of the true scores. A number of difficulties arise when considering non-linear regression with the regressor measured subject to error.First of all, the outcome variable can no longer be normally distributed because the model equation involves non-linear functions of normally distributed random terms. Whereas a linear function can be a good approximation for an increasing function in a short interval, the same linear function may not be applicable for the entire range of scores. A simple procedure for checking the model involves splitting the examinees into a small number of subsets grouped by the score x and fitting separate models for each subset of data. Any trend in the model fits for these subsets is an indication that the transformation of x^* by a non-linear function would get us much closer to y^*. This suggests that linear equating generally overestimates the distance between the equated test forms. As an alternative, the observed scores x and y can be subjected to transformations that promote linearity of the association of the corresponding true scores. Note that a transformation of the true scores may correspond to a substantially different transformation of the observed scores.

6.5   Summary

A measurement error model was applied to make inference about the association of the true scores from pairs of tests assumed to measure the same trait. The residual variance in the regression of the true scores, and the corresponding proportion of variation explained, R^2, are informative measures of the distance of the traits underlying the two tests. The example from the SAT testing programme shows that it is very difficult to measure the same underlying trait by tests with different formats. The hypothesis that the forms with grid-in items are closer to the forms with multiple-choice items is not supported for either achievement level. Ignoring the measurement error of the scores, or estimating their variance with bias, leads to substantially biased estimation of the distance between two forms. The analysis of the SAT experiment highlights the counterbalancing effects of the measurement error and of the proximity of the true scores to the trait of interest. Although constructed-response tests may be more valid, that is, their true scores are more highly correlated with the domain-true score, this advantage is eroded by the greater measurement error variance of the corresponding observed scores.

The method presented makes a distinction between the true and observed scores. It is a generalization of the true score theory (Gulliksen, 1950; Lord and Novick, 1968) to bivariate scores. The method can be applied to the assessment of the impact on the scores of other alterations of the tests, for instance, to study how examinee performance is affected by limiting the time allowed or by controlling other conditions (such as availability of calculators).

Measurement error models are more comprehensively discussed in Fuller (1987). An extension of the measurement models for clustered (grouped) data is presented in Longford (1993c). Holland and Rubin (1982) present a comprehensive account of the equating methods used in educational testing; see also Lord (1980).

7

Inference from surveys with complex sampling design

7.1 Introduction

Monitoring the quality of education is an important concern for educational researchers, politicians, and economists, as well as parents and organizations representing them. Large-scale surveys are probably the most important source of inference about the educational system of a country. Not infrequently, conclusions drawn from educational surveys make the news headlines and are used to support and justify policies that affect the educational system.

Educational surveys present a considerable challenge for educational researchers, for survey statisticians, and for public relations, as well as for public funds. First, a single survey is insufficient for most purposes because the educational system comprises several distinct populations of subjects (students), defined, for example, by age, grade, or the type of school. Each population requires a different survey instrument tailored to the expected distribution of ability of the subjects. The school curriculum comprises several academic subjects that may be of interest for the survey. Of course, teachers also represent a population relevant to such surveys.

Next, the surveyed population is a moving target because, say, most of this year's first-graders will be the next year's second-graders. In fact, a survey is likely to be useful only in comparison with other surveys since it can provide only a snapshot of a dynamic system. Also, there are no absolute criteria for what constitutes satisfactory education, other than the unrealistic ideal of all the students mastering every aspect of the hypothetical perfect curriculum.

Further, a typical outcome variable, such as knowledge of a well-defined domain, is measured indirectly, by means of questions (items), and imperfectly, because a complete representation of the domain could be achieved only by a very large number of items. Other elements of imperfect measurement are sampling (only a sample of the target population is administered the survey instrument), motivation (the subjects are informed that they have no personal stake in their contribution to the survey, and so may not perform as well as they would in a high-stakes setting), missing responses (subjects selected into the survey may be unavailable on the day; a student may fail to respond to some of the questionnaire items), and definition of the scale ('scoring' of the items).

The subject of this chapter is estimation of population and subpopulation means of indirectly observed quantities. In the spirit of the earlier chapters, we will consider not only estimation of the mean of a variable for one (sub-)population but also estimation of the means for several related variables, subpopulations, and surveys. In particular, we will explore how information from one survey can be exploited for inference from a different (but closely related) survey. We see the key in defining compact data summaries that capture certain aspects of the sampling design and are stable across contexts. The within- and between-cluster variances (variance components) fulfill this niche and mediate in the model-based estimation of (sub-)population means. The commonality of this approach with the rater reliability and score adjustment issues discussed in Chapters 2–4 is in the central role of the variance parameters. In surveys with clustered sampling design, the variances are summaries of the consistent differences among the clusters. Although these differences are a nuisance feature of the survey, the variances are full-fledged parameters of interest.

The chapter is motivated by a particular survey, the National Assessment of Educational Progress (NAEP), funded by the U.S. Department of Education, and carried out and analysed at ETS. NAEP is an extensive programme of surveys for several academic subjects (Mathematics, Writing, Reading, History, Geography, and so on) and age/grade groups, carried out according to a regular schedule over the last two decades.

Estimation of the population mean will be expedited rather quickly and the focus will be on estimation of the sampling variance of the estimator of the mean. We will contrast two approaches: jackknife, which does not assume explicitly a model underlying the survey data, and a model-based approach, which relies on a description of the sampling design by a statistical model. Unlike the jackknife, the model-based method enables, at least in principle, pooling information across subpopulations and surveys. This is of particular importance for the estimation of the means for subpopulations sparsely represented in the survey sample.

The chapter concentrates on the issues of estimation and computing; how to make substantive inferences based on the estimated quantities is beyond its scope and would involve exhaustive research of how the results are used and interpreted by the sponsors of the surveys. Kish (1965) and Cochran (1974), classic monographs on survey sampling, contain sufficient bakcground for this chapter.

Section 7.2 describes the design of a typical NAEP survey. We make a distinction between the *realized* design, that is, the description of how the survey sample was drawn, and the *model* design, which is an idealized description of the sampling design. Section 7.3 gives details of the outcome variable and of the procedures for its estimation. Section 7.4 describes a jackknife procedure for estimating population means for a directly observed variable in such a survey. Section 7.5 presents the model-based approach. The jackknife and model-based methods are illustrated on several examples in Section 7.6. Section 7.7 deals with model-based estimation of proportions and percentiles or quantiles, and Section 7.8 deals with fitting ordinary regression. In Section 7.9, the problem of estimating a large number of subpopulation means, many of them based on very few subjects, is considered. Section 7.10 describes a simulation-based method for comparing the efficiency of the estimators. The chapter concludes with a summary.

7.2 Sampling design

Because of relative simplicity and tractability, much of the classical statistical theory revolves around the assumptions of stochastic independence and simple random sampling. In surveys of large populations, such as in nationwide surveys, the complex structure of the population and relative inaccessibility of the sampled subjects make simple random sampling infeasible. On the other hand, complexity of the sampling design invalidates statistical analyses based on the routinely adopted assumption of simple random sampling.

The design and execution of a survey are rarely a smooth and easily described affair. Contingencies are encountered at most stages, leading to a variety of compromises of the original design, the consequences of which are difficult to evaluate. In the analysis of a survey, an important decision has to be made as to which features, planned or unforeseen, are to be taken into account in the analysis and which are to be ignored. This can be described as a balancing act between the conflicting requirements of adequacy and parsimony of the statistical model. As an illustration of these problems, we give details of the 1990 NAEP Math State Trial Assessment, a set of statewide surveys for eighth-grade students. The designs of the surveys differ from state to state in several features; we describe the survey design for New Jersey.

First, the realized design giving an account of the process of how schools and students were selected into the survey, and then the idealized, or the 'model', version used for analysis is presented.

7.2.1 The realized sampling design

At the planning stage, it was set as a target to draw a sample of about 105 schools with about 25 students per school on average. The sampling frame, consisting of the list of all schools in the state that have eighth-grade students, was constructed using several official sources. For each school, either the exact or an approximate number of eighth-graders in the previous academic year was obtained. The school districts (groups of schools) were stratified according to three categorical variables:

- urbanicity (urban, rural, and other);

- median household income (three ordinal categories);

- minority enrollment (high, medium, and low enrollment of Black and Hispanic students).

Schools with fewer than 20 eighth-grade students were aggregated into clusters containing at least 20 students each. A natural ordering of the strata was defined, combining urbanicity and minority enrollment. The schools were sorted in a 'serpentine' order from the lowest median income to the highest in the first stratum, from the highest median income to the lowest in the next stratum, and so on.

A large urban school was included in the survey sample with certainty. From the sorted list of the rest of the schools, a systematic sample was drawn, using a random starting point, with probability proportional to school enrollment, and a step-length such as to ensure that 104 schools would be selected. Cooperation of these schools was solicited with the corresponding school district authorities. Anticipating imperfect cooperation, a scheme for finding 'substitute' schools was designed, and it was applied whenever a good match was available for the school that declined to cooperate.

The selected clusters (schools, or unions of small schools) were assigned, on an ad hoc basis, to 53 replicate groups, most of them consisting of two clusters each. The replicate groups play the role of strata; we do not refer to them as such so as to avoid the confusion with the stratification defined by urbanicity, median income, and minority enrollment. The procedure of forming the replicate groups is described by Koffler (1991) and justified by Johnson and Rust (1992).

The school districts were requested to compile lists of all the eighth-grade students in the selected schools. From each selected school with enrollment

TABLE 7.1. Clustering structure of the New Jersey sample.

Replicate groups	Counts of students within clusters						
1 – 7	29+20	23+28	22+26	23+19	25+23	30+23	39+27
8 – 14	23+29	25+29	28	24+24	29+28	26+29	25
15 – 21	26+26	29+27	26	26+29	29+26	23+22	22
22 – 28	28+28	29+26	22+25	26+23	26+25+25	13+14	21+26
29 – 35	28+23	22+26	26+28	22+26	22+24	27+25	22+55
36 – 42	23+23	23+19	22+25	23+29	28+27	24+26	28+26
43 – 49	29+29	29+26	29+26	25+23	28+26	24+25	54+27
50 – 53	27+29	28+29	27+27	25+27+25			

Notes: Each entry of the table contains the numbers of selected students within the clusters in each group 1–53. For example, group 1 has a cluster with 29 and one with 20 students in the sample. Groups 26 and 53 have three clusters each in the sample. The sample is comprised of 104 clusters with 2710 students.

of more than 35 eighth-graders, a random sample of 30 students was drawn without replacement. From schools with fewer than 36 students, all students were included in the sample.

Giving the complete details as well as a rationale for some of the features of this sampling design is beyond the scope of this section. The interested reader is referred to Koffler (1991), Rust and Johnson (1992), or Longford (1995). Our purpose is to contrast the realized and 'model' sampling designs.

7.2.2   The 'model' sampling design

The procedures for estimating the sample means and their standard errors are derived assuming the following sampling scheme. The clusters (schools) are stratified into 53 replicate groups with 1–3 clusters drawn with replacement from each group (from most groups, two clusters are drawn). Three empty replicate groups were formally added to the design for administrative reasons and to enable the analysis of all the participating states by the same software. The sampling process is independent across the groups. From each selected cluster, a random sample of students is selected with replacement, with sample sizes as described in the previous section. The sampling process of students in the selected clusters is independent across the clusters. Table 7.1 summarizes the realized clustering design.

The significance of selection with replacement is that the sampled units are statistically independent. A unit (a cluster or a student) may be selected more than once, in which case the unit is regarded as two distinct sampled units. For instance, if a school is selected twice, two independent samples from that school are drawn, and there may be an overlap of students in the two draws. Data from such students will be entered twice, once with each formally selected unit. Of course, even if a student is drawn more than once, he/she will be assigned only one survey questionnaire.

We see that, on the surface, the realized and model designs have little in common; we will keep this fact in mind, and in Section 7.11, we will critically evaluate the validity of inferences that rely on the assumption of the model sampling design.

7.2.3   Sampling weights and non-response

A number of intended purposes of the survey as well as practical consider-ations lead to unequal chances of the sampling units being included in the survey. For instance, it is important to make comparisons of the means of outcome variables for various ethnic categories, some of which are sparsely and unevenly represented in the population. With equal sampling weights, such a category would be represented in the sample by too few subjects. The unequal probabilities of inclusion are reflected by the sampling weights. The *design* sampling weights are set prior to sampling and are inversely propor-tional to the probabilities of inclusion conditional on perfect participation, adherence to the sampling design, and the sampling frame being exact.

The sampling weights for the clusters are set first. Within each selected school, simple random sampling is used, and so the conditional sampling weights for subjects within clusters are equal. Since the selection stages are independent, the (unconditional) sampling weights for the subjects are equal to the products of the cluster-level and the conditional subject-level weights. In our case, the design sampling weights are constant within clus-ters.

As a by-product, the sampling procedure may yield additional informa-tion about the sampling frame (recall that at the outset a complete list of all the eighth-graders in the state was not available). This may lead to a better assessment of the actual probabilities of inclusion of the units that happened to have been selected. The process of adjusting the weights to reflect this information is called *poststratification*. Non-response is an-other factor that has an impact on the probabilities of inclusion and so it warrants further adjustment of the sampling weights. Non-response may be differentially distributed among the units and may be associated with some of the recorded variables, such as proficiency and socio-demographic background.

Most of the weight adjustments are multiplicative; the design weights are multiplied by a variety of correction factors. Unlike the design weights, the adjusted weights are random variables because they are affected by the sample drawn. Again, we omit the technical details; see Koffler (1991) and Rust and Johnson (1992) for a complete account. Our purpose is to point out that the adjusted sampling weights are merely *estimates* of the

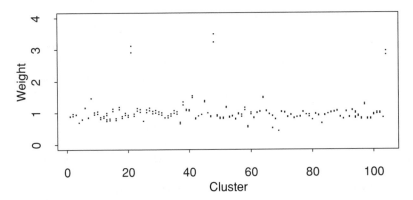

FIGURE 7.1. Adjusted weights for New Jersey. The horizontal axis is the cluster index (1, ..., 104) and the vertical axis is the adjusted sampling weight. Duplicate values of the weight in a cluster are represented by a single dot.

reciprocals of the probabilities of inclusion, and so they are another element of imperfection of the survey design.

Figure 7.1 displays the adjusted weights for the New Jersey sample. Note that there are at most two distinct values of the weight in each cluster, and the pairs of values are not substantially different. Subjects in three clusters have much greater weights than the rest of the sample, for which the weights are in a narrow range.

Cooperation of school districts, schools, and students in New Jersey was very good; only two schools and 5.7 percent of the selected students failed to cooperate. In contrast, the non-cooperation rate among the selected students in Oklahoma was 20 percent, because of parental consent requirements. In New Jersey (104 clusters with 2710 students), there are only three distinct cluster-level adjustment factors: 1.000 (no adjustment), 1.027, and 1.046, for 46, 37, and 21 clusters, respectively. The student-level adjustment factors are in the range 1.016–1.150 (22 distinct values), with mean and median equal to 1.06 and standard deviation 0.024.

The design weights for Oklahoma (108 clusters with 2222 students) are constant. The student-level adjustment factors have 35 distinct values, 2 in most clusters, in the range 1.00–1.95, with mean 1.25, median 1.18, and standard deviation 0.185. There are only three essentially distinct values of the school-level adjustment factor: no adjustment for 60 schools, 1.015–1.016 for 42 schools, and 1.160 for 6 schools.

Section 7.6.2 discusses the importance of the weights and of their adjustment.

7.3 Proficiency scores

The student questionnaire contains several sections, one of which is intended for measurement of ability in mathematics. Each student can be presented only a limited number of such questionnaire items, and so any inference about an individual's ability is subject to considerable uncertainty. With large samples of students, this uncertainty does not preclude making reliable inferences about the population summaries of ability and about the precision of these estimates. Of course, if the individual's abilities were measured with more precision, a reduction in the sample size could be afforded.

The outcome variable of principal interest is the *proficiency score* for a domain of knowledge (mathematics). It is not observed directly but is itself estimated from the responses to the cognitive items. Briefly, the probability of correct response of subject i to item k is modelled as

$$P(Z_{ik} = 1 \mid \theta_i; a_k, b_k, c_k) = \frac{c_k + \exp(a_k + b_k\theta_i)}{1 + \exp(a_k + b_k\theta_i)} ;$$

the responses Z_{ik} are assumed to be conditionally independent given the proficiency scores θ_i and the triplets of *item parameters* (a_k, b_k, c_k). The item parameters can be interpreted as the difficulty (a_k), discrimination (b_k), and the probability of guessing (c_k). Note that $\{\theta_i\}$ are confounded with $\{a_k, b_k\}$; a linear transformation of $\{\theta_i\}$ can be compensated by a linear reparametrization of $\{a_k, b_k\}$.

Usually, there are many examinees i, and it is meaningful to regard them as a sample from a population. It is expedient, with unimportant restriction to generality, to assume that $\{\theta_i\}$ is a random sample from $\mathcal{N}(0, 1)$ that can be regarded as a *prior* distribution of the proficiency scores. In an application, or in reporting, a linear transformation of these scores can be applied so that the scores would be comparable (equated) to a scale used, for instance, in another survey.

The proficiency scores and the item parameters are estimated by a marginal maximum likelihood approach; see Bock and Aitkin (1981) and Mislevy and Bock (1983).

7.3.1 Imputed values

Instead of a point estimate for each θ_i, its posterior distribution is estimated. This is of importance because precision of the estimates $\hat{\theta}_i$ has an impact on the sampling variation of the estimator of a population summary of $\{\theta_i\}$. In the analysis of the survey, each proficiency score θ_i is represented by a set of five *imputed* values drawn at random from the approximate posterior distribution of θ_i. See Mislevy (1991) for details.

Any analysis referring to the proficiency scores (such as estimation of the population mean) involves five identical analyses using each set of imputed values. Let $\hat{\beta}_h$, $h = 1, \ldots, 5$, be a quintet of such estimates. Then the estimate that refers to the proficiency scores is their arithmetic mean,

$$\hat{\beta} = \frac{1}{5} \sum_{h=1}^{5} \hat{\beta}_h \,.$$

The sampling variance of this estimator, $\mathrm{var}(\hat{\beta})$, is estimated similarly, but it has to be inflated by the variance of the estimates across the five analyses. Let s_h^2 be the estimated sampling variance of $\hat{\beta}_h$; then the estimated sampling variance of $\hat{\beta}$ is

$$s^2 = \frac{1}{5} \sum_{h=1}^{5} s_h^2 + \frac{1}{4} \sum_{h=1}^{5} \left(\hat{\beta}_h - \hat{\beta} \right)^2 \,.$$

In the remainder of the chapter, we consider the sets of five imputed values as given. Of course, instead of five, a greater number of imputed values could be used. Appropriateness of five imputations was established by extensive simulation studies.

7.4   Jackknife

The jackknife is a general prescription for reduction of bias of estimators and for estimation of their standard errors. Jackknife is not a uniquely defined method but a general estimation approach based on resampling ideas. Wolter (1985) is a suitable reference for a detailed background. In this section, we describe a particular implementation of the jackknife method used for analysis of the 1990 NAEP Math State Trial Assessment.

We will adopt the 'model' sampling design described in Section 7.2.2 and will use the subscripts i, j, and k for subject $i = 1, \ldots, n_{jk}$ in cluster $j = 1, \ldots, m_k$ of replicate group $k = 1, \ldots, K$. Apart from a few exceptions, the cluster sample sizes n_{jk} are in the range 20–30; the numbers of sampled clusters within replicate groups, m_k, are 0–3, and the number of replicate groups is $K = 56$; see Table 7.1.

In general, we will use capital letters for objects defined for the population and lowercase for objects defined for the sample. Thus, Y_h, $h = 1, \ldots, N$, is the outcome (the proficiency score) for eighth-grader h in the state, and y_{ijk} is the outcome for student i in cluster j of replicate group k. To simplify the description, we assume first that the proficiency scores y_{ijk} are observed without error.

The mean proficiency for the state is estimated by the ratio estimator

$$\hat{\mu} = \frac{\sum_k \sum_j \sum_i w_{ijk} y_{ijk}}{\sum_k \sum_j \sum_i w_{ijk}} \,. \tag{7.1}$$

Because of the complexity of the sampling design, the sampling variance of this estimator cannot be established in any straightforward manner. Unequal probabilities of selection, clustered sampling design, and adjustment for non-response exert a non-trivial impact on the sampling variance.

In the jackknife analysis, each replicate group (whether empty or not) is associated with a *pseudoanalysis* carried out on a *pseudosample*. The pseudosamples are formed as follows: the clusters are randomly assigned order $j = 1, 2, \ldots, m_k$ within replicate groups; of course, any randomness is involved only when $m_k > 1$. For replicate groups with no more than one cluster, the pseudosample coincides with the original sample. If replicate group k contains two clusters, then the pseudosample k is created by replacing the first cluster in group k by the other cluster in the group. This is equivalent to doubling the weights for all subjects in the second cluster. These weights are referred to as the *replicate weights*. For groups with three clusters, the first cluster is removed and the weights for the subjects in the other two clusters are multiplied by 1.5. Thus, each subject in the sample is associated with $K + 1$ replicate weights. If poststratification were applied, the replicate weights would have to be adjusted by poststratification applied to the pseudosample. Clearly, this represents a considerable computational load.

The kth pseudoanalysis evaluates the estimator (7.1) for the kth pseudosample using the kth set of replicate weights. Let the resulting estimators, called the *pseudoestimators*, be $\hat{\mu}^{(k)}$, $k = 1, 2, \ldots, K$. The jackknife estimator of the mean μ is defined as the arithmetic mean of the pseudoestimators $\hat{\mu}^{(k)}$:

$$\hat{\mu}_J = \frac{\sum_{k=1}^{K} \hat{\mu}^{(k)}}{K}. \tag{7.2}$$

The sampling variance of $\hat{\mu}_J$ is estimated as the sum of squares of the deviations of the pseudoestimators from the jackknife estimator:

$$\widehat{\mathrm{var}}\left(\hat{\mu}_J\right) = \sum_{k=1}^{K} \left(\hat{\mu}^{(k)} - \hat{\mu}_J\right)^2. \tag{7.3}$$

In practice, $\hat{\mu}$ is (nearly) unbiased, and it differs from $\hat{\mu}_J$ only slightly. Therefore, as a convention, $\hat{\mu}$ is reported instead of $\hat{\mu}_J$. Note that for replicate groups with $m_k \leq 1$, $\hat{\mu}^{(k)} = \hat{\mu}$; such replicate groups make an ignorable contribution to the sum of squares in (7.3).

The jackknife method given by (7.2) and (7.3) is easy to implement once the replicate weights have been computed. When a large number of means are estimated, the relative computational load of calculating these weights is reduced because the same set of weights apply for each jackknife analysis.

The jackknife method has a straightforward extension for estimating subpopulation means. Simply, the ratio estimator is applied to the appropriate subpopulation using the same set of replicate weights. Note that the subpopulation may not be represented in several sampled clusters or even in some replicate groups.

The main purpose of this description is to contrast it with the model-based approach presented in the next section. We do not attempt any justification of these procedures. Several elements are merely conventions set for the sake of definiteness and uniformity. See Johnson and Rust (1992) for details and further background.

The jackknife method has a straightforward extension to other statistical methods, such as regression, ANOVA, and contingency table analysis. The general prescription, given by (7.2) and (7.3), is applied to the estimators derived by the pseudoanalyses of the K pseudosamples.

7.5 Model-based method

In this section, we apply the model-based approach of Potthoff, Woodbury, and Manton (1992) to the stratified clustered sampling design employed in the NAEP surveys.

7.5.1 Stratification and clustering

A typical survey is conducted to collect information and to enable inference about a population heterogeneous with respect to one or several variables. Without heterogeneity, large-scale surveys would not be necessary ('all the subjects are the same'). At the same time, heterogeneity precludes precise estimation of population quantities; given a sample, more heterogeneity is associated with less precise inference.

Stratification can be an effective tool for improved inference in the presence of substantial heterogeneity. The key to successful stratification is to identify in the target population relatively homogeneous subpopulations, called *strata*, and then, in essence, to carry out independent surveys within each subpopulation. Within-stratum means are then estimated with relatively high precision because within-stratum variances are small. The population means are estimated by combining these estimators.

Clustering is an indispensable feature of the design of most large-scale surveys. For example, it would be very difficult, expensive, and impractical to collect a random sample from the population of eighth-graders in a state. In our case, it may even be impossible to produce a complete list of all eighth-graders. Instead, a list of all the schools is compiled and a (weighted) random sample drawn from this list; schools play the role of clusters. Students are then selected from each school included in the survey.

The trade-off for easier data collection is more complex statistical analysis of the collected data. In general, there is a fair amount of agreement about the estimators of the basic summaries, such as population means, but there are a variety of approaches to estimation of the sampling variance of such estimators. We adopt, without discussion, the ratio estimator $\hat{\mu}$ given by (7.1) as the estimator of the population mean μ and focus on estimating the sampling variance of this estimator. Conceptually, the sampling variance $\mathrm{var}(\hat{\mu})$ is defined as the variance of the estimators $\hat{\mu}$ over a large number of hypothetical replications of the survey using the same sampling design. Clearly, such a definition cannot be exploited operationally; conducting a single survey is expensive enough. The role of replication is taken up by a model that, in ideal circumstances, faithfully describes how the data are generated. As usual, there is no unique model; the only criteria for a 'good' model are its realistic nature and that it captures the salient features of the sampling design.

We consider separate within-group population means μ_k, and we assume that each cluster's population mean deviates from the group mean by a quantity that is a realization of a random variable. This naturally leads to the model

$$y_{ijk} = \mu_k + \delta_{jk} + \varepsilon_{ijk}, \qquad (7.4)$$

where the group means μ_k, $k = 1, \ldots, K$, are unknown constants and δ_{jk} and ε_{ijk} are independent random variables with zero expectations. The cluster-level deviations δ_{jk} are assumed to have a common between-cluster variance σ_B^2. It would be impractical to have group-specific variances $\sigma_{Bk}^2 = \mathrm{var}(\delta_{.k})$ because each random sample $\{\delta_{1,k}, \ldots, \delta_{m_k,k}\}$ would be realized not more than three times, and so each variance σ_{Bk}^2 would be estimated with little precision. The common variance σ_B^2 can also be interpreted as the within-cluster covariance since

$$\mathrm{cov}\left(y_{ijk}, y_{i'jk}\right) = \sigma_B^2$$

for any two distinct subjects $i \neq i'$ in an arbitrary cluster jk.

We assume that the subject-level deviations ε_{ijk} have cluster-specific variances $\sigma_{W,jk}^2$. Provided there is empirical evidence to support it, common variances within groups, $\sigma_{W,k}^2$, or even a single common variance σ_W^2, can be considered. Note that we make no assumptions about the distributions of the random terms other than their mutual independence and homogeneity (common variances).

To avoid cumbersome notation, we introduce the within-cluster totals of weights $w_{+jk} = \sum_i w_{ijk}$, the within-group totals $w_{++k} = \sum_j w_{+jk}$, and the sample total $w_+ = \sum_k w_{++k}$. In a similar vein, we introduce the within-cluster weighted sample means

$$\bar{y}_{.jk} = \frac{1}{w_{+jk}} \sum_{i=1}^{n_{jk}} w_{ijk} y_{ijk}$$

and the within-group sample means

$$\bar{y}_{\cdot\cdot k} = \frac{1}{w_{++k}} \sum_{j=1}^{m_k} w_{+jk} \bar{y}_{\cdot jk} ,$$

so that $\hat{\mu} = w_+^{-1} \sum_k \sum_j w_{+jk} \bar{y}_{\cdot jk} = (w_{++1} \bar{y}_{\cdot\cdot 1} + \ldots + w_{++K} \bar{y}_{\cdot\cdot K})/w_+$.

We assume that the sampling weights are proportional to the reciprocals of the sampling probabilities. Then $\hat{\mu}$ is an unbiased estimator of the 'model' population mean

$$\mu^* = \frac{1}{w_+} \sum_{k=1}^K \mathbf{E}(\mu_k + \delta_{jk} + \varepsilon_{ijk}) = \frac{1}{w_+} \sum_{k=1}^K w_{++k} \mu_k .$$

We draw a distinction between this population mean μ^* and the mean of the finite (existing, or realized) target population. The latter, obtainable if a 100 percent sample were drawn, is equal to

$$\mu = \frac{1}{W_+} \sum_{k=1}^K W_{++k} \mu_k + \frac{1}{W_+} \sum_{k=1}^K \sum_{j=1}^{M_k} W_{+jk} \delta_{jk} + \frac{1}{W_+} \sum_{k=1}^K \sum_{j=1}^{M_k} \sum_{i=1}^{N_{jk}} \varepsilon_{ijk} ;$$

the capital letters refer to the entire population. In such a design, the sample weights W_{ijk} would be identical, $W_{ijk} = 1$. The model in (7.4) implies that the population mean is a random variable, with variance

$$\mathrm{var}(\mu) = \frac{\sigma_B^2}{W_+^2} \sum_{k=1}^K \sum_{j=1}^{M_k} W_{+jk}^2 + \frac{\sigma_{W,jk}^2}{N} . \tag{7.5}$$

Thus, μ^* and μ coincide only when the population is comprised of infinitely many clusters. Recall that the purpose of stratification is to reduce the within- and between-cluster differences (within groups). The variance in (7.5) is an increasing function of the variance parameters σ_B^2 and $\sigma_{W,jk}^2$, and so good stratification reduces the need for a distinction between μ^* and μ. We will ignore this distinction, although, in estimating means of small subpopulations in particular, the variance in (7.5) may be non-trivial.

In the next three sections, we derive the sampling variance of $\hat{\mu}$ and find that it is a linear function of the variances σ_B^2 and $\sigma_{W,jk}^2$. These variances are then estimated from weighted sum-of-squares statistics by the method of moments, and the estimate of $\mathrm{var}(\hat{\mu})$ is derived by replacing the variances σ_B^2 and $\sigma_{W,jk}^2$ by their estimates.

7.5.2 Sampling variance of the ratio estimator

According to the model in (7.4), the within-cluster means have variances

$$\mathrm{var}(\bar{y}_{\cdot jk}) = \frac{1}{w_{+jk}^2} \left\{ w_{+jk}^2 \mathrm{var}(\delta_{jk}) + \sum_{i=1}^{n_{jk}} w_{ijk}^2 \mathrm{var}(\varepsilon_{ijk}) \right\}$$

$$= \sigma_B^2 + \frac{\sigma_{W,jk}^2}{w_{+jk}^2} w_{jk}^{(2)}, \tag{7.6}$$

where $w_{jk}^{(2)} = \sum_i w_{ijk}^2$. The clusters are mutually independent, and so

$$\mathrm{var}\,(\hat{\mu}) = \frac{1}{w_+^2} \sum_{k=1}^{K} \sum_{j=1}^{m_k} w_{+jk}^2 \mathrm{var}\,(\bar{y}_{.jk})$$

$$= \frac{\sigma_B^2}{w_+^2} \sum_{k=1}^{K} \sum_{j=1}^{m_k} w_{+jk}^2 + \frac{1}{w_+^2} \sum_{k=1}^{K} \sum_{j=1}^{m_k} \sigma_{W,jk}^2 w_{jk}^{(2)}. \tag{7.7}$$

The variances σ_B^2 and $\sigma_{W,jk}^2$ are not known, and so $\mathrm{var}\,(\hat{\mu})$ is not known either but can be estimated by substituting estimates in place of the exact values of σ_B^2 and $\sigma_{W,jk}^2$. In the next two sections, we derive method-of-moments estimators of these variances.

7.5.3   Within-cluster variance

To estimate the within-cluster variance $\sigma_{W,jk}^2$, we consider the weighted within-cluster sum of squares,

$$v_{jk} = \sum_{i=1}^{n_{jk}} w_{ijk} (y_{ijk} - \bar{y}_{jk})^2 .$$

Its expectation, assuming the model in (7.4), is

$$\mathrm{E}(v_{jk}) = \sum_{i=1}^{n_{jk}} w_{ijk} \mathrm{var}\left(\varepsilon_{ijk} - \frac{1}{w_{+jk}} \sum_{i'=1}^{n_{jk}} w_{i'jk} \varepsilon_{i'jk} \right)$$

$$= \sigma_{W,jk}^2 \sum_{i=1}^{n_{jk}} w_{ijk} \left\{ \left(1 - \frac{w_{ijk}}{w_{+jk}}\right)^2 + \frac{1}{w_{+jk}^2} \sum_{i' \neq i} w_{i'jk}^2 \right\}$$

$$= \sigma_{W,jk}^2 \sum_{i=1}^{n_{jk}} w_{ijk} \left(1 - \frac{2w_{ijk}}{w_{+jk}} + \frac{w_{jk}^{(2)}}{w_{+jk}^2} \right)$$

$$= \sigma_{W,jk}^2 \left(w_{+jk} - \frac{w_{jk}^{(2)}}{w_{+jk}} \right) . \tag{7.8}$$

The familiar identity for the unweighted sum of squares is obtained by setting all weights equal to unity, $w_{ijk} \equiv 1$:

$$\mathrm{E}\left\{ \sum_{i=1}^{n_{jk}} (y_{ijk} - \bar{y}_{jk})^2 \right\} = \sigma_{W,jk}^2 (n_{jk} - 1) ;$$

note that in this equation $\bar{y}_{jk}$ has a meaning different from that in (7.8) because different sampling weights are used. For unweighted samples, the within-cluster sum of squares is associated with $n_{jk} - 1$ degrees of freedom. The term 'degrees of freedom' has roots in the analysis of variance (ANOVA) for normally distributed outcomes: when y_{ijk} are normally distributed, $v_{jk}/\sigma^2_{W,jk}$ has the χ^2 distribution with $n_{jk} - 1$ degrees of freedom.

Potthoff *et al.* (1992) extend the notion of the degrees of freedom to weighted survey samples by defining a normalization of the set of weights. Suppose u_i, $i = 1,\ldots,n$, are sample weights for a probability random sample. Then their normalization is defined as

$$u_i^* = u_i \frac{\sum_{i'} u_{i'}}{\sum_{i'} u_{i'}^2}.$$

The normalized weights u_i^* have the property that their total is equal to the total of their squares:

$$\sum_{i=1}^n u_i^* = \sum_{i=1}^n u_i^{*2}.$$

The total weight $n_u = u_1^* + \ldots + u_n^*$ can be interpreted as the *effective* sample size; that is, the arithmetic mean of a simple random sample of size n_u would have *approximately* the same distribution as the probability random sample with weights $u_1, \ldots, u_n$; see Potthoff *et al.* (1992) for details.

When all weights are positive and $n > 1$, then $1 < n_u \le n$, and the identity $n_u = n$ holds only when all the weights are equal. The effective sample size n_u is close to unity when the weight of a single subject dominates the rest of the sample. Obviously, when all the weights vanish, except for one observation, $n_u = 1$.

Let $n_{W,jk}$ be the effective sample size of cluster jk, that is,

$$n_{W,jk} = \frac{w_{+jk}^2}{w_{jk}^{(2)}}.$$

Then

$$\mathbf{E}\left(v_{jk}\right) = \sigma^2_{W,jk} w_{+jk} \left(1 - \frac{1}{n_{W,jk}}\right).$$

By matching the sum-of-squares statistic v_{jk} with its expectation,

$$v_{jk} = \hat{\sigma}^2_{W,jk} w_{+jk} \frac{n_{W,jk} - 1}{n_{W,jk}},$$

we obtain the method-of-moments estimator of $\sigma^2_{W,jk}$:

$$\hat{\sigma}^2_{W,jk} = \frac{v_{jk}}{w_{+jk}} \frac{n_{W,jk}}{n_{W,jk} - 1}. \tag{7.9}$$

Had we defined the within-cluster sum of squares statistic v_{jk}^* using the normalized weights $w_{ijk}^* = w_{ijk} n_{W,jk} / w_{+jk}$,

$$v_{jk}^* = \sum_{i=1}^{n_{jk}} w_{ijk}^* \left(y_{ijk} - \bar{y}_{jk} \right)^2 ,$$

the same estimator of the within-cluster variance would be obtained:

$$\hat{\sigma}_{W,jk}^2 = \frac{v_{jk}^*}{n_{W,jk} - 1} .$$

To estimate the common within-cluster variance $\sigma_{W,k}^2$ for each group k, the cluster-specific estimators $\hat{\sigma}_{W,jk}^2$ can be pooled:

$$\hat{\sigma}_{W,k}^2 = \frac{\sum_{j=1}^{m_k} (n_{W,jk} - 1) \hat{\sigma}_{W,jk}^2}{\sum_{j=1}^{m_k} n_{W,jk} - m_k} .$$

The estimator for the variance common to all the clusters in the sample, σ_W^2, is derived similarly.

7.5.4   Between-cluster variance

The between-cluster variance σ_B^2 is estimated by a similar approach. We define the (weighted) between-cluster sum of squares as

$$v_B = \sum_{k=1}^{K} \sum_{j=1}^{m_k} u_{jk} \left(\bar{y}_{jk} - \bar{y}_k \right)^2 , \tag{7.10}$$

where $\{u_{jk}\}$ is a suitable set of non-negative coefficients (weights). We postpone the discussion of how to set these weights until later. We derive the expectation of v_B and use it to define a method-of-moments estimator of σ_B^2. The expectation of v_B is

$$\mathbf{E}(v_B) = \sum_{k=1}^{K} \sum_{j=1}^{m_k} u_{jk} \left\{ \mathrm{var}(\bar{y}_{jk}) - 2\mathrm{cov}(\bar{y}_{jk}, \bar{y}_k) + \mathrm{var}(\bar{y}_k) \right\}$$

$$= \sum_{k=1}^{K} \sum_{j=1}^{m_k} u_{jk} U_{jk} \mathrm{var}(\bar{y}_{jk})$$

$$= \sum_{k=1}^{K} \sum_{j=1}^{m_k} u_{jk} U_{jk} \left(\sigma_B^2 + \frac{\sigma_{W,jk}^2}{n_{W,jk}} \right) , \tag{7.11}$$

where

$$U_{jk} = 1 - \frac{2w_{+jk}}{w_{++k}} + \frac{1}{w_{++k}^2} \sum_{j=1}^{m_k} w_{+jk}^2 . \tag{7.12}$$

For a given set of constants $\{u_{jk}\}$, moment matching yields the estimator

$$\hat{\sigma}_B^2 = \frac{v_B - \sum_{k=1}^{K} \sum_{j=1}^{m_k} u_{jk} U_{jk} \hat{\sigma}_{W,jk}^2 / n_{W,jk}}{\sum_{k=1}^{K} \sum_{j=1}^{m_k} u_{jk} U_{jk}} . \qquad (7.13)$$

The choice of the weights u_{jk} should reflect the relative importance and precision of the contributions of the clusters in (7.10). The total of the sampling weights w_{+jk} is an obvious candidate. For $u_{jk} = w_{+jk}$, equation (7.13) simplifies somewhat since

$$\sum_{k=1}^{K} \sum_{j=1}^{m_k} w_{+jk} U_{jk} = w_+ - \sum_{k=1}^{K} \frac{1}{w_{++k}} \sum_{j=1}^{m_k} w_{+jk}^2 .$$

If the variances σ_B^2 and $\sigma_{W,jk}^2$ were known, the weights u_{jk} could, at least in principle, be set in such a way as to minimize the sampling variance of v_B. To avoid the trivial solution $u_{jk} \equiv 0$, a constraint has to be imposed on u_{jk}. A practical choice is that $\sum_k \sum_j u_{jk}$ be a specified positive constant.

Even when the observations $\{y_{ijk}\}$ are not normally distributed, the within-cluster weighted means $\bar{y}_{jk}$ are approximately normally distributed, and so the squared deviations $(\bar{y}_{jk} - \bar{y}_k)^2$ are approximately χ^2-distributed. The variances of $(\bar{y}_{jk} - \bar{y}_k)^2$ are approximately proportional to the squares of their expectations. Ignoring the dependence of the squared deviations, and assuming that the variances σ_B^2 and $\sigma_{W,jk}^2$ are known, the optimal coefficients would be the reciprocals of the factors in (7.11),

$$u_{jk}^* = \frac{1}{U_{jk}(\sigma_B^2 + \sigma_{W,jk}^2 / n_{W,jk})} . \qquad (7.14)$$

As a further approximation, $\sigma_{W,jk}^2$ can be replaced by $\hat{\sigma}_{W,jk}^2$ for some or all the clusters. For σ_B^2, a guess can be made, which yields the 'optimal' weights u_{jk}^*, which in turn provide through (7.13) an (improved) estimate of σ_B^2. Iterations of (7.14) and (7.13) can be carried out until convergence is achieved. As an alternative, the procedure may start with the weights $u_{jk} = w_{+jk}$. Although convergence is usually achieved after fewer than five iterations, it appears that the additional computational load is not rewarded by more efficient estimation of either σ_B^2 or $\mathrm{var}(\hat{\mu})$. See Longford (1995) for details.

In many surveys with stratified clustered design, a pair of clusters is selected from each stratum. For such a design, an alternative sum-of-squares statistic is defined using the squared differences of the cluster means:

$$v_2 = \sum_{k=1}^{K} u_k \left(\bar{y}_{1k} - \bar{y}_{2k}\right)^2 , \qquad (7.15)$$

where u_k are non-negative constants. This definition can be extended to the design in which each stratum is represented by a small number of clusters; simply, the summation in (7.15) would be over all strata that are represented by at least two clusters. Of course, the method based on v_2 may be inefficient because the third and consecutive clusters from a stratum do not contribute to the sum of squares in (7.15).

For completeness, we derive the estimator of σ_B^2 based on v_2. First, the mean squared difference of two cluster means is

$$
\mathbf{E} \left(\hat{\mu}_{1k} - \hat{\mu}_{2k} \right)^2 = \operatorname{var} \left(\hat{\mu}_{1k} \right) + \operatorname{var} \left(\hat{\mu}_{2k} \right)
$$
$$
= 2\sigma_B^2 + \frac{\sigma_{W,1k}^2}{n_{W,1k}} + \frac{\sigma_{W,2k}^2}{n_{W,2k}} .
$$

Hence,

$$
\mathbf{E}(v_2) = \sum_{k; m_k \geq 2} u_k \left(2\sigma_B^2 + \frac{\sigma_{W,1k}^2}{n_{W,1k}} + \frac{\sigma_{W,2k}^2}{n_{W,2k}} \right) . \tag{7.16}
$$

(The summation is over all strata that are represented in the sample by at least two clusters.) The method of moments yields the estimator

$$
\hat{\sigma}_B^2 = \frac{v_2 - \sum_{k; m_k \geq 2} u_k \sum_{j=1}^2 \hat{\sigma}_{W,jk}^2 / n_{W,jk}}{2 \sum_{k; m_k \geq 2} u_k} , \tag{7.17}
$$

which is somewhat simpler than the estimator based on v_B, (7.13). The obvious choice for the weights u_k are the group-level totals of weights, w_{++k}. Even when there are no groups represented by more than two clusters, the estimators of σ_B^2 with $u_{jk} = w_{+jk}$ in (7.10) and $u_k = w_{++k}$ in (7.16) are substantially different. The latter scheme is inefficient when the sample sizes of the pairs of clusters within groups are very discrepant because the differences $\hat{\mu}_{1k} - \hat{\mu}_{2k}$ have large variances in such cases. Iterative schemes, analogous to those discussed for the statistic v_B, can be designed, but they do not lead to a uniform improvement in the estimation of σ_B^2 or, indeed, of the estimator of the sampling variance of the ratio estimator of the population mean.

In conclusion, the estimator of the sampling variance of the ratio estimator of the population mean is

$$
\widehat{\operatorname{var}} \left(\hat{\mu} \right) = \frac{\hat{\sigma}_B^2}{w_+^2} \sum_{k=1}^K \sum_{j=1}^{m_k} w_{+jk}^2 + \frac{1}{w_+^2} \sum_{k=1}^K \sum_{j=1}^{m_k} \hat{\sigma}_{W,jk}^2 w_{jk}^{(2)} , \tag{7.18}
$$

where the estimators of the variances $\hat{\sigma}_B^2$ and $\hat{\sigma}_{W,jk}^2$ are defined by (7.9) and (7.13), respectively.

7.5.5 Multivariate outcomes

Both the jackknife and model-based methods have direct extensions for multivariate outcomes. Suppose $\mathbf{y}_{ijk}$ is a vector of outcomes for subject

ijk. The population mean of $\mathbf{y}$, denoted by $\boldsymbol{\mu}$, can be estimated component-wise; for each component, the jackknife or the model-based methods can be applied. The sampling variance matrix of the vector of estimated means for the jackknife estimator is

$$\widehat{\mathrm{var}}\left(\boldsymbol{\mu}_J\right) = \sum_{k=1}^{K} \left(\hat{\boldsymbol{\mu}}^{(k)} - \hat{\boldsymbol{\mu}}_J\right)\left(\hat{\boldsymbol{\mu}}^{(k)} - \hat{\boldsymbol{\mu}}_J\right)^\top ,$$

using the notation analogous to that in Section 7.4. For the model-based method, equations (7.8), (7.11), (7.16), and (7.18) carry over to the multivariate case (with variances replaced by variance matrices and squares, e^2, replaced by matrix products $\mathbf{ee}^\top$). The multivariate version of (7.18) is

$$\widehat{\mathrm{var}}\left(\hat{\mu}\right) = \frac{1}{w_+^2}\hat{\boldsymbol{\Sigma}}_B \sum_{k=1}^{K}\sum_{j=1}^{m_k} w_{+jk}^2 + \frac{1}{w_+^2}\sum_{k=1}^{K}\sum_{j=1}^{m_k}\hat{\boldsymbol{\Sigma}}_{W,jk} w_{jk}^{(2)} , \qquad (7.19)$$

where $\hat{\boldsymbol{\Sigma}}_W$ and $\hat{\boldsymbol{\Sigma}}_B$ are the estimated within- and between-cluster variance matrices for the outcome vectors $\mathbf{y}$.

7.6 Examples

Estimation of the population means for the states of New Jersey and Oklahoma using the jackknife method is summarized in Table 7.2. The data were extracted from public-release tapes by Thomas Jirele of ETS. The ratio estimator of the population mean, evaluated for each set of imputed values, is given in the row 'Weighted mean'. The rightmost column is the arithmetic mean of the preceding five estimates in the row. The jackknife mean for each imputed value is calculated as the mean of the 56 pseudoestimates, each based on a separate set of replicate (sampling) weights. We see that the difference between the jackknife and the ratio estimates is trivial for each imputed value. The standard error is available only for the jackknife estimator, but it is a good approximation also for the ratio estimator.

Table 7.3 summarizes model-based estimation of the population mean for the two states. We consider four estimators, two each based on the between-cluster sum-of-squares statistics v_2 and v_B. For v_2, we apply the weights $u_k = w_{++k}$ (the method is denoted by **BI**) and set the weights to the reciprocals of the contributions to $\mathrm{E}(v_2)$, assuming the values of the variances σ_B^2 and $\sigma_{W,jk}^2$ equal the estimates obtained by the method **BI**. This method, denoted by **BR**, corresponds to one iteration of the scheme approximating the optimal weights.

Similarly, for v_B we apply the weights $u_{jk} = w_{+jk}$ (the method denoted by **CI**) and set the weights to the reciprocals of the contributions to $\mathrm{E}(v_B)$

TABLE 7.2. Jackknife analysis. Estimation of the population mean of proficiency scores.

	Set of imputed values					
	1	2	3	4	5	Overall
New Jersey						
Weighted mean	269.47	269.42	269.37	269.40	269.65	269.46
Jackknife mean	269.48	269.43	269.37	269.42	269.65	269.47
JK stand. error	1.04	1.07	1.03	1.06	1.04	1.05
Oklahoma						
Weighted mean	262.95	262.74	262.78	262.71	262.63	262.76
Jackknife mean	262.91	262.71	262.71	262.68	262.60	262.73
JK stand. error	1.23	1.27	1.21	1.24	1.22	1.24

using the values of the variances σ_B^2 and $\sigma_{W,jk}^2$ estimated by the method **CI**. This method is denoted by **CR**.

The table gives the estimates of the between-cluster variance σ_B^2 for each method and each set of imputed values. The estimates are around 100 for New Jersey and around 120 for Oklahoma. For orientation, the estimates of the within-cluster variances (specific to each cluster) are in the range 400–1200, with the means around 650 for both states.

The estimates of the standard errors in the four model-based methods differ only slightly. However, they are in a considerable disagreement with their jackknife counterparts for New Jersey (say, 1.19 versus 1.05). On the other hand, there is a close agreement for Oklahoma (1.24). The next section attempts to arbitrate between these estimators in a more general context.

Suppose we accept, say, the estimates using method **CI** at face value. What interpretation and usefulness can we attach to the results? First, we find that New Jersey's mean proficiency is about 6.5 points higher than the mean proficiency for Oklahoma and that this difference is highly significant (the standard error of the difference is $\sqrt{1.19^2 + 1.23^2} \doteq 1.7$).

Of course, the real meaning of the quantity 6.5 depends on the definition of the proficiency scale. It is impossible to generate an 'absolute' description for it; at best, we can compare this difference with some other quantities, such as the differences for some other pairs of states. The standard deviation of a cluster-level mean is about 10 units, and so the New Jersey clusters (schools) by no means have uniformly higher mean proficiency than the Oklahoma clusters. In fact, it is likely that many schools in Oklahoma (although much fewer than one-half of them) are above the New Jersey average. Certainly, there are many students in Oklahoma who are above

TABLE 7.3. Model-based estimators of standard error of the weighted mean of proficiency scores for New Jersey and Oklahoma.

	Set of imputed values					
	1	2	3	4	5	Overall
New Jersey						
Weighted mean	269.47	269.42	269.37	269.40	269.65	269.46
Method **BI**						
$\hat{\sigma}_B^2$	99.36	104.17	97.83	100.40	98.26	100.01
Standard error	1.19	1.21	1.17	1.19	1.18	1.19
BR						
$\hat{\sigma}_B^2$	96.85	99.29	90.20	97.59	96.20	96.02
Standard error	1.17	1.18	1.14	1.18	1.17	1.17
CI						
$\hat{\sigma}_B^2$	107.40	108.29	100.07	101.32	103.91	104.20
Standard error	1.22	1.22	1.18	1.19	1.21	1.21
CR						
$\hat{\sigma}_B^2$	104.53	104.91	95.29	100.65	102.02	101.48
Standard error	1.21	1.21	1.16	1.19	1.20	1.19
Oklahoma						
Weighted mean	262.95	262.74	262.78	262.71	262.63	262.76
BI						
$\hat{\sigma}_B^2$	114.60	119.77	112.67	116.81	114.08	115.58
Standard error	1.22	1.25	1.22	1.24	1.22	1.23
BR						
$\hat{\sigma}_B^2$	120.18	199.58	114.54	118.70	115.25	117.65
Standard error	1.25	1.25	1.23	1.24	1.23	1.24
CI						
$\hat{\sigma}_B^2$	121.29	128.09	118.91	120.82	119.20	121.66
Standard error	1.25	1.28	1.25	1.25	1.24	1.26
CR						
$\hat{\sigma}_B^2$	124.14	125.58	118.95	120.73	118.50	121.58
Standard error	1.26	1.27	1.25	1.15	1.24	1.26

the New Jersey average, and many New Jersey students who are below the Oklahoma mean.

What we have learned is that students vary a great deal, schools in a state vary much less, and the two surveyed states differ *on average* even less. Nevertheless, the small between-state difference is of considerable importance because it is a difference after averaging over many students.

Finding causes and explanations for the observed differences is a difficult and politically sensitive issue. Socioeconomic background of the students is often used as a descriptor of the differences in proficiency. Expenditure on education, teachers' qualifications, and other professional background are other candidates. The surveys collect a wealth of related information, and so there is some cause for optimism. However, the collected data enable us to make no inferences about the causes of the observed (estimated) differences because we have had no control over the assignment of students to classrooms or over the assignment of background and other variables to students, teachers, and schools.

A principal hurdle to unequivocal answers about causes of differences is our inability to implement experimental design. Experimental design requires randomized allocation of students to values or categories of the explanatory variables. In a very limited context, we can assign students to schools (within a small area), but assigning students to different socioeconomic backgrounds is clearly infeasible.

Linear regression, dealt with in Section 7.8, provides a general framework for relating differences in proficiencies to these variables. In principle, it gives answers to hypothetical questions such as

> Would the students in New Jersey achieve higher/lower proficiency if they attended schools in Oklahoma?

If the answer is 'higher', would it make sense to implement changes in the educational system in New Jersey to bring it closer to the system in Oklahoma? Here we are on a shaky ground; every system has a number of imperfections and bringing in changes modelled by a relatively good yet imperfect system may be detrimental. Also, a system that works in one location and context may be much less effective elsewhere. Our view is that any sterile statistical analysis, however well justified on technical grounds, becomes problematic if its conclusions are formed without input from the substantive domain of the survey and without a thorough mutual understanding among the statistician(s), educational researchers, and administrators.

The fact that several analyses confirm a particular conclusion does not add much confidence to our inference because the methods are closely related, are applied to the same dataset, and they share the deficiency of being applicable only in an experimental design setting.

In the next section, we illustrate estimation of subpopulation means.

TABLE 7.4. Questionnaire items and response options that define the subpopulations analysed in Table 7.5.

Item	Nr.	Response options
Derived race/ethnicity	28	1 — White 2 — Black 4 — Asian
Minority stratum	31	1 — High proportion 2 — Low proportion
Parents' educational level	183	2 — Graduated from high school 4 — Graduated from college
Teacher's graduate major	193	1 — Mathematics 2 — Education 3 — Other 9 — Missing

7.6.1 Subpopulation means

The data collected by the surveys are summarized in the form of estimated means of proficiencies for the students belonging to a variety of categories defined by the questionnaires (personal and parental background, teacher professional background, school and home experiences, and the like). For instance, item 28 of the student-background questionnaire inquires about the student's ethnicity (response options are White, Black, Hispanic, Asian, Native American, and 'other'). The results contain the estimates of the subpopulation mean and its standard error for each response category that is represented in the sample by sufficient data. The sample size (2710 for New Jersey) may be adequate for estimation of the population mean, but many subpopulations defined by the responses to such items are represented very sparsely in the survey sample. For instance, there are only 131 Asian students in the New Jersey sample, and they are not represented in 47 clusters (45 percent). The questionnaire items and response options are given in Table 7.4. Table 7.5 gives the estimates and related details for several subpopulations.

The results confirm that the differences between the jackknife and ratio estimators of the mean are trivial. Differences among the three estimators of the standard error are more substantial, and not only for small subpopulations. Certainly, little additional insight into the relative efficiency of these estimators can be gained by comparing their values for further subpopulations. Section 7.10 describes a method for comparing alternative estimators by simulations.

TABLE 7.5. Jackknife and model-based estimates for a selected set of subpopulations; New Jersey.

Item and response	Students and clusters	Weighted mean	Mean $\hat{\sigma}^2_W$	Jackknife	CI	CR
28,1	1789/95	279.49	662.56	279.54 (1.06)	(1.19) [67.50]	(1.33) [90.74]
28,2	398/61	240.79	397.64	240.83 (2.30)	(2.34) [73.73]	(3.20) [110.41]
28,4	131/57	296.97	655.03	296.99 (4.92)	(5.04) [116.43]	(4.83) [17.96]
31,1	656/25	279.25	719.71	279.24 (2.36)	(2.20) [72.66]	(1.97) [53.68]
31,2	1170/45	274.79	690.37	274.84 (2.10)	(1.54) [63.62]	(1.58) [68.10]
183,2	633/102	258.87	574.89	258.89 (1.59)	(1.76) [138.10]	(1.56) [95.48]
183,4	1225/104	281.38	716.87	281.38 (1.35)	(1.40) [96.56]	(1.41) [98.19]
193,1	386/34	281.73	515.23	281.70 (4.13)	(4.48) [364.58]	(4.02) [306.86]
193,2	677/64	272.97	560.91	273.00 (2.55)	(2.11) [150.46]	(2.60) [223.46]
193,3	1346/91	265.80	580.20	265.83 (1.97)	(1.89) [193.71]	(2.06) [233.36]
193,9	301/39	261.36	523.84	261.35 (4.61)	(3.88) [79.09]	(5.29) [103.27]

Notes: For each method, the estimates of σ^2_B are given in brackets, [ ], and the estimated standard errors in parentheses, ( ). The items and response options are given in Table 7.4.

There is some indication that the variances $\sigma^2_{W,jk}$ and σ^2_B may be the same for some of the subpopulations. In small datasets, there are many clusters with small sample sizes, and so their variances $\sigma^2_{W,jk}$ are estimated with a lot of uncertainty. Considerable advantage could be gained by pooling information about such variances across subpopulations. This idea is exploited in Section 7.9 for the improved estimation of a large number of subpopulation means.

A major deficiency of the estimators is that they ignore the possibility of students' incorrect responses to the items. Although, presumably, most students declare their gender, ethnicity, and the like correctly, information about their parents is probably declared with less precision, and the extent of television watching, the amount of homework, and the like is at best a guess, affected by a number of subjective and temporal influences. This problem can be tackled only by gaining an intimate knowledge of the students' mental processes when responding to questionnaire items and by assessing all the elements of uncertainty involved.

7.6.2   How much do weights matter?

It is easy to show that the sampling weights cannot be ignored in estimation of the population mean. For instance, there are 1789 White students in the New Jersey sample, that is, 77.6 percent of the sample. However, the weights of these students account for only 66.6 percent of the total. A finer issue is whether the adjustment of the weights matters and whether it has the desired effect. Certainly, the impact of the weight adjustment is, in general, much smaller than that of introducing the weights. For instance, the adjusted weights of the White students, using the adjusted weights, are 66.4 percent, a drop of 0.2 percent.

Adjustment of the weights is subject to uncertainty because it depends on the sample drawn. With the exception of the jackknife and other resampling methods, approaches to the analysis of survey data regard the adjusted weights as the design weights, ignoring the stochastic nature of the adjustment. Whether this is justified for the model-based estimators can be assessed by a Monte Carlo study in which the sampling weights are replaced by perturbed values imitating other sets of adjusted weights that could have equally been realized.

Instead of the realized weights w_{ijk}, we consider a set of 'perturbed' weights, $w^{(p)}_{ijk}$, generated by the variance component model

$$\log\left(w^{(s)}_{ijk}\right) = \log\left(w^*_{ijk}\right) + \delta^{(w)}_{jk} + \varepsilon^{(w)}_{ijk},$$

where $\delta^{(w)}_{jk}$ and $\varepsilon^{(w)}_{ijk}$ are mutually independent normally distributed random variables with zero means and respective variances $\sigma^2_{w,B}$ (**between-cluster**) and $\sigma^2_{w,W}$ (**within-cluster**); w^*_{ijk} is the (geometric) mean weight for student

ijk averaged over the samples. We choose the logarithmic scale because multiplicative sources of variation are more realistic for modelling of the uncertainty in weight adjustment. The variances $\sigma^2_{w,B}$ and $\sigma^2_{w,W}$ are chosen so as to make the realized weight adjustment appear realistic.

It is instructive to consider two kinds of weight adjustment factors: the realized adjustments and the hypothetical adjustments that would convert the design weights into the weights that correspond to the unconditional probabilities of inclusion in the survey. Note that $\exp(\delta^{(w)}_{jk})$ and $\exp(\varepsilon^{(w)}_{ijk})$ are not equal to the respective cluster- and student-level adjustments. These adjustments aim at changing the weights w^s_{ijk} to the unknown 'ideal' weights w^*_{ijk}.

Suppose the realized weight adjustment factors are such that most of their observed variation is due to the discrepancy between the ideal and the design weights. Then the sampling variation of each realized adjustment is much smaller than the observed variance of the adjustments. Thus, realistic values of $\sigma^2_{w,B}$ and $\sigma^2_{w,W}$ can be set as certain fractions of the within- and between-cluster variances of logarithms of the weight adjustments. The sample variances of the cluster- and student-level log-weight adjustments are suitable estimators of these variances.

The weight adjustment in New Jersey is so modest that only very small variances $\sigma^2_{w,W}$ and $\sigma^2_{w,B}$ are realistic. As a consequence, the impact of weight perturbation is negligible.

7.7   Estimating proportions

The jackknife method described in Section 7.4 can be used for estimating (sub-)population proportions because they correspond to the means of dichotomous variables. For example, to estimate the population proportion p of students who gave the correct answer to a certain questionnaire item, we define the variable Y by setting $Y_h = 1$ if student h gives the correct answer, and $Y_h = 0$ otherwise. The values of Y are available for the survey sample, and are denoted by y_{ijk}. The population proportion sought is equal to the population mean of Y, $p = (Y_1 + \ldots + Y_N)/N$. The ratio estimator of p is given by (7.1), and its sampling variance can be estimated by (7.3) or (7.18).

For variables that take on values of only zero and unity, the population mean and variance are related: the variance of such a variable Y with mean p is

$$\mathrm{var}(Y) = p(1-p).$$

Therefore, in the model-based approach there is a considerable redundancy in estimating the within-cluster variances $\sigma^2_{W,jk}$. They may be more efficiently estimated from the within-cluster proportions. In this section, we describe an adaptation of the model-based approach for population proportions that dispenses with estimation of the within-cluster variances and makes full use of the binary nature of the data.

Let p_k be the probability of a positive outcome ($Y = 1$) in stratum k, $p_k = \mathrm{P}(Y = 1 \mid k)$. The conditional probabilities for clusters in stratum k, $p_{jk} = \mathrm{P}(Y = 1 \mid j, k)$, are assumed to have expectation p_k and variance σ_B^2:

$$
\begin{aligned}
\mathbf{E}(p_{jk} \mid p_k) &= p_k, \\
\mathrm{var}(p_{jk} - p_k) &= \sigma_B^2.
\end{aligned}
\tag{7.20}
$$

Given the cluster-level probabilities p_{jk}, the outcomes y_{ijk}, $i = 1, \ldots, n_{jk}$, are conditionally independent.

In models for binary data, it is customary to assume that the *logits* of the conditional probabilities are normally distributed with a common variance; see Chapter 9 for an example. The choice in (7.20) is motivated by computational expediency and freedom from distributional assumptions.

Let $\hat{p}_{jk} = \sum_i w_{ijk} y_{ijk} / w_{+jk}$; this is the ratio estimator of the within-cluster proportion p_{jk}. Its variance (not conditional on p_{jk}) is

$$
\begin{aligned}
\mathrm{var}(\hat{p}_{jk}) &= \mathrm{var}\left\{\mathbf{E}\left(\hat{p}_{jk} \mid p_{jk}\right)\right\} + \mathbf{E}\left\{\mathrm{var}\left(\hat{p}_{jk} \mid p_{jk}\right)\right\} \\
&= \frac{p_k(1 - p_k)}{n_{W,jk}} + \left(1 - \frac{1}{n_{W,jk}}\right)\sigma_B^2,
\end{aligned}
\tag{7.21}
$$

and the variance of the population proportion estimator $\hat{p}$ is

$$
\begin{aligned}
\mathrm{var}(\hat{p}) &= \frac{1}{w_+^2} \sum_{k=1}^{K} \sum_{j=1}^{m_k} w_{+jk}^2 \mathrm{var}(\hat{p}_{jk}) \\
&= \frac{1}{w_+^2} \left\{ \sum_{k=1}^{K} p_k(1 - p_k) \sum_{j=1}^{m_k} w_{jk}^{(2)} + \sigma_B^2 \sum_{k=1}^{K} \sum_{j=1}^{m_k} \left(w_{+jk}^2 - w_{jk}^{(2)} \right) \right\}.
\end{aligned}
\tag{7.22}
$$

The sampling variance depends on the between-cluster variance σ_B^2 and the stratum-level probabilities p_k. We estimate the sampling variance in (7.22) by replacing the unknown parameters by their estimates. The stratum-probability p_k is estimated as

$$
\hat{p}_k = \frac{1}{w_{++k}} \sum_{j=1}^{m_k} w_{+jk} \hat{p}_{jk}.
$$

For σ_B^2, we derive a method-of-moments estimator. The development parallels that in Section 7.5.4. Let

$$
v_B = \sum_{k=1}^{K} \sum_{j=1}^{m_k} u_{jk} \left(\hat{p}_{jk} - \hat{p}_k \right)^2.
$$

The expectation of this statistic is

$$\mathbf{E}(v_B) = \sum_{k=1}^{K} \sum_{j=1}^{m_k} u_{jk} U_{jk} \mathrm{var}\,(\hat{p}_{jk})\;,$$

where U_{jk} is given by (7.12). Substituting for $\mathrm{var}(\hat{p}_{jk})$ and solving the moment-matching equation yields

$$\hat{\sigma}_B^2 = \frac{v_B - \sum_{jk} u_{jk} U_{jk} \hat{p}_k (1 - \hat{p}_k)/n_{W,jk}}{\sum_{jk} u_{jk} U_{jk} (1 - 1/n_{W,jk})}\;;\qquad(7.23)$$

the probabilities p_k have been replaced by their estimators. Note that the expectation $\mathbf{E}(v_B)$ is a non-linear function of p_k; in fact, it is linear in the variances $p_k(1-p_k)$. The bias of $\hat{p}_k(1-\hat{p}_k)$ as an estimator of $p_k(1-p_k)$ is

$$\mathbf{E}\{\hat{p}_k(1-\hat{p}_k) - p_k(1-p_k)\} = \mathbf{E}(\hat{p}_k^2 - p_k^2) = \mathrm{var}(\hat{p}_k)\,,$$

and it can be estimated by

$$\widehat{\mathrm{var}}(\hat{p}_k) = \hat{p}_k(1-\hat{p}_k)f_k + \hat{\sigma}_B^2 \left(\sum_{j=1}^{m_k} \frac{w_{+jk}^2}{w_{++k}^2} - f_k \right),$$

where $f_k = \sum_j w_{jk}^{(2)}/w_{++k}^2$. Subtracting this term from $\hat{p}_k(1-\hat{p}_k)$ may be detrimental, though, because while reducing the bias it inflates the sampling variance of the adjusted estimator. However, when the stratum contains many subjects and p_k is not too close to zero or unity, the bias is trivial.

This method for estimation with binary data can be extended to data with other distributions for which the mean and variance are related. For instance, for Poisson distributed data the variance is equal to the expectation. Equations (7.20)–(7.23) carry over for Poisson data with the following changes: replace the probability $p.$ with the mean $\lambda.$ and the variance $p.(1-p.)$ with $\lambda..$

Example

Of interest is the percentage of students whose proficiency is above various thresholds. Denote this percentage, as a function of the proficiency x, by $G(x)$. Note that $1 - G(x)/100$ is the population-distribution function of proficiency at x. Table 7.6 gives the estimates of these percentages for thresholds 220, 240, ..., 320 for New Jersey. Although the jackknife and model-based estimates (using the weights $u_{jk} = w_{+jk}$) are in close agreement, the estimated standard errors differ, especially for the extreme thresholds which involve very small or very large percentages. For completeness, we give the estimates of the between-cluster variance σ_B^2; note

TABLE 7.6. The jackknife and model-based estimates of the percentages of eighth-grade students in New Jersey with proficiency values above the thresholds of 220, 240, 260, 280, 300, and 320 points.

	Proficiency threshold					
	220	240	260	280	300	320
Ratio estimate	93.56	80.98	60.33	37.09	18.94	6.70
Jackknife estimate	93.57	81.00	60.33	37.09	18.93	6.70
Jackknife st.err.	0.90	1.26	1.54	1.45	1.15	0.65
Model-based st.err.	1.00	1.36	1.56	1.43	1.07	0.53
Between-cluster $\hat{\sigma}_B^2$	0.89	1.62	2.16	1.79	0.88	0.22

that they vary a great deal over the range of thresholds. Clearly, the estimates are of limited utility without a good understanding of what the threshold proficiency values represent.

We postpone the assessment of the relative merits of the jackknife and model-based methods to Section 7.10.

7.7.1 Percentiles

Estimates of percentiles are often reported in educational surveys as easy-to-interpret descriptors of the distribution of an outcome variable in the surveyed population. Of interest is, say, the proficiency value that is exceeded by the top 5 percent of the eighth-grade students in the state. The $100p$ percentile of variable Y is defined as the value Y_p^* such that $100p$ percent of the population has values of Y smaller than or equal to Y^*:

$$P(Y \leq Y_p^*) = p.$$

Quantiles have definitions equivalent to percentiles; quantile p is defined as the $100p$ percentile. The percentiles can be estimated by the jackknife method: the sample percentiles (*pseudopercentiles*) for each pseudosample are averaged to obtain the jackknife estimate of the percentile. In an alternative approach, the percentiles are considered as the inverses of the distribution function. The distribution function $F(x)$, or its complement $G(x) = 1 - F(x)$, can be estimated at any point x by the jackknife or a model-based method.

The population proportion of subjects with proficiency above the threshold x is $p = G(x)$. Given a proportion p, the corresponding threshold is found as $x = G^{-1}(p)$. The estimator of the threshold x for this proportion is found as the value of x that yields the estimate of the proportion equal to p. An approximation to the sampling variance of this estimator $\hat{x}$ is obtained by the delta method:

$$\text{var}(\hat{x}) \approx \frac{\text{var}(\hat{p})}{\{G'(\hat{p})\}^2} \, . \tag{7.24}$$

The derivative of G can be estimated as a finite difference, say, by estimating p for thresholds x and $x+1$. For estimating the variance $\text{var}(\hat{p})$, either the jackknife or the model-based method can be used.

A percentile of a sample can be found by rank ordering the subjects in the sample according to the outcome variable and finding the value corresponding to the appropriate rank. For large samples, this may be computationally very demanding. A more efficient procedure is based on the Newton method. Starting with two guesses, say, x_0 and x_1, the next guess is found by linear interpolation. Let $p_0 = G(x_0)$ and $p_1 = G(x_1)$; then the next approximation is

$$p_2 = p_1 + \frac{p_1 - p_0}{G(x_1) - G(x_0)} \, . \tag{7.25}$$

Iterations of this equation are applied until convergence, with appropriately changed indices and with $G(x)$ replaced by its estimator $\hat{G}(x)$. Usually, fewer than six iterations suffice even when very poor initial guesses are made. Since at convergence $G(x_1) = G(x_0)$, it may be useful to add a small constant in the denominator of (7.25) to avoid expressions of the form $0/0$.

By way of illustration, we describe the estimation of the 90th percentile of the distribution of proficiency scores in New Jersey. The jackknife method requires an analysis of each combination of 57 replicate weights and five sets of imputed values. The outcome of each analysis is the estimated percentile obtained from the cumulative totals of weights for the proficiencies sorted in ascending order. The jackknife estimate of the 90th percentile is 314.30, based on the percentiles for the sets of imputed values equal to 313.43, 312.72, 312.77, 313.56, and 314.05. The standard error of the jackknife estimate is 0.84. The estimate of the 90th percentile based on the adjusted weights w_{ijk} is 313.24.

Suppose we start the model-based estimation with guesses 310 and 325. The corresponding percentiles are 87.80 and 95.16. Linear approximation yields the proficiency value 314.49, which corresponds to 90.64 percent. Two more iterations home in on the value of 313.40, which is the estimated 90th percentile. The corresponding standard eror is 0.74.

7.8   Regression with survey data

Linear regression is an important method for exploring associations of variables. In the case of simple regression, it is assumed that variables X and

Y are linearly related, barring a normally distributed disturbance:

$$Y_i = a + bX_i + \varepsilon_i ; \tag{7.26}$$

$i = 1, \ldots, I$ are the observed units, a and b are unknown constants, and $\{\varepsilon_i\}$ is assumed to be a random sample from $\mathcal{N}(0, \sigma^2)$. The residual variance σ^2 is usually unknown. If the values $(X_1, Y_1), \ldots, (X_N, Y_N)$ were available for the entire population, the parameters a, b, and σ^2 could be estimated using the familiar *ordinary least squares* (OLS) method. Much of the appeal of OLS is due to its natural interpretation; the OLS estimator $(\hat{a}, \hat{b})$ minimizes the sum of squares of the deviations of the outcomes from the regression line, $\sum_i (Y_i - a - bX_i)^2$. When looking at a scatterplot of two variables, the analyst's first instinct is to overlay a straight line through the middle of the cloud of points. The constants a (the intercept) and b (the slope) define this line. The standard deviation σ is the average vertical distance of a point from the regression line.

In finite populations, we may conceive a regression model by considering a random process that gives rise to the disturbances ε_i. Since the population is usually structured, with subjects in clusters, the assumption of independence and homogeneity of the disturbances is questionable. Nevertheless, for the entire population, the ordinary least squares fit is well defined, and it is meaningful to estimate this fit from the sample data.

Jackknife and model-based methods for fitting regression with survey data are described in this section. In the jackknife method, the ordinary least squares is applied to each pseudosample constructed in the same manner as for population mean estimation (Section 7.4). The resulting K sets of estimates and estimated sampling variances are summarized as follows:

- Parameter estimates are the means of the corresponding pseudoestimates.

- Estimates of the sampling variances are the corrected sums of squares of the pseudoestimates.

An alternative approach is based on direct estimation of the quantity of interest, namely,

$$b^{(p)} = \frac{\sum_i X_i Y_i - N \bar{X} \bar{Y}}{\sum_i X_i^2 - N \bar{X}^2}, \tag{7.27}$$

where $\bar{X}$ and $\bar{Y}$ are the respective population means of X and Y. We distinguish between the underlying regression parameter b, as in (7.26), and its would-be estimator $b^{(p)}$ (if X and Y were available for the entire population). The latter estimator can be expressed as a function of population means:

$$b^{(p)} = \frac{\overline{XY} - \bar{X}\bar{Y}}{\overline{X^2} - \bar{X}^2} ; \tag{7.28}$$

the corresponding intercept is $a^{(p)} = \bar{Y} - b^{(p)}\bar{X}$. Each of the population means, $\bar{X}$, $\bar{Y}$, $\overline{XY}$ (mean of the products X_iY_i), and $\overline{X^2}$ (mean of the squares X_i^2), can be estimated by the jackknife, model-based, or another method. An estimator of $b^{(p)}$ is obtained by substituting the estimates for the population means:

$$\hat{b}^{(p)} = \frac{\widehat{\overline{XY}} - \hat{\bar{X}}\hat{\bar{Y}}}{\widehat{\overline{X^2}} - \hat{\bar{X}}^2}.\tag{7.29}$$

Since $\hat{b}^{(p)}$ is a non-linear function of the population mean estimators, even when these estimators are unbiased, $\hat{b}^{(p)}$ may not be. The bias of $\hat{b}^{(p)}$ and its sampling variance can be approximated using the delta method.

Let $\mathbf{u} = \left(\hat{\bar{X}}, \hat{\bar{Y}}, \widehat{\overline{X^2}}, \widehat{\overline{Y^2}}, \widehat{\overline{XY}}\right)$ and $\mathbf{U} = \left(\bar{X}, \bar{Y}, \overline{X^2}, \overline{Y^2}, \overline{XY}\right)$, and let f be the function such that $\hat{b}^{(p)} = f(\mathbf{u})$. The Taylor expansion of the estimator $f(\mathbf{u})$ around the estimand $f(\mathbf{U})$ yields the approximation (by ignoring all but the first three terms of the expansion):

$$\hat{b}^{(p)} \approx f(\mathbf{U}) + \frac{\partial f}{\partial \mathbf{U}}(\mathbf{u} - \mathbf{U})^{\top} + \frac{1}{2}(\mathbf{u} - \mathbf{U})\frac{\partial^2 f}{\partial \mathbf{U}^{\top}\partial \mathbf{U}}(\mathbf{u} - \mathbf{U})^{\top}.\tag{7.30}$$

Hence, the approximate bias of $\hat{b}^{(p)}$ is

$$\mathbf{E}\left\{\hat{b}^{(p)} - f(\mathbf{U})\right\} \approx \frac{1}{2}\mathrm{tr}\left\{\frac{\partial^2 f}{\partial \mathbf{U}^{\top}\partial \mathbf{U}}\mathrm{var}(\mathbf{u})\right\}.\tag{7.31}$$

The sampling variance of $f(\mathbf{u})$ can be approximated as

$$\mathrm{var}\left(\hat{b}^{(p)}\right) = \frac{\partial f}{\partial \mathbf{U}}\mathrm{var}(\mathbf{u})\left(\frac{\partial f}{\partial \mathbf{U}}\right)^{\top},\tag{7.32}$$

derived from (7.30) by ignoring the contribution of the quadratic term.

Equation (7.31) suggests an improvement of the estimator $\hat{b}^{(p)}$ by adjusting it for the estimated bias. Such an adjustment may be detrimental when the estimate of the quantity in (7.31) is subject to considerable uncertainty.

The residual variance, defined for the population, is

$$\hat{\sigma}^2 = \overline{Y^2} - \frac{\overline{XY}^2 - \bar{X}\bar{Y}}{\overline{X^2} - \bar{X}^2}.$$

It can be estimated by substituting the estimates in place of population means. Its bias can be estimated using (7.31) for the appropriate function f.

The described method can be extended to multiple regression by estimating $f(\mathbf{U}) = \left(\mathbf{X}^{\top}\mathbf{X}\right)^{-1}\mathbf{X}^{\top}\mathbf{Y}$ from the weighted sample means of squares and cross-products of all the variables. The general outline can be extended further to any estimator that is a function of a small number of sufficient statistics. An alternative approach to multiple regression with survey data, based on random-effects models, is applied in Chapter 8.

Example

For illustration, we construct a covariate by adding up all the non-missing responses to items 231–238 of the student questionnaire. The items, headed by the text

In Math class how often do you ... ?,

inquire about the frequency of various classroom activities associated with good teaching practices (doing problems from textbooks; on worksheets; in small groups; using rulers, blocks, or solids; calculators; a computer; taking math tests; and writing reports or doing projects). The responses to each item are coded on a 5-point scale (5 — almost every day; 4 — several times a week; 3 — about once a week; 2 — less than once a week; and 1 — never).

Because of missing responses, the covariate is not defined for 87 subjects (3.2 percent of the sample). The values of the covariate are in the range 11–40, although only 10 students have scores lower than 15, and 12 students have scores higher than 35. The mean score is 28.45 and the standard deviation is 3.85. The distribution of the scores is unimodal, with the mode at 30 points, attained by 306 students. About 60 percent of the students have scores in the range 27–32, and each of these scores is attained by more than 200 students. The median score is 29.

The results of the regression analysis are summarized in Table 7.7. There is a close agreement between the jackknife and model-based methods. The jackknife method involves $57 \times 5 = 285$ weighted least squares fits, whereas in the model-based method, the population means (the means, the means of squares, and the means of the cross-products of X and Y) are estimated for each set of imputed values. Clearly, the latter requires much less computing.

The estimated regression slope has the expected sign and is highly significant, as assessed by the t-ratio statistic ($1.432/0.232 \doteq 6.2$). The difference of 20 points on the covariate (say, from 15 points to 35 points) is associated with the difference of 28.6 points on the proficiency scale. However, even this difference, which corresponds to the two extremes, is only of the same order as the residual standard deviation, $\sqrt{1036.44} = 32.2$.

Two factors are likely to reduce the 'explanatory power' of the fitted regression. First, the covariate is defined in a rather arbitrary fashion, with emphasis on convenient definition and easy description, and second, the responses of the students are far from perfectly reliable. Also, there may be a number of other covariates that would yield a better regression model for the proficiency scores.

7.9 Estimating many subpopulation means

Large-scale surveys serve a multitude of purposes; different agencies are interested in inference about a variety of subpopulations defined by re-

TABLE 7.7. Regression analysis using the jackknife and model-based methods.

| Parameter | Set of imputed values | | | | | |
	1	2	3	4	5	Overall
			Jackknife			
Intercept	230.03	230.02	229.63	230.33	226.66	229.34
Slope	1.403	1.401	1.414	1.390	1.524	1.426
	(0.227)	(0.218)	(0.218)	(0.225)	(0.235)	(0.235)
Res. var.	1042.05	1031.51	1015.88	1043.62	1048.37	1036.47
		Model-based method CI	$(u_{jk} = w_{+jk})$			
Intercept	230.03	229.02	229.62	230.16	226.61	229.28
Slope	1.407	1.406	1.418	1.395	1.528	1.432
	(0.224)	(0.216)	(0.219)	(0.223)	(0.236)	(0.232)
Res. var.	1040.12	1028.51	1013.17	1040.37	1048.33	1036.44

Notes: The covariate is constructed as the total of the response codes for the student questionnaire items 231–238. The estimated standard errors are given in parentheses.

sponses to the background questionnaire items. It may be more expedient to estimate subpopulation means and their sampling variances for a whole array of subpopulations rather than to respond to individual requests for estimation or hypothesis testing. From a different perspective, estimation of a subpopulation mean can be improved by 'borrowing strength', that is, incorporating information about means of other subpopulations.

For small subsamples, especially those with only a few strata represented by more than one large cluster, the jackknife method often breaks down, and the estimate of the sampling variance is clearly incorrect. The main problem with the model-based method is that the estimates of the within- and between-cluster variances are subject to a lot of uncertainty, which is ignored in estimating the sampling variance of the subpopulation mean estimator. Estimation of σ_B^2 is particularly problematic when only a small number of random terms δ_i is realized, and some of them only on a small number of subjects.

An attractive proposition to deal with this problem is to pool information across the subpopulations. Although it is not reasonable to assume that all the subpopulations have the same between-cluster variance, suitably selected sets of subpopulations may have values of the variance σ_B^2 in a narrow range. In a simplistic approach, the estimator $\hat{\sigma}_B^2$ based on the data from a single subpopulation would be replaced by the mean of such estimators, $\bar{\hat{\sigma}}_B^2$, from the entire set of subpopulations. In calculating this average variance, the contributing estimators can be assigned differential weights, so as to reflect differential precision of estimation. Also, the estimator for the reference subpopulation can be given greater weight, so as to increase its influence on the estimation of the subpopulation mean.

An alternative approach is based on regression smoothing. We observed earlier that the sampling variance of the ratio estimator is a linear combination of the between-cluster and the within-cluster variances:

$$\text{var}(\hat{\mu}_a) = S_{a,2}\sigma_B^2 + \sum_{k=1}^{K}\sum_{j=1}^{m_k} S_{a,1jk}\sigma_{W,jk}^2 \qquad (7.33)$$

for subpopulation-specific constants $S_{a,2}$ and $\{S_{a,1jk}\}$, where

$$
\begin{aligned}
S_{a,2} &= \frac{1}{w_{a,+}^2}\sum_{k=1}^{K}\sum_{j=1}^{m_k} w_{a,+jk}^2\,, \\[2mm]
S_{a,1jk} &= \frac{w_{a,jk}^{(2)}}{w_{a,+}^2}\,;
\end{aligned}
\qquad (7.34)
$$

see (7.7). The totals of weights $w_{a,+jk}$, $w_{a,+}$, and $w_{a,jk}^{(2)}$ are defined as in Section 7.5.1, with all summations restricted to the subpopulation a. Suppose an *estimated* sampling variance, $\widehat{\text{var}}(\hat{\mu}_a)$, is available for each subpopulation; it could be obtained by the jackknife, model-based, or any other method. These estimates satisfy the linear regression model

$$\widehat{\text{var}}(\hat{\mu}_a) = S_{a,2}\sigma_B^2 + \sum_{k=1}^{K}\sum_{j=1}^{m_k} S_{a,1jk}\sigma_{W,jk}^2 + \varepsilon_a\,, \qquad (7.35)$$

where ε_a is a random term. It is comprised of two components: the error of estimation, $\widehat{\text{var}}(\hat{\mu}_a) - \text{var}(\hat{\mu}_a)$, and the model deviation

$$\text{var}(\hat{\mu}_a) - S_{a,2}\sigma_B^2 - \sum_{jk} S_{a,1jk}\sigma_{W,jk}^2\,,$$

which may be due to varying within- and between-cluster variances or due to a departure from the 'model' sampling design. The variances σ_B^2 and $\sigma_{W,jk}^2$, now in the role of regression parameters, may be assumed known or unknown. If unknown, they can be estimated by standard regression techniques, assuming normality of ε_a. Differential precision of the estimates $\widehat{\text{var}}(\hat{\mu}_a)$ can be accounted for by introducing suitable regression weights (dependent on the sample size).

The regression estimates $\tilde{\sigma}_B^2$ and $\tilde{\sigma}_{W,jk}^2$ for the model in (7.35) can be used to define the 'smoothed' estimates of the sampling variances as the fitted values:

$$\widehat{\text{var}}(\hat{\mu}_a) = S_{a,2}\tilde{\sigma}_B^2 + \sum_{k=1}^{K}\sum_{j=1}^{m_k} S_{a,1jk}\tilde{\sigma}_{W,jk}^2\,,$$

setting $S_{a,1jk} = 0$ when subpopulation a is not represented in cluster jk. When there are a large number of clusters, it is expedient to substitute the estimates $\hat{\sigma}^2_{W,jk}$ for the corresponding variances in (7.35), thus obtaining a simple regression on σ^2_B with a specified intercept.

Extensions of this approach are easy to devise, for instance, by introducing different variances σ^2_B for disjoint subsets of the subsamples. The regression equation (7.35) can be supplemented by other data summaries, not only functions of the sampling weights, even if the original interpretation in terms of a common between-cluster variance would no longer apply. Usual regression diagnostic methods can be applied to assess appropriateness of the selected model.

7.10   Jackknife and model-based estimators

We have seen that analyses of real data are inconclusive about the merits of the jackknife and model-based estimators of the sampling variance. In this section, we demonstrate how simulations can be used to compare the efficiency of these estimators. We point out that simulations would not be a method of choice if the sampling distribution of the estimators could be evaluated analytically.

To outline the approach, the observed data are replaced by data generated according to an adopted model, with realistic values of the model parameters, and the two competitor estimators are evaluated. This process is carried out a large number of times, so that the observed distribution of the simulated values of each estimator is close enough to the theoretical sampling distribution of the estimator.

Although this scheme appears to present a level plane for the alternative estimators, it is somewhat unfair to the jackknife method, because the model adopted for simulating the data is in accordance with the model-based method, whereas the assumptions underlying the jackknife method are less stringent (model flexibility is an advantage of the jackknife).

As the 'data frame', we take the New Jersey sample, with its sampling weights and clustering and stratification structure, and replace the outcome variable by a set of values generated according to the variance component model in (7.4). The model parameters are themselves drawn at random: the stratum means μ_k are drawn from $\mathcal{N}(250, \Sigma_{str})$, the within-cluster standard deviations $\sigma_{W,jk}$ are drawn from the uniform distribution on (V_L, V_H), and the draws are mutually independent. The settings for Σ_{str}, V_L, and V_H, as well as σ^2_B, are discussed below. The simulated set of stratum means μ_k is common to all simulations (representing *fixed* effects), but different sets of cluster-level deviations δ_{jk} and subject-level deviations ε_{ijk} are drawn in each simulation, representing *random* effects. The simulated deviations are independently drawn from the respective distributions $\mathcal{N}(0, \sigma_B^2)$ and $\mathcal{N}(0, \sigma_{W,jk}^2)$.

The choice of the normal and uniform distributions is arbitrary; other, less familiar distributions may be just as suitable, but the setting of some of the simulation parameters may then be more difficult. After some trial and error, we chose the following settings:

$$\Sigma_{str} = 100, \quad V_L = 10, \quad V_H = 40, \quad \sigma_B^2 = 100.$$

The dispersion of the simulated stratum means Σ_{str} was obtained as the rounded sampling variance of the estimated stratum-level means, adjusted for the uncertainty of the means. The cluster-level variance σ_B^2 is set to the rounded value of its estimate from the survey data. The distribution of the simulated within-cluster variances $\sigma_{W,jk}^2$ was set by trial and error.

Suppose, for the moment, that the simulated variances are the variance parameters in the survey. Given the survey data, these variances would be estimated, and each estimator $\sigma_{W,jk}^2$ would have approximately a χ^2 distribution with $n_{W,jk}$ degrees of freedom. Ignoring the approximation, the estimators of $\sigma_{W,jk}^2$ can be simulated directly and the simulated values compared with the realized values of $\hat{\sigma}_{W,jk}^2$, say, by a quantile plot. Our aim was to match the distribution of the simulated $\hat{\sigma}_{W,jk}^2$, over the 104 clusters, with the distribution of the realized values $\hat{\sigma}_{W,jk}^2$. Figure 7.2 contains the quantile plots of the within-cluster variance estimates based on each of the five sets of imputed values against their simulated counterparts. The logarithmic scale is used so as to improve the resolution of the plots. For orientation, each plot contains 104 points. The simulated estimates of the within-cluster variance are sorted in ascending order and plotted against the sorted within-cluster variance estimates for each set of imputed values in the New Jersey survey. In each plot, a different set of simulated within-cluster variance estimates is used. The distribution of the simulated estimates does not match the data-based estimates perfectly, but the deviations of the quantiles are moderate throughout the range.

For each set of generated proficiency scores, we apply the jackknife estimator, with the replicate weights from the survey, and the model-based estimators **CI** and **CR**. Furthermore, we apply the optimal weights u_{jk} assuming the value $\sigma_B^2 = 100$. It is useful to explore this method, denoted by **C100**, to assess how well the model-based approach would fare if the between-cluster variance were known exactly. The difference in efficiency of the estimators **CI** and **C100** represents the potential improvement of model-based estimation by incorporating external information about σ_B^2.

Table 7.8 summarizes the results of 100 simulations. For each estimator, the minimum, maximum, mean, median, and the observed standard deviation of the estimates are given. The realized values are approximately normally distributed for each estimator. The simulations confirm that the ratio and jackknife estimators are nearly identical. The observed sampling

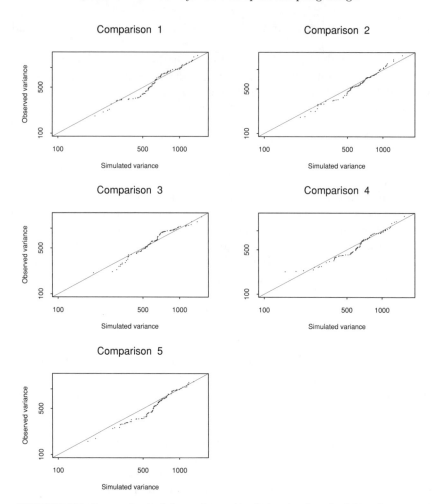

FIGURE 7.2. Comparison of the estimated and the simulated within-cluster variances. 'Comparison' k, $k = 1, \ldots, 5$, is the plot of the ordered values of the simulated within-cluster variances against the ordered values of the estimated within-cluster variances for the kth set of imputed values. The five simulations are mutually independent. In the plots, both axes are on the logarithmic scale.

TABLE 7.8. Summary of simulations of model-based estimators.

Estimator	Minimum	Mean	Median	Maximum	Std. dev.	df
Wtd mean	248.14	250.27	250.29	252.67	1.20	
Jack. mean	248.14	250.28	250.28	252.66	1.20	
Jack. var.	0.72	1.35	1.33	2.25	0.34	31.6
CI var	0.66	1.41	1.37	2.26	0.32	38.7
CI σ_B^2	32.23	100.28	97.04	180.14	29.09	
C100 var	0.64	1.42	1.39	2.29	0.32	40.1
C100 σ_B^2	30.55	101.33	98.73	182.21	28.81	

Notes: The estimators of the sampling variance of the weighted mean are denoted by the method and the symbol 'var' in the first column. The estimators of the between-cluster variance are denoted by the method and the symbol σ_B^2. The sampling standard deviation ('Std. dev.') and the fitted number of degrees of freedom ('df') are given in the rightmost columns. One hundred simulations were carried out.

variance of these estimators is $1.20^2 = 1.44$. The jackknife estimator of this variance has the observed mean of 1.33, a bias of –0.11. The model-based estimators **CI** and **CR** are also biased, but to a lesser degree (respective biases –0.04 and –0.05). The model-based estimators of the sampling variance also have smaller sampling variances (0.32^2 versus 0.34^2).

Estimators of variances, for instance, in ANOVA and ordinary regression, are often χ^2 distributed, and the associated numbers of degrees of freedom can be readily interpreted as a measure of efficiency of the estimator. The greater the number of degrees of freedom, the more efficient the estimator. The estimators of the sampling variance of $\hat{\mu}$ are approximately χ^2 distributed, and the associated numbers of degrees of freedom can be estimated by matching the moments of the estimator with the moments of a χ^2 distribution. Since the mean of the χ_d^2 distribution is d and the variance is $2d$, moment matching leads to the equation

$$\widehat{df} = \frac{2 \times (\text{mean estimate of variance})^2}{\text{variance of MSE}}.$$

The estimated numbers of degrees of freedom are given in the rightmost column of Table 7.8. The jackknife estimator of the sampling variance of $\hat{\mu}$ is associated with 31.6 degrees of freedom, whereas the **CI** estimator has 38.7 degrees of freedom. Even if the between-cluster variance σ_B^2 were known, only 1.4 additional degrees of freedom (toward 40.1) would be gained.

Conclusions from these simulations apply neither to other subpopulations nor to other estimators; the simulations have to be carried out for each specific context (data frame). In general, the model-based estimator

CI is more efficient than its jackknife counterpart, particularly for sparse and unevenly distributed subpopulations. For estimating proportions and regression parameters, model-based estimators are also more efficient. See Longford (1995) for details of several sets of simulations.

7.11 Summary

We described a class of model-based estimators of the sampling variance of the ratio estimator of the population and subpopulation means in surveys with stratified clustered sampling design. The estimators are derived by matching the moments of the theoretical distribution of certain sum-of-squares statistics with their observed values. Simulations attest to the efficiency of these estimators in comparison with the jackknife estimator. The model-based method is distribution-free, assuming, in essence, only variance homogeneity within clusters.

A general approach to deriving estimators of more complex population summaries and parameters by expressing the summaries as functions of population means was illustrated on ordinary regression. Next to efficiency, the most important advantage of the model-based methods is that they dispense with the replicate weights, which may take up a substantial proportion of the survey data. The model-based approach can be extended to more complex sampling designs by adopting an appropriate superpopulation model.

The role of the weight adjustment and its impact on estimation was explored. It is important to distinguish between the need for weight adjustment and the need for adjusting for the uncertainty involved in this adjustment.

The model-based approach presented in this chapter is in contrast with *design-based* approaches, which rely solely on the information encoded in the sampling design. The obvious criticism of the model-based design is the vulnerability of *every* statistical model. However, in NAEP as well as in other large-scale surveys, the 'advertised' sampling design is rarely implemented accurately because a number of contingencies, organizational problems, and instances of incomplete information about the target population are encountered. Therefore, the assumptions of the design-based approach are usually not pristine either. An undoubted advantage of the model-based approach is that it enables collating information across surveys and subpopulations, which is of great importance in regularly conducted surveys. Also, the approach is readily applicable to more complex population summaries such as ordinary regression. Although design-based approaches can accommodate some of these methods, 'borrowing strength' across surveys cannot be accomplished in a design-based approach in any straightforward manner.

Whichever method of estimation is applied, great care has to be exercised in interpreting the estimated quantities, because a number of sources of uncertainty cannot be formally incorporated in the analysis. Imperfection of the measurement instrument and deviations from the 'model' sampling design are due to the practicalities of data collection. The multiple imputation method takes care of the uncertainty about the proficiency scores but assumes that the cognitive questionnaire items are a perfect representation of the surveyed domain of knowledge. Any inference of causal or explanatory nature is justified only in an experimental design framework which cannot be imposed in the context of a large-scale survey. Thus, even if the difference between two subpopulation means is estimated with high precision, it does not imply superiority of one subpopulation in any way. Adjustment for some relevant background variables still does not warrant such inference, because assignment of the values of the background variables is not under external control. Some of the background variables may be interpreted as a 'treatment' in the sense of the experimental design. Comparisons of these treatment groups are of interest for policy decisions (for instance, for recommendations about teaching styles). The principal hurdle to straightforward interpretation of between-group differences is the informative assignment of subjects to groups and the presence of informative choices in education in general. Therefore, the estimates and their standard errors, even if estimated with high precision, require informal adjustments to take account of the features of the studied process that are ignored by the formal statistical analysis.

8

Small-area estimation

8.1 Introduction

Large-scale educational and literacy surveys, such as the National Assessment of Educational Progress (NAEP), the National Education Longitudinal Survey (NELS), and the National Adult Literacy Survey (NALS), often provide sufficient information about their target populations and certain well-represented subpopulations, but they cannot be used directly for inferences about small areas, such as states, counties, or other geographical units. National surveys do contain some information about small areas, but such information may be difficult to extract and, on its own, may be insufficient for inferences with a desired level of confidence.

States, or even smaller administrative units, often conduct smaller-scale surveys for their jurisdictions. These surveys are patterned on the national surveys and frequently use the same or only slightly altered survey instruments (questionnaires). The cost of such surveys could be reduced if information from the national surveys were incorporated in the analysis of the small-scale survey.

The subject of this chapter is inference about small areas using data from large-scale surveys and methods for combining information from several surveys. Our general approach can be concisely described as follows: if all the small areas were 'similar', then inference on the large scale (say, about the country) would be directly applicable to the small area. 'Similarity' means a small or vanishing variance of the small-area population means of the outcome variable. For a moderate small-area-level variance, information about the other small areas is useful for inference about a particular small area, but, in general, the larger the variance, the smaller the contribution of the other small areas to the information about the particular small area.

Even if the outcome variable has substantial small-area-level variation, there may be an explanation for the differences among the small areas. Thus, after adjusting for a suitable set of covariates, the (adjusted) differences among the small areas may diminish. In other words, the association of the outcome variables with a set of covariates is similar across the small areas. This similarity can be effectively utilized for improved inference about small areas.

Central to the development of this chapter is inference about between-cluster variation, which plays an important role in estimation for a small area. There are several parallels with Chapter 7, where we found that the sampling variance of the estimate of the population mean depends on the within- and between-cluster variances. In this chapter, we switch our attention to clusters, or small areas, and explore how population summaries, the estimates of the population mean and of the variance components, can contribute to improved estimation of the small-area mean. In common with estimation of raters' severities in Chapter 3 and improved estimation of item DIF in Chapter 5, we apply shrinkage estimators to optimally combine information from the small area and from the entire population.

In order to avoid any conflict or confusion with the terms introduced in the previous chapter, we will continue to use the term 'cluster' for a sampling unit but will restrict it to the collection of the elementary units (subjects) drawn into the sample. The term 'small area' will refer to the population represented by the cluster. For instance, in the application discussed in Section 8.7, U.S. states are small areas, whereas the samples drawn from each state are clusters.

Section 8.2 describes a simple scheme for pooling information across small areas. Section 8.3 extends this approach by incorporating adjustment for covariates, which reduces (evens out) the between-small-area differences. Computational and algorithmic issues are discussed in Section 8.4. Section 8.5 deals with prediction of the mean for a small area, and Section 8.6 discusses model selection issues. Section 8.7 presents an application to two literacy surveys conducted by the U.S. Department of Labor. The chapter is concluded by a summary.

8.2 Shrinkage estimation

Suppose variable Y is defined for each subject in a target population by values Y_i, $i = 1, 2, \ldots, N$, and these values have been observed in a survey with stratified clustered sampling design for a sample y_{ijk}, $i = 1, \ldots, n_{jk}$, $j = 1, \ldots, m_k$, and $k = 1, \ldots, K$. We use the same notation as in Chapter

7: y denotes the outcome variable, w the sampling weights, μ the population mean, and the subscripts ijk denote subject i in cluster j of stratum k. Of interest is estimation of the population mean of small area j, not necessarily represented in the survey.

It would seem irresponsible even to attempt to estimate the mean of a cluster that has not been included in the survey. However, if all the clusters have identical means, then the estimator of the population mean is an efficient estimator of the cluster mean. Since the survey sample contains data from several clusters, we can assess whether equality of the cluster-level (population) means is a realistic hypothesis.

We represent the stratification and clustering by the variance component model

$$y_{ijk} = \mu_k + \delta_{jk} + \varepsilon_{ijk}, \tag{8.1}$$

where $\{\delta_{jk}\}_{jk}$ and $\{\varepsilon_{ijk}\}_i$ are mutually independent random samples from centred distributions with respective variances σ_B^2 and $\sigma_{W,jk}^2$. For a cluster represented in the data, the ratio estimator of its population mean $\mu_{jk} = \mu_k + \delta_{jk}$ was introduced in Section 7.4:

$$\bar{y}_{\cdot jk} = \frac{1}{w_{+jk}} \sum_{i=1}^{n_{jk}} w_{ijk} y_{ijk}. \tag{8.2}$$

Assuming the model in (8.1), this estimator is conditionally unbiased, $\mathbf{E}(\bar{y}_{\cdot jk} - \mu_{jk} \mid \mu_{jk}) = 0$, and its conditional sampling variance is

$$\mathrm{var}(\bar{y}_{\cdot jk} \mid \mu_{jk}) = \frac{\sigma_{W,jk}^2}{n_{W,jk} - 1}, \tag{8.3}$$

where $n_{W,jk}$ is the effective sample size of cluster j in stratum k (as defined in Section 7.5.3). When the sample from the cluster is a small part of the survey sample from the stratum, $\mathrm{var}(\bar{y}_{\cdot jk})$ is much greater than the variance of the population mean estimator $\hat{\mu}_k$ because $\hat{\mu}_k$ is based on a much larger dataset.

On the one hand, in the special case of 'similarity' there is an efficient estimator for the mean of a cluster not represented in the sample; on the other hand, the mean of a cluster represented in the survey sample by a small number of subjects has a large sampling variance. This is counterintuitive; data from the cluster appear to be detrimental to the estimation of the cluster mean! This contradiction is reconciled by combining the two estimators, $\hat{\mu}_k$ and $\bar{y}_{\cdot jk}$. Typically, the former is biased but has a small variance, whereas the latter is unbiased but has a large variance.

We consider the linear combination

$$\hat{\mu}_{jk} = c_{jk}\hat{\mu}_k + (1 - c_{jk})\bar{y}_{\cdot jk} \tag{8.4}$$

and find the constant $c_{jk} \in [0, 1]$ which minimizes the mean squared error (MSE) of $\hat{\mu}_{jk}$. Let $w_{jk}^{(2)} = \sum_i w_{ijk}^2$ be the sum of squares of the weights for cluster jk. The MSE of $\hat{\mu}_{jk}$ is derived by elementary operations. In its derivation, we condition on the realized value of the cluster-level deviation δ_{jk};

$$
\mathbf{E}\left\{(\hat{\mu}_{jk} - \mu_{jk})^2 \mid \delta_{jk}\right\}
$$

$$
= \mathbf{E}\left[\{c_{jk}(\hat{\mu}_k - \mu_{jk}) + (1 - c_{jk})(\bar{y}_{\cdot jk} - \mu_{jk})\}^2 \mid \delta_{jk}\right]
$$

$$
= c_{jk}^2 \mathbf{E}\left\{(\hat{\mu}_k - \mu_{jk})^2 \mid \delta_{jk}\right\}
$$

$$
+ 2c_{jk}(1 - c_{jk})\,\mathrm{cov}\,(\hat{\mu}_k - \mu_{jk}, \bar{y}_{\cdot jk} - \mu_{jk} \mid \delta_{jk})
$$

$$
+ (1 - c_{jk})^2\,\mathrm{var}(\bar{y}_{\cdot jk} - \mu_{jk} \mid \delta_{jk}).
$$

Substituting the model equations for $\hat{\mu}_k$ and $\bar{y}_{\cdot jk}$ and exploiting the properties of independence, we obtain

$$
\mathbf{E}\left\{(\hat{\mu}_{jk} - \mu_{jk})^2 \mid \delta_{jk}\right\}
$$

$$
= c_{jk}^2 \mathbf{E}\left\{\left(\frac{1}{w_{++k}}\sum_{j'=1}^{m_k}\sum_{i=1}^{n_{j'k}} w_{ij'k}\varepsilon_{ij'k} + \frac{1}{w_{++k}}\sum_{j'=1}^{m_k} w_{+j'k}\delta_{j'k} - \delta_{jk}\right)^2 \mid \delta_{jk}\right\}
$$

$$
+ 2c_{jk}(1 - c_{jk})\,\mathrm{cov}\left(\frac{1}{w_{++k}}\sum_{j'=1}^{m_k}\sum_{i=1}^{n_{j'k}} w_{ij'k}\varepsilon_{ij'k}\,, \; \frac{1}{w_{+jk}}\sum_{i=1}^{n_{jk}} w_{ijk}\varepsilon_{ijk}\right)
$$

$$
+ (1 - c_{jk})^2\,\mathrm{var}\left(\frac{1}{w_{+jk}}\sum_{i=1}^{n_{jk}} w_{ijk}\varepsilon_{ijk}\right)
$$

$$
= \frac{c_{jk}^2}{w_{++k}^2}\sum_{j'=1}^{m_k}\sigma_{W,j'k}^2 w_{j'k}^{(2)} + (1 - c_{jk})\sigma_{W,jk}^2 \frac{w_{jk}^{(2)}}{w_{+jk}}\left\{\frac{2c_{jk}}{w_{++k}} + \frac{(1 - c_{jk})}{w_{+jk}}\right\}
$$

$$
+ \sigma_B^2\frac{c_{jk}^2}{w_{++k}^2}\sum_{j'\neq j} w_{+j'k}^2 + c_{jk}^2\frac{(w_{++k} - w_{+jk})^2}{w_{++k}^2}\delta_{jk}^2.
$$

This is a quadratic function of the coefficient c_{jk}, and so its maximum is easily located as the root of the first-order derivative:

$$
c_{jk}^* = \frac{\sigma_{W,jk}^2}{D_{jk}}\frac{w_{jk}^{(2)}}{w_{+jk}^2}\left(1 - \frac{w_{+jk}}{w_{++k}}\right),
$$

where

$$
D_{jk} = \sigma_{W,jk}^2\frac{w_{jk}^{(2)}}{w_{+jk}^2}\left(1 - \frac{2w_{+jk}}{w_{++k}}\right) + \frac{1}{w_{++k}^2}\sum_{j'=1}^{m_k}\sigma_{W,j'k}^2 w_{j'k}^{(2)}
$$

$$
+ \frac{\sigma_B^2}{w_{++k}^2}\sum_{j'=1}^{m_k} w_{+j'k}^2 + \left(1 - \frac{w_{+jk}}{w_{++k}}\right)^2 \delta_{jk}^2.
$$

Note that D_{jk} is a linear and increasing function of the variances σ_B^2 and $\sigma_{W,jk}^2$. The optimal coefficient c_{jk}^* can be shown to be in the range $[0, 1)$; $\hat{\mu}_{jk}$ can be interpreted as a shrinkage estimator. The coefficient vanishes only when $\sigma_{W,jk}^2 = 0$ or when $w_{+jk} = w_{++k}$, that is, when stratum k is represented in the sample by a sole cluster. The MSE of the estimator in (8.4) with $c_{jk} = c_{jk}^*$ is

$$\mathbf{E}(\hat{\mu}_{jk} - \mu_{jk})^2 = \frac{\sigma_{W,jk}^2 w_{jk}^{(2)}}{w_{+jk}^2} - \frac{\sigma_{W,jk}^4 \left(w_{jk}^{(2)}\right)^2}{D_{jk} w_{+jk}^2} \left(\frac{1}{w_{+jk}} - \frac{1}{w_{++k}}\right)^2 .$$

This MSE depends on the between-cluster variance σ_B^2 only through D_{jk}, and so it is an increasing function of σ_B^2; for a given sampling design and within-cluster variances $\sigma_{W,jk}^2$, the greatest improvement in estimation of μ_{jk} takes place when between-cluster variance vanishes.

Optimality is unlikely to be eroded substantially if δ_{jk}^2 is replaced by its unconditional variance σ_B^2. In practice, the unknown variances σ_B^2 and $\sigma_{W,jk}^2$ are replaced by their estimates. The difference $\bar{y}_{.jk} - \bar{y}_{..k}$ is a trivial estimator of δ_{jk}. However, $(\bar{y}_{.jk} - \bar{y}_{..k})^2 - \widehat{\text{var}}(y_{jk})$ is a more appropriate estimator of δ_{jk}^2 because it is less affected by the sampling variance of $\bar{y}_{.jk} - \bar{y}_{..k}$. Alternatively, a shrinkage estimator of δ_{jk} can be used.

8.3   Regression with survey data

In the previous section, we explored how all clusters from a stratum can contribute to estimation of the population mean of a cluster in the stratum, that is, how we can 'borrow strength' from the other clusters to estimate a cluster-population mean more efficiently. One conclusion, supported by intuition, is that between-cluster differences are detrimental to inference about clusters.

In this section, we consider two avenues of improvement in small-area estimation. First, not only clusters within the stratum but all the clusters in the sample should contribute to estimation of a cluster mean. Second, between-cluster differences can be reduced by adjustment for important covariates using linear regression. The two avenues essentially coincide because adjustment for stratum differences is a special case of the adjustment by linear regression.

We start by describing a general approach for data from a clustered sample with no stratification, or equivalently, a single stratum, and then extend the approach to stratified clustered samples. For notational simplicity, we omit the index k (stratum) throughout.

We consider a two-level linear regression model

$$y_{ij} = \mathbf{x}_{ij}\boldsymbol{\beta} + \delta_j + \varepsilon_{ij} , \tag{8.5}$$

where $\boldsymbol{\beta}$ is a vector or parameters, and $\{\delta_j\}$ and $\{\varepsilon_{ij}\}$ are mutually independent random samples from respective normal distributions $\mathcal{N}(0, \sigma_B^2)$ and $\mathcal{N}(0, \sigma_W^2)$. The subscripts refer to individuals $i = 1, 2, \ldots, n_j$ in small areas $j = 1, 2, \ldots, m$. The covariates in $\mathbf{x}$ can be defined for subjects or clusters. Variables on which stratification is based are an example of the latter.

The model in (8.5) can be interpreted as that of analysis of covariance with the term δ_j representing the difference of the regression for small area j from the average regression $\mathbf{x}\boldsymbol{\beta}$. These differences vanish when $\sigma_B^2 = 0$. With a known population mean of the covariates for small area j, denoted by $\bar{\mathbf{x}}_j$, the population mean of the outcome variable in the small area could be estimated as

$$\hat{y}^{(j)} = \bar{\mathbf{x}}_j \hat{\boldsymbol{\beta}}, \tag{8.6}$$

where $\hat{\boldsymbol{\beta}}$ is an estimator of $\boldsymbol{\beta}$, say, based on the large-scale survey. Suppose $\hat{\boldsymbol{\beta}}$ is unbiased. Assuming an infinite population (a *super*population) in the small area, the sampling variance of this estimator is

$$\mathrm{var}(\hat{y}^{(j)}) = \bar{\mathbf{x}}_j \boldsymbol{\Sigma}_b \bar{\mathbf{x}}_j^\top,$$

where $\boldsymbol{\Sigma}_b$ is the sampling variance matrix of the regression estimator $\hat{\boldsymbol{\beta}}$ based on the large-scale survey. Naturally, the precision of this estimator plays an important role in the estimation for a small area.

When $\delta_j \neq 0$, the estimator in (8.6) is biased; letting $\bar{y}_j$ be the population mean of Y in small-area j, we have

$$\mathbf{E}(\bar{\mathbf{x}}_j \hat{\boldsymbol{\beta}} - \bar{y}_j \mid \delta_j) = -\delta_j,$$

so that when σ_B^2 is large, the estimator in (8.6) is biased for many small areas (for those with large values of $|\delta_j|$). Therefore, unless the small-area-level variance vanishes, information about δ_j is another element contributing to the estimation of $y^{(j)}$. The MSE conveniently combines the two measures of imperfection of an estimator. Assuming infinite population size of the small area or, equivalently, ignoring the variance of the mean residual, $\mathrm{var}(\bar{\varepsilon}_j)$, the conditional MSE of $\bar{\mathbf{x}}_j \hat{\boldsymbol{\beta}}$ is

$$\mathbf{E}\left\{ \left(\bar{\mathbf{x}}_j \hat{\boldsymbol{\beta}} - \bar{y}_j \right)^2 \mid \delta_j \right\} = \bar{\mathbf{x}}_j \boldsymbol{\Sigma}_b \bar{\mathbf{x}}_j^\top + \delta_j^2.$$

In the absence of any information about δ_j, other than information mediated by σ_B^2 or its estimator, the MSE can be summarized by its expectation $\bar{\mathbf{x}}_j \boldsymbol{\Sigma}_b \bar{\mathbf{x}}_j^\top + \sigma_B^2$. In practice, the mean of the vectors of covariates for the small area is itself estimated, and so it represents another element of uncertainty in estimating $\bar{y}_j$.

We consider first the estimation of the population mean for a small area not represented in the national survey. We assume first that the set of covariates is given; (model) selection of the covariates is discussed in Section 8.7.4.

The estimation of population means and regression parameters using data from surveys with stratified clustered sampling design was described in Chapter 7. In the next section, we describe an alternative method for estimation of regression parameters. Its principal advantage is that for complex regression models it is much simpler than the model-based method. We describe an algorithm for fitting the regression model in (8.5), assuming equal weights, and then adapt the algorithm for fitting these models for sampling weights.

8.4   Fitting two-level regression

Assuming equal sampling weights, the log-likelihood for the model in (8.5) is

$$l = -\frac{1}{2}\left\{ n\log(2\pi) + \sum_{j=1}^{m}\log\det(\mathbf{V}_j) + \sum_{j=1}^{m}\mathbf{e}_j^\top\mathbf{V}_j^{-1}\mathbf{e}_j\right\}, \tag{8.7}$$

where $n = n_1 + \ldots + n_m$ is the sample size, $\mathbf{e}_j = \mathbf{y}_j - \mathbf{X}_j\boldsymbol{\beta}$ is the vector of residuals for cluster j, and $\mathbf{V}_j$ is the variance matrix of the outcome vector $\mathbf{y}_j = \left(y_{1j}, \ldots, y_{n_j j}\right)^\top$. Outcomes within clusters are correlated, $\mathrm{cov}(y_{ij}, y_{i'j}) = \sigma_B^2$, and so

$$\mathbf{V}_j = \sigma_W^2\mathbf{I}_{n_j} + \sigma_B^2\mathbf{J}_{n_j};$$

$\mathbf{I}_n$ is the $n \times n$ identity matrix and $\mathbf{J}_n$ is the $n \times n$ matrix of ones. Note that $\mathbf{J}_n = \mathbf{1}_n\mathbf{1}_n^\top$, where $\mathbf{1}_n$ is the $n \times 1$ vector of ones.

Since some of the clusters may have large sample sizes n_j, it is useful to have analytic equations for the determinant and the inverse of $\mathbf{V}_j$, so that operations with large matrices are avoided in the evaluation of the log-likelihood in (8.7). The pattern of the matrices $\mathbf{V}_j$ is effectively exploited by the formulae

$$\begin{aligned}\mathbf{V}_j^{-1} &= \frac{1}{\sigma_W^2}\mathbf{I}_{n_j} - \frac{1}{\sigma_W^2}\frac{\sigma_B^2}{\sigma_W^2 + n_j\sigma_B^2}\mathbf{J}_{n_j}, \\[4pt] \det(\mathbf{V}_j) &= \sigma_W^{2(n_j-1)}(\sigma_W^2 + n_j\sigma_B^2).\end{aligned} \tag{8.8}$$

The inversion formula is proved by multiplication:

$$\left(\sigma_W^2\mathbf{I}_{n_j} + \sigma_B^2\mathbf{J}_{n_j}\right)\left(\frac{1}{\sigma_W^2}\mathbf{I}_{n_j} - \frac{1}{\sigma_W^2}\frac{\sigma_B^2}{\sigma_W^2 + n_j\sigma_B^2}\mathbf{J}_{n_j}\right) = \mathbf{I}_{n_j},$$

using the identity $\mathbf{J}_n^2 = n\mathbf{J}_n$. To prove the formula for the determinant, we find all the eigenvalues of $\mathbf{V}_j$. First, $\mathbf{V}_j\mathbf{1}_{n_j} = (\sigma_W^2 + n_j\sigma_B^2)\mathbf{1}_{n_j}$, and so

$\sigma_W^2 + n_j \sigma_B^2$ is an eigenvalue of $\mathbf{V}_j$. Next, let $\mathbf{a}$ be a $n_j \times 1$ vector containing zeros except for one element each equal to 1 and -1. Since $\mathbf{V}_j \mathbf{a} = \sigma_{W,j}^2 \mathbf{a}$, any such vector $\mathbf{a}$ is an eigenvector of $\mathbf{V}_j$. There are $n-1$ linearly independent vectors $\mathbf{a}$, and so $\sigma_{W,j}^2$ is an $(n-1)$-multiple eigenvalue of $\mathbf{V}_j$. That implies the second identity in (8.8).

Equations for the Fisher scoring algorithm are derived by formal differentiation of the log-likelihood. In Section 5.8, we discussed maximization of a log-likelihood function similar to that in (8.7), in a slightly different context and using a different notation. For completeness, we give the equations for the first- and expected second-order partial derivatives of the log-likelihood l. As in Section 5.8, it is advantageous to estimate the variance ratio $\tau = \sigma_B^2/\sigma_W^2$ instead of the variance σ_B^2, because the subject-level variance σ_W^2 can be separated out of the log-likelihood:

$$l = -\frac{1}{2}\left\{ n\log(2\pi\sigma_W^2) + \sum_{j=1}^{m}\log\det(\mathbf{W}_j) + \frac{1}{\sigma_W^2}\sum_{j=1}^{m}\mathbf{e}_j^\top \mathbf{W}_j^{-1}\mathbf{e}_j \right\},$$

where $\mathbf{W}_j = \sigma_W^{-2}\mathbf{V}_j = \mathbf{I}_{n_j} + \tau\mathbf{J}_{n_j}$, as a function of the variance ratio τ, does not depend on σ_W^2. When all the other parameters are known, the score function for σ_W^2,

$$\frac{\partial l}{\partial \sigma_W^2} = -\frac{1}{2\sigma_W^4}\left(n\sigma_W^2 - \sum_{j=1}^{m}\mathbf{e}_j^\top \mathbf{W}_j^{-1}\mathbf{e}_j \right),$$

has the unique root

$$\hat{\sigma}_W^2 = \frac{1}{n}\sum_{j=1}^{m}\mathbf{e}_j^\top \mathbf{W}_j^{-1}\mathbf{e}_j. \tag{8.9}$$

For the other parameters, we have

$$\frac{\partial l}{\partial \beta} = \frac{1}{\sigma_W^2}\sum_{j=1}^{m}\mathbf{X}_j^\top \mathbf{W}_j^{-1}\mathbf{e}_j,$$

$$\frac{\partial l}{\partial \tau} = -\frac{1}{2}\sum_{j=1}^{m}\mathbf{1}_{n_j}^\top \mathbf{W}_j^{-1}\mathbf{1}_{n_j} + \frac{1}{2\sigma_W^2}\sum_{j=1}^{m}\left(\mathbf{e}_j^\top \mathbf{W}_j^{-1}\mathbf{1}_{n_j} \right)^2 \tag{8.10}$$

and

$$-\frac{\partial^2 l}{\partial \beta \partial \beta^\top} = \frac{1}{\sigma_W^2}\sum_{j=1}^{m}\mathbf{X}_j^\top \mathbf{W}_j^{-1}\mathbf{X}_j,$$

$$\frac{\partial^2 l}{\partial \beta \partial \tau} = \mathbf{0}_p,$$

$$-\mathbf{E}\left(\frac{\partial^2 l}{\partial \tau^2} \right) = \frac{1}{2}\sum_{j=1}^{m}\left(\mathbf{1}_{n_j}^\top \mathbf{W}_j^{-1}\mathbf{1}_{n_j} \right)^2. \tag{8.11}$$

The Fisher scoring algorithm starts with the ordinary least squares (OLS) fit $\hat{\boldsymbol{\beta}}_0 = (\mathbf{X}^\top \mathbf{X})^{-1} \mathbf{X}^\top \mathbf{y}$ and a guess for $\hat{\tau}$, say, $\hat{\tau}_0 = 0.1$. At each iteration, the current estimate of $\boldsymbol{\beta}$ is the generalized least squares (GLS) solution

$$\hat{\boldsymbol{\beta}}_{new} = \left(\sum_{j=1}^{m} \mathbf{X}_j^\top \hat{\mathbf{W}}_j^{-1} \mathbf{X}_j \right)^{-1} \sum_{j=1}^{m} \mathbf{X}_j^\top \hat{\mathbf{W}}_j^{-1} \mathbf{y}_j \, ,$$

where $\hat{\mathbf{W}}_j$ is the scaled variance matrix $\mathbf{W}_j$ evaluated at the current value of $\hat{\tau}$. The estimate of the subject-level variance σ_W^2 is

$$\hat{\sigma}_{W,new}^2 = \frac{1}{n} \sum_{j=1}^{m} \mathbf{e}_j^\top \hat{\mathbf{W}}_j^{-1} \mathbf{e}_j \, .$$

The estimate of the variance ratio τ is updated as

$$\hat{\tau}_{new} = \hat{\tau}_{old} - \left\{ \mathbf{E} \left(\frac{\partial^2 l}{\partial \tau^2} \right) \right\}^{-1} \frac{\partial l}{\partial \tau} \, ,$$

with the partial derivatives evaluated at $\tau = \hat{\tau}_{old}$. The convergence criteria discussed in Sections 5.4 and 5.8.1 (change of the log-likelihood and the norm of the correction vector) are also applicable for this algorithm.

The quadratic forms in $\mathbf{W}_j^{-1}$ are evaluated using the inversion formula in (8.8). For arbitrary $n_j \times 1$ vectors $\mathbf{a}_1$ and $\mathbf{a}_2$,

$$\mathbf{a}_1^\top \mathbf{W}_j^{-1} \mathbf{a}_2 = \mathbf{a}_1^\top \mathbf{a}_2 - \frac{\tau}{1 + n_j \tau} \mathbf{a}_1^\top \mathbf{1}_{n_j} \, \mathbf{a}_2^\top \mathbf{1}_{n_j} \, , \qquad (8.12)$$

and so the inverse matrices $\mathbf{W}_j^{-1}$ need not be formed. For $\mathbf{a}_2 = \mathbf{1}_{n_j}$, further simplification takes place:

$$\mathbf{a}_1^\top \mathbf{W}_j^{-1} \mathbf{1}_{n_j} = \frac{\mathbf{a}_1^\top \mathbf{1}_{n_j}}{1 + n_j \tau} \, . \qquad (8.13)$$

The Fisher scoring algorithm involves computing the log-likelihood in (8.7), the estimate of the within-cluster variance σ_W^2, (8.9), the first-order partial derivatives in (8.10), and the information about $\boldsymbol{\beta}$ and τ, (8.11). These quantities depend on the data $(\mathbf{X}, \mathbf{y})$ only through the totals of cross-products $(\mathbf{X}, \mathbf{y})^\top (\mathbf{X}, \mathbf{y})$ and the within-cluster totals $(\mathbf{X}_j, \mathbf{y})^\top \mathbf{1}_{n_j}$. It is practical to compute these summaries at the beginning of the algorithm and store them throughout. Then the original data do not have to be accessed throughout the iterations.

8.4.1   Restricted maximum likelihood

An important criticism of the maximum likelihood estimator is that the estimator of the variance is not affected by the uncertainty about $\boldsymbol{\beta}$. This is easiest to demonstrate on the ordinary regression. Suppose $\tau = 0$; then the maximum likelihood estimator of β coincides with the OLS estimator $\hat{\beta} = (\mathbf{X}^\top\mathbf{X})^{-1}\mathbf{X}^\top\mathbf{y}$, and the maximum likelihood estimate of the residual variance is $\hat{\sigma}_W^2 = \mathbf{e}^\top\mathbf{e}/n$. If the regression parameters β were known, $\hat{\sigma}_W^2$ would be unbiased. When β is estimated, the bias of $\hat{\sigma}_W^2$ is corrected by replacing the denominator n with $n - p$. This is commonly referred to as taking account of the p degrees of freedom due to the estimated regression parameters.

When β is unknown, the estimator of σ_W^2 is based on a linear transformation of the outcomes $\mathbf{y}$ that does not depend on β. One such transformation is $\mathbf{Py} = \mathbf{X}\left(\mathbf{X}^\top\mathbf{X}\right)^{-1}\mathbf{X}^\top\mathbf{y}$; then

$$\hat{\sigma}_W^2 = \frac{1}{n}\mathbf{y}^\top(\mathbf{I}_n - \mathbf{P})\mathbf{y}.$$

The matrix $\mathbf{P}$ is known as the projection operator. It 'projects' the outcomes $\mathbf{y}$ to the fitted values: $\mathbf{Py} = \mathbf{X}\hat{\beta}$. The matrices $\mathbf{P}$ and $\mathbf{I}_n - \mathbf{P}$ are idempotent; that is, $\mathbf{P}^2 = \mathbf{P}$ and $(\mathbf{I}_n - \mathbf{P})^2 = \mathbf{I}_n - \mathbf{P}$. The rank of $\mathbf{P}$ is p. In fact, it can be shown that $\mathbf{P}$ has eigenvalues 0, with multiplicity $n - p$, and 1, with multiplicity p. For further background on the projection operators, see Seber (1977) or Searle (1987).

A linear combination of the outcomes, $\mathbf{c}^\top\mathbf{y}$, is called an error contrast if $\mathbf{E}(\mathbf{c}^\top\mathbf{y}) = 0$. The error contrasts form a $(n - p)$-dimensional linear space. Since $\mathbf{E}(\mathbf{y} - \mathbf{Py}) = \mathbf{0}_n$, the columns of the matrix $\mathbf{I}_n - \mathbf{P}$ form error contrasts, and since the rank of $\mathbf{I}_n - \mathbf{P}$ is $n - p$, a linear basis for the space of error contrasts can be selected from these columns.

The fact that the estimator of σ_W^2 depends on y only through $(\mathbf{I}_n - \mathbf{P})\mathbf{y}$ implies that all the information about σ_W^2 is contained in a set of $n - p$ linearly independent error contrasts. It can be shown that the actual choice of the error contrasts is unimportant.

The deficiency of the maximum likelihood estimator of the residual variance carries over to the variances in random coefficient models. Maximizing the likelihood for a set of $n-p$ linearly independent error contrasts appears to be a rather cumbersome task because the error contrasts do not have the same patterned correlation structure as the original outcomes $\mathbf{y}$. It turns out that the log-likelihood for $(\mathbf{I}_n - \mathbf{P})\mathbf{y}$ is equal to

$$l_R = l + C - \frac{1}{2}\log\left\{\det\left(\sum_{j=1}^m \mathbf{X}_j^\top\mathbf{V}_j^{-1}\mathbf{X}_j\right)\right\}, \tag{8.14}$$

where l is the log-likelihood given by (8.7) and C is a constant. This result is due to Harville (1974). See Patterson and Thompson (1971) and Harville (1977) for further background on the estimation of variance components using error contrasts. Note that different regression designs $\mathbf{X}$ imply essentially different sets of error contrasts, and so the values of the 'restricted' log-likelihood given by (8.14) cannot be used for comparing two models with different regression designs. For a comparison of two models with the same regression design, the value of C is immaterial because it cancels out in the likelihood ratio test statistic.

The Fisher scoring algorithm described above can be adapted for maximization of the log-likelihood in (8.14). The generalized least squares (GLS) equation for estimating $\boldsymbol{\beta}$ is applicable because $l - l_R$ does not involve $\boldsymbol{\beta}$. However, different estimates of the variances, and therefore different values of $\hat{\mathbf{W}}_j$, imply a different estimator $\hat{\boldsymbol{\beta}}$.

Using the variance ratio τ, the variance σ_W^2 can be extracted from the determinant in (8.14):

$$
\det\left(\sum_{j=1}^{m} \mathbf{X}_j^\top \mathbf{V}_j^{-1} \mathbf{X}_j\right) = (\sigma_W^2)^p \det\left(\sum_{j=1}^{m} \mathbf{X}_j^\top \mathbf{W}_j^{-1} \mathbf{X}_j\right).
$$

By setting the partial derivative of l_R to zero, we obtain the restricted maximum likelihood (REML) estimator of σ_W^2:

$$
\hat{\sigma}_W^2 = \frac{1}{n-p} \sum_j \mathbf{e}_j^\top \hat{\mathbf{W}}_j^{-1} \mathbf{e}_j,
$$

which has the appropriate denominator $n - p$. To estimate the variance ratio τ, the score function in (8.10) has to be adjusted:

$$
\frac{\partial l_R}{\partial \tau} = \frac{\partial l}{\partial \tau} + \frac{1}{2} \sum_{j=1}^{m} \mathbf{1}_{n_j}^\top \mathbf{W}_j^{-1} \mathbf{X}_j \mathbf{X}_j^\top \mathbf{W}_j^{-1} \mathbf{1}_{n_j}.
$$

The adjustment of the second-order partial derivative is usually negligible and can be omitted.

The random terms δ_j characterize the differences among the clusters. Their realizations can be estimated using their conditional expectations given the outcomes $\mathbf{y}_j$,

$$
\mathbf{E}\left(\delta_j \mid \mathbf{y}_j; \boldsymbol{\beta}, \sigma_W^2, \tau\right) = \tau \mathbf{1}_{n_j}^\top \mathbf{W}_j^{-1} \mathbf{e}_j = \frac{\tau}{1 + n_j \tau} \mathbf{1}_{n_j}^\top \mathbf{e}_j. \tag{8.15}
$$

The first identity follows from the property of the normal distribution; the second is obtained by substituting (8.13). Similarly, the conditional variance of δ_j is

$$
\mathrm{var}\left(\delta_j \mid \mathbf{y}_j; \boldsymbol{\beta}, \sigma_W^2, \tau\right) = \sigma_B^2 - \sigma_W^2 \tau^2 \mathbf{1}_{n_j}^\top \mathbf{W}_j^{-1} \mathbf{1}_{n_j} = \frac{\sigma_B^2}{1 + n_j \tau}. \tag{8.16}
$$

Since the conditional distribution of δ_j given $\mathbf{y}_j$ is normal, it is completely determined by its mean and variance. An estimator of δ_j is obtained by substituting (restricted) maximum likelihood estimates for the parameters in the equation for $\mathbf{E}(\delta_j \mid \mathbf{y}_j)$. The estimated conditional variance is a measure of uncertainty about δ_j.

8.4.2 Sampling weights

Sampling weights are an important feature of the sampling design in most surveys. Ignoring the sampling weights is likely to lead to substantial biases in the estimation of population and small-area quantities because it renders the realized sample unrepresentative of the sampled (target) population. For a profound discussion, see Pfefferman (1993).

For illustration, the commonly used estimator of the mean of a random sample (equal weights) is the arithmetic mean $\bar{y} = (y_1 + \ldots + y_n)/n$. For independent data (no clustering), with sampling weights w_i, $i = 1, \ldots, n$, the 'weighted' mean, or the ratio estimator,

$$\bar{y} = \frac{\sum_i w_i y_i}{\sum_i w_i}, \tag{8.17}$$

is unbiased. Similarly, the regression parameter vector $\boldsymbol{\beta}$, estimated for independent observations with equal weights as

$$\hat{\boldsymbol{\beta}} = \left(\sum_{i=1}^n \mathbf{x}_i \mathbf{x}_i^\top\right)^{-1} \sum_{i=1}^n y_i \mathbf{x}_i,$$

has the 'weighted' version

$$\hat{\boldsymbol{\beta}}_w = \left(\sum_{i=1}^n w_i \mathbf{x}_i \mathbf{x}_i^\top\right)^{-1} \sum_{i=1}^n w_i y_i \mathbf{x}_i. \tag{8.18}$$

In Chapter 7, we discussed an alternative estimator of the regression parameters. The estimator given by (8.18) is much more simplistic and less principalled because it is derived purely by an analogy, and it does not distinguish between imperfect estimation owing to the incomplete nature of the data (vis-à-vis a census) and the imperfect fit of the regression model for the entire population had a census been conducted. Nevertheless, in many contexts, the estimator in (8.18), and, more generally, the analogy implied, is satisfactory.

The estimators in (8.17) and (8.18) do not depend on how the weights are normalized. However, the weighted versions of the information matrix, $\sum_i w_i \mathbf{x}_i \mathbf{x}_i^\top$, do require an appropriate normalization. We will use the normalization of Potthoff et al. (1992) introduced in Section 7.5. Recall that in this normalization the total of the weights is equal to the total of the squared weights. We will assume that the weights, denoted by w_{ijk}, have already been subjected to such a normalization.

We are interested in fitting the variance component model in (8.5) for a clustered sample with sampling weights. For that, we adapt the Fisher scoring algorithm by replacing all the cross-products by their weighted versions. Thus, for a pair of variables $x^{(1)}$ and $x^{(2)}$, we use the weighted total $\sum_j \sum_i w_i x_{ij}^{(1)} x_{ij}^{(2)}$ instead of the sample total of cross-products $\left(\mathbf{x}^{(1)}\right)^\top \mathbf{x}^{(2)}$, and the within-cluster totals $\left(\mathbf{x}_j^{(1)}\right)^\top \mathbf{1}_{n_j}$ are replaced by $\left(\mathbf{x}_j^{(1)}\right)^\top \mathbf{w}_j$, where $\mathbf{w}_j = (w_{1j}, \ldots, w_{n_jj})^\top$ is the vector of weights for cluster j. Note that, in particular, the sample sizes n_j and $\sum_j n_j$ are replaced by the respective *effective* sample sizes $\sum_i w_{ij} = \mathbf{w}_j^\top \mathbf{1}_{n_j}$ and $\sum_j \sum_i w_{ij} = \mathbf{w}^\top \mathbf{1}_n$.

The restricted maximum likelihood can be adapted for sampling weights similarly.

8.5   Small-area mean prediction

In Section 8.2, we discussed how two estimates of the small-area mean can be combined. In this section, we develop estimators based exclusively on the large-scale survey, assuming that both $\bar{\mathbf{x}}_j$ and $\boldsymbol{\beta}$ are estimated. Such an estimator can be a component of the shrinkage estimator derived in Section 8.2.

First we consider the estimator $\hat{y}_j = \hat{\bar{\mathbf{x}}}_j \hat{\boldsymbol{\beta}}$, which is appropriate for clusters j that are not represented in the large-scale survey (our best guess being $\delta_j = 0$). In such a case, information about the covariates has to be obtained from a different source. When an estimator of the mean $\hat{\bar{\mathbf{x}}}_j$ is based on data not used for estimating $\boldsymbol{\beta}$, $\hat{\bar{\mathbf{x}}}_j$ and $\hat{\boldsymbol{\beta}}$ are independent. Then

$$\mathbf{E}(\hat{y}_j) = \mathbf{E}(\hat{\bar{\mathbf{x}}}_j)\mathbf{E}(\hat{\boldsymbol{\beta}}),$$

and so unbiasedness of $\hat{\bar{\mathbf{x}}}_j$ and $\hat{\boldsymbol{\beta}}$ implies unbiasedness of $\hat{y}_j$ as an estimator of the small-area population mean $\bar{y}_j$. Let $\boldsymbol{\Sigma}^{(j)}$ be the sampling variance matrix of $\hat{\bar{\mathbf{x}}}_j$. The sampling variance of $\hat{y}_j$ is derived by conditioning on $\hat{\boldsymbol{\beta}}$ (conditioning on $\hat{\bar{\mathbf{x}}}_j$ would achieve the same goal):

$$\begin{aligned} \mathrm{var}(\hat{y}_j) &= \mathbf{E}\left\{ \mathrm{var}(\hat{\bar{\mathbf{x}}}_j\hat{\boldsymbol{\beta}} \mid \hat{\boldsymbol{\beta}}) \right\} + \mathrm{var}\left\{ \mathbf{E}(\hat{\bar{\mathbf{x}}}_j\hat{\boldsymbol{\beta}} \mid \hat{\boldsymbol{\beta}}) \right\} \\ &= \mathbf{E}\left(\hat{\boldsymbol{\beta}}^\top \boldsymbol{\Sigma}^{(j)}\hat{\boldsymbol{\beta}} \right) + \mathrm{var}\left(\bar{\mathbf{x}}_j\hat{\boldsymbol{\beta}} \right) \\ &= \mathrm{tr}(\boldsymbol{\Sigma}_b\boldsymbol{\Sigma}^{(j)}) + \boldsymbol{\beta}^\top\boldsymbol{\Sigma}^{(j)}\boldsymbol{\beta} + \bar{\mathbf{x}}_j\boldsymbol{\Sigma}_b\bar{\mathbf{x}}_j^\top . \end{aligned} \tag{8.19}$$

Each term in (8.19) is non-negative and equal to zero only in a degenerate case. When $\bar{\mathbf{x}}_j$ is known, $\boldsymbol{\Sigma}^{(j)} = \mathbf{0}$ and $\mathrm{var}(\hat{y}_j) = \mathbf{x}_j\boldsymbol{\Sigma}_b\mathbf{x}_j^\top$; uncertainty about $\bar{\mathbf{x}}$ inflates the sampling variance of the predictor $\hat{y}_j$. Some inflation takes place even when $\boldsymbol{\beta} = \mathbf{0}$.

Next, suppose $\hat{\boldsymbol{\beta}}$ and $\hat{\bar{\mathbf{x}}}_j$ are correlated, and let $\boldsymbol{\Sigma}_{b,j}$ be their covariance matrix. The predictor $\hat{y}_j$ is no longer unbiased because

$$\mathbf{E}(\hat{y}_j) = \boldsymbol{\beta}\bar{x}_j + \mathrm{tr}\left(\boldsymbol{\Sigma}_{b,j} \right) . \tag{8.20}$$

When the estimators $\hat{\boldsymbol{\beta}}$ and $\hat{\bar{x}}_j$ are based on a common dataset and the cluster is a dominant part of the dataset, the correlations in $\boldsymbol{\Sigma}_{b,j}$ may be substantial. In addition, if there is a lot of uncertainty about β, $\bar{x}_j$, or both, the predictor $\hat{y}_j$ is seriously biased.

To derive the sampling variance of $\hat{y}_j$, we will use the following identities:

$$\mathbf{E}\left(\hat{\beta}\mid \hat{\bar{x}}_j\right) = \beta + \Sigma_{b,j}\left(\Sigma^{(j)}\right)^{-1}(\hat{\bar{x}}_j - \bar{x}_j)^\top,$$

$$\operatorname{var}\left(\hat{\beta}\mid \hat{\bar{x}}_j\right) = \Sigma_b - \Sigma_{b,j}\left(\Sigma^{(j)}\right)^{-1}\Sigma_{b,j}^\top.$$

By conditioning on $\hat{\bar{x}}_j$, the sampling variance of $\hat{y}_j$ is expressed as

$$\operatorname{var}(\hat{y}_j) = \mathbf{E}\left[\hat{\bar{x}}_j\left\{\Sigma_b - \Sigma_{b,j}\left(\Sigma^{(j)}\right)^{-1}\Sigma_{b,j}^\top\right\}\hat{\bar{x}}_j^\top\right]$$

$$+ \operatorname{var}\left[\hat{\bar{x}}_j\left\{\beta + \Sigma_{b,j}\left(\Sigma^{(j)}\right)^{-1}(\hat{\bar{x}}_j - \bar{x}_j)^\top\right\}\right].$$

To evaluate the expectations and (co-)variances involving quadratic forms, we need the following identities:

$$\mathbf{E}\left(\hat{\bar{x}}_j\Sigma\hat{\bar{x}}_j^\top\right) = \operatorname{tr}\left(\Sigma\Sigma^{(j)}\right) + \bar{x}_j\Sigma\bar{x}_j^\top,$$

$$\operatorname{cov}\left(\hat{\bar{x}}_j, \hat{\bar{x}}_j\Sigma\hat{\bar{x}}_j^\top\right) = \Sigma^{(j)}\left(\Sigma + \Sigma^\top\right)\bar{x}_j^\top,$$

$$\operatorname{var}\left(\hat{\bar{x}}_j\Sigma\hat{\bar{x}}_j^\top\right) = \operatorname{tr}\left(\Sigma\Sigma^{(j)}\Sigma\Sigma^{(j)}\right) + \operatorname{tr}\left(\Sigma\Sigma^{(j)}\Sigma^\top\Sigma^{(j)}\right)$$

$$+ 2\bar{x}_j\Sigma\Sigma^{(j)}\Sigma\bar{x}_j^\top + 2\bar{x}_j\Sigma\Sigma^{(j)}\Sigma^\top\bar{x}_j^\top.$$

These identities are well known for symmetric matrices Σ; see, for instance, Seber (1977, Ch. 2). Their general versions given above are derived by application of the symmetric versions to $\Sigma + \Sigma^\top$, noting that the quadratic form $q(\mathbf{x}, \Sigma) = \mathbf{x}\Sigma\mathbf{x}^\top$ is invariant with respect to transposition; $q(\mathbf{x}, \Sigma) = q(\mathbf{x}, \Sigma^\top)$. Application of these identities yields

$$\operatorname{var}\left(\hat{y}_j\right) = \bar{x}_j\Sigma_b\bar{x}_j^\top + \operatorname{tr}\left(\Sigma_b\Sigma^{(j)}\right) - \bar{x}_j\Sigma_{b,j}\left(\Sigma^{(j)}\right)^{-1}\Sigma_{b,j}^\top\bar{x}_j^\top$$

$$- \operatorname{tr}\left\{\Sigma_{b,j}\left(\Sigma^{(j)}\right)^{-1}\Sigma_{b,j}^\top\Sigma^{(j)}\right\}$$

$$+ \left\{\beta - \Sigma_{b,j}\left(\Sigma^{(j)}\right)^{-1}\bar{x}_j^\top\right\}^\top\Sigma^{(j)}\left\{\beta - \Sigma_{b,j}\left(\Sigma^{(j)}\right)^{-1}\bar{x}_j^\top\right\}$$

$$+ 2\bar{x}_j\left\{\Sigma_{b,j} + \left(\Sigma^{(j)}\right)^{-1}\Sigma_{b,j}^\top\Sigma^{(j)}\right\}\left\{\beta - \Sigma_{b,j}\left(\Sigma^{(j)}\right)^{-1}\bar{x}_j^\top\right\}$$

$$+ \operatorname{tr}\left\{(\Sigma_{b,j})^2\right\} + \operatorname{tr}\left\{\left(\Sigma^{(j)}\right)^{-1}\Sigma_{b,j}^\top\Sigma^{(j)}\Sigma_{b,j}\right\}$$

$$+ 2\bar{\mathbf{x}}_j \left(\boldsymbol{\Sigma}^{(j)} \right)^{-1} (\boldsymbol{\Sigma}_{b,j})^2 \, \bar{\mathbf{x}}_j^{\top}$$

$$+ 2\bar{\mathbf{x}}_j \left(\boldsymbol{\Sigma}^{(j)} \right)^{-1} \boldsymbol{\Sigma}_{b,j} \boldsymbol{\Sigma}^{(j)} \boldsymbol{\Sigma}_{b,j}^{\top} \left(\boldsymbol{\Sigma}^{(j)} \right)^{-1} \bar{\mathbf{x}}_j^{\top} \, ,$$

which after elementary operations simplifies to

$$\text{var} \left(\hat{y}^{(j)} \right) = \text{tr} \left(\boldsymbol{\Sigma}_b \boldsymbol{\Sigma}^{(j)} \right) + \boldsymbol{\beta}^{\top} \boldsymbol{\Sigma}^{(j)} \boldsymbol{\beta} + \bar{\mathbf{x}}_j \boldsymbol{\Sigma}_b \bar{\mathbf{x}}_j^{\top}$$
$$+ \text{tr} \left\{ (\boldsymbol{\Sigma}_{b,j})^2 \right\} + 2\bar{\mathbf{x}}_j \boldsymbol{\Sigma}_{b,j} \boldsymbol{\beta} \, . \tag{8.21}$$

In a typical application, estimation of the covariance matrix $\boldsymbol{\Sigma}_{b,j}$ is problematic because the regression estimator $\hat{\boldsymbol{\beta}}$ is a complex function of the data. We can argue, though, that unless the cluster j forms a substantial fraction of the data in the large-scale survey, the covariances in $\boldsymbol{\Sigma}_{b,j}$ are very small. Otherwise, little efficiency is lost by discarding the data from outside cluster j. Of course, the intermediate case may arise when the cluster forms, say, about a quarter of the large-scale survey data. Various forms of sensitivity analysis can be carried out to assess the impact of the (unknown) correlation structure on the sampling variance of $\hat{y}_j$. For instance, the sampling variance in (8.21) may be evaluated for $\boldsymbol{\Sigma}_{b,j}$ corresponding to correlations equal to 0.25. The sampling variance is likely to be unduly affected by the covariance matrix $\boldsymbol{\Sigma}_{b,j}$ only when there is substantial uncertainty about both $\boldsymbol{\Sigma}_b$ and $\boldsymbol{\Sigma}^{(j)}$. Note that the bias of $\hat{y}_j$ depends on $\boldsymbol{\Sigma}_{b,j}$, (8.20). Correction of the bias is fraught with the danger of inflating the sampling variance of the resulting (approximately unbiased) estimator because the correction may have a large sampling variance. Of course, when $\boldsymbol{\Sigma}_{b,j}$ vanishes, (8.21) collapses to (8.19).

When $\sigma_B^2 > 0$, the sampling variance in (8.21) has to be supplemented by the squared bias, or its estimate, to obtain the MSE of $\hat{y}^{(j)}$. The bias can be estimated as the weighted version of the conditional expectation in (8.15), with the parameters replaced by their estimates:

$$\hat{\delta}_j = \frac{\hat{\tau}}{1 + \hat{\tau} w_{+j}} \sum_{i=1}^{n_j} w_{ij} (y_{ij} - \mathbf{x}_{ij} \hat{\boldsymbol{\beta}}) \, ,$$

where $w_{+j} = w_{1j} + \ldots + w_{n_j j}$ is the total weight in cluster j. Instead of $\hat{\delta}^2$, the squared deviation δ_j^2 is more efficiently estimated as $\hat{\delta}_j^2 - \widehat{\text{var}}(\delta_j \mid \mathbf{y}_j)$, where the estimated conditional variance is obtained from (8.16);

$$\widehat{\text{var}}(\delta_j \mid \mathbf{y}_j) = \frac{\hat{\sigma}_B^2}{1 + \hat{\tau} w_{+j}} \, .$$

8.6   Selection of covariates

Ideally, the covariates in $\mathbf{x}$ would be selected so that the outcomes y are closely fit by a linear regression, that is, both variances σ_W^2 and σ_B^2 are small. In most contexts, this is an unrealistic proposition because of the limited understanding of the processes that influence the outcome y and because of the imperfect survey instruments used to elicit the values of y and $\mathbf{x}$.

Human subjects are notorious for imperfect cooperation in surveys, and missing information is pervasive throughout data from sample surveys. In our approach, we require complete records from each subject. Listwise deletion, that is, deletion of every surveyed subject with an incomplete record, is a simple way to bypass the problem of incomplete data. If a large proportion of the subjects is thus excluded, a lot of information is lost and the advantage of a better fitting regression model may be more than negated by increased uncertainty about $\boldsymbol{\beta}$. Fewer variables are associated with the loss of fewer subjects due to listwise deletion, and so a careful balance has to be struck between model adequacy (appropriate covariates) and effective sample size.

Apart from the loss of information, exclusion of subjects is problematic because the remaining sample may be a poorer representation of the sampled population. Non-response in a survey may be more prevalent in one subpopulation than in another and patterns (frequencies) of non-response may be different and differently interrelated in the various subpopulations. Poststratification (adjustment of the sampling weights) is a potential remedy for this problem, although it is associated with additional uncertainty.

Schemes that impute values in place of missing data can be successful only if they are modelled on the processes that give rise to non-response. Models for non-response usually involve considerable uncertainty, which is difficult to reflect in the imputed data. (An imputed value contains less information than a value obtained directly from the subject.) In practice, the most effective resolution of this problem is to ensure that as few subjects as possible are discarded. Chapter 10 describes a method for analysis of incomplete data based on the EM algorithm. Its application in the present context (clustered observations and sampling weights) is not straightforward, though.

An important constraint is that an estimate of the mean of the covariates has to be available for the small area ($\hat{\bar{\mathbf{x}}}_j$). Again, a delicate balance has to be struck between the need for covariates as good predictors and covariates with known or well-estimated small-area means. The improvement in the regression fit due to a covariate may be offset by a large sampling variance of the estimator of the small-area mean of the covariate.

This concern is related to the utility of reducing the between-cluster variance σ_B^2. Covariates defined for clusters, or covariates that have small within-cluster variance, are likely to reduce the between-cluster variance, whereas covariates with substantial within-cluster variance may not. Cluster-level variables are easier to handle because they are defined for clusters, and their small-area mean is defined with certainty from a single observation on the cluster. On the other hand, σ_W^2 is usually much greater than σ_B^2, and so elementary-level covariates have greater potential to improve prediction for small areas.

Of course, the selection of a suitable regression model for small-area estimation has to be complemented by a host of practical considerations about the survey data. We illustrate some of these in the next section.

8.7   Application

We analyse data from two national and two statewide surveys of adult literacy. The main purpose of the surveys was to assess the nature and extent of literacy skills in the adult population (aged 16 and over) in the United States. The national surveys were conducted on behalf of the U.S. Department of Labor in 1991, and the statewide surveys, carried out in Mississippi and Oregon, used a subset of the background questionnaire items. The data were kindly provided by Peter Pashley of ETS.

Estimation of each subject's proficiency score is based on a 45-minute set of exercises. Methods for estimating the underlying proficiency scores and for taking account of the uncertainty in their estimation were described in Section 7.3. As in Chapter 7, we assume that a set of five imputed values is given for each subject. In particular, we ignore the issue of missing responses to the items in the exercises. The additional uncertainty about the proficiency of a subject who did not respond to several items is reflected in the more dispersed posterior distribution of proficiency. This distribution is represented in the data by a set of five imputed values.

The national surveys were conducted as part of the U.S. Employment Service/Unemployment Insurance (ES/UI) and Job Training Partnership Act (JTPA) programmes. The target populations for the surveys were the subjects benefiting from the respective programmes. They were mostly unemployed, and the target populations had substantial overlap. The target populations in the statewide surveys were all the residents drawing unemployment benefit.

The national surveys used (regionally) stratified clustered designs with states as clusters. In fact, an unemployment benefit centre was selected from each state included in the survey, and a weighted random sample of beneficiaries attending the centre was drawn. There are some minor differences between the two surveys which are of no significance for our illustration. For details, see Kirsch and Jungeblut (1992).

The sampling weights were derived by adjusting the design weights due to poststratification. We treat the poststratified weights as if they were

TABLE 8.1. Raw and effective sample sizes in the adult literacy surveys.

	Survey			
	ES/UI	JTPA	Mississippi	Oregon
Sample size	3277	2501	1804	1993
Effective sample size	1403	1046	1629	1854
Coefficient of variation	1.34	1.39	0.11	0.08

the design weights and assume that the between-stratum differences are fully accounted for in the regression models used. Throughout, we will use the normalized weights. The sample sizes (numbers of subjects) and the effective sample sizes (the totals of the normalized weights) for the four surveys are given in Table 8.1. The third row of the table gives the coefficient of variation of the weights, defined as the ratio of the sample variance and the square of the sample mean of the weights:

$$\rho = \frac{\text{var}(w_\cdot)}{\bar{w}^2}.$$

It is a simple and useful indicator of how much smaller the effective sample size is compared to the raw sample size. In the national surveys, the weights vary considerably; for instance, the ratio of the largest and smallest weights is 86.5 in ES/UI and 53.5 in JTPA. These ratios are much smaller in the statewide surveys: 10.6 in Mississippi and 3.9 in Oregon. The four panels in Figure 8.1 display the histograms of the sampling weights. To enable easy comparisons, each histogram has the same scale for the horizontal axis. To maintain good resolution of the diagram, 24 observations in the JTPA survey with normalized weights in the range 3.25–3.28 and 4 observations in the Mississippi survey with normalized weights equal to 5.46 are omitted from the histograms.

The within-state homogeneity relative to U.S.-wide variation in the background variables is only a minor contributor to the smaller variation in the weights; rather, the national surveys focussed much more on certain rare combinations of background variables. As a consequence, some subjects were assigned extremely large sampling weights. Although the raw sample sizes for the national surveys are greater than the raw sample sizes in the statewide surveys, the inequality is reversed for the effective sample sizes.

Table 8.2 gives the raw and effective sample sizes for each state in the ES/UI survey. To emphasize the nature of variation of the sampling weights, we give the mean weights within states. They vary from 0.125 to 2.00. The identification of the states is not important, and so it is omitted. A similar pattern can be observed in the corresponding summaries for the JTPA survey; we omit the details to conserve space and avoid repetitiveness.

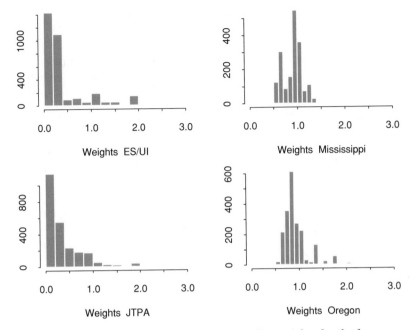

FIGURE 8.1. Histograms of the normalized sampling weights for the four surveys. The same scale for the horizontal axis is used in all four histograms.

Figure 8.2 displays the histograms of the first imputed values for the subjects in the four surveys. It may be inappropriate to read too much into the observed differences in the distributions for the two national and the two statewide surveys because the surveys involve different distributions of weights.

There is no strong association of the proficiency scores and the sampling weights. Figure 8.3 presents the scatterplot of the sampling weights and the estimated proficiency scores (averages of the sets of five imputed values) in the left-hand panel and the corresponding scatterplot for the within-state means in the right-hand panel. Note that among the larger weights there are only a small number of distinct values. Clearly, the statewide means of proficiencies vary much less than the individual proficiencies.

We are concerned with validation of the small-area prediction procedure described above. For this purpose, we will use the national survey data to fit a regression model (to estimate β), estimate the population mean of the regressors in the states of Mississippi and Oregon ($\hat{\bar{\mathbf{x}}}_j$), and then assess the validity of the method by comparing the prediction based on these estimates ($\hat{y}_j = \hat{\bar{\mathbf{x}}}_j \hat{\beta}$) with the estimate of the state mean of the outcome based on the statewide survey, $\hat{\bar{y}}_j$:

TABLE 8.2. State-level sample sizes in ES/UI survey.

States	Sample size	Raw and effective sample sizes and their ratios							
	Raw	121	140	200	162	129	182	61	219
1– 8	Effective	68.13	25.67	27.87	49.03	107.47	32.62	49.13	71.12
	Ratio	0.56	0.18	0.14	0.30	0.83	0.18	0.81	0.32
	Raw	173	217	56	56	224	180	210	204
9–16	Effective	49.60	32.16	8.06	20.34	49.59	39.43	28.05	49.22
	Ratio	0.29	0.15	0.14	0.36	0.22	0.22	0.13	0.24
	Raw	56	56	31	57	57	39	56	57
17–24	Effective	85.81	61.11	11.68	8.32	20.17	23.61	10.68	7.14
	Ratio	1.53	1.09	0.38	0.15	0.35	0.61	0.19	0.13
	Raw	56	56	56	56	56	54		
25–30	Effective	111.71	77.26	54.73	104.21	56.66	61.97		
	Ratio	1.99	1.38	0.98	1.86	1.01	1.15		

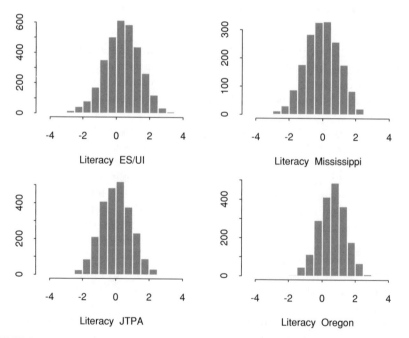

FIGURE 8.2. Histograms of the first sets of imputed values for the four surveys. The same scale for the horizontal axis is used in all four histograms.

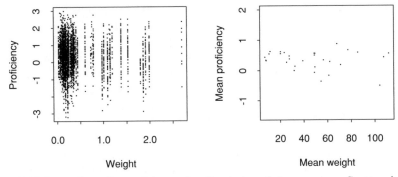

FIGURE 8.3. Sampling weights and estimated proficiency scores. Scatterplots of the individual values (left-hand panel) and of the statewide means (right-hand panel).

> How would we fare in estimating the state-level means of outcomes if the outcomes were not available for the subjects in the statewide surveys?

8.7.1   No adjustment

We consider first the estimation of the (national) population mean. For the two states, this corresponds to small-area estimation with an adjustment for no covariates; the estimator of the national mean is also an estimator of the state-level mean. To avoid duplication, we discuss only the analysis for the ES/UI data. Chapter 7 dealt with estimation of the population mean and its sampling variance. For illustration, we contrast it with estimation using random coefficient models.

Since the outcomes (proficiency scores) are represented by five imputed values, we analyse each set of imputed values separately and then summarize them to obtain estimates that refer to the proficiency scores. The ratio estimator of the population mean in the ES/UI survey has the following values for the sets of imputed values (standard errors are given in parentheses):

$$\begin{array}{ccccc} 0.299 & 0.303 & 0.299 & 0.310 & 0.322 \text{ ,} \\ (0.088) & (0.086) & (0.081) & (0.075) & (0.074) \end{array}$$

and so the estimate of the population mean proficiency score is 0.307, with the standard error 0.081.

We fit the 'empty' two-level model

$$y_{ij} = \mu + \delta_j + \varepsilon_{ij} .$$

Six iterations of the Fisher scoring algorithm were carried out for each set of imputed values. The log-likelihood changed by less than 10^{-3} after the fifth iteration for each analysis. In fact, three iterations are adequate for the precision to three significant digits required for reporting. The maximum likelihood estimate of the population mean proficiency is 0.327 (standard error 0.064). The estimates of the within- and between-cluster variances are 1.192 and 0.089. The standard error of the latter is 0.031; there is considerable uncertainty about the between-cluster variance because the number of clusters is rather small.

The model-based estimate of the between-cluster variance is 0.105, much higher than the maximum likelihood estimate. The standard error of the population mean is 0.081, also higher than its ML counterpart. The discrepancy between the model-based and maximum likelihood methods has several potential explanations. First, in the model-based approach, we estimated cluster-specific variances, whereas in the maximum likelihood approach, a common within-cluster variance is estimated. Second, the maximum likelihood method ignores the degree of freedom due to estimation of the population mean. Note that, because of clustering, this is 1 out of the 30 degrees of freedom, and so it does make a non-trivial difference. Third, an explanation may be in the heuristic nature of the 'weighted' likelihood.

The degree of freedom due to estimation of the mean can be accounted for by maximizing the restricted log-likelihood. The resulting estimate of the between-cluster variance is only slightly higher, 0.090, and the standard error of the population mean, using this estimate of σ_B^2, is 0.086, nearly identical to its maximum likelihood counterpart.

In our experience, the discrepancy between the model-based and maximum likelihood estimates is much smaller when adjustment for covariates is applied. Model-based estimation is rather cumbersome when a large number of covariates is used, and so we will use only maximum likelihood estimation in the next section. Also, for model-based estimation, there are no formal (regression) model selection procedures.

8.7.2 Adjustment for covariates

In this section, we give details of regression fitting for the survey data. In the first round, we use the regressors listed in Table 8.3.

The variables *More English* and *More Maths* code the expressed perceptions of the subjects about the usefulness of additional training in English and Mathematics. The variables related to income and parents' education are regarded throughout as quantitative variables (otherwise too many parameters would have to be estimated). We selected these variables because they are common questionnaire items, involve little non-response, and they are likely to be associated with the outcome variable. We used listwise deletion of subjects. The sample size for the ES/UI data was reduced from 3277 to 3219, and the effective sample size from 1402.5 to 1378.4. Listwise deletion for the same covariates in the JTPA dataset resulted in reduction

TABLE 8.3. Regressor variables used for adjustment in small-area estimation.

Variable	Type	Details
Sex	Dichotomous	0 for men and 1 for women
Ethnicity	Nominal	Six categories
Age category	Ordinal	Five categories
More English	Dichotomous	2 – useful, 1 – not useful
More Maths	Dichotomous	2 – useful, 1 – not useful
Mother's education	Ordinal	Eleven categories, 1–11
Father's education	Ordinal	Eleven categories, 1–11
Personal income	Ordinal	Eleven categories 1–11
Household income	Ordinal	Eleven categories 1–11
C. age	Quantitative	Age in years
Q. age	Quantitative	Transformation $C. age^2/1000$

of the sample size from 2501 to 2455 and of the effective sample size from 1047.6 to 1023.9.

The means and proportions (as applicable) of the covariates for the four surveys are given in Table 8.4. The counts for the categories of the variables do not add up to the sample size because of non-response. The proportion of missing data does not exceed 2 percent for any variable in either survey, and the data are complete for several variables.

The regression model fit for the ES/UI survey using the first set of imputed values and the set of covariates listed in Table 8.3 is summarized in Table 8.5. For comparison, the weighted least squares fit (WLS) and the maximum likelihood fit (MLE) are given. We prefer to use the 'full' maximum likelihood over the restricted maximum likelihood (REML) because likelihood ratio testing for competing regression models is possible only with the former.

For categorical regressor variables, we use the parametrization in which the first category is assigned value zero, so that the estimates for the other categories are their contrasts with the first category. Each regression estimate is accompanied by its standard error. We see that there is little difference between the WLS and MLE results. This similarity can be attributed to the small (adjusted) between-cluster variance. By adjusting for the 23 regressor variables, the within-cluster variance is reduced from about 1.10 to 0.74, but the between-cluster variance is almost erased; it is reduced from 0.09 to less than 0.001 (0.074×0.010). The regression parameter estimates vary a great deal across the sets of imputed values because they are rather unstable, but there is a close agreement of WLS and MLE throughout. The estimates of the model variances are much more stable.

The estimates that refer to the proficiency scores are obtained by averaging over the analyses for the five sets of imputed values. Their utility is

TABLE 8.4. Weighted sample means and proportions of the covariates.

Variable		ES/UI Propt'n or mean	ES/UI Count	JTPA Propt'n or mean	JTPA Count	Mississippi Propt'n or mean	Mississippi Count	Oregon Propt'n or mean	Oregon Count
Sex	1	0.56	1756	0.41	1008	0.47	761	0.50	1064
	2	0.44	1515	0.58	1484	0.53	1043	0.50	929
Ethnicity	1	0.63	2394	0.69	1556	0.66	1300	0.92	1845
	2	0.12	375	0.21	663	0.32	473	0.01	16
	3	0.20	384	0.06	159	0.01	20	0.03	57
	4	0.02	40	0.00	17	0.00	2	0.02	28
	5	0.01	48	0.03	76	0.00	5	0.02	28
	6	0.02	36	0.01	30	0.00	4	0.01	19
Education	1	0.03	135	0.07	202	0.13	217	0.02	34
	2	0.18	619	0.33	871	0.19	349	0.15	282
	3	0.59	2006	0.55	1295	0.48	872	0.56	1104
	4	0.19	513	0.06	130	0.19	362	0.27	570
	5	0.00	4	0.00	3	0.00	1	0.00	1
Age categ.	1	0.10	314	0.17	489	0.09	140	0.09	138
	2	0.18	616	0.19	485	0.11	173	0.12	183
	3	0.22	727	0.21	505	0.13	238	0.17	301
	4	0.32	1059	0.31	733	0.27	477	0.35	778
	5	0.17	546	0.10	259	0.40	776	0.28	593
More Engl	1	0.57	1792	0.66	1717	0.52	889	0.39	745
	2	0.42	1461	0.33	762	0.47	901	0.61	1246
More Math	1	0.69	2231	0.79	2002	0.61	1054	0.52	1003
	2	0.30	1020	0.20	473	0.38	732	0.48	988
Mother ed.		3.77	3273	3.67	2494	4.38	1801	4.31	1993
Father ed.		4.37	3271	4.32	2497	5.07	1801	4.86	1992
Pers. income		3.29	3268	2.29	2489	3.99	1782	3.86	1992
Hous. income		5.04	3262	3.41	2468	4.95	1759	5.55	1984
Age (years)		33.84	3266	30.67	2492	42.64	1804	37.91	1993
Quadr. age		1.29	3266	1.06	2492	2.11	1804	1.61	1993

TABLE 8.5. Regression model fits for ES/UI survey data using WLS and MLE.

Parameter (contrast)		WLS		MLE	
		Estimate	Std. error	Estimate	Std. error
Intercept		−1.148	(0.470)	−1.171	(0.465)
Sex	2–1	−0.199	(0.050)	−0.204	(0.052)
Ethnicity	2–1	−0.648	(0.080)	−0.641	(0.064)
	3–1	−0.522	(0.067)	−0.449	(0.072)
	4–1	−0.702	(0.174)	−0.679	(0.173)
	5–1	−0.575	(0.212)	−0.592	(0.210)
	6–1	−0.124	(0.200)	−0.102	(0.199)
Education	2–1	0.806	(0.155)	0.813	(0.153)
	3–1	1.184	(0.148)	1.187	(0.147)
	4–1	1.685	(0.158)	1.686	(0.157)
	5–1	−0.111	(0.689)	−0.130	(0.681)
Age category	2–1	−0.287	(0.117)	−0.287	(0.116)
	3–1	−0.257	(0.172)	−0.271	(0.170)
	4–1	−0.373	(0.250)	−0.386	(0.247)
	5–1	−0.198	(0.322)	−0.021	(0.318)
More English		0.547	(0.063)	0.539	(0.063)
More Maths		−0.055	(0.067)	−0.053	(0.067)
Mother's educ.		0.0190	(0.0093)	0.0187	(0.0092)
Father's educ.		0.0037	(0.0078)	0.0043	(0.0077)
Personal income		0.031	(0.014)	0.030	(0.014)
Household income		0.033	(0.011)	0.034	(0.011)
Age (years)		0.02236	(0.02810)	0.02288	(0.02777)
Quadratic age		−0.00038	(0.00029)	−0.00038	(0.00029)
σ_1^2		0.7414		0.7404	
τ				0.0098	(0.0083)
Deviance		3380.50		3354.89	

limited because small-area estimation is based on the regressions for the imputed values. The five 'predictions' will be averaged at the end.

The likelihood ratio test statistic can be used to compare the WLS and MLE fits. Instead of the value of the log-likelihood, Table 8.5 gives its -2-multiple, called the *deviance*, so that the likelihood ratio is the difference of deviances for the maximum likelihood fits of a suitable pair of models. To test the hypothesis that the variance ratio $\tau = 0$ or, equivalently, that $\sigma_B^2 = 0$, we compare the models with $\tau = 0$ (fitted by WLS) and with τ estimated (MLE) using the same set of covariates. Thus, the value of the likelihood ratio statistics is $3380.50 - 3354.89 = 25.61$. The null-distribution of this statistic is χ_1^2, and so it is statistically significant at any reasonable level of significance (say, 1 percent). Note however, that the t-ratio statistic, $0.0098/0.0083 = 1.2$, is not significant.

Since the sole purpose of the regression analysis is to provide an improved prediction method for state-level means, we do not seek any interpretation for the estimated regression parameters. Note that, for instance, the estimates associated with the levels of Education are not in monotone order; in fact, they fail to align even after averaging over the five analyses.

Analysis of the JTPA survey data leads to similar observations and conclusions, and so we omit the details.

8.7.3   Prediction and cross-validation

We proceed to the estimation of the means of proficiency scores for the two states, using the national surveys (the fitted regressions) and the covariate information from the statewide surveys. The within-state means $\bar{\mathbf{x}}_j$ are estimated using the (multivariate) ratio estimator with the poststratified weights, and the sampling variance matrices are obtained under the assumption of weighted random sampling in each state.

The input to the analysis that yields the small-area estimate of the state-level mean proficiency score comprises the five sets of regression parameter estimates ($\hat{\boldsymbol{\beta}}$) and their estimated sampling variance matrices ($\hat{\boldsymbol{\Sigma}}_b$), based on the national survey data, and the vector of estimated means of the covariates ($\hat{\bar{\mathbf{x}}}_j$) and their estimated sampling variance matrix ($\hat{\boldsymbol{\Sigma}}^{(j)}$) for state j, based on the statewide survey data.

For illustration, we assume first that the between-cluster variance σ_B^2 is equal to zero and then discuss its contribution to the uncertainty about the estimation of the state-level means. Recall that σ_B^2 was estimated subject to a lot of uncertainty. Since the national and statewide surveys do not overlap, we set $\boldsymbol{\Sigma}_{b,j} = \mathbf{0}$ throughout. Then the estimator $\hat{\bar{\mathbf{x}}}_j \hat{\boldsymbol{\beta}}$ has bias $-\delta_j$ and its sampling variance is given by (8.19).

The estimated means and their standard errors (assuming $\sigma_B^2 = 0$) are given in Table 8.6 for each imputed value, for the two statewide and two national surveys. The estimates based on the imputed values are sum-

TABLE 8.6. Prediction of the means of the proficiency scores for Mississippi and Oregon.

Survey	Quantity	Set of imputed values					Prof-cy score
		1	2	3	4	5	
		Mississippi					
ES/UI	Mean	0.135	0.112	0.169	0.154	0.161	0.146
	Std. error	0.065	0.068	0.062	0.060	0.058	0.067
JTPA	Mean	0.067	0.084	0.099	0.109	−0.006	0.071
	Std. error	0.084	0.081	0.082	0.083	0.085	0.095
Miss.	Obs. mean	−0.117	−0.122	−0.108	−0.127	−0.124	−0.120
	Std. error	0.026	0.026	0.026	0.027	0.026	0.027
		Oregon					
ES/UI	Mean	0.624	0.603	0.625	0.629	0.641	0.624
	Std. error	0.043	0.047	0.039	0.035	0.032	0.042
JTPA	Mean	0.486	0.516	0.539	0.495	0.467	0.501
	Std. error	0.062	0.059	0.060	0.061	0.063	0.067
Oregon	Obs. mean	0.575	0.561	0.567	0.579	0.572	0.571
	Std. error	0.019	0.019	0.019	0.019	0.019	0.020

marized in the rightmost column to give the estimates that refer to the proficiency scores.

Having estimated the proficiency scores for the subjects in the statewide surveys, their state-level means can be estimated directly from these surveys. The results for the two states are summarized at the bottom of each panel. We can now compare the small-area estimate based on the national survey data with the estimate based on the statewide survey.

First, without adjustment, that is, using the estimate of the national mean proficiency score, the small-area estimate would be hopelessly inadequate. The states of Mississippi and Oregon happen to be close to the extremes of the state-level means. Mississippi's estimated mean is lower than that of any state represented in the ES/UI survey, and in the JTPA survey only Missouri has a lower mean (−0.29). Oregon is among the states with the highest mean proficiency scores; in the ES/UI data, only Maryland (0.62), Utah (0.63), and Massachusetts (0.89) have higher estimated means, and in JTPA none of the states exceeds Oregon's estimated mean.

Clearly, adjustment for the selected covariates is instrumental in improved prediction for the two states, although the prediction is far from perfect. The estimates for Mississippi (0.146 and 0.071) are much higher than the estimated mean from the statewide survey (−0.120); the estimated standard errors are too small to account for this discrepancy. The predictions for Oregon appear to be much more successful; the discrepancy between the small-area and the statewide estimates is well within the estimated sampling errors.

These standard errors ignore the state-level variation of the proficiency scores. The estimates of these variances (averaged over the five analyses) are 0.00322 (standard error 0.00480) for ES/UI and 0.00095 (0.00414) for JTPA. If we regard these estimated variances as the underlying parameters and combine them with the standard errors quoted in Table 8.6, they inflate the average standard errors (averaged over δ_j^2) from 0.067 to $\sqrt{0.067^2 + 0.00322} = 0.087$ for ES/UI and from 0.095 to 0.099 for JTPA. The corresponding increases for Oregon are from 0.042 to 0.070 (for ES/UI) and from 0.067 to 0.074 (for JTPA).

8.7.4 Refinement

The covariates $\mathbf{x}$ were chosen by two important criteria: adequacy of the model fit (reduction of the within- and between-cluster variances) and pattern of missing data (so as not to lose too many subjects by listwise deletion). Here we explore how the predictions are altered when a different set of covariates is used. First, we supplement the regression model by a number of variables that have been observed both in the national and the statewide surveys and then apply informal model selection criteria to reduce the list of covariates with the intention of maintaining the model fit but increasing the sample size obtained by listwise deletion.

Table 8.7 lists a set of suitable covariates to supplement the list given in Table 8.3. Listwise deletion using these variables leads to a reduction of the sample size by about 900 subjects for both datasets; from 3277 to 2367 for ES/UI and from 2501 to 1604 for JTPA. Inclusion of these variables in the regression model results in small changes of the state-level variance for both datasets, but the standard errors of the prediction based on this model are greater than for the original model. The estimates for Mississippi are 0.178 (standard error 0.067) based on ES/UI survey data, and 0.035 (0.105) based on JTPA, ignoring the between-cluster variation in both cases.

The improvement in the model fit is more than offset by the reduced effective sample size. Also, the 900 or so subjects discarded by listwise deletion are informative subsamples of the respective datasets. Clearly, too high a price is paid for inclusion of so many variables in the prediction model.

In the next round of model refinement, we drop the 'quadratic age' term (it has a low t-ratio for all model fits), collapse the categories 4–6 of Ethnicity (Native Americans, Asian Americans, and 'other', each with small counts), collapse the categories 4 and 5 of Education (there are very few

TABLE 8.7. List of additional regressor variables for small-area estimation.

Description	Abbreviation	Number of categories	Values
Enrolled in school?	Sch.	2	Yes/No
High school diploma?	H. S.	2	Yes/No
Military service?	Mil. S.	2	Yes/No
Registered to vote?	Rg Vot	2	Yes/No
How often use Math on job?	MathU	5	Ordinal
Reading skills good enough for job?	ReadJ	3	Ordinal
Math skills good enough for job?	MathJ	3	Ordinal
Better job if more training in English?	Mor En	2	Yes/No
Better job if more training in Maths?	Mor Mt	2	Yes/No
How often read English newspaper?	ENews	5	Ordinal
How many people in household?	#Hhld		Quantitative
How often read/use reports on job?	Reps	5	Ordinal
How often write memos on job?	Mems	5	Ordinal

subjects in category 5), and discard variables H. S., Mil. S., MathU, ReadJ, MathJ, #Hhld, Reps, and Mems because their values are missing for large numbers of subjects, they are not important in the regression model, or both.

The new regression model contains 25 regression parameters. The respective raw and effective sample sizes after listwise deletion are 3089 and 1323 for ES/UI and 2364 and 991 for JTPA. This model appears to be a good compromise of adequacy (more covariates) and small loss of observations due to listwise deletion.

Table 8.8 gives the maximum likelihood fits to the two national survey datasets. These estimates are averaged over the five analyses for the sets of imputed values of y; the standard errors are adjusted for the variance across the five analyses, as described in Section 7.3.1.

The within- and between-cluster variances are reduced only slightly; we are interested in the impact of this reduction on the sampling variances of the predictors of the statewide means. The predictions based on the original and refined models, summarized in Table 8.9, differ only slightly. The standard errors are smaller, but the gains are not substantial. For comparison, the right-hand side of the table gives the estimates of the statewide means based solely on the state-level surveys. These estimates are not identical because they are based on the subsamples defined by the corresponding listwise deletion.

We see that the method of prediction using regression adjustment is robust with respect to the choice of covariates. This is a very important property because there may be important variables that have not been measured or observed in the survey. In particular, the pattern of missing

TABLE 8.8. Regression model fits for ES/UI and JTPA; maximum likelihood estimates.

Parameter (contrast)		ES/UI		JTPA	
		Estimate	Std. error	Estimate	Std. error
Intercept		−0.236	(0.245)	−0.345	(0.264)
Sex	2–1	−0.197	(0.050)	−0.125	(0.069)
Ethnicity	2–1	−0.703	(0.079)	−0.689	(0.078)
	3–1	−0.510	(0.069)	−0.555	(0.080)
	(>3)–1	−0.443	(0.116)	0.367	(0.145)
Education	2–1	0.751	(0.159)	0.690	(0.171)
	3–1	1.091	(0.151)	1.051	(0.151)
	(>3)–1	1.528	(0.160)	1.489	(0.168)
Age category	2–1	−0.028	(0.106)	−0.032	(0.104)
	3–1	0.060	(0.120)	0.089	(0.120)
	4–1	0.058	(0.163)	0.126	(0.171)
	5–1	0.198	(0.262)	0.244	(0.269)
Sch.		−0.259	(0.072)	−0.212	(0.077)
Rg Vot		−0.234	(0.055)	−0.181	(0.068)
Mor En		0.461	(0.066)	0.437	(0.065)
Mor Mt		−0.018	(0.067)	−0.041	(0.071)
ENews	2–1	0.062	(0.057)	0.067	(0.057)
	3–1	−0.140	(0.083)	−0.127	(0.082)
	4–1	−0.231	(0.110)	−0.165	(0.122)
	5–1	−0.329	(0.175)	−0.293	(0.178)
Mother's educ.		0.0163	(0.0093)	0.0176	(0.0086)
Father's educ.		−0.0026	(0.0077)	−0.0030	(0.0075)
Personal income		0.026	(0.014)	0.015	(0.013)
Household income		0.027	(0.011)	0.021	(0.011)
Age (years)		−0.0128	(0.0067)	−0.0109	(0.0069)
σ_1^2		0.7332		0.5825	
τ		0.0068	(0.0078)	0.0039	(0.0078)

TABLE 8.9. Predictions for Mississippi and Oregon based on the original model (see Table 8.6) and the refined model.

State	ES/UI		JTPA		State	
Model	Mean	Std. error	Mean	Std. error	Mean	Std. error
Mississippi						
Original	0.146	(0.067)	0.071	(0.095)	−0.120	(0.027)
Refined	0.140	(0.060)	0.091	(0.084)	−0.107	(0.027)
Oregon						
Original	0.624	(0.042)	0.501	(0.067)	0.571	(0.020)
Refined	0.648	(0.039)	0.499	(0.067)	0.570	(0.021)

data does not have an overwhelming impact on the results. This 'robustness' feature is very important because the prediction relies heavily on expediency (availability of data) in addition to familiarity with the subject matter, theoretical considerations, and formal statistical procedures.

The apparent bias of the prediction for Mississippi remains unexplained, though.

8.8   Summary and literature review

A prediction method for estimating small-area means of outcome variables from national surveys, based on a random-effects regression model, was presented and illustrated on a cross-validation study of literacy proficiency scores in two U.S. states, Mississippi and Oregon. For these states, statewide surveys have been carried out, and so the predictions from the national surveys can be compared with more reliable estimates based on the statewide surveys. Uncertainty about the prediction is assessed by the standard error of the predictor.

The procedure involves the selection of a regression model for the outcome variable. The covariates for this model should be selected so as to reduce the (adjusted) within- and between-cluster variances as much as possible. In particular, the latter is a component of the average MSE of prediction for a state not represented in the national survey.

Fitting these regression models, with random coefficients due to clusters (states), requires an iterative procedure. We described an adaptation of the Fisher scoring algorithm that takes into account the sampling weights. The prediction of the population mean for a state is based on the regression parameter estimates, their estimated sampling variance matrix, an estimate of the state-level population mean of the covariates, their estimated sampling variance matrix, and the covariance matrix of the regression and covariate mean estimates. The latter matrix vanishes when the data for the regression and the covariate information do not overlap; otherwise considerable difficulties are encountered. Nevertheless, when the state is a small part of the survey data used in the regression the covariance matrix can be set to zero.

Assumptions of normality are adopted throughout. This is reasonable for the regression parameter and population mean estimates, and in the particular application also for the outcomes.

Various schemes for collating information across surveys can be employed. Combining national and statewide surveys is a special case. By comparing the sampling variances of the small-area prediction and the direct estimator of the population mean for a state, we can see that the national survey is not as informative about a state as the statewide survey of comparable effective sample size. However, the contribution of the national surveys can be non-trivial.

For small-area estimation using a large number of clusters, there may be scope for more detailed modelling of between-cluster variation. As a generalization of the models discussed in this chapter, the between-cluster differences may depend on some of the covariates. Between-cluster variation in such a model is described by the variance matrix of the within-cluster regression coefficients. See Longford (1993b) for details.

There are two identifiable strains in the literature on small-area estimation: adjustment by regression and combining information across small areas. We have combined the two approaches in an attempt to benefit from both. Adjustment for regression was explored by Ericksen (1974). Holt and Scott (1982) discuss regression analysis using survey data.

Combining information across clusters to improve estimation for each cluster was pioneered by Fay and Herriot (1979), and application of the approach was greatly encouraged by the development of empirical Bayes methods (Morris, 1983) and enabled by proliferation of modern computers. The random-effects element of our approach is motivated by Battese, Harter, and Fuller (1988). For another case study in agricultural research using small-area estimation, see Stasny, Goel, and Rumsey (1991). See also Prasad and Rao (1990) and Wolter and Causey (1991). Tsutakawa (1988) presents a study of geographic variation with non-normally distributed outcomes.

Platek *et al.* (1987) is an edited volume of contributions to small-area estimation. Ghosh and Rao (1994) present a comprehensive review of the latest developments in small-area estimation. Adaptation of missing data methods (Little and Rubin, 1987) to surveys with complex sampling design is another element in improving estimation for small areas.

9

Cut scores for pass/fail decisions

9.1 Introduction

Many educational and licencing tests are used for classifying examinees into a small number of categories, such as 'satisfactory', 'borderline', and 'unsatisfactory'. In such tests, each possible response pattern has to be assigned to one of the categories. This task is often simplified by defining a scoring rule for the responses, so that the examinees are ordered on a unidimensional scale. Then it suffices to set the cut scores that separate the categories. When several test forms are used, separate sets of cut scores have to be set for each of them because the forms are likely to have different score distributions.

Without substantial loss of generality, we consider the case of a single cut point separating two categories of examinees. For instance, a test may be used to assign examinees to a 'pass' and a 'fail' category, and the cut score can be interpreted as the minimal acceptable competence. We refer to the examinees with scores above the cut score as *competent*. It is important to distinguish between observed-score and true-score competence because of the two kinds of incorrect decisions that can be made about each examinee: failing a true-score competent examinee and passing an examinee whose true-score is below the cut point.

If we knew that a given percentage of the examinees were competent, or simply wished to pass a certain percentage of the examinees, we could assign that percentage of the examinees with the highest observed scores to the 'pass' and the remainder to the 'fail' category. If there are costs associated with each incorrect decision, this assignment scheme has to be adjusted. For example, if passing an examinee who should have been failed is associated with extremely high costs, only examinees who have performed very well should be passed.

In a more realistic setting, experts are engaged to set the cut score for passing. Of course, the experts could classify every examinee by his/her responses. This is not a workable proposition in large-scale tests because a large number of experts would be required. Also, the objectivity of the classification process would be undermined, unless the examinees were classified by several experts. Procedures for resolving disagreement among the experts assessing the same examinee would have to be introduced. The adjustment schemes discussed in Chapter 3 provide one avenue for doing this.

The objectivity of the classification process remains intact if the experts are engaged merely to set the rules for classification. There are two distinct approaches. In the first approach, each expert is assumed to have a good idea about the kind of examinee who is on the borderline between 'fail' and 'pass'. For each item of the test form, the expert gives his/her view of the chance that such a borderline examinee would give the correct response. For items such as essays, scored on an ordinal scale, the expert guesses the average grade for such examinees. The cut score is set to the expected test score for a borderline examinee. The experts' expectations are averaged in the obvious fashion. Such schemes have been extensively explored by Nedelsky (1954) and Subkoviak (1978); see Angoff (1971) and Hambleton *et al.* (1978) for reviews.

The principal drawback of such schemes is that the experts are often very inconsistent in their perception of percentages or fractions. Their task can be made easier by asking them to classify each item into one of an ordered set of categories, such as 'almost nobody', 'some', 'about half', and 'almost everybody', according to the proportion of borderline examinees who they believe would give the correct response. The analyst's task is to attach 'typical' percentages to these categories. In this way, some consistency in the experts' assessments may be introduced at the price of a coarse classification.

The subject of this chapter is another scheme for eliciting and reconciling experts' proposals for cut scores. In this scheme, the experts inspect the sets of responses of a small number of examinees and classify each examinee as 'fail' or 'pass'. Independently, the responses of each of these examinees are scored. The experts' classifications are then related to the scores and the (fitted) association is applied to all the examinees, including those whose response sheets were inspected by the experts. In this way, the experts are engaged only for a limited time and the classification procedure is objective. Note the pivotal role played by the test score.

The topic of this chapter is closely related to that of Chapters 2–4. We are interested in reconciling experts' ratings and, as a form of quality control, in assessing the degree of disagreement among the experts. The statistical development is closely related to these two elements. First, we introduce the model that relates an expert's assessment to the test scores, and then we extend this model to express the differences among the experts in terms of variation.

For the former, we apply logistic regression. Differences among the experts are accommodated by introducing random regression coefficients. We prefer to model differences among the experts by a random variable (or vector), so as to capture the random nature of the process of selecting the experts. In pursuit of objectivity, we aim to make inferences with respect to the population of experts, not merely the experts who happen to have been selected for the cut-score setting exercise.

Logistic regression with random coefficients is a natural extension of the random regression coefficient models from the normal framework introduced in Chapter 8. The 'pass/fail' verdicts of each expert are a cluster of observations with a correlation structure induced by the severity of the expert. The ideal case of full agreement among the experts corresponds to each examinee being rated unanimously as either 'pass' or 'fail' by all the experts. No variation in severity corresponds to *equal probabilities* of a classification of each examinee by all the experts. Clearly, this is a much less stringent condition than full agreement.

Unlike in Chapter 8, where we focussed on estimation of realizations of random variables, here the random variables representing experts' severities are a nuisance, and they are of interest only for diagnostic purposes. Nevertheless, the severity variance is of central interest as a measure of agreement among the experts. In the approach we follow, this variance is estimated by maximum likelihood. Several issues carry over from the discussion in Chapters 2 and 3. In particular, it would be useful to establish whether this measure of agreement is consistent across test forms of a test, so that the level of agreement in future standard setting exercises could be predicted. This would facilitate well-informed decisions about the numbers of experts to be engaged and the numbers of essays to be examined by the experts.

The experts' severities are transparent through the proportions of examinees they classify as 'pass' and 'fail'. Disagreement with the score scale, that is, failing an examinee who has a higher score than a passed examinee, is referred to as inconsistency. Although variation in severity in this context is closely related to that in essay rating (Chapter 2), inconsistency has an essentially different meaning in the two contexts.

The next section introduces and motivates the logistic regression model with random coefficients. Section 9.3 describes algorithms for fitting this model. In Section 9.4, three examples are analysed and the results are compared with a simpler approach in which differences among the experts are ignored. The chapter is concluded with a summary.

9.2   Models

A random sample of examinees $i = 1, \ldots, I$ from an administration is selected and their responses are presented to each expert $j = 1, \ldots, J$. The outcome of the inspection of the response sheet i by expert j is the rating y_{ij}; $y_{ij} = 1$ for 'pass' and $y_{ij} = 0$ for 'fail'.

For each expert, we consider a model that relates the chance of a 'pass' as a function of the test score:

$$P(y_{ij} = 1 \mid x_i \,; a_j \,, b_j) = g(a_j + b_j x_i), \qquad (9.1)$$

where a_j and b_j are expert-specific coefficients, and g is an increasing function, common to all the experts. The inverse of g, g^{-1}, is commonly called the link function. The ordinary regression corresponds to the identity, $g(x) = x$. For binary data, it is advantageous to consider functions g that map the real axis $(-\infty, +\infty)$ to the interval $(0, 1)$, so that having estimated the coefficients a_j and b_j, the fitted probabilities, $g(\hat{a}_j + \hat{b}_j x_i)$, would lie in the range $(0, 1)$. Also, the probability scale, being bounded, is distinctly non-additive. Improvement from a 50 percent chance to a 70 percent chance is, intuitively, much less substantial than, say, from 80 percent to 100 percent. In fact, from a high percentage, there is only a limited scope for improvement as measured in percentage points.

In many settings, it is appropriate and convenient to use the log-odds ratio scale. The log-odds ratio, or the *logit* of probability p, is defined as

$$\mathrm{logit}(p) = \log\left(\frac{p}{1-p}\right) = \log(p) - \log(1-p).$$

Its inverse is

$$\mathrm{logit}^{-1}(x) = \frac{\exp(x)}{1 + \exp(x)}.$$

Linearity on the logit scale corresponds to $g(x) = \mathrm{logit}^{-1}(x)$ in (9.1). We will use this scale throughout the chapter. Much of the development in this and the next section carries over to other link functions, although some simplification is derived in the computational algorithm for model fitting with the logit link.

The regression in (9.1) can be extended to non-linear regression, such as

$$P(y_{ij} = 1 \mid x_i \,; a_j \,, b_j) = g(a_j + b_j x_i + c_j x_i^2),$$

and the regression model can be supplemented by other covariates, defined for examinees, experts, or even by their interactions. In practice, binary data with small to moderate sample size contain very sparse information about complex associations, such as in multiple regression, and so the scope of regression modelling is rather limited.

The model in (9.1) assumes that the regression lines relating the chances of a pass as a function of the test score differ among the experts in both their slopes and intercepts. The slope b_j can be interpreted as *discrimination* of the expert. High slope indicates that the examinees have a wide range of chances of passing with the expert, while with an expert with a shallow slope, the examinees's chances are in a narrower range. In particular, an expert with $b_j = 0$ appears to be not very useful because each examinee's chance of passing is equal to $g(a_j)$, independent of the score x. Of course, the scores may not be a good reflection of the examinees' abilities, in which case the expert is beyond reproach. Assuming valid scores, high discrimination is preferred because it corresponds to most examinees having probabilities of 'pass' close to either zero or unity.

As a summary of the differences among the experts, we consider the variance matrix $\mathbf{\Omega} = \text{var}(a., b.)$. For simplicity, we consider first the case of no variation in discrimination, $\text{var}(b.) = 0$. Let b be the common value of the discrimination and $a = \mathbf{E}(a.)$ be the expected intercept. In the absence of variation in discrimination, the deviation $\delta_j = a_j - a$ can be interpreted as the severity of expert j. The variance Ω_a has an interpretation similar to the severity variance of essay raters in Chapters 2–3. The 'measurement error' associated with the score x_i is assumed to be negligible and is ignored throughout.

The hypothetical average expert corresponds to $\delta_j = 0$. For such an expert, the probability of a 'pass' for a given score x is equal to $\text{logit}^{-1}(a+bx)$. Note that this is different from the proportion of passes in the population of experts;

$$\int \text{logit}^{-1}(a + bx + \delta\sqrt{\Omega_a})\phi(\delta)d\delta \neq \text{logit}^{-1}(a + bx)$$

(ϕ is the density function of $\delta_j/\sqrt{\Omega_a}$), unless the integrand on the left-hand side is a symmetric function of δ. For instance, when ϕ is the standard normal density, the identity above holds only when $a + bx = 0$.

9.3   Fitting logistic regression

The average regression parameters a and b and the variance matrix $\mathbf{\Omega}$ are estimated by maximum likelihood. We describe first the estimation of the regression parameters asuming $\mathbf{\Omega} = \mathbf{0}$, that is, when

$$P(y_{ij} = 1) = g(a + bx_{ij}), \tag{9.2}$$

independently, and then describe an algorithm for estimating the regression and variation parameters in the model with random coefficients:

$$P(y_{ij} = 1 \mid a_j, b_j) = g(a_j + b_jx_{ij}), \tag{9.3}$$

assuming that, marginally, (a_j , b_j) is a random sample from $\mathcal{N}_2(\mathbf{0}, \mathbf{\Omega})$. Finally, we apply the delta method to approximate the sampling distribution of the estimator of the cut score.

9.3.1   Generalized linear models

A more general formulation of the model in (9.2) is as follows: the observations y_{ij} are independent, have respective densities (or probabilities) $\xi(y; a + bx_{ij})$, and

$$\mathbf{E}(y_{ij}) = g(a + bx_{ij}). \tag{9.4}$$

Note that the indices ij can be replaced by a single index. We maintain the former for notational consistency; in the next section, both indices will be essential. For binary data, ξ is the function on $\{0, 1\}$ assigning 1 with probability $p = \text{logit}^{-1}(a+bx_{ij})$, and 0 with the complementary probability.

Alternatively, the distribution of the observations can be specified by the expectation $\mathbf{E}(y_{ij})$ as a function of the linear predictor, as in (9.4), and the function that relates the variance of an observation to its expectation:

$$\text{var}(y_{ij}) = v \left\{ \mathbf{E}(y_{ij}) \right\} .$$

The function v is called the variance function. For example, in the logistic regression, $v(p) = p(1 - p)$.

Generalized linear models are closely connected to the *exponential family* of distributions. This family is defined by the general formula for their densities:

$$\xi(y; \theta, \tau) = \exp \left\{ \frac{y\theta - b(\theta)}{\tau} + c(y; \tau) \right\} , \tag{9.5}$$

where b and c are some real twice differentiable functions and $\tau > 0$ is a known constant, usually referred to as the *scale*. The mean and variance of this distribution are

$$\mathbf{E}(y) = b'(\theta) ,$$
$$\text{var}(y) = \tau b''(\theta) ,$$

where b' and b'' are the first- and second-order partial derivatives of b. Necessarily, $b''(\theta) > 0$ throughout the range of θ. The variance function is defined by the equation

$$v\{b'(\theta)\} = \tau b''(\theta) .$$

In generalized linear models, the observations y_{ij} are independent with densities (probabilities) $\xi(\theta_{ij})$, where ξ is given by (9.5) and $\theta_{ij} = \eta(\mathbf{x}_{ij}\boldsymbol{\beta})$ is a function of the linear predictor. Each function η corresponds to a link. The link associated with the identity function η, $\theta_{ij} = a + bx_{ij}$, is called the *canonical link*.

The log-likelihood for such a model is

$$l(\boldsymbol{\beta}) = \left[\frac{1}{\tau} \sum_{ij} \{y_{ij}\theta_{ij} - b(\theta_{ij})\} + \sum_{ij} c(y_{ij}; \tau) \right].$$

Its maximum is found by the Newton-Raphson algorithm. The vector of the first-order partial derivatives is

$$(\mathbf{h} =) \quad \frac{\partial l}{\partial \boldsymbol{\beta}} = \frac{1}{\tau} \sum_{ij} \{y_{ij} - b'(\theta_{ij})\} \frac{\partial \theta_{ij}}{\partial \eta_{ij}} \mathbf{x}_{ij}, \tag{9.6}$$

and the matrix of the negative second-order partial derivatives is

$$(\mathbf{H} =) \quad - \frac{\partial^2 l}{\partial \boldsymbol{\beta} \partial \boldsymbol{\beta}^{\mathsf{T}}} = \sum_{ij} \left[b''(\theta_{ij}) \left(\frac{\partial \theta_{ij}}{\partial \eta_{ij}} \right)^2 - \{y_{ij} - b'(\theta_{ij})\} \frac{\partial^2 \theta_{ij}}{\partial \eta_{ij}^2} \right] \mathbf{x}_{ij} \mathbf{x}_{ij}^{\mathsf{T}}, \tag{9.7}$$

where $\eta_{ij} = \mathbf{x}_{ij}\boldsymbol{\beta}$. Note that since $\mathbf{E}(y_{ij}) = b'(\theta_{ij})$, the expected information matrix for $\boldsymbol{\beta}$ is

$$(\mathbf{H}^* =) \quad - \mathbf{E} \left(\frac{\partial^2 l}{\partial \boldsymbol{\beta} \partial \boldsymbol{\beta}^{\mathsf{T}}} \right) = \sum_{ij} b''(\theta_{ij}) \left(\frac{\partial \theta_{ij}}{\partial \eta_{ij}} \right)^2 \mathbf{x}_{ij} \mathbf{x}_{ij}^{\mathsf{T}}. \tag{9.8}$$

For the logistic regression, $b(\theta) = - \log(1 - p)$, so that $p = \text{logit}^{-1}(\theta)$ and $\tau = 1$. Further, $b'(\theta) = p$ and $b''(\theta) = p(1 - p)$, and so equations (9.6)–(9.8) simplify to

$$\mathbf{h} = \sum_{ij} \mathbf{x}_{ij} (y_{ij} - p_{ij}),$$
$$\mathbf{H}^* = \mathbf{H} = \sum_{ij} p_{ij}(1 - p_{ij}) \mathbf{x}_{ij} \mathbf{x}_{ij}^{\mathsf{T}}. \tag{9.9}$$

The particularly simple form of the partial derivatives is due to the fact that the logit is the canonical link for the binary distribution; $\partial \theta_{ij}/\partial \boldsymbol{\beta} = \mathbf{x}_{ij}$. That is a prominent reason why the logit link is preferred over other alternatives for binary data.

Estimation of the regression parameters $\boldsymbol{\beta}$ starts with an initial solution, such as $\boldsymbol{\beta}_0 = \left(\sum_{ij} y_{ij}/n, 0, \ldots, 0 \right)^{\mathsf{T}}$, and proceeds with adjustments

$$\boldsymbol{\beta}_{new} = \boldsymbol{\beta}_{old} + \mathbf{H}^{-1}\mathbf{h},$$

with $\mathbf{H}$ and $\mathbf{h}$ evaluated at $\boldsymbol{\beta}_{old}$. The matrix $\mathbf{H}$ is positive semidefinite, but may be singular (that is, have a zero eigenvalue). It can be shown, though, that in the simple regression model (9.4), the eigenvalues of $\mathbf{H}$ are positive whenever the covariate x is not constant and none of the fitted probabilities p_{ij} are equal to zero or unity.

The criterion for convergence can be based on the norm of the correction $\mathbf{H}^{-1}\mathbf{h}$, the increment of the log-likelihood $l(\boldsymbol{\beta}_{new}) - l(\boldsymbol{\beta}_{old})$, the norm of the scoring vector $\mathbf{h}$, or their combination. In well-conditioned problems, the number of iterations is usually smaller than ten, even for a very stringent convergence criterion.

McCullagh and Nelder (1989) is a comprehensive text on generalized linear models.

9.3.2   Random coefficients

The maximum likelihood estimation for the generalized linear model given by (9.4), commonly referred to as generalized least squares (GLS), is a weighted least squares procedure in which the weights are a function of the linear predictor, and so they have to be adjusted in each iteration. This description motivates the following procedure for *approximate* maximum likelihood estimation for the logistic regression with random coefficients.

Consider the Fisher scoring algorithm described in Section 8.5. We observed that the procedure for fitting normal random coefficient models uses the data only through certain within-cluster cross-products. To take account of the sampling weights, we replaced these cross-products by their weighted versions. A natural adaptation for non-normally distributed outcomes is to replace the cross-products by their *iteratively reweighted* versions. Thus, we start with the GLS fit (ignoring within-cluster dependence) and proceed with iterations of the Fisher scoring algorithm, with the cross-products replaced by their weighted versions. The same weight function is used as in GLS, and so the weights have to be recalculated in each iteration in which the regression parameters are adjusted. This procedure is formally justified by deriving an approximation to the log-likelihood; see Longford (1994a) for details.

Alternatively, we may consider the exact log-likelihood

$$l = \sum_{j=1}^{J} \log \int \cdots \int \prod_{i=1}^{I_j} \xi\left(\theta_{ij}; \boldsymbol{\delta}_j \boldsymbol{\Omega}^{-\frac{1}{2}}\right) \phi(\boldsymbol{\delta}_j) d\boldsymbol{\delta}_j . \tag{9.10}$$

When the number of dimensions in the integration above is small, this integral can be approximated by Gaussian (numerical) quadrature. The first- and second-order partial derivatives can be derived by exchanging the order of integration and differentiation, and the resulting integrals can also be evaluated using Gaussian quadrature. Thus, the (approximate) Newton-Raphson algorithm can be implemented. This approach has been followed by Im and Gianola (1988) and Longford (1994a); see the latter or Longford (1993a) for technical details.

9.3.3   Cut score estimation

Since $\text{logit}^{-1}(0) = \frac{1}{2}$, a 50 percent chance of a pass corresponds to the cut score $x^* = -a/b$. The cut score corresponding to $100c$ percent chance of a pass is $\{\text{logit}(c) - b\}/a$. For brevity, we denote $C = \text{logit}(c)$.

In practice, the regression parameters a and b are estimated, with their sampling variance matrix $\mathbf{S}$ itself estimated by a positive definite matrix $\hat{\mathbf{S}}$. In further development, we assume that estimates of a, b, and $\mathbf{S}$ are available, and denote the elements of $\mathbf{S}$ by $S_a = \text{var}(\hat{a})$, $S_b = \text{var}(\hat{b})$, and $S_{ab} = \text{cov}(\hat{a}, \hat{b})$.

The natural estimator of the ratio $(C - a)/b$ is $(C - \hat{a})/\hat{b}$. The sampling distribution of this estimator can be approximated by the delta method. Let

$$\frac{C - \hat{a}}{\hat{b}} = \frac{C - a - \varepsilon_a}{b + \varepsilon_b},$$

where ε_a and ε_b are random terms representing the deviations of the estimators from the corresponding parameters. Writing

$$\frac{C - \hat{a}}{\hat{b}} = \frac{\frac{C-a}{b} - \frac{\varepsilon_a}{b}}{1 + \frac{\varepsilon_b}{b}},$$

and assuming that ε_b is small in absolute value in relation to b, the expansion of the factor $(1 + \varepsilon_b/b)^{-1}$ into a geometric series yields

$$\frac{C - \hat{a}}{\hat{b}} = \left(\frac{C - a}{b} - \frac{\varepsilon_a}{b}\right)\left(1 - \frac{\varepsilon_b}{b} + \frac{\varepsilon_b^2}{b^2} - \frac{\varepsilon_b^3}{b^3} + \cdots\right)$$

$$= \frac{C - a}{b} - \frac{\varepsilon_a}{b} - \frac{(C - a)\varepsilon_b}{b^2} + \frac{\varepsilon_a\varepsilon_b}{b^2} + \frac{(C - a)\varepsilon_b^2}{b^3} + \cdots.$$

Taking expectations, while ignoring all but the leading terms in the expansion, we obtain

$$\mathbf{E}\left(\frac{C - \hat{a}}{\hat{b}}\right) \approx \frac{C - a}{b} + \frac{\Sigma_{ab}}{b^2} + \frac{(C - a)\Sigma_b}{b^3}. \tag{9.11}$$

By taking the expectation of the squares in the approximation

$$\frac{C - \hat{a}}{\hat{b}} - \frac{C - a}{b} \approx -\frac{\varepsilon_a}{b} - \frac{(C - a)\varepsilon_b}{b^2},$$

we obtain

$$\text{var}\left(\frac{C - \hat{a}}{\hat{b}}\right) \approx \frac{\Sigma_a}{b^2} + \frac{2(C - a)\Sigma_{ab}}{b^3} + \frac{(C - a)^2\Sigma_b}{b^4}. \tag{9.12}$$

Equation (9.11) enables an approximate correction for bias by replacing the estimator $(C - \hat{a})/\hat{b}$ with $(C - \hat{a})/\hat{b} - \hat{\Sigma}_{ab}/\hat{b}^2 - (C - \hat{a})\hat{\Sigma}_b/\hat{b}^3$. Equation (9.12) can be used for estimating the standard error of either estimator of $(C - a)/b$.

9.4 Examples

In each of the three examples of standard setting analysed in this section, the cut score is estimated for $c = \frac{1}{2}$, that is, $C = 0$. The data were provided by Skip Livingston and Jerry Melican from ETS.

9.4.1 PPST Writing test

Pre-Professional Skills Test (PPST) is a test for U.S. students entering teacher training programmes. In some states, it is also used for licencing new teachers. The test consists of three batteries of tests (Reading, Writing, and Mathematics). The Writing component of the test consists of a set of items that are scored as right or wrong. A new form is used for every administration, and each examinee in an administration is presented the same test form. The number of correct responses is adopted as the test score, and it is the basis for either passing or failing the examinee on this component of the test. No equating procedures are employed, but a cut-score study is conducted after each administration.

Sixteen experts were engaged to set the cut score for the PPST Writing test in summer 1992. They rated the response sheets of 17 randomly selected examinees. The selected examinees had scores in the range 4–12. The strictest expert gave only 6 passes (11 fails), whereas the most lenient one gave only 1 fail. One examinee received a pass from only one expert, while another examinee received passes from all but one expert. However, these two examinees did not have respectively the lowest and the highest scores. The data and its summary are displayed in Table 9.1.

The examinees' scores are given in the first row and the numbers of passes received in the bottom row. Each examinee's ratings are given in a column. Each expert is represented by a row (except the top and bottom rows). The last column contains the numbers of passes given by each expert. Among the $16 \times 17 = 272$ ratings, there were 193 passes (71 percent).

If the severity variance vanished, $\sigma^2 = 0$, the logistic regression for independent observations would be applicable. The corresponding GLS fit is

$$-2.264 \quad + \quad 0.382x$$
$$(0.519) \qquad (0.067)$$

(the standard errors are given in parentheses). Based on this equation, the estimate of the cut score is equal to $2.264/0.382 = 5.93$. Bias correction using the delta method yields the estimate 5.88. The standard error associated with these estimates is equal to 0.45.

We consider first fitting separate regressions for each expert. The fitted regressions are plotted in Figure 9.1 on the logit scale (the left-hand panel) and the probability scale (the right-hand panel). Fitting each logistic regression required four to seven iterations of GLS, with the exception of

TABLE 9.1. Data from the cut-score setting exercise for the PPST Writing test.

	Examinee																	
Reader	1	2	3	4	5	6	7	8	9	10	11	12	13	14	15	16	17	Passes
Score	8	4	5	11	8	10	6	9	7	12	11	10	6	9	8	6	7	
1	1	0	0	0	1	1	1	1	1	1	1	0	1	1	1	1	0	12
2	1	1	0	1	1	1	1	0	1	1	1	1	1	1	1	1	1	15
3	1	0	0	1	1	1	0	0	1	1	1	1	1	0	0	0	0	9
4	1	0	0	1	1	1	1	0	1	1	1	0	0	1	1	0	1	11
5	1	0	0	1	1	1	0	1	1	1	1	1	1	1	1	1	0	13
6	1	1	0	1	1	1	1	1	1	1	1	1	1	1	1	1	1	16
7	1	0	0	1	1	1	0	1	1	1	1	1	1	1	1	1	0	13
8	0	0	0	0	1	1	0	0	0	1	1	1	1	1	0	1	1	9
9	1	0	0	1	1	1	0	1	1	1	1	1	1	1	1	1	0	13
10	1	0	0	1	0	1	0	1	0	1	0	1	1	1	1	0	0	9
11	1	1	0	1	1	1	1	1	1	1	1	1	1	1	1	1	0	15
12	1	0	0	1	1	1	1	1	1	1	1	1	1	1	1	1	1	15
13	1	0	1	1	0	1	0	0	0	0	0	0	0	1	1	0	0	6
14	0	0	0	1	1	1	1	1	1	1	1	1	1	1	0	1	1	13
15	1	0	0	1	0	1	1	1	1	1	0	0	1	1	1	0	1	11
16	1	0	0	0	1	1	1	1	1	1	1	1	0	1	1	1	1	13
Passes	14	3	1	13	13	16	9	11	13	15	13	12	13	15	13	11	8	193

Notes: The first row of the table gives the examinees' scores (say, examinee 1 scored 8 points). The first column of the table is the expert number. In the main body of the table, '1' stands for 'pass' and '0' for 'fail' rating. The bottom row gives the within-examinee totals of passes, and the rightmost column gives the number of passes given by each expert.

expert 12. This expert failed the 2 examinees with the lowest scores and passed the other 14 examinees. The logistic regression is attempting to fit zero probability of passing for scores below 5.5 and zero probability of failing above 5.5. The iterations of GLS keep increasing the fitted slope and adjusting the intercept accordingly. The GLS procedure fails to converge, but there is a good reason why it does so.

For illustration, the pointwise confidence band for expert 1 is drawn by dashed lines in both panels of Figure 9.1. Although there is a considerable uncertainty about the fitted regression line for each expert, the fitted lines are dispersed more than what would be expected if the underlying regressions were identical. The estimates of the slopes are in the range 0.14–1.14 (except for expert 12); although some of the experts stand out as having higher or lower fitted slopes than the rest, this variation can be attributed

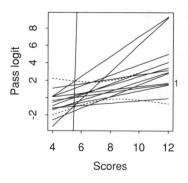 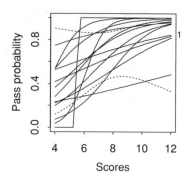

FIGURE 9.1. Separate logistic regressions for each expert; PPST Writing test data. Each solid line represents an expert. The horizontal axis is the score of the examinee and the vertical, the fitted logit of the probability of passing (the left-hand panel) and the corresponding probability (the right-hand panel). The pointwise 95 percent confidence band for expert 1 is drawn by dashed lines.

to errors of estimation. The standard errors of the slope estimates are in the range 0.24–1.00 (except for expert 12).

The data are not extensive enough to explore the differences in discrimination, and so we assume from now on that the experts have equal discrimination. The regressions fitted by GLS are not very useful for setting the cut score because they still have to be averaged over the experts. The average (marginal) regression is obtained directly by fitting the random coefficient model.

The maximum likelihood fit for the random coefficient model in (9.1) that allows for variation in severity but assumes constant discrimination is

$$-2.852 \quad + \quad 0.504x \,.$$
$$(0.645) \qquad (0.083)$$

This is a substantial departure from the GLS fit; a steeper estimated slope is obtained, with a noticeable increase of the standard errors. The estimates of the cut score are 6.56 (without bias correction) and 6.51 (with bias correction), with the standard error equal to 0.55. The fitted probabilities, as a function of the score x, are plotted in Figure 9.2, together with a confidence band generated from pointwise confidence intervals. For completeness, the GLS fit is plotted in the diagram by a dashed line. Allowing for varying discrimination changes the regression fit only slightly and leads to a slight inflation of the standard error of the cut score (to 0.60).

Varying discrimination corresponds to unrelated within-expert regressions, each based on only 17 binary responses. Although borrowing strength across the experts (clusters) enables more efficient estimation, the discrimination variance is estimated with very little precision. Varying discrimination represents too fine a pattern in the outcomes, which cannot be reliably estimated from such a small dataset.

PPST Writing

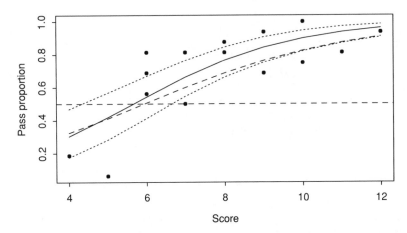

FIGURE 9.2. The logistic regression fit pointwise confidence band for PPST Writing test. Each point represents an examinee. The horizontal axis is the score of the examinee and the vertical the proportion of passes given by the experts. The GLS regression fit is drawn by a dashed line and the ML fit by a solid line. The 95 percent pointwise confidence bounds are drawn by dotted lines.

The maximum likelihood estimate of the standard deviation s is 0.775 (standard error 0.245). It implies substantial variation in the experts' standards. For illustration, the difference of $2\hat{s} = 1.55$ logits corresponds to the change of probabilities from $\text{logit}^{-1}(0) = 0.5$ to $\text{logit}^{-1}(1.55) = 0.825$, or to $\text{logit}^{-1}(-1.55) = 0.175$.

Five iterations of the approximate Newton-Raphson algorithm were required to achieve convergence. The orderly manner of convergence is documented in Table 9.2. The deviance stands for the value of -2 log-likelihood at the previous solution. In the first row, the GLS deviance (329.02) is given.

9.4.2   Physical Education

A similar standard setting exercise was conducted for the two parts (I and II) of the Physical Education component of the Praxis II test administered in Hawaii in September 1992. The same 11 experts were engaged for both parts, to rate 12 examinees on Part I, and a different set of 13 examinees on Part II. The datasets and their summaries for the two parts are displayed in Tables 9.3 and 9.4, respectively.

In rating Part I, all experts rated the two examinees with the lowest scores and another examinee as 'fail'. One examinee was rated as 'pass' by all experts and another one was rated as 'pass' by all but one expert. The

TABLE 9.2. Convergence of the maximum likelihood solution for PPST Writing test.

Iter.	$\hat{a}$	$\hat{b}$	$\hat{s}$	Deviance	Δ	$s(\hat{a})$	$s(\hat{b})$	$s(\hat{s})$
	−2.264	0.382	0.500	329.02				
1	−2.774	0.479	0.674	278.62	0.557	7.061	70.302	3.219
2	−2.853	0.502	0.759	274.13	0.145	1.714	15.115	1.079
3	−2.852	0.504	0.775	273.76	0.023	0.228	1.764	0.167
4	−2.852	0.504	0.775	273.75	0.001	0.006	0.042	0.005
5	−2.852	0.504	0.775	273.75	$< 10^{-5}$	$< 10^{-5}$	$< 10^{-4}$	$< 10^{-5}$

Notes: The first row gives the starting solution; the regression parameter estimates, $\hat{a}$ and $\hat{b}$, are set to the GLS estimates, and the standard deviation $\hat{s}$ is set to 0.5 (arbitrarily chosen). The deviance is the value of the $-2 \log$-likelihood for the previous iteration. (The first row contains the GLS deviance.) Δ is the mean squared difference of the parameters and the deviance of two consecutive solutions; $s(\hat{\theta})$ is the value of the score function for the parameter estimate $\hat{\theta}$ evaluated at the previous iteration. The proximity of these values to zero is a suitable criterion for convergence of the algorithm.

experts' ratings are not consistent with the scores at the high end of the score scale; the examinee with the highest score, 60 points, received two 'fail' ratings, while the examinee with the sixth highest score, 40 points, received only one 'fail' rating.

The GLS and maximum likelihood regression fits are

$$-4.71 \quad + \quad 0.116x$$
$$(0.85) \qquad (0.020)$$

and

$$-5.92 \quad + \quad 0.153x,$$
$$(1.17) \qquad (0.038)$$

respectively. The scores x are in the range 10–60. The difference in the fitted slopes is substantial, and the standard error of the maximum likelihood estimator is almost twice as large as the nominal GLS standard error. The estimate of the between-expert (severity) standard deviation is 0.86 with standard error 0.38.

The GLS estimate of the cut score is 40.66 with standard error 1.77; the correction for bias is unimportant. Using the maximum likelihood fit, the estimate of the cut score is 38.59 with standard error 2.32. It is of interest that an examinee used in the standard setting exercise scored 40 points (close to the cut score) but received passes from all but one expert. Figure 9.3 presents a graphical summary of the results.

TABLE 9.3. The data for the standard setting exercise for the Physical Education test, Part I.

Reader						Examinee							Passes
	1	2	3	4	5	6	7	8	9	10	11	12	
Score	60	56	52	49	47	40	38	37	32	30	15	14	
1	1	1	1	1	1	1	1	1	0	0	0	0	8
2	0	1	1	1	1	1	1	0	0	0	0	0	6
3	1	1	1	1	1	1	0	0	0	0	0	0	6
4	1	1	1	1	1	1	1	0	0	1	0	0	8
5	1	1	1	1	1	1	1	1	0	0	0	0	8
6	1	1	1	1	1	1	1	1	0	1	0	0	9
7	1	1	1	1	0	1	1	1	0	0	0	0	7
8	1	1	1	0	1	1	0	0	0	0	0	0	5
9	1	1	0	0	1	1	1	0	0	1	0	0	6
10	0	1	0	0	1	0	0	0	0	0	0	0	2
11	1	1	1	0	0	1	0	0	0	1	0	0	5
Passes	9	11	9	7	9	10	7	4	0	4	0	0	70

Note: The same layout as in Table 9.1 is used.

In rating Part II, the same 11 experts were engaged using 13 selected examinees. The pass/fail ratings are inconsistent with the scores to a considerable degree. For instance, the fourth lowest scoring examinee in the exercise (25 points) was rated as 'pass' by all but one expert, better than the highest scoring examinee (56 points, three 'fails'). Also, the fourth and fifth examinees (50 and 48 points, respectively) received 'pass' ratings from only about half the experts, whereas the sixth examinee (42 points) was rated as 'pass' by all the experts. The data are displayed in Table 9.4.

The GLS and the maximum likelihood regression fits are

$$\begin{matrix} -1.75 & + & 0.047x \\ (0.44) & & (0.011) \end{matrix}$$

and

$$\begin{matrix} -1.85 & + & 0.062x, \\ (0.53) & & (0.014) \end{matrix}$$

respectively. The scores x are in the range 10–60. Unlike in the other two standard setting exercises, here the regression slope is rather shallow. In this case, the change in the estimate of the slope from GLS to the maximum likelihood has a sizeable impact on the estimate of the cut score. Based on GLS, the cut score is estimated as 37.24 (standard error 3.47),

Physical Education Part I

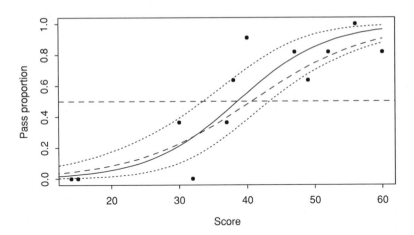

FIGURE 9.3. The logistic regression fit and pointwise confidence band for Physical Education, Part I. Each point represents an examinee. The horizontal axis is the score of the examinee and the vertical is the proportion of passes given by the experts. The GLS regression fit is drawn by a dashed line.

while the maximum likelihood solution yields 29.84 (4.10). The bias correction reduces this figure to 29.62. The estimate of the severity variation is 0.52 (standard error 0.30). Figure 9.4 presents a graphical summary of the results.

This example demonstrates that the GLS and the maximum likelihood solutions can differ substantially. It seems that the shallow regression slope and the inconsistency of the expert's decisions brought about this difference. Certainly, the shallow slope exacerbates the difference between the two solutions measured parallel to the x-axis. Reexamination of the scoring rules as well as of the experts' decisions may uncover that the inconsistency is due to some of the items that certain experts regarded as important and others did not.

The scope for diagnostic procedures in standard setting exercises, as with binary data in general, is rather limited. Since the outcomes take on only two distinct values, they cannot contain any outliers. However, outlying experts may be of considerable interest. They are easily identified by the extreme number of 'passes' or 'fails' they have awarded. Their exclusion from the exercise reduces the severity variance and makes the standard setting appear to have higher quality. Substantive considerations, such as evidence that the expert does not belong to the designated population or that he/she has departed from the protocol, should accompany a decision to exclude the expert.

TABLE 9.4. The data for the standard setting exercise for the Physical Education test, Part II.

Reader	Examinee													Passes
	1	2	3	4	5	6	7	8	9	10	11	12	13	
Score	56	55	55	50	48	42	35	32	27	25	21	15	11	
1	1	1	1	1	1	1	1	1	1	1	0	1	0	11
2	1	1	1	1	0	1	1	1	0	1	0	0	0	8
3	1	1	1	0	0	1	1	0	0	1	1	0	0	7
4	0	1	1	0	1	1	0	0	1	1	1	0	1	8
5	1	1	1	1	1	1	0	1	0	1	0	1	1	10
6	1	1	1	1	0	1	0	0	0	1	0	1	1	8
7	1	1	1	1	1	1	1	1	0	1	0	0	0	9
8	1	1	1	0	1	1	0	1	0	1	0	0	0	7
9	1	1	1	0	1	1	1	0	1	0	0	0	0	7
10	0	1	1	0	0	1	0	0	0	1	0	0	0	4
11	0	1	1	0	0	1	0	0	0	1	0	0	0	4
Passes	8	11	11	5	6	11	5	5	3	10	2	3	3	83

Notes: The same layout as in Tables 9.1 and 9.3 is used. The same experts were engaged as in Table 9.3.

Throughout, we assumed that the test scores x involve no measurement error. Usually, this is not a realistic assumption. Multiple imputations, as applied in Chapters 7 and 8, provide a simple prescription for assessing the impact of the measurement error when its variance is available (or estimated). We replace each realized score with several draws (imputed values) from its posterior distribution of the corresponding true scores and carry out separate analyses for each set of imputed values. The results are then averaged over the analyses, with the obvious adjustment for the estimates of sampling variation. The impact of the measurement error is much weaker than in an analysis of ordinal (continuous) data because each elementary outcome ('pass' or 'fail') is itself associated with a lot of uncertainty.

More complex standard-setting exercises can be organized by employing incomplete designs. For instance, the experts may assess non-identical (but overlapping) sets of response sheets. The methods presented in this chapter carry over to such designs when non-informative assignment of response sheets to experts is applied.

Physical Education Part II

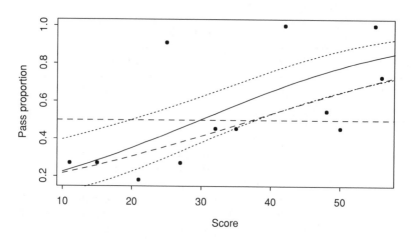

FIGURE 9.4. The logistic regression fit and pointwise confidence band for Physical Education, Part II. Each point represents an examinee. The horizontal axis is the score of the examinee and the vertical the proportion of passes given by the experts. The GLS regression fit is drawn by a dashed line.

9.5   Summary

Data from three standard setting exercises were analysed using the logistic regression model that assumes interchangeable experts, that is, no variation in severity, and the results were compared with those obtained by using logistic regression with random coefficients representing differences in severity. Although substantially different regression fits were obtained in each case, the differences are of importance only in one case in which the pass/fail decisions are very inconsistent with the scores.

The analyses indicate that the experts tend to apply vastly different standards. Some would pass only a small fraction of the examinees, whereas others would fail only a small fraction. Confirming intuition, the estimation of the cut score is least precise and most problematic when there is a lot of inconsistency between the scores and the experts' verdicts.

Simulation studies reported in Longford (1993a) indicate that the GLS estimator for the logistic regression model with random coefficients is much less efficient than the maximum likelihood estimator when the between-cluster variation is substantial. Application of the maximum likelihood in standard setting exercises improves the efficiency of the estimator of the cut score, reduces the bias in estimating the sampling variation of this estimator, and provides a measure of the between-expert differences in severity.

Logistic regression with random coefficients is often applied for much larger datasets than those analysed in this chapter. For such data, it is meaningful to consider models with a much more complex pattern of between-cluster differences. For such models, the method described in Section 9.3 requires evaluation of a large number of multidimensional integrals. This may be computationally infeasible. There are a number of approaches to approximate maximum likelihood estimation with non-normal random coefficient models. An approximation to the log-likelihood, which involves no integration, can be derived directly; see Longford (1994a). A computationally appealing method, called the generalized estimating equations, due to Zeger and Liang (1986), defines the estimate of the regression vector by the GLS formula

$$\hat{\beta} = \left(\mathbf{X}^{\top} \mathbf{V}^{-1} \mathbf{X} \right)^{-1} \mathbf{X}^{\top} \mathbf{V}^{-1} \mathbf{y} \tag{9.13}$$

where the matrix $\mathbf{V}$ is, typically, a block-diagonal matrix, with the patterns in the diagonal blocks described by the covariance structure parameters. Since these parameters are estimated, equation (9.13) has to be applied iteratively, each time with the updated estimate of $\mathbf{V}$.

The EM algorithmic approach provides yet another avenue to fitting random coefficient models. Their drawback, however, is slow convergence and the fact that in this approach certain conditional expectations have to be evaluated numerically unless an approximation is applied. See Laird and Ware (1982) for details. Fitzmaurice, Laird, and Rotnitzky (1993) review methods for fitting random coefficient models for discrete data with a focus on longitudinal analysis.

10

Incomplete longitudinal data

10.1 Introduction

In most statistical applications, we expect that a set of relevant variables is available for each subject. However, human subjects are notorious for imperfect cooperation with surveys, especially when they have little or no stake in the outcome of the data collection exercise. Pervasive examples of imperfect cooperation are failure to answer an item from the background questionnaire and, more generally, failure to adhere to the protocol of the survey. For instance, examinees may lose motivation half-way through the test and abandon the test without attending to a segment of items, or they may mark the responses to these items arbitrarily. More radical forms of incomplete cooperation are not turning up for the appointment and rejecting the approach of the data collector. Such instances are not uncommon because educational surveys typically demand a substantial commitment, in terms of time and mental effort, from the examinees. Our concern in this chapter is not with alleviating these problems, such as providing incentives to examinees and improving the presentation of the survey instruments, but rather with facing the problem of missing data as a fact of life and devising methods of analysis that make full use of data from all subjects, however incomplete their records may be.

Nowhere is the problem of missing data more acute than in longitudinal surveys, where subjects are contacted on several occasions over a period of months or years. Some subjects may become unavailable due to circumstances not related to their performance at the previous contacts with the study (moved out of the area, deceased), may refuse cooperation directly because of a previous contact (embarrassment with the performance or some other lasting unpleasant impression), or may be unwilling to take part in the study more than a very limited number of times. Of course, a myriad of everyday reasons also contribute to missingness.

Most statistical methods for analysis of longitudinal data rely on the rectangular structure of the data; that is, the value of each variable is available for every subject. Typically, the same outcome variable or vector is measured on each occasion because the changes in this variable (vector) over time are of interest. The observation of a subject at one time point, however accurate, can at best provide only a snapshot of a continually developing skill, knowledge, or ability. Yet, development of these traits is a central theme of much educational research. For instance, the effectiveness of a learning programme cannot be assessed without observing a sample of individuals both at the beginning and at the end of the programme.

Longitudinal analysis is indispensable in studying mental, academic, and physical development of children and young adults, even when the subjects take part in no specific programme. The school, home, neighbourhood, mass media, and other social institutions can be regarded as a complex treatment containing several interacting components.

Keeping track of the subjects in a longitudinal study requires considerable resources, and the return for the effort may be less than satisfactory when the original sample is eroded by attrition and incomplete cooperation. Given these problems, the best that can be accomplished by statistical analysis is to make full use of the available data. This includes inferring from the available data what the conclusions of the analysis would have been had each subject cooperated fully.

The next section outlines approaches to dealing with incomplete data and discusses their advantages and drawbacks. Section 10.3 deals with longitudinal analysis and motivates the EM algorithm for efficient use of incomplete records, derived in Section 10.4. Section 10.5 describes the data from the National Education Longitudinal Survey (NELS) and the purpose of the survey. The data are then analysed in Section 10.6. The chapter concludes with a summary.

10.2   Informative missingness

The data from a subject are called a *record*. A record may contain some missing values (say, the subject did not respond to some of the questions); such a record is called *incomplete*. A record with no missing data is said to be *complete*. In a typical longitudinal dataset, a record may consist of several sections. Data collected at each time point form a section. In addition, some data may be constant over time, such as socioeconomic background, sex, and date of birth, and so the time point when they were collected is not relevant. Such variables form another section.

There are two conceptually simple approaches to dealing with incomplete records. When there are only a few such records, they could be omitted from the analysis. This approach is most unsatisfactory when a lot of records are almost complete because then a lot of data are discarded. In general, discarding subjects from the study is problematic because the remaining subjects may be a non-representative sample of the studied population. A simple example is, say, a study of income of the adult population. If we ignore the homeless and illiterate, because they cannot complete the questionnaire asking for their home address, we are likely to underrepresent subjects in the lowest income category. As a consequence, the mean income would be overestimated.

An alternative approach is to fill in some judiciously selected values in place of the missing data. The obvious choice would be the sample mean of all the available values for that variable. Several problems immediately arise. First, if such 'completed' or *imputed* data were used in place of the missing data, the variances of the variables would be underestimated because the imputation has contributed to the centre of the distribution. Second, the completed data would appear to have more information than they really contain because the imputed data would be treated on par with the data obtained from the subjects. Third, the studied variables are often highly correlated, and so the values of the available variables hold some clues about the missing data. For instance, imputing the average income for the subjects who did not volunteer the information may result in a substantial overestimate of the mean income.

In Chapters 7 and 8, we came across multiple imputations as a method for completing datasets and yet preserving the uncertainty associated with missingness. In this chapter, we consider a computationally less extensive method that avoids generating large datasets due to multiply imputed values.

Suppose the values of the variables are collected in chronological order. Consider the subsample of subjects who have complete records after the first p variables have been collected. This subsample can be further split into two subsamples according to the availability of the value on variable $p+1$. In the most optimistic, and yet realistic, scenario, these two subsamples represent populations with the same conditional distribution; that is, given the data from the first p components, missingness of the $(p+1)$st component will occur at random. Such a process of missingness is referred to as *missing at random*. Its advantage is that the missing data can, in principle, be estimated without bias because their distribution depends on the complete data only through the available data.

Missing at random can be regarded as an extreme case. Non-cooperation of some subjects may be related to the values of the variables they fail to provide only through the values of the variables they have provided or will provide in future. In the other extreme scenario, the subjects who did not cooperate in the observation of a variable would have had values completely different from what would be expected based on the values of the available variables. For instance, a subject with high scores on the history tests administered on the previous occasions did not cooperate at the latest time point because he/she knew that he/she would be given a low score this time. Fortunately, this is quite an unrealistic scenario because the subject is unlikely to assess his/her future performance with a lot of precision (not knowing the content of the test), or indeed, remember the performance from a year or so ago! However, some more subtle and difficult to understand processes may be at work, which make the patterns of non-cooperation depart from missingness at random. The data at hand provide no clues about these processes, and so the assumptions of missingness at random, routinely adopted in analyses of incomplete data as well as in this chapter, are untestable by formal statistical procedures based on the available data. Protection against substantial violation of this assumption is provided by collecting variables relevant to the studied processes, so that after conditioning on them, the processes of missingness are, *hopefully*, random.

The next section gives an outline of longitudinal analysis assuming complete data.

10.3   Longitudinal analysis

Suppose variables $p = 1, \ldots, P$ are observed on subjects $i = 1, \ldots, n$. Let the resulting data matrix be $\mathbf{Y}$ $(n \times P)$. Its ith row $\mathbf{y}_i$ is the vector of outcomes for subject i, and its column $\mathbf{Y}_p$ is the vector of the values of variable p. For simplicity, we assume that the data from the subjects are a random sample from a multivariate normal distribution, $\mathcal{N}_P(\boldsymbol{\mu}, \boldsymbol{\Sigma})$. The P components may be one from each time point or some other configuration (for instance, four test scores from each of three time points). The population average increases of the scores are functions of the vector $\boldsymbol{\mu}$, and $\boldsymbol{\Sigma}$ describes the covariance structure of the scores.

It may be appropriate to define a parametrization (model) for both $\boldsymbol{\mu}$ and $\boldsymbol{\Sigma}$, more parsimonious than using P and $P(P+1)/2$ parameters, respectively, especially when the sample size is small to moderate. For large-scale surveys, such as NELS, analysed in Section 10.5, such parametrization is not necessary, and, in any case, a formal hypothesis test is likely to reject any such model in favour of a less parsimonious one because of the high precision of all the estimates. It is more practical to explore the estimates of the mean vector and of the variance matrix and generate hypotheses about the underlying processes.

In many contexts, the differences among the subpopulations defined by background variables are of interest, or it is desirable to adjust the outcomes for these variables. Multivariate regression provides a general framework for incorporating such information. Let $\mathbf{X}$ be the $n \times R$ matrix of such variables, defined for the subjects. In multivariate regression, the outcomes are related to the background variables through the model

$$\mathbf{Y} = \mathbf{XB} + \boldsymbol{\Xi},\tag{10.1}$$

where $\mathbf{B}$ is an $R \times P$ matrix of parameters and $\boldsymbol{\Xi}$ is a matrix, the rows of which form a random sample from $\mathcal{N}_P(\mathbf{0}, \boldsymbol{\Sigma})$. Denote the pth row and column of $\mathbf{B}$ by $\mathbf{B}_{p\cdot}$ and $\mathbf{B}_{\cdot p}$, respectively. The model in (10.1) is, in essence, a set of P regressions, $\mathbf{Y}_p = \mathbf{XB}_{\cdot p}$, sharing the same set of regressor variables in $\mathbf{X}$ and having model deviations ($\boldsymbol{\Xi}$) correlated within subjects. As in univariate regression, let the first column of $\mathbf{X}$ be the vector of ones, $\mathbf{1}_n$, so that $\mathbf{B}_{1\cdot}$ represents the intercept.

The parameter matrices $\mathbf{B}$ and $\boldsymbol{\Sigma}$ can be estimated by multivariate least squares:

$$\begin{aligned}
\hat{\mathbf{B}} &= \left(\mathbf{X}^\top \mathbf{X}\right)^{-1} \mathbf{X}^\top \mathbf{Y}, \\
\hat{\boldsymbol{\Sigma}} &= \frac{1}{n-P}\left(\mathbf{Y}^\top \mathbf{Y} - \mathbf{Y}^\top \mathbf{X}\hat{\mathbf{B}}\right).
\end{aligned}\tag{10.2}$$

When the subjects are associated with sampling weights, w_i, these estimators are adapted by computing all the cross-products in a weighted fashion,

$$\begin{aligned}
\hat{\mathbf{B}} &= \left(\mathbf{X}^\top \mathbf{W}\mathbf{X}\right)^{-1} \mathbf{X}^\top \mathbf{W}\mathbf{Y}, \\
\hat{\boldsymbol{\Sigma}} &= \frac{1}{w_+ - P}\left(\mathbf{Y}^\top \mathbf{W}\mathbf{Y} - \mathbf{Y}^\top \mathbf{W}\mathbf{X}\hat{\mathbf{B}}\right),
\end{aligned}\tag{10.3}$$

where $\mathbf{W}$ is the $n \times n$ diagonal matrix of weights, $(\mathbf{W})_{ii} = w_i$, and $w_+ = w_1 + \ldots + w_n = \text{tr}(\mathbf{W})$ is the total of the weights. We assume throughout that the weights w_i are normalized so that their total and the total of their squares coincide. The same normalization was used in Chapters 7 and 8.

When the survey employs a clustered or stratified clustered sampling design, using, say, schools or classrooms as clusters, the assumption of independence of the subjects may not be realistic because, reflecting the shared environment, the responses of the subjects within the clusters may be more homogeneous than those of the subjects at large. This phenomenon can be effectively accommodated in the model in (10.2) by decomposing the random terms in $\boldsymbol{\Xi}$ into their cluster- and subject-level components. Let $\boldsymbol{\varepsilon}_{ij}$ be the vector of model deviations for subject i from cluster j; this is a row of the matrix $\boldsymbol{\Xi}$. This vector is decomposed as

$$\boldsymbol{\varepsilon}_{ij} = \boldsymbol{\gamma}_j + \boldsymbol{\delta}_{ij},$$

where $\{\gamma_j\}_j$ and $\{\delta_{ij}\}_{ij}$ are two independent random samples from the centred normal distributions with respective variance matrices $\Sigma^{(2)}$ and $\Sigma^{(1)}$. Then the variance matrix of the vector of observations on a subject is $\Sigma^{(1)} + \Sigma^{(2)}$, but the conditional (within-cluster) variance matrix, given the cluster-level vector γ_j, is $\Sigma^{(1)}$. This model is the multivariate version of the models considered in Chapters 7 and 8.

10.4   EM algorithm

The EM algorithm is a general prescription for analysis of incomplete data. The term 'EM algorithm' was coined by Dempster, Laird, and Rubin (1977), although its principles have been used by many statisticians since long ago; see, for instance, Hartley (1958) and Orchard and Woodbury (1972). The letters 'E' and 'M' stand for the two steps of the algorithm: expectation and maximization. In fact, the algorithm is iterative and each iteration consists of these two steps.

The basic idea of the EM algorithm is that the available data are embedded in a larger set of *complete* data for which maximum likelihood estimation would be relatively simple. For instance, in the case of longitudinal data analysed in Section 10.5, the natural complete dataset would be realized if all the subjects cooperated fully. The statistics required for maximum likelihood estimation with such data are various (weighted) totals and cross-products. They depend on the missing data through a small number of statistics. The weighted totals are

$$\mathbf{Y}_k^\top \mathbf{w} = \mathbf{Y}_k^{(a,k)^\top} \mathbf{w}^{(a,k)} + \mathbf{Y}_k^{(m,k)^\top} \mathbf{w}^{(m,k)} ,$$

where the superscripts $^{(a,k)}$ and $^{(m,k)}$ stand for the subsets of subjects for whom the variable y_k is available and missing, respectively. We estimate the statistic $\mathbf{Y}_k^{(m,k)^\top} \mathbf{w}^{(m,k)}$ by its conditional expectation, given the estimated model parameters and the available data:

$$\widehat{\mathbf{Y}_k^\top \mathbf{w}} = \mathbf{Y}_k^{(a,k)^\top} \mathbf{w}^{(a,k)} + \mathbf{E}\left(\mathbf{Y}_k^{(m,k)^\top} \mathbf{w}^{(m,k)} \mid \hat{\boldsymbol{\mu}}, \hat{\Sigma}, ; \mathbf{Y} \right) .$$

This is a linear function of the missing data, and so the conditional expectation above can be evaluated as the linear combination of the recordwise conditional expectations.

Similarly, we decompose the cross-products in the weighted sampling variance matrix for the complete data

$$\frac{1}{\operatorname{tr}(\mathbf{W}) - 1} \left\{ \mathbf{Y}^\top \mathbf{W} \mathbf{Y} - \operatorname{tr}(\mathbf{W}) \overline{\mathbf{Y}}^\top \overline{\mathbf{Y}} \right\}$$

into its components that depend solely on the available data, on the missing data, and those that require both available and missing data:

$$\mathbf{Y}_k^\top \mathbf{W} \mathbf{Y}_h = \mathbf{Y}_k^{(a,kh)^\top} \mathbf{W}^{(a,kh)} \mathbf{Y}_h^{(a,kh)} + \mathbf{Y}_k^{(a,k;m,h)^\top} \mathbf{W}^{(a,k;m,h)} \mathbf{Y}_h^{(a,k;m,h)}$$

$$+ \mathbf{Y}_k^{(a,h;m,k)^\top} \mathbf{W}^{(a,h;m,k)} \mathbf{Y}_h^{(a,h;m,k)}$$

$$+ \mathbf{Y}_k^{(m,kh)^\top} \mathbf{W}^{(m,kh)} \mathbf{Y}_h^{(m,kh)},$$

where the superscripts $^{(a,kh)}$, $^{(m,kh)}$, and $^{(a,k;m,h)}$ stand for the respective subsets of subjects for whom y_k and y_h are both available, both missing, and y_k is available but y_h is missing. The first term depends only on available data, and so it is available. The second and third terms are linear functions of the missing data, and so they can be estimated as the same linear functions of the conditional expectations of the missing data, given the available data. The fourth term is a quadratic function of the missing data, and so its conditional expectation is somewhat more involved. The elementary contribution, $w_i y_{k,i} y_{h,i}$, is estimated by its conditional expectation as

$$w_i \operatorname{cov}(y_{k,i}, y_{h,i} \mid \hat{\boldsymbol{\mu}}, \hat{\boldsymbol{\Sigma}}; \mathbf{y}_i) + w_i \mathbf{E}(y_{k,i} \mid \hat{\boldsymbol{\mu}}, \hat{\boldsymbol{\Sigma}}; \mathbf{y}_i) \mathbf{E}(y_{h,i} \mid \hat{\boldsymbol{\mu}}, \hat{\boldsymbol{\Sigma}}; \mathbf{y}_i).$$

In summary, the EM algorithm consists of *maximizing* the likelihood, in our case computing the sampling means and (co)variances, preceded by computing the conditional *expectations* of the statistics that depend on the missing data. These steps have to be iterated because the conditional expectations depend on model parameters which are updated in the M-step. Many applications of the EM algorithm are notorious for slow convergence. Intuitively, convergence is slower the larger the fraction of missing data or, more generally, of the information associated with the missing data.

The choice of the complete dataset is up to the analyst, and convenience of the resulting likelihood maximization is the main consideration, because that procedure will have to be carried out several times. For a given incomplete dataset, smaller complete datasets are preferable because less missing information results in faster convergence.

For completeness, we give the equations for the conditional expectations and variance matrices required for the E-step of the EM algorithm. Let a_i and m_i be the respective vectors of indices of the available and the missing data for subject i. For instance, $\boldsymbol{\Sigma}_{m_i a_i}$ is the submatrix of $\boldsymbol{\Sigma}$ formed by its missing-index rows and available-index columns for subject i. The conditional distribution of the missing data given the available data for subject i is normal with the mean vector

$$\boldsymbol{\mu}_{m_i} + \boldsymbol{\Sigma}_{m_i a_i} \boldsymbol{\Sigma}_{a_i a_i}^{-1} (\mathbf{y}_{a_i} - \boldsymbol{\mu}_{a_i}) \tag{10.4}$$

and the variance matrix

$$\boldsymbol{\Sigma}_{m_i m_i} - \boldsymbol{\Sigma}_{m_i a_i} \boldsymbol{\Sigma}_{a_i a_i}^{-1} \boldsymbol{\Sigma}_{a_i m_i}. \tag{10.5}$$

Subjects with the same pattern of missingness share the same conditional variance matrix of the missing data, and so it is computationally more efficient to evaluate the conditional expectations of the required missing-data statistics separately for each pattern of missingness.

10.5 Application

The National Education Longitudinal Survey (NELS) administered four tests to a national sample of eighth-graders in 1988, and then further sets of four tests to the same subjects in 1990 (as tenth-graders) and in 1992 (as twelfth-graders). The domains of the four tests were Reading Comprehension, Mathematics, Science, and History/Citizenship/Geography. A probability weighted clustered sampling design was used, with schools as clusters.

In 1988, the sample comprised 16 488 students, 8349 women and 8140 men, from 1011 schools, with the schools represented in the sample by between 1 and 49 students. However, by 1990, most of these students attended different (high) schools as tenth-graders, and so the number of combinations of secondary and high schools is several thousand. The participation and cooperation of the students in 1988 was very good, but in 1990, and in 1992 in particular, fewer students were tested. Many non-cooperating students were unavailable on the day(s) when a set of four tests was scheduled, and so the corresponding set of four scores is missing. For instance, 3737 students had no scores from the 1992 follow-up; 3002 of them had all 8 scores from 1988 and 1990. Table 10.1 summarizes the extent of missingness.

The sample size appears to be so large that we could use listwise deletion and reduce our attention to the 11 467 students (69.5 percent of the sample) with complete records from all 12 tests. Of the $16\,488 \times 12 \doteq 198\,000$ test scores, about 176 000 (88.9 percent) are observed; it would appear somewhat frivolous to exclude $176\,000 - 12 \times 11\,467 \doteq 38\,400$ scores (19.4 percent), as a matter of statistical and computational convenience. Indeed, the sampling variation of the estimates may not be a concern. However, the bias incurred by excluding such a large proportion of the sample, very likely an informative subsample, may be substantial.

The subjects in the sample are associated with sampling weights, and so it is more appropriate to consider the effective sample size, as in Chapters 7 and 8. The sampling weights are in the range 0.24–73.88, with mean 1.80 (median 1.47) and standard deviation 2.25. The large variation of the sampling weights is reflected in the reduced effective sample size. The effective sample size for the 16 488 subjects is 6426.4, and for the sample obtained by listwise deletion, it is merely 4890.9.

TABLE 10.1. Summary of missing test scores in NELS.

		Missingness in NELS		
	Year	No missing	Some missing	All missing
	1988	15 778	126	584
	1990	15 265	286	937
	1992	12 526	225	3737
1988 and 1990		14 643	1794	51
1990 and 1992		11 928	4065	495
1988, 1990, and 1992		11 467	4988	33

Note: The total number of students (total within each row) is 16 488.

10.6   Estimation

To illustrate the informative nature of missingness, we consider three simple estimators of the mean vector and of the variance matrix of the four scores in the 1992 follow-up. First, the estimates based on the 11 467 complete records for all three years are

$$\begin{pmatrix} 33.24 \\ 48.41 \\ 23.51 \\ 34.84 \end{pmatrix} \begin{pmatrix} 99.77 & 104.13 & 44.32 & 40.12 \\ 104.13 & 203.43 & 68.63 & 54.90 \\ 44.32 & 68.63 & 37.89 & 25.35 \\ 40.12 & 54.90 & 25.35 & 28.63 \end{pmatrix}.$$

Next we consider the 12 526 subjects with complete records from 1992. The corresponding estimates are

$$\begin{pmatrix} 32.80 \\ 47.66 \\ 23.22 \\ 34.59 \end{pmatrix} \begin{pmatrix} 102.70 & 107.39 & 45.82 & 41.35 \\ 107.39 & 207.91 & 70.48 & 56.80 \\ 45.82 & 70.48 & 38.58 & 26.03 \\ 41.35 & 56.80 & 26.03 & 29.30 \end{pmatrix}.$$

Each component of the estimate of the mean is reduced, and each element of the estimated variance matrix is increased, although the pattern of the means and correlations is largely unchanged. However, this should be regarded as a warning; supplementing the sample by just over 9 percent of the data brought about perceptible changes. What would happen if we enlarged the sample by another 30 percent?

Another simple improvement on estimating the means and (co)variances is achieved by considering all the subjects for whom the required data are observed. Thus, each estimated mean is based on a different sample. However, these samples have substantial overlaps; in fact, data from additional

TABLE 10.2. Estimates of the population means and standard deviations.

	Subject areas			
Year	Reading	Mathematics	Science	History
1988	26.45	35.14	18.44	29.25
	8.61	*11.79*	*4.84*	*4.60*
1990	29.69	42.10	21.03	31.00
	10.13	*13.96*	*6.05*	*5.24*
1992	31.92	46.28	22.64	34.11
	10.27	*14.62*	*6.29*	*5.50*

Note: Each cell contains the estimate of the mean (at the top) and the estimate of the standard deviation (at the bottom, in italics).

191, 187, 104, and 45 subjects only are used for computing the estimates for the respective means of Reading, Mathematics, Science, and History scores in 1992. The estimates of the means and of the variance matrix are

$$
\begin{pmatrix} 32.75 \\ 47.59 \\ 23.20 \\ 34.58 \end{pmatrix}
\begin{pmatrix} 103.07 & 108.52 & 46.59 & 42.93 \\ 108.52 & 208.34 & 71.46 & 58.56 \\ 46.59 & 71.46 & 38.64 & 26.65 \\ 42.93 & 58.56 & 26.65 & 29.28 \end{pmatrix}.
$$

Of course, the changes are only slight, because only a few data points are added. However, the trend of decreasing means and increasing (co)variances persists (with one exception, element [4,4]). It seems that the students who tend to miss out on tests in the survey have lower ability in each subject area. Similar patterns can be observed for 1988 and 1990.

Next we apply the EM algorithm. A starting solution is required for the model parameters μ and Σ. For simplicity, we set it to the estimates based on the 11 467 subjects with complete records. The E-step loops over the patterns of missingness and computes the conditional means and the common conditional variance matrix of the missing data for records with each pattern. This avoids a great deal of duplication since the 5021 incomplete records involve only 104 patterns of missingness.

The iterations of the EM algorithm converge very fast to a stationary solution. The first iteration reduces the estimates of the means by between 0.55 and 2.08. The second iteration alters the estimates by no more than ±0.035, and the corrections by the subsequent iterations are even smaller.

The estimate of the variance matrix converges somewhat slower. The corrections for the estimates of the variances and covariances at the first iteration are in the range 0.40 to 9.11, at the second iteration −0.19 to

0.90, and after eight iterations the estimates change by less than 0.001. The resulting estimates of the population means are given in Table 10.2. The means increase over time. This cannot be interpreted as evidence of domain knowledge improving over time (although that is very likely) because of the arbitrariness of the scales of the tests. In NELS, the test scores are equated so as to enable such comparisons, but the equating procedures are associated with a lot of uncertainty. Of course, comparisons of the nominal scores across the four domains are meaningless, even within years.

Instead of the estimate of the variance matrix, it is more effective to present the estimated standard deviations and the correlation matrix. The estimated standard deviations are given in Table 10.2 (in italics). The estimated correlation matrix is

$$
\begin{pmatrix}
1.00 & 0.71 & 0.71 & 0.73 & 0.80 & 0.69 & 0.67 & 0.68 & 0.74 & 0.67 & 0.64 & 0.67 \\
0.71 & 1.00 & 0.73 & 0.69 & 0.69 & 0.88 & 0.73 & 0.66 & 0.66 & 0.83 & 0.70 & 0.65 \\
0.71 & 0.73 & 1.00 & 0.73 & 0.68 & 0.70 & 0.74 & 0.68 & 0.65 & 0.68 & 0.72 & 0.67 \\
0.73 & 0.69 & 0.73 & 1.00 & 0.71 & 0.68 & 0.69 & 0.76 & 0.67 & 0.66 & 0.66 & 0.72 \\
0.80 & 0.69 & 0.68 & 0.71 & 1.00 & 0.76 & 0.75 & 0.76 & 0.82 & 0.73 & 0.70 & 0.72 \\
0.69 & 0.88 & 0.70 & 0.68 & 0.76 & 1.00 & 0.79 & 0.72 & 0.72 & 0.93 & 0.76 & 0.70 \\
0.67 & 0.73 & 0.74 & 0.69 & 0.75 & 0.79 & 1.00 & 0.77 & 0.70 & 0.78 & 0.81 & 0.73 \\
0.68 & 0.66 & 0.68 & 0.76 & 0.76 & 0.72 & 0.77 & 1.00 & 0.72 & 0.71 & 0.71 & 0.79 \\
0.74 & 0.66 & 0.65 & 0.67 & 0.82 & 0.72 & 0.70 & 0.72 & 1.00 & 0.74 & 0.73 & 0.76 \\
0.67 & 0.83 & 0.68 & 0.66 & 0.73 & 0.93 & 0.78 & 0.71 & 0.74 & 1.00 & 0.79 & 0.73 \\
0.64 & 0.70 & 0.72 & 0.66 & 0.70 & 0.76 & 0.81 & 0.71 & 0.73 & 0.79 & 1.00 & 0.78 \\
0.67 & 0.65 & 0.67 & 0.72 & 0.72 & 0.70 & 0.73 & 0.79 & 0.76 & 0.73 & 0.78 & 1.00
\end{pmatrix}
$$

The gaps delineate the three time points. Alternatively, the correlation matrix could be presented by clumping together the triplets of scores for the same domain. The correlations within these triplets are somewhat higher. For instance, the correlation matrix for Reading Comprehension (rows and columns 1, 5, and 9) is

$$
\begin{pmatrix}
1.00 & 0.80 & 0.74 \\
0.80 & 1.00 & 0.82 \\
0.74 & 0.82 & 1.00
\end{pmatrix}.
$$

The variance matrix Σ has two components: the measurement error variance matrix and the variance matrix of the true scores. The former is estimated from half-forms by the method described in Chapter 6. The issues of missingness in estimating the measurement error variances can be ignored because the students could not identify the half-forms. The estimated measurement error variances are given in Table 10.3. Note that they are quite consistent within the subject areas. Assuming that the measurement errors are independent, the variance matrix for the underlying ('true') scores is obtained by subtracting the measurement error variances from the diagonal of the estimated variance matrix for the observed scores. The resulting matrix may not be positive definite because all the estimates are subject

TABLE 10.3. Estimates of the measurement error variances in NELS.

Year	Subject areas			
	Reading	Mathematics	Science	History
1988	7.82	7.87	3.41	1.77
1990	7.45	6.95	3.66	2.14
1992	8.24	6.51	3.74	2.36

to uncertainty. The eigenvalues of the estimated observed-score variance matrix are

$$
\begin{matrix}
800.3 & 69.20 & 35.98 & 22.13 & 19.54 & 15.97 \\
11.53 & 10.23 & 7.35 & 6.50 & 5.08 & 4.53
\end{matrix} \quad . \tag{10.6}
$$

The eigenvalues of the estimated true-score variance matrix are

$$
\begin{matrix}
793.7 & 62.01 & 28.89 & 17.96 & 12.45 & 8.79 \\
7.29 & 4.53 & 3.78 & 3.01 & 2.33 & 1.69
\end{matrix} \quad . \tag{10.7}
$$

It is instructive to inspect the conditional variance matrices because they indicate the extent of information about missing data contained in the available data. For instance, the conditional variance matrix for the scores at the third time point (1992), given the scores at the first two time points (1988 and 1990) is

$$
\begin{pmatrix}
29.56 & 7.58 & 5.21 & 5.22 \\
5.22 & 28.88 & 5.69 & 4.42 \\
5.21 & 5.69 & 11.28 & 3.81 \\
5.22 & 4.42 & 3.81 & 9.25
\end{pmatrix} ;
$$

the variances are 28, 14, 28, and 31 percent or the respective unconditional variances. The radical reduction of the variances as a result of conditioning indicates that the available data contain a lot of information about the missing data. Even when most of the scores are missing for a subject, the few available scores are informative about the missing scores, although to a lesser extent than in the example discussed.

Devotees of factor analysis are interested in approximating either of these variance matrices by a sum of a diagonal matrix and a matrix of small rank. Since the eigenvalues cannot be naturally split into those that almost vanish and those that are large, and the sample size is very large, no parsimonious factor analysis model is likely to be accepted by a formal hypothesis test. Graphical models (Whittaker, 1990) provide another general approach to searching for patterns in variance matrices. The first step in this approach is to inspect the inverse of the correlation matrix, $\mathbf{R}^{-1}$, for small entries. The results are entirely as expected; the elements of $\mathbf{R}^{-1}$ corresponding to rows and columns from different years and different domains are all smaller than 0.025 in absolute value. On the other hand, some entries corresponding to domains in the same year are greater than 0.10 in absolute value. This implies that two scores from different subject areas (A and B, say) and different years (K and L) are (nearly) conditionally independent given either the score from subject area A in year L or the score from subject area B in year K.

10.6.1 Variation in growth

Growth of knowledge can be assessed from longitudinal data only if the measurements of a variable refer to the same scale at each time point. We demonstrate here that this assumption is in conflict with the assumption that the knowledge of most students grows over time.

The fitted distribution for the scores on Reading Comprehension is normal with mean (26.45, 29.69, 31.92) and variance matrix

$$\begin{pmatrix} 74.08 & 70.09 & 65.76 \\ 70.09 & 102.57 & 85.73 \\ 65.76 & 85.73 & 105.52 \end{pmatrix},$$

The estimated measurement error variances for the scores at time points 1, 2, and 3 are 7.82, 7.45, and 8.24, respectively, and so the variance matrix for the true scores is

$$\begin{pmatrix} 68.26 & 70.09 & 65.76 \\ 70.09 & 95.12 & 85.73 \\ 65.76 & 85.73 & 97.28 \end{pmatrix}.$$

The mean difference between time points 1 and 2 is $29.69-26.45 = 3.24$, but the standard deviation of these differences is $\sqrt{95.12 + 68.26 - 2 \times 70.09} = 4.82$. Thus, $100\Phi^{-1}(3.24/4.82) \doteq 25$ percent of the subjects have lower true score at the second time point than at the first one. That is difficult to believe, or to ascribe to estimation error. Comparisons for the other subject areas and time points lead to similar conclusions.

However, a finer understanding of the measured quantity may provide an alternative (or complementary) explanation. We think of human *ability* in any particular domain as a variable changing very smoothly over time. For instance, the proficiency in mathematics of a typical student steadily increases over the four years of attending high school. We distinguish between *ability* and *performance*. The latter characterizes the momentary (daily) disposition of the student, as related to the domain, and is affected by everyday influences such as practice, engagement in activities not related to the domain, fluctuation in the state of physical and mental health, and various distractions. Tests measure performance, and interpretation of the corresponding true scores as ability is subject to uncertainty. The variance associated with this source of uncertainty could, in principle, be measured by repeated testing on consecutive days. However, such an experiment would wear down most cooperating subjects and would thus defeat the object of the study. Yet another source of uncertainty is the actual test form administered. Again, any form of replication to obtain an estimate of the corresponding variance is, in practice, not feasible on any meaningful scale because it requires several alternative test forms.

The sources of uncertainty due to temporal variation in performance and due to the choice of the test form are non-trivial barriers to monitoring of ability over time. Experiments to assess these sources of uncertainty are difficult to design and conduct without compromising their realistic nature.

10.6.2   Covariate adjustment

The EM algorithm for regression raises no additional conceptual difficulties, although a larger number of functions of the missing data have to be estimated. In the NELS dataset, four categorical variables are available: gender (dichotomous), ethnicity (Asian, Hispanic, Black, White, and American Asian; not available for 154 subjects), socioeconomic status (SES, ordinal categorical, 1–4, not available for one subject), and parental education (ParEd, ordinal categorical, 1–6, not available for 228 subjects). Parental education and socioeconomic status are highly correlated. Their cross-tabulation, for the entire sample and for the subsample of Hispanic students, is displayed in Table 10.4. The table shows that Hispanic students tend to have lower socioeconomic status, and their parents have less education than the population at large.

We focus first on the subpopulation of Hispanic students, represented in the NELS sample by 2010 subjects (981 men and 1029 women). The EM algorithm can be applied to this subsample. The resulting estimates of the subpopulation means are displayed in Table 10.5. The estimates of the means are lower than their population counterparts by 2–6 points and so are the estimates of the standard deviations (given in italics); compare with Table 10.2.

There are a number of alternative explanations for this finding. A natural one is that Hispanic students are disproportionately represented in the lower socioeconomic categories, and their parents tend to have poorer educational background. This and similar hypotheses cannot be tested using solely the present dataset because its collection involved no experimental design. A rigorous experimental design could be implemented only in the unrealistic setting in which we would have control over the educational background and SES of the subjects' parents. In the present setting, the best we can aim for is as good a description of the data as possible. One way of achieving this is to consider a specific pattern of differences among

TABLE 10.4. Cross-tabulation of parental education and socioeconomic status.

SES	No HS	HS/GED	College	Col. deg.	MA/MS	PhD	NA
				Parental education			
1	1521	1391	767	13	2	0	99
	631	*201*	*137*	*7*	*2*	*0*	*34*
2	107	1326	2289	120	12	3	50
	36	*114*	*286*	*9*	*4*	*1*	*10*
3	3	399	2736	652	95	6	34
	0	*28*	*243*	*39*	*11*	*2*	*2*
4	1	6	659	1720	1463	969	44
	0	*1*	*44*	*69*	*66*	*30*	*3*
NA	0	0	0	0	0	0	1
	0	*0*	*0*	*0*	*0*	*0*	*0*

Notes: The following abbreviations are used: HS — high school degree, GED — General Educational Development (high school degree equivalent in the USA), College — attended college, no degree obtained, Col. deg. — college degree, MA/MS — masters degree, PhD — doctoral degree, NA — not available. SES=1 stands for the lowest and SES=4 for the highest socioeconomic category. The counts for the entire sample are in plain type, those for the Hispanic students are in italics.

the mean vectors for each combination of the background variables while assuming the same variance matrix for each combination. Since there are 480 different combinations of the background variables, it is advantageous to consider a simpler pattern of differences. Each combination would be associated with 12 parameters.

If we discard all the interactions of the background variables, the number of parameters associated with the means is reduced to $16 \times 12 = 192$. This is by no means a large number relative to the number of datapoints, about 176 000, although orientation in the results would be very difficult. We combine parental background and socioeconomic status into a single categorical variable with six categories, according to the recoding scheme described by the following matrix:

SES	1	2	3	4	5	6
			Parental education			
1	1	2	3	3	4	5
2	2	2	3	4	4	5
3	2	3	3	4	5	6
4	3	3	4	5	6	6

TABLE 10.5. Estimates of the means and standard deviations of the subpopulation of Hispanic students.

Year	Subject areas			
	Reading	Mathematics	Science	History
1988	22.89	29.90	16.39	27.20
	7.30	*9.49*	*3.94*	*4.28*
1990	25.90	35.98	18.18	28.86
	8.93	*12.04*	*5.00*	*4.55*
1992	28.32	40.22	19.82	32.06
	9.35	*13.03*	*5.65*	*5.21*

Note: The same layout as in Table 10.2 is used.

For instance, the combination of SES=3 and parental education category 4 (college degree) is recoded into the new 'socioeducational' category 4 (printed in boldface). The definition of this variable does not have any profound theoretical basis; it is based solely on intuition and common sense. The categories of this synthetic variable have respective effective sample sizes 625, 1176, 2525, 598, 627, and 837, and the total weight for the subjects with missing values is 38. With this variable replacing SES and parental education, the number of estimated means (regression parameters) is reduced to $11 \times 12 = 132$.

Of course, the background variables also contain missing values. In the NELS sample, 379 students (2.3 percent) have some background variable not available (ethnicity for 154, socioeconomic status for 1, and parental education for 228 students). More generally, we should be concerned that some of the available data are not accurate because the assignment to a category involves judgement, and in some cases it is ambiguous. For simplicity, we ignore this issue and discard the subjects with incomplete background information. We discuss this problem in Section 10.6.3.

We apply the EM algorithm to fit the regression model described above. For the starting solution, we fit the model to the data with complete records (11 255 subjects). The first iteration updates the starting estimates by between –1.61 and 0.93 for the regression parameters and –1.89 to 3.92 for the (co)variance parameters. The corrections are smaller than $\pm 10^{-3}$ for the regression parameters by the sixth iteration and for the (co)variances by the seventh iteration.

The fitted residual variance matrix has more or less uniformly smaller elements than the estimated raw variance matrix. The ratios of the corresponding elements are in the range 0.68–0.82; the ratios for the diagonal elements are in the range 0.75–0.82. Eigenvalue decomposition reveals a similar structure of the two fitted matrices. The eigenvalues of the fitted residual variance matrix are

$$
\begin{array}{cccccc}
587.6 & 67.18 & 35.30 & 20.09 & 17.99 & 16.03 \\
11.55 & 9.97 & 7.35 & 6.46 & 5.05 & 4.50 \; ;
\end{array}
$$

compare with (10.6). The explanation for this similarity has little to do with the domains and structure of the tests. Simply, the dominant eigenvector of both variance matrices is a vector akin to the total score, and the uniform reduction of the fitted variances and covariances due to adjustment for covariates corresponds to a reduction in the dominant eigenvalue of the matrix. A similar phenomenon can be observed for the fitted true-score variance matrix, obtained from the observed-score version by subtracting the measurement error variances from the corresponding diagonal elements.

The regression parameter estimates are displayed in Table 10.6. Several patterns are readily identified in this matrix. Women score on average higher on Reading Comprehension than men. Men are somewhat better in the Science tests. However, these differences are much smaller than the residual standard deviation. There are many women whose Reading Comprehension scores are lower and whose Science scores are higher than the corresponding averages for men. The mean scores of the minorities other than Asian are lower than the means for White students. The mean score for Mathematics is higher for Asian students than for White students. The socioeducational categories line up in the expected order for each test and time point, and the differences are very consistent within tests.

Although the matrix of regression parameters has a strong pattern, its presentation in Table 10.6 is somewhat unappealing. An easier to digest alternative is illustrated in Figure 10.1. The fitted means for the socioeducational categories are drawn for each time point and domain of knowledge. The quintets of points for a socioeducational category are connected by dashed lines; the domain is marked by the initial letter ('R', 'M', 'S', and 'H'), with the smallest type for the first, medium for the second, and the largest type for the third time point. For comparison, the linear scale (the left-hand panel) is contrasted with the logarithmic scale (the right-hand panel). On the linear scale, the subpopulation means appear to fan out — higher socioeducational categories are associated with greater differences. The differences are much more even on the logarithmic scale, suggesting that instead of differences, we should have considered multiplicative increments. In hindsight, this should have been clear from Table 10.5, where we pointed out the strong association of the means and standard deviations. The entire analysis can be rerun using the logarithm transformation. The conclusions are largely unaltered, and so we omit the details.

Normality of the scores is a diagnostic concern because we made essential use of the properties of the normal distribution in the EM algorithm. The scores are distinctly non-normally distributed. For illustration, the normal quantile plots for a random subsample of the scores from the third time

TABLE 10.6. Multivariate regression parameter estimates for the NELS data.

	Rd 1	Ma 1	Sc 1	Hi 1	Rd 2	Ma 2	Sc 2	Hi 2	Rd 3	Ma 3	Sc 3	Hi 3
1	21.4	32.5	16.8	27.3	23.9	38.5	19.4	29.1	27.7	43.6	21.5	32.7
Women	1.9	0.1	−0.7	−0.4	2.2	0.0	−1.3	−0.6	2.3	−0.9	−1.7	−0.7
Hisp	−2.1	−6.2	−1.4	−1.3	−2.3	−7.4	−2.3	−1.4	−3.4	−8.0	−2.6	−1.8
Black	−3.7	−9.1	−2.7	−1.8	−4.8	−11.3	−4.2	−2.2	−6.1	−12.4	−5.0	−3.0
White	0.9	−2.0	0.4	0.3	0.4	−2.9	0.2	0.2	−0.6	−3.8	−0.2	−0.4
Am. In.	−3.8	−8.0	−1.9	−2.3	−5.3	−10.6	−3.0	−2.4	−5.9	−11.3	−3.6	−3.7
Sc-Ed 2	1.4	2.3	0.7	0.9	2.1	3.3	1.1	0.9	1.6	3.4	1.2	0.9
Sc-Ed 3	3.8	5.0	1.9	2.1	4.8	7.2	2.6	2.2	4.2	7.4	2.7	2.3
Sc-Ed 4	6.6	8.3	3.2	3.4	7.7	10.7	4.3	3.8	7.2	11.4	4.5	4.1
Sc-Ed 5	7.3	11.0	3.9	4.1	9.4	14.7	5.6	4.8	8.7	15.6	5.6	5.1
Sc-Ed 6	9.7	14.4	5.0	5.2	11.9	17.8	7.0	6.0	11.2	19.1	7.0	6.2

Notes: The columns represent the tests (Rd — Reading Comprehension, Ma — Mathematics, Sc — Science, Hi — History/Citizenship/Geography, at time points 1, 2, and 3) and the rows represent the covariates: *1* stands for the intercept that corresponds to a Male Asian student in the socioeducational category 1. The other rows represent the contrasts with the corresponding reference group; for instance, 'White' stands for the contrast (adjusted difference) of the White and Asian students; 'Sc-Ed k' stands for the contrast of categories k and 1 of the socioeducational status.

point are drawn in Figure 10.2. The plots depart from the straight line substantially, and none of the obvious transformations (such as log, square root, or other powers) promote normality. Normality could be achieved only by difficult-to-interpret transformations specific to each variable. Clearly, this is not a practical proposition.

This raises the issue of robustness of the algorithm vis-à-vis departures from normality. The formula for the conditional expectation, (10.4), can be interpreted as predicting the missing data from the available data using ordinary regression, and so the robustness properties of the ordinary least squares carry over to our EM algorithm. Similarly, the conditional variance given by (10.5) can be interpreted as the residual variance in this regression. It may be estimated suboptimally when the assumptions of normality are violated, but it is fairly robust also.

10.6.3 Missing covariate data

In pursuit of efficient use of all available information, we may attempt to incorporate the data from the 379 subjects whose background information is incomplete. Since the background variables are all categorical, the E-step

Linear scale

Log-scale

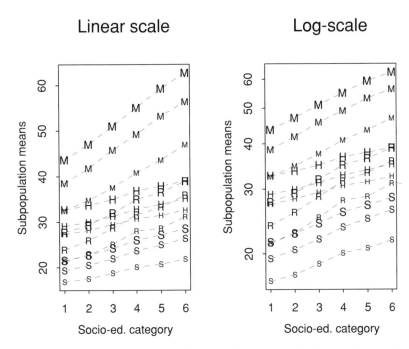

FIGURE 10.1. Estimates of the subpopulation means for the socioeducational categories. Linear and logarithmic scale. The means corresponding to a knowledge domain and time point are joined by a dashed line. The symbols used are: R — Reading Comprehension, M — Mathematics, S — Sciences, H — History/Citizenship/Geography. The smallest type is used for the first, the medium for second, and the largest type for the third time point. All the plotted points represent the means for Asian men (reference category).

of the algorithm consists of estimating the conditional probabilities of the categories to which the subjects belong. Here, we can combine information contained in the available scores and in the population proportions of the categories. For instance, men and women have very similar mean scores on each variable and are evenly represented in each ethnicity and socioeducational category, and so these variables are not very informative about the gender of the examinee. In the E-step, the conditional expectation of the dummy variable representing gender is close to one-half. However, the scores contain non-trivial information about the ethnicity and socioeducational categories because these categories have distinctly different means. Also, since ethnicity and socioeducational status are correlated, one contains information about the other; Table 10.4 provides a case in point.

Suppose a subject is known to belong to one of K categories that are represented in the population in proportions p_k, $k = 1, \ldots K$. Suppose that conditional on belonging to category k the available scores (or other variables) have joint density f_k (we suppress dependence of f_k on the model

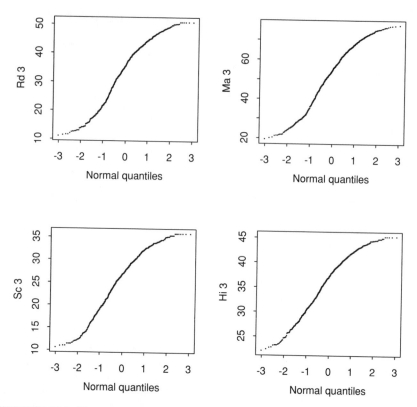

FIGURE 10.2. Normal quantile plots of the scores at time point 3 for a random subsample of size 800; NELS data.

parameters). Then the conditional probability of belonging to category h is

$$r_h = \frac{p_h f_h}{p_1 f_1 + \ldots + p_K f_K}$$

The conditional expectation of any contribution to a statistic involving missing data is a linear combination of the conditional probabilities r_k and of the conditional expectations, given that the subject belongs to category k. Such a scheme is rather difficult to implement and yet it is imperfect because it does not accommodate the association of the categorical variables. In our case, the returns in terms of more efficient estimation are likely to be diminishing since a small fraction of the examinees are involved and their participation in the test is sparser than that of the entire sample. See Little and Schluchter (1985) for details and an example.

10.6.4   Standard errors

One apparent weakness of the EM algorithm is that it does not provide standard errors in any direct way as, say, the Fisher scoring algorithm does. In the application analysed, the standard errors are of little importance when estimating the population means because the sample sizes are so large and the proportion of missing data is rather modest. However, in the regression, standard errors would be more useful because some of the background categories, American Indians in particular, are represented in the sample by small numbers of subjects and small effective sample sizes.

The issue of estimating standard errors when using the EM algorithm has been addressed by Louis (1982) and Meilijson (1989), among others. Neither approach is practical in the analysis of NELS data. However, the following simple rule-of-thumb can be applied. If the data were complete, any standard error would be easily computed. Since some data are missing, this would be an overestimate of the 'true' standard error. Similarly, we could consider a rectangular subset of the data for which the corresponding standard error could be easily computed. The listwise deletion provides such a subset. Since the ratio of the (effective) sample sizes of these two datasets is about 0.70, the two rough estimates of a particular standard error are about 0.84:1, which in many settings is sufficient for a rough guide. The value of precision of the standard errors is severely eroded when a large number of parameter estimates is considered, and so complex calculations of unbiased estimators of the standard errors are often not justified.

10.6.5   Clustering

Surveys often employ clustered sampling design so as to take advantage of the nested structure of the studied population. For instance, in NELS, students are nested within classrooms or high schools. Modelling survey data could be enhanced by taking account of this nesting structure. This is done by assuming a correlation structure of the vectors of observations from subjects in the same classroom (or school). For simplicity, constant correlation or constant covariance can be assumed. More realistic models assume higher correlations (covariances) between scores for the same variable. The EM algorithm has to be adjusted because information about a missing value is contained not only in the available data for the subject but also in the available data for the other subjects in the classroom, in particular for the corresponding variables. This leads to a rather complex and difficult-to-implement algorithm.

10.7   Summary

The EM algorithmic approach to efficient analysis of incomplete data was demonstrated on the National Education Longitudinal Survey. Although the approach is by no means a foolproof protection against the vagaries of imperfect cooperation of the subjects, it does not discard any incomplete records and, assuming multivariate normality, introduces no bias in estimation of regression (location) or (co)variance parameters.

Unlike many other applications of the EM algorithm, the computational algorithm described involves no convergence problems. Some complications arise in multivariate regression analysis when some values of both continuous and categorical variables are missing.

The Gibbs sampler is a method for generating samples from multivariate distributions defined only by certain conditional and marginal distributions. In principle, it can be applied in place of the equations (10.4) and (10.5) for evaluating the conditional means and expectations of the missing data with assumptions more appropriate than multivariate normality. In this respect, it is much more general than the approach discussed here. Although its implementation is relatively straightforward, its requirement on computing time may be prohibitive for a data set as large as the NELS survey. Gelfand and Smith (1990) and Gelfand *et al.* (1990) are a suitable introduction to Gibbs sampling.

References

Agresti, A. (1988). A model for agreement between ratings on an ordinal scale. *Biometrics* **44**, 539–548.

Angoff, W. (1971). Norms, scales, and equivalent scores. In Thorndike, R.L. (Ed.) *Educational Measurement*. American Council of Education, Washington, DC.

Battese, G. E., Harter, R. M., and Fuller, W. A. (1988). An error-component model for prediction of county crop areas using survey and satellite data. *Journal of the American Statistical Association* **83**, 28–36.

Becker, R. A., Chambers, J. M., and Wilks, A. R. (1988). *The New S Language. A Programming Environment for Data Analysis and Graphics*. Wadsworth and Brooks/Cole, Pacific Grove, CA.

Bennett, R. E., Rock, D. A., and Wang, M. (1991). Equivalence of free-response and multiple-choice items. *Journal of Educational Measurement* **28**, 77–92.

Bock, R. D., and Aitkin, M. (1981). Marginal maximum likelihood estimation of item parameters: An application of an EM algorithm. *Psychometrika* **46**, 443–459.

Braun, H. I. (1988). Understanding scoring reliability: Experiments in calibrating essay readers. *Journal of Educational Statistics* **13**, 1–18.

Brennan, R. L. (1983). *Elements of Generalizability Theory*. American College Testing Program, Iowa City, IA.

Chambers, J. M., and Hastie, T. J. (1992). *Statistical Models in S.* Wadsworth and Brooks/Cole Advanced Books & Software, Pacific Grove, CA.

Cochran, W. (1974). *Sampling Techniques.* Wiley and Sons, New York, NY.

Cox, D. R., and Hinkley, D. V. (1974). *Theoretical Statistics.* Chapman and Hall, London, UK.

Cronbach, L. J., Gleser, G. C., Nanda, H., and Rajaratnam, N. (1972). *The Dependability of Behavioral Measurements: Theory of Generalizability of Scores and Profiles.* Wiley and Sons, New York, NY.

Dempster, A. P., Laird, N. M., and Rubin, D. B. (1977). Maximum likelihood from incomplete data via the EM algorithm. *Journal of the Royal Statistical Society*, Ser. B, **39**, 1–38.

Dorans, N. J., and Kulick, E. (1986). Demonstrating the utility of the standardization approach to assessing unexpected differential item performance on the Scholastic Aptitude Test. *Journal of Educational Measurement* **23**, 355–368.

Edwards, A. W. F. (1972). *Likelihood.* Cambridge University Press, Cambridge, UK.

Efron, B. (1995). The statistical century. *RSS News* **22** No. 5, 1–2.

Ericksen, E. P. (1974). A regression method for estimating populations of local areas. *Journal of the American Statistical Association* **69**, 867–875.

Fay, R. E., and Herriot, R. A. (1979). Estimates of income for small places: an application of James-Stein procedures to census data. *Journal of the American Statistical Association* **74**, 269–277.

Fitzmaurice, G. M., Laird, N. M., and Rotnitzky, A. G. (1993). Regression models for discrete longitudinal responses. *Statistical Science* **8**, 284–309.

Fuller, W. A. (1987). *Measurement Error Models.* Wiley and Sons, New York, NY.

Gelfand, A. E., and Smith, A. F. M. (1990). Sampling-based approaches to calculating marginal densities. *Journal of the American Statistical Association* **85**, 398–409.

Gelfand, A. E., Hills, S. E., Racine-Poon, A., and Smith, A. F. M. (1990). Illustration of Bayesian inference in normal data models using Gibbs sampling. *Journal of the American Statistical Association* **85**, 972–985.

Ghosh, M., and Rao, J. N. K. (1994). Small area estimation: An appraisal. *Statistical Science* **9**, 55–93.

Gulliksen, H. (1950). *Theory of Mental Tests.* Wiley, New York, NY.

Hambleton, R. K., Swaminathan, H., Algina, J., and Coulson, D. B. (1978). Criterion-referenced testing and measurement: A review of technical issues and developments. *Review of Educational Research* **48**, 1–47.

Hartley, H. O. (1958). Maximum likelihood estimation from incomplete data. *Biometrics* **14**, 174–194.

Harville, D. A. (1974). Bayesian inference for variance components using only error contrasts. *Biometrika* **61**, 383–385.

Harville, D. A. (1977). Maximum likelihood approaches to variance component estimation and to related problems. *Journal of the American Statistical Association* **72**, 320–340.

Hedeker, D., and Gibbons, R. D. (1994). A random-effects ordinal regression model for multilevel analysis. *Biometrics* **50**, 933–944.

Holland, P. W., and Rubin, D. B. (1982). *Test Equating*. Academic Press, New York.

Holland, P. W., and Thayer, D. T. (1988). Differential item performance and the Mantel-Haenszel procedure. In Wainer, H., and Braun, H. (Eds.) *Test Validity*, pp. 129–145. Lawrence Erlbaum Associates, Hillsdale, NJ.

Holland, P. W., and Wainer, H. (Eds.) (1993). *Differential Item Functioning*. Lawrence Erlbaum Associates, Hillsdale, NJ.

Holt, D., and Scott, A. J. (1982). Regression analysis using survey data. *The Statistician* **30**, 169–177.

Im, S., and Gianola, D. (1988). Mixed models for binomial data with an application to lamb mortality. *Applied Statistics* **37**, 196–204.

Johnson, E. G., and Rust, K. F. (1992). Population inferences and variance estimation. *Journal of Educational Statistics* **17**, 179–190.

Kirsch, I. S., and Jungeblut, A. (1992). Profiling the literacy proficiencies of JTPA and ES/UI populations. Final report to the Department of Labor. Educational Testing Service, Princeton, NJ.

Kish, L. (1965). *Survey Sampling*. Wiley and Sons, New York, NY.

Koffler, S. L. (1991). The Techical Report of NAEP's 1990 Trial State Assessment Program. Report No. 21–ST01, National Center for Education Statistics, Washington, DC.

Laird, N. M., and Ware, J. H. (1982). Random effects models for longitudinal data. *Biometrics* **38**, 963–974.

Landis, R. J., and Koch, G. G. (1977). The measurement of observer agreement for categorical data. *Biometrics* **33**, 159–174.

Little, R. J. A., and Rubin, D. B. (1987). *Statistical Analysis with Missing Data*. Wiley and Sons, New York, NY.

Little, R. J. A., and Schluchter, M. D. (1985). Maximum likelihood for mixed continuous and categorical data with missing values. *Biometrika* **72**, 497–512.

Longford, N. T. (1993a). Logistic regression with random coefficients. ETS Technical Report 93–30. Educational Testing Service, Princeton, NJ.

Longford, N. T. (1993b). *Random Coefficient Models.* Oxford University Press, Oxford, UK.

Longford, N. T. (1993c). Regression analysis of multilevel data with measurement error. *British Journal of Mathematical and Statistical Psychology,* **46**, 301–311.

Longford, N. T. (1994a). Logistic regression with random coefficients. *Computational Statistics and Data Analysis* **17**, 1–15.

Longford, N. T. (1994b). Reliability of essay rating and score adjustment. *Journal of Educational Statistics* **19**, 171–201.

Longford, N. T. (1995). Model-based methods for analysis of data from 1990 NAEP Trial State Assessment. Research and Development Report NCES 95–696. National Center for Education Statistics, Washington, DC.

Longford, N. T., Holland, P. W., and Thayer, D. T. (1993). Stability of the MH D-DIF statistics across populations. In Holland, P. W., and Wainer, H. (Eds.) *Differential Item Functioning,* pp. 171–196. Lawrence Erlbaum Associates, Hillsdale, NJ.

Lord, F. M. (1980). *Application of Item Response Theory to Practical Testing Problems.* Lawrence Erlbaum Associates, Hillsdale, NJ.

Lord, F. M., and Novick, M. (1968). *Statistical theories of Mental Test Scores.* Addison-Wesley, Reading, MA.

Louis, T. A. (1982). Finding the observed information matrix when using the EM algorithm. *Journal of the Royal Statistical Society* Ser. B, **44**, 226–233.

Lunz, M. E., Wright, B. D., and Linacre, J. M. (1990). Measuring the impact of judge severity on examination scores. *Applied Measurement in Education* **3**, 331–345.

Mantel, N., and Haenszel, W. (1959). Statistical aspects of the analysis of data from retrospective studies of disease. *Journal of the National Cancer Institute* **22**, 719–748.

Mardia, K. V., Kent, J. T., and Bibby, J. M. (1979). *Multivariate Analysis.* Academic Press, London, UK.

McCullagh, P., and Nelder, J. A. (1989). *Generalized linear models* (2nd edition). Chapman and Hall, London, UK.

Meilijson, I. (1989). A fast improvement to the EM algorithm on its own terms. *Journal of the Royal Statistical Society* Ser. B, **51**, 127–138.

Mislevy, R. J. (1991). Randomization-based inferences about latent variables from complex samples. *Psychometrika* **56**, 177–196.

Mislevy, R. J., and Bock, R. D. (1983). *BILOG: Item Analysis and Test Scoring with Binary Logistic Models.* Scientific Software, Inc., Mooresville, IN.

Morris, C. N. (1983). Parametric empirical Bayes inference: Theory and applications. *Journal of the American Statistical Association* **78**, 47–65.

Nedelsky, L. (1954). Absolute grading standards for objective tests. *Educational and Psychological Measurement* **14**, 3–19.

Orchard, T., and Woodbury, M. A. (1972). A missing information principle: theory and applications. *Proceedings of the 6th Berkeley Symposium on Mathematical Statistics and Probability* **1**, 697–715.

Patterson, H. O., and Thompson, R. (1971). Recovery of inter-block information when block sizes are unequal. *Biometrika* **58**, 545–554.

Pfeffermann, D. (1993). The role of sampling weights when modeling survey data. *International Statistical Review* **61**, 317–337.

Phillips, A., and Holland, P. W. (1987). Estimators of the variance of the Mantel-Haenszel log-odds-ratio estimate. *Biometrics* **43**, 425–431.

Platek, R., Rao, J. N. K., Särndal, C.-E., and Singh, M. P. (Eds.) (1987). *Small Area Statistics.* Wiley and Sons, New York, NY.

Potthoff, R. F., Woodbury, M. A., and Manton, K. G. (1992) "Equivalent sample size" and "equivalent degrees of freedom" refinements for inference using survey weights under superpopulation models. *Journal of the American Statistical Association* **87**, 383–396.

Prasad, N. G. N., and Rao, J. N. K. (1990). The estimation of mean squared errors of small-area estimators. *Journal of the American Statistical Association* **85**, 163–171.

Robins, J., Breslow, N., and Greenland, S. (1986). Estimators of the Mantel-Haenszel variance consistent in both sparse data and large-strata limiting models. *Biometrics* **42**, 311–323.

Robinson, G. K. (1991). That BLUP is a good thing: The estimation of random effects. *Statistical Science* **6**, 15–32.

Rust, K. F., and Johnson, E. G. (1992). Sampling and weighting in the National Assessment. *Journal of Educational Statistics* **17**, 111–129.

Searle, S. R. (1987). *Linear Models for Unbalanced Data.* Wiley and Sons, New York, NY.

Searle, S. R., Casella, G., and McCulloch, C. E. (1992). *Variance Components.* Wiley and Sons, New York, NY.

Seber, G. A. F. (1977). *Linear Regression Analysis.* Wiley and Sons, New York, NY.

Shavelson, R. J., and Webb, N. (1991). *Generalizability Theory. A Primer. Volume 1.* Sage Publications, Newbury Park, CA.

Shealy, R. T., and Stout, W. F. (1993). An item-response theory model for test bias and differential test functioning. In Holland, P. W., and Wainer, H. (Eds.) *Differential Item Functioning*, pp. 197–239. Lawrence Erlbaum Associates, Hillsdale, NJ.

Skaggs, G., and Lissitz, L. W. (1992). The consistency of detecting item bias across different test administrations: Implications of another failure. *Journal of Educational Measurement* **29**, 227–242.

Stasny, E. A., Goel, P. K., and Rumsey, D. J. (1991). County estimates of wheat production. *Survey Methodology* **17**, 211–225.

Subkoviak, M. (1978). Empirical investigation of procedures for estimating reliability for mastery tests. *Journal of Educational Measurement* **15**, 111–116.

Tsutakawa, R. K. (1988). Mixed model for analyzing geographic variability in mortality rates. *Journal of the American Statistical Assoociation* **83**, 37–42.

Uebersax, J. S. (1990). Latent class analysis of diagnostic agreement. *Statistics in Medicine* **9**, 559–572.

Uebersax, J. S. (1993). Statistical modeling of expert ratings on medical treatment appropriateness. *Journal of the American Statistical Association* **88**, 421–427.

Wainer, H., and Thissen, D. (1994). On examinee choice in educational testing. *Review of Educational Research* **64**, 159–195.

Wang, X.-B., Wainer, H., and Thissen, D. (1993). On the viability of some untestable assumptions in equating exams that allow for examinee choice. ETS Technical Report 93-31. Educational Testing Service, Princeton, NJ.

Whittaker, J. (1990). *Graphical Models in Applied Multivariate Statistics.* Wiley and Sons, Chichester, UK.

Wolter, K.M. (1985). *Introduction to Variance Estimation.* Springer-Verlag, New York, NY.

Wolter, K. M., and Causey, B. D. (1991). Evaluation of procedures for improving population estimates for small areas. *Journal of the American Statistical Association* **86**, 278–284.

Zeger, S. L., and Liang, K.-Y. (1986). Longitudinal data analysis for discrete and continuous outcomes. *Biometrics* **42**, 121–130.

Index

Springer Series in Statistics

(continued from p. ii)

DATE DUE

DEC 18			

Demco, Inc. 38-293